Register for Free Membership to

s o l u t i o n s @ s y n g r e s s . c o m

Over the last few years, Syngress has published many best-selling and critically acclaimed books, including Tom Shinder's *Configuring ISA Server 2004*, Brian Caswell and Jay Beale's *Snort 2.1 Intrusion Detection*, and Angela Orebaugh and Gilbert Ramirez's *Ethereal Packet Sniffing*. One of the reasons for the success of these books has been our unique **solutions@syngress.com** program. Through this site, we've been able to provide readers a real time extension to the printed book.

As a registered owner of this book, you will qualify for free access to our members-only solutions@syngress.com program. Once you have registered, you will enjoy several benefits, including:

- Four downloadable e-booklets on topics related to the book. Each booklet is approximately 20-30 pages in Adobe PDF format. They have been selected by our editors from other best-selling Syngress books as providing topic coverage that is directly related to the coverage in this book.

- A comprehensive FAQ page that consolidates all of the key points of this book into an easy-to-search web page, providing you with the concise, easy-to-access data you need to perform your job.

- A "From the Author" Forum that allows the authors of this book to post timely updates and links to related sites, or additional topic coverage that may have been requested by readers.

Just visit us at **www.syngress.com/solutions** and follow the simple registration process. You will need to have this book with you when you register.

Thank you for giving us the opportunity to serve your needs. And be sure to let us know if there is anything else we can do to make your job easier.

SYNGRESS®

SYNGRESS®

Practical VoIP Security

Thomas Porter

Jan Kanclirz
Andy Zmolek
Antonio Rosela
Michael Cross
Larry Chaffin
Brian Baskin
Choon Shim

KEY	SERIAL NUMBER
001	HJIRTCV764
002	PO9873D5FG
003	829KM8NJH2
004	BNNERHJC7B
005	CVPLQ6WQ23
006	VBP965T5T5
007	HJJJ863WD3E
008	2987GVTWMK
009	629MP5SDJT
010	IMWQ295T6T

PUBLISHED BY
Syngress Publishing, Inc.
800 Hingham Street
Rockland, MA 02370

Practical VoIP Security

Printed in Canada
1 2 3 4 5 6 7 8 9 0
ISBN: 1597490601

Publisher: Andrew Williams   Page Layout and Art: Patricia Lupien
Acquisitions Editor: Gary Byrne   Copy Editor: Adrienne Rebello
Cover Designer: Michael Kavish   and Mike McGee
Technical Editors: Andy Zmolek, Thomas Porter,   Indexer: Julie Kawabata
      and Stephen Watkins

Distributed by O'Reilly Media, Inc. in the United States and Canada.
or information on rights, translations, and bulk sales, contact Matt Pedersen, Director of Sales and Rights, at Syngress Publishing; email matt@syngress.com or fax to 781-681-3585.

Acknowledgments

Syngress would like to acknowledge the following people for their kindness and support in making this book possible.

Syngress books are now distributed in the United States and Canada by O'Reilly Media, Inc. The enthusiasm and work ethic at O'Reilly are incredible, and we would like to thank everyone there for their time and efforts to bring Syngress books to market: Tim O'Reilly, Laura Baldwin, Mark Brokering, Mike Leonard, Donna Selenko, Bonnie Sheehan, Cindy Davis, Grant Kikkert, Opol Matsutaro, Mark Wilson, Rick Brown, Tim Hinton, Kyle Hart, Sara Winge, Peter Pardo, Leslie Crandell, Regina Aggio Wilkinson, Pascal Honscher, Preston Paull, Susan Thompson, Bruce Stewart, Laura Schmier, Sue Willing, Mark Jacobsen, Betsy Waliszewski, Kathryn Barrett, John Chodacki, Rob Bullington, Kerry Beck, Karen Montgomery, and Patrick Dirden.

The incredibly hardworking team at Elsevier Science, including Jonathan Bunkell, Ian Seager, Duncan Enright, David Burton, Rosanna Ramacciotti, Robert Fairbrother, Miguel Sanchez, Klaus Beran, Emma Wyatt, Krista Leppiko, Marcel Koppes, Judy Chappell, Radek Janousek, Rosie Moss, David Lockley, Nicola Haden, Bill Kennedy, Martina Morris, Kai Wuerfl-Davidek, Christiane Leipersberger, Yvonne Grueneklee, Nadia Balavoine, and Chris Reinders for making certain that our vision remains worldwide in scope.

David Buckland, Marie Chieng, Lucy Chong, Leslie Lim, Audrey Gan, Pang Ai Hua, Joseph Chan, June Lim, and Siti Zuraidah Ahmad of Pansing Distributors for the enthusiasm with which they receive our books.

David Scott, Tricia Wilden, Marilla Burgess, Annette Scott, Andrew Swaffer, Stephen O'Donoghue, Bec Lowe, Mark Langley, and Anyo Geddes of Woodslane for distributing our books throughout Australia, New Zealand, Papua New Guinea, Fiji, Tonga, Solomon Islands, and the Cook Islands.

Lead Author
and Technical Editor

Thomas Porter, Ph.D. (CISSP, IAM, CCNP, CCDA, CCNA, ACE, CCSA, CCSE, and MCSE) is the Lead Security Architect in Avaya's Consulting & Systems Integration Practice. He also serves as Director of Network Security for the FIFA World Cup 2006.

Porter has spent over 10 years in the networking and security industry as a consultant, speaker, and developer of security tools. Porter's current technical interests include VoIP security, development of embedded microcontroller and FPGA Ethernet tools, and H.323/SIP vulnerability test environments. He is a member of the IEEE and OASIS (Organization for the Advancement of Structured Information Standards). Porter recently published Foundation articles for SecurityFocus titled "H.323 Mediated Voice over IP: Protocols, Vulnerabilities, and Remediation"; and "Perils of Deep Packet Inspection."

Tom lives in Chapel Hill, North Carolina, with his wife, Kinga, an Asst. Professor of Internal Medicine at the University of North Carolina, and two Chesapeake Bay retrievers.

Contributing Authors

Brian Baskin (MCP, CTT+) is a researcher and developer for Computer Sciences Corporation, on contract to the Defense Cyber Crime Center's (DC3) Computer Investigations Training Program (DCITP). Here, he researches, develops, and instructs computer forensic courses for members of the military and law enforcement. Brian currently specializes in Linux/Solaris intrusion investigations, as well as investigations of various network applications. He has designed and implemented networks to be used in scenarios, and has also exercised penetration testing procedures.

Brian has been instructing courses for six years, including presentations at the annual DoD Cyber Crime Conference. He is an avid amateur programmer in many languages, beginning when his father purchased QuickC for him when he was 11, and has geared much of his life around the implementations of technology. He has also been an avid Linux user since 1994 and enjoys a relaxing terminal screen whenever he can. He has worked in networking environments for over 10 years from small Novell networks to large, mission-critical, Windows-based networks.

Brian lives in the Baltimore, MD, area with his lovely wife and son. He is also the founder and president of the Lightning Owners of Maryland car club. Brian is a motor sports enthusiast and spends much of his time building and racing his vehicles. He attributes a great deal of his success to his parents, who relinquished their household 80286 PC to him at a young age and allowed him the freedom to explore technology.

Brian cowrote Chapter 8.

Joshua Brashars is a security researcher for the External Threat Assessment Team at Secure Science Corporation. Before that, Joshua spent many years in the telecommunications industry as an implementation consultant for traditional and VoIP PBX systems. Joshua would like to extend heartfelt thanks to his family, friends, Lance James and SSC, Johnny Long and all of johnny.ihackstuff.com, and a special nod to Natas, Strom Carlson, and lucky225 for fueling the fire in his passion for telephone systems.

Joshua contributed to Chapter 3.

Larry Chaffin (CISSP, PMP, JNCIE, MBCP, CWNP, NNCSE, NNCDE, CCNP, CCDP, CCNP-WAN, CCDP-WAN) is the CEO/Chairman of Pluto Networks and the Vice President of Advanced Network Technologies for Plannet Group. He is an accomplished author; he cowrote *Managing Cisco Network Security* (ISBN: 1-931836-56-6) and has also been a coauthor/ghost writer for 11 other technology books for VoIP, WLAN, security, and optical technologies. Larry has more than 29 vendor certifications such as the ones already listed, plus Cisco VoIP, Optical, Security, VPN, IDS, Unity, and WLAN. He is also certified by Nortel in DMS Carrier Class Switches along with CS100'S, MCS5100, Call Pilot, and WLAN. Many other certifications come from vendors such as Avaya, HP, IBM, Microsoft, PeopleSoft, and VMware. Larry has been a Principal Architect around the world in 22 countries for many Fortune 100 companies designing VoIP, Security, WLAN, and optical networks. His next project is to write a book on Nortel VoIP and a new security architecture book he has designed for VoIP and WLAN networks.

Larry cowrote Chapter 7.

Michael Cross (MCSE, MCP+I, CNA, Network+) is an Internet Specialist/Computer Forensic Analyst with the Niagara Regional Police Service (NRPS). He performs computer forensic examinations on computers involved in criminal investigation. He also has consulted and assisted in cases dealing with computer-related/Internet crimes. In addition to designing and maintaining the NRPS Web site at www.nrps.com and the NRPS intranet, he has provided support in the areas of programming, hardware, and network administration. As part of an information technology team that provides support to a user base of more than 800 civilian and uniform users, he has a theory that when the users carry guns, you tend to be more motivated in solving their problems.

Michael also owns KnightWare (www.knightware.ca), which provides computer-related services such as Web page design, and Bookworms (www.bookworms.ca), where you can purchase collectibles and other interesting items online. He has been a freelance writer for several years, and he has been published more than three dozen times in numerous books and anthologies. He currently resides in St. Catharines, Ontario, Canada, with his lovely wife, Jennifer, his darling daughter, Sara, and charming son, Jason.

Michael wrote Chapter 6.

Bradley Dunsmore (CCNP, CCDP, CCSP, INFOSEC, MCSE+I, MCDBA) is a Software/QA engineer for the Voice Technology Group at Cisco Systems Inc. He is part of the Golden Bridge solution test team for IPT based in RTP, NC. His responsibilities include the design, deployment, testing, and troubleshooting of Cisco's enterprise voice portfolio. His focus area is the integration of Cisco's network security product line in an enterprise voice environment. Bradley has been working with Cisco's network security product line for four years and he is currently working on his CCIE lab for Security. Prior to his six years at Cisco, Bradley worked for Adtran, Bell Atlantic, and as a network integrator in Virginia Beach, Va.

Bradley has authored, co-authored, or edited several books for Syngress Publishing and Cisco Press for network security, telecommunication, and general networking. He would like to thank his fiancée, Amanda, for her unwavering support in everything that he does. Her support makes all of this possible.

Bradley contributed to Chapter 8.

Jan Kanclirz Jr. (CCIE #12136-Security, CCSP, CCNP, CCIP, CCNA, CCDA, INFOSEC Professional, Cisco WLAN Support/Design Specialist) is currently a Senior Network Information Security Architect at IBM Global Services. Jan specializes in multivendor designs and post-sale implementations for several technologies such as VPNs, IPS/IDS, LAN/WAN, firewalls, content networking, wireless and VoIP. Beyond network designs and engineering Jan's background includes extensive experience with open source applications and Linux. Jan has contributed to *Managing and Securing Cisco SWAN* (ISBN: 1-932266-91-7), a Syngress publication.

In addition to Jan's full-time position at IBM G.S., Jan runs a security portal, *www.MakeSecure.com,* where he dedicates his time to security awareness and consulting. Jan lives with his girl friend, Amy, and her daughter, Abby, in Colorado, where they enjoy outdoor adventures.

Jan wrote Chapter 2.

Tony Rosela (PMP, CTT+) is a Senior Member Technical Staff with Computer Sciences Corporation working in the development and delivery of technical instructional material. He provides leadership through knowledge and experience with the operational fundamentals of PSTN architecture and how the PSTN has evolved to deliver high-quality services, including VoIP. His other specialties include IP enabling voice networks, WAN voice and data network design, implementation and troubleshooting, as well as spending a great deal of time in the field of computer forensics and data analysis.

Tony cowrote Chapter 4.

Mark Spencer founded Linux Support Services in 1999 while still a Computer Engineering student at Auburn University. When faced with the high cost of buying a PBX, Mark simply used his Linux PC and knowledge of C code to write his own. This was the beginning of the worldwide phenomenon known as Asterisk, the open source PBX, and caused Mark to shift his business focus from Linux support to supporting Asterisk and opening up the telecom market. Linux Support Services is now known as Digium, and is bringing open source to the telecom market while gaining a foothold in the telecom industry.

Mark strongly believes that every technology he creates should be given back to the community. This is why Asterisk is fully open source. Today, that model has allowed Asterisk to remain available free of charge, while it has become as robust as the leading and most expensive PBXs.

The Asterisk community has ambassadors and contributors from every corner of the globe. Recently Mark was named by *Network World* as one of the 50 Most Powerful People in Networking, next to Cisco's John Chambers, Microsoft's Bill Gates, and Oracle's Larry Ellison. A renowned speaker, Mark has presented and delivered keynotes at a number of industry conferences, including Internet Telephony, SuperComm, and the VON shows.

Mark holds a degree in Computer Engineering from Auburn University, and is now president of Digium, Inc. He has also led the creation of several Linux-based open source applications, most notably Asterisk, the Open Source PBX, and Gaim Instant Messenger.

Mark wrote the IAX section of Chapter 7.

Choon Shim is responsible for the Qovia's technology direction and development of the Qovia product line.

Choon was previously President at Widearea Data Systems, where he designed and developed collaboration platform software. Prior to joining Widearea Data Systems, he was the Senior Development Manager and Principal Engineer for Merant.

Choon is a successful technology leader with 20+ years' experience architecting, building, and delivering large-scale infrastructure software products. He has extensive hands-on technical development skills and has successfully managed software teams for well-known enterprise software companies, including BMC Software and EMC Corporation.

Choon is the author of *Community Works and Express/OS* shareware used widely throughout the world. He is a frequent speaker at VoIP and networking conferences for academic and industry. He recently gave a keynote speech to SNPD conference and chaired VoIP Security Panel at Supercomm05. Choon holds a B.S. in Computer Science from Kyoungpook National University and an M.S in Electrical Engineering from the University of Wisconsin.

Choon wrote Chapters 14 and 16.

Stephen Watkins (CISSP) is an Information Security Professional with more than 10 years of relevant technology experience, devoting eight of these years to the security field. He currently serves as Information Assurance Analyst at Regent University in southeastern Virginia. Before coming to Regent, he led a team of security professionals providing in-depth analysis for a global-scale government network. Over the last eight years, he has cultivated his expertise with regard to perimeter security and multilevel security architecture. His Check Point experience dates back to 1998 with FireWall-1 version 3.0b. He has earned his B.S. in Computer Science from Old Dominion University and M.S. in Computer Science, with Concentration in Infosec, from James Madison University. He is nearly a life-long resident of Virginia Beach, where he and his family remain active in their church and the local Little League.

Stephen was the technical editor for Chapter 15.

Andy Zmolek is Senior Manager, Security Planning and Strategy at Avaya. In that role, Andy drives product security architecture and strategy across Avaya's voice and data communications products. Previously at Avaya, he helped launch the Avaya Enterprise Security Practice, led several Sarbanes-Oxley-related security projects within Avaya IT, and represented Avaya in standards bodies (IETF, W3C) as part of the Avaya CTO Standards Group. Avaya Inc. designs, builds and manages communications networks for more than one million businesses worldwide, including over 90 percent of the FORTUNE 500®.

Andy has been involved with network security for over a decade, and is an expert on Session Initiation Protocol (SIP) and related VoIP standards, Presence systems, and firewall traversal for VoIP. He holds a degree in Mathematics from Brigham Young University and is NSA IAM certified.

Prior to joining Avaya, he directed network architecture and operations at New Era of Networks, a pioneer of enterprise application integration (EAI) technology, now a division of Sybase. Andy got his start in the industry as a systems architect responsible for the design and operation of secure real-time simulation networks for missile and satellite programs at Raytheon, primarily with the Tomahawk program.

Andy wrote Chapter 15, cowrote Chapters 3 and 4, and was a technical editor for several chapters.

Contents

Chapter 1

Introduction to VoIP Security

Solutions in this chapter:

- The Switch Leaves the Basement
- What Is VoIP?
- VoIP Isn't Just Another Data Protocol
- Security Issues in VoIP Networks
- A New Security Model

☑ Summary
☑ Solutions Fast Track
☑ Frequently Asked Questions

Introduction

The business of securing our private data is becoming more important and more relevant each day. The benefits of electronic communication come with proportionate risks. Critical business systems can be and are compromised regularly, and are used for illegal purposes. There are many instances of this: Seisint (Lexis-Nexis research), Choicepoint, Bank of America, PayMaxx, DSW Shoe Warehouses, Ameriprise, and T-Mobile are all recent examples.

- Seisint (Lexis-Nexis research) was hacked, potentially compromising names, addresses, and social security and driver's license information relating to 310,000 people.

- Choicepoint, one of the nation's largest information aggregators, allowed criminals to buy the private identity and credit information of more than 150,000 customer accounts. Besides the harm done to Choicepoint's reputation, in late January, 2006, Choicepoint was fined $15 million by the FTC for this breach. This figure does not include the millions of dollars spent by Choicepoint on the cleanup of this debacle. This settlement makes it clear that the FTC is increasingly willing to escalate security-related enforcement actions.

WARNING

Victims of personal data security breaches are showing their displeasure by terminating relationships with the companies that maintained their data, according to a new national survey sponsored by global law firm White & Case. The independent survey of nearly 10,000 adults, conducted by the respected privacy research organization Ponemon Institute, reveals that nearly 20 percent of respondents say they have terminated a relationship with a company after being notified of a security breach.

"Companies lose customers when a breach occurs. Of the people we surveyed who received notifications, 19 percent said that they have ended their relationship with the company after they learned that their personal information had been compromised due to security breach. A whopping 40 percent say that they are thinking about terminating their relationship," said Larry Ponemon, founder and head of the Ponemon Institute.

- Bank of America announced that it had "lost" tapes containing information on over 1.2 million federal employee credit cards, exposing the individuals involved and the government to fraud and misuse.

- PayMaxx Inc., a Tennessee payroll management company, suffered a security lapse that may have exposed financial data on as many as 100,000 workers.

- DSW Shoe Warehouses revealed that credit card data from about 100 of its stores had been stolen from a company computer over the past three months.

- A hacker even attacked T-Mobile, the cellular telephone network used by actress Paris Hilton, and stole the information stored on Hilton's phone, including private phone numbers of many other celebrities.

These are just a few examples from one month in 2005. Everyone "knows" that information security is important, but what types of damage are we talking about? Certainly, Paris Hilton's phone book is not critical information (except, perhaps to her). Table 1.1 lists the types of losses resulting from attacks on data networks.

Table 1.1 Losses Resulting from Attacks on Data Networks

Direct Losses	Indirect Losses
Economic theft	Loss of sales
Theft of trade secrets	Loss of competitive advantage
Theft of digital assets	Brand damage
Theft of consumer data	Loss of goodwill
Theft of computing resources	Failure to meet contract obligations
Productivity loss due to data corruption	Noncompliance with privacy regulations
Productivity loss due to spam	Officer liability
Recovery expenses	Reparations

The aforementioned bullet points are based on data network examples. VoIP networks simply haven't existed long enough to provide many real-world examples of information breaches. But they will.

The practice of information security has become more complex than ever. By Gartner's estimates, one in five companies has a wireless LAN that the CIO doesn't know about, and 60 percent of WLANs don't have their basic security functions enabled. Organizations that interconnect with partners are beginning to take into account the security environment of those partners. For the unprepared, security breaches and lapses are beginning to attract lawsuits. "It's going to be the next asbestos," predicts one observer.

The daily challenges a business faces—new staff, less staff, more networked applications, more business partner connections, and an even more hostile Internet environment—should not be allowed to create more opportunities for intruders. The fact is, all aspects of commerce are perilous, and professional security administrators realize that no significant gain is possible without accepting significant risk. The goal is to intelligently, and economically, balance these risks.

This book is based on the premise that in order to secure VoIP systems and applications, you must first understand them. In addition, efficient and economical deployment of security controls requires that you understand those controls, their limitations, and their interactions with one another and other components that constitute the VoIP and supporting infrastructure.

The Switch Leaves the Basement

Telephone networks were designed for voice transmission. Data networks were not. Recently—within the last three to five years—PBX functionality has moved logically (and even physically) from the closet or fenced room in the basement into the data networking space, both from physical connectivity and management standpoints. Additionally, the components of the converged infrastructure (gateways, gatekeepers, media servers, IP PBXes, etc.) are no longer esoteric variants of VxWorks, Oryx-Pecos, or other proprietary UNIXs, whose operating systems are not well enough known or distributed to be common hacking targets; but instead run on well-known, commonly exploited Windows and Linux OSes. SS7, which hardly any data networking people understand, is slowly being replaced by SIGTRAN (which is basically SS7 over IP), H.323 (which no one understands ☺), and SIP (which is many things to many people), running over TCP/IP networks. By the way, hackers understand TCP/IP.

Most people, if they even think about it, consider the traditional public switched telephone network (PSTN) secure. On the PSTN the eavesdropper requires physical access to the telephone line or switch and an appropriate hardware bugging device.

NOTE

"Whenever a telephone line is tapped, the privacy of the persons at both ends of the line is invaded, and all conversations between them upon any subject, and although proper, confidential, and privileged, may be overheard. Moreover, the tapping of one man's telephone line involves the tapping of the telephone of every other person whom he may call, or who may call him. As a means of espionage, writs of assistance and general warrants are but puny instruments of tyranny and oppression when compared with wire tapping."
—Justice Louis Brandeis, Olmstead v. United States, 1928.

Toll fraud occurs more frequently than most people realize (one source estimates damages at $4 billion per year) primarily due to improperly configured remote access policies (DISA—Direct Inward System Access) and voicemail; however, strong authentication codes and passwords, active call detail record accounting, and physical security controls reduce the risk of damage due to toll fraud to reasonable levels. Although it is theoretically possible to "hack" SS7, only sophisticated techniques and direct access to the signaling channel make this possible.

Unlike most standards in data networking—for example, TCP/IP has been relatively stable for more than 20 years now—there is a high degree of inconsistency in support and implementation of VoIP-related standards, due in part to the rapid evolution in the standards themselves, and due in part to vendors attempting to lock in customers to nonstandard protocol implementations. The consequence of this is that, in some cases, immature (vulnerable) applications reach the market. Vendors are oftentimes only familiar with their specific application's protocol implementation, and when designing a security solution, aren't always concerned about interoperability. This is actually quite ironic because these same vendors tout standards to foster interoperability.

An additional difference between VoIP and more common protocols is that both major VoIP protocols separate signaling and media on different channels. These channels run over dynamic IP address/port combinations. This has significant security implications that will be detailed later in this book. If you combine this fact (separate signaling and data channels) with the reality that users naturally expect to be able to simply make both inbound and outbound calls, then you should begin to realize that VoIP is more challenging to secure technically than common protocols that initiate with outbound client requests.

VoIP is difficult to firewall. Additionally, since IP addressing information is cascaded within the signaling stream of H.323 and within SIP control packets, encryption of these streams—an obvious security measure—wreaks havoc with NAT implementations. IPv4 was not invented with real-time communications and NAT in mind.

In addition to the vulnerabilities and difficulties that we have summarized, converged networks offer an array of new vectors for traditional exploits and malware. This is due in part to the unique performance requirements of the voice fraction of converged networks, and in part to the fact that more intelligence (particularly in the case of SIP) is moved from the guarded center to the edge of the network. Increased network points of access equals increased network complexity—and complexity is the bane of security engineers. In addition, SIP may become particularly attractive as hacking target, due to its HTTP based underpinnings, and the ease with which ASCII encoded packets can be manipulated.

Are these new problems? Not really. Information systems have long been at some risk from malicious actions or inadvertent user errors, and from natural and man-made disasters. In recent years, systems have become more susceptible to these threats because computers have become more interconnected and, thus, more interdependent, and these systems have become accessible to a larger number of individuals. In addition, the number of individuals with computer skills is increasing, more automated tools are available, and intrusion, or hacking, techniques are becoming more widely known via the Internet and other media.

Converged VoIP and data networks inherit all the security weaknesses of the IP protocol—including spoofing, sniffing, denial of service attacks, replay attacks, and message integrity attacks. All the legacy application servers that serve as adjuncts in converged networks (DNS, SNMP, TFTP, etc.) will also be targets of attack as they have been on data networks. Viruses and worms will become a real threat to the entire telecommunication infrastructure.

Hacking will converge as well.

Unfortunately, even though the overwhelming majority of VoIP calls will occur uneventfully between two or more trusted individuals—in much the same way that most data sessions take place securely today—the public will focus on extraordinary examples of "the call that went bad." Our challenge is to restrict these incidents to the best of our abilities.

What Is VoIP?

Although VoIP, IP Telephony, and Converged Networks all have slightly different definitions, they often are used interchangeably. In this book, we will do the same. When using any of these terms, we are talking about the structures and processes that result from design and implementation of a common networking infrastructure that accommodates data, voice, and multimedia communications. Today, it is all about voice. There are plenty of examples of streaming video, but the enthusiasm today is to replace circuit-switched voice with packet-switched voice within the enterprise and at home across broadband connections.

Why is this happening now? IP telephony adoption is ramping up dramatically for a number of reasons: traditional PBXs and related telco equipment that was upgraded as organizations prepared for Y2K is beginning to reach end-of-life; IP switches are cheaper and potentially offer more features than traditional PBXs; data system administrators and their networks have become more mature, and thus, can support the quality of service that VoIP services require; and VoIP technology (particularly the products) have gotten better. VoIP is attractive to organizations and to broadband end-users as they attempt to derive more value from an infrastructure that is already paid for.

VoIP Benefits

What does converging voice and data on the same physical infrastructure promise? First, we may actually lower costs after all, due to the economies of supporting one network instead of two. Organizations also will save money on toll bypass, intralata regional toll (also known as local toll) charges, and all the "extra" services that POTS providers currently bill for.

Tools & Traps…

VoIP Saves Me $$$

Because of my work on the FIFA World Cup, I spend a part of each month in Europe, primarily in Germany. My cell phone bill averaged about $450.00 US per month—mostly talking with individuals in the United States—for the first few months I was working here. Now I use either a headset and softphone or a USB IP phone and connect over wireless to a U.S.-based IP-PSTN gateway provider. My cell phone bill has decreased by more than 90 percent and expense reporting of my telephone charges is not as painful as in the past. If you are a road warrior, and you incur significant long-distance toll charges, then there is no excuse for not switching to some type of VoIP-based communications.

VoIP, from a management and maintenance point of view, is less expensive than two separate telecommunications infrastructures. Implementation can be expensive and painful, but is repaid in the form of lower operating costs and easier administration. The pace and quality of IP application development is increasing in step with VoIP adoption. Features that were unavailable on traditional systems, such as "click-to-talk" with presence awareness, can rapidly be modified and deployed. Even voice encryption, which in the past was limited to select organizations, can now be used by anyone in a VoIP environment.

An often overlooked benefit of converging data and voice is that organizational directories often are updated and consolidated as part of the VoIP deployment process. This not only enables economies in and of itself but also makes features such as Push Directories possible. Push is the capability of an application using the WML protocol to send content to the telephone. IP transforms the everyday telephone into an applications-enabled appliance. The addition of push enables phone displays and/or audio to support a variety of applications (Web browsing, time reporting, emergency alerts, travel reservations, account code entry, announcements, branding via screensaver, inventory lookups, scheduling, etc.).

> ### NOTE
>
> **Presence:** Oftentimes, when discussing VoIP, the term "presence" is thrown around. What is presence? Presence is a system for determining whether or not an individual is available to communicate. In its simplest form, presence has nothing to do with location. In traditional telephony, presence can be determined to some extent by the status of the remote handset after a call is attempted. If the remote handset fails to go off-hook after eight to 10 rings, then the callee is probably not present. A busy tone indicates that the callee is probably present but unavailable. A better example of presence is instant messaging (IM). Instant messaging brought presence—the ability to tell when others are available to chat—to the masses. The next logical step was to incorporate location information into the context of presence. Presence as a source of users' state information has been maturing over the past few years. In the enterprise the notion of presence is broader. Presence can refer to the type of position a person has (for example, management or call center operator), their physical and organizational location, and a constellation of other personal information.

Convergence should simplify telecommunications management. For example, a single management station or cluster can be used to monitor both data and voice components and performance via SNMP. As mentioned earlier in this chapter, directory management will be simplified as well.

VoIP Protocols

Two major VoIP and multimedia suites dominate today: SIP and H.323. Others (like H.248) exist, and we will discuss some of them in this book, but these are the two major players. For simplicity, I will define SIP and H.323 as signaling protocols. However, whereas H.323 explicitly defines lower level signaling protocols, SIP is really more of an application-layer control framework. The SIP Request line and header field define the character of the call in terms of services, addresses, and protocol features.

Voice media transport is almost always handled by RTP and RTCP, although SCTP (Stream Control Transmission Protocol) has also been proposed and ratified by the IETF (and is used for the IP version of SS7, known as SIGTRAN). The transport of voice over IP also requires a large number of supporting protocols that are used to ensure quality of service, provide name resolution, allow firmware and software upgrades, synchronize network clocks, efficiently route calls, monitor performance, and allow firewall traversal. We talk about these and others in more detail in Chapter 8.

SIP is a signaling protocol for Internet conferencing, telephony, presence, events notification, and instant messaging. SIP is an IETF-ratified response-request protocol whose message flow closely resembles that of HTTP. SIP is a framework in that its sole purpose is to establish sessions. It doesn't focus on other call details. SIP messages are ASCII encoded. A number of open source SIP stacks exist.

H.323, on the other hand, is an ITU protocol suite similar in philosophy to SS7. The H.323 standard provides a foundation for audio, video, and data communications across IP-based networks, including the Internet. The H.323 protocols are compiled using ASN.1 PER. PER (Packed Encoding Rules)—a subset of BER—is a compact binary encoding that is used on limited-bandwidth networks. Also, unlike SIP, H.323 explicitly defines almost every aspect of call flow. The only open source H.323 stack I am aware of is the OpenH323 suite.

Both protocol suites rely upon supplementary protocols in order to provide ancillary services. Both protocols utilize TCP and UDP, and both open a minimum of five ports per VoIP session (Call signaling, two RTP, and two RTCP.) Both protocols offer comparable features, but they are not directly interoperable. Carriers tend to prefer H323 because the methods defined by H.323 make translation from ISDN or SS7 signaling to VoIP more straightforward than for SIP. SIP, on the other hand, is text-based, works better with IM, and typically is implemented on less expensive hardware. H.323 has been the market leader, but SIP rapidly is displacing H.323.

In Table 1.2, many of the more recent protocols that you will find in a VoIP environment are listed. We will talk about these and others in more detail in Chapters 8 and 13.

Table 1.2 VoIP-Related Protocols

Acronym	Support VoIP Protocol
RTSP	Real Time Streaming Protocol for media play-out control
RSVP	Resource Reservation Protocol
STUN	Simple Traversal of UDP through NAT
TURN	Traversal Using Relay NAT
ICE	Interactive Connectivity Establishment
SDP	Session Discovery Protocol
TLS	Transport Layer Security

VoIP Isn't Just Another Data Protocol

IP Telephony utilizes the Internet architecture, similar to any other data application. However—particularly from a security administrator's point-of-view—VoIP is different. There are three significant reasons for this:

- Voice conversations can be initiated from outside the firewall. Most client-driven protocols initiate requests from inside the firewall. Figure 1.1 shows the basic message flow of a typical Web browsing, e-mail, or SSH session.

- The real-time nature of VoIP—get there a second too late, and the packet is worthless.

- Separation of data and signaling. Sessions, particularly unknown inbound sessions, that define addressing information for the data (media) channel in a discrete signaling channel do not interact well with NAT and encryption.

Figure 1.1 Normal Message Flow

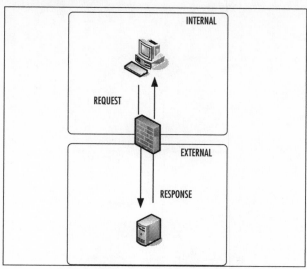

In Figure 1.1, a request is initiated by a client on the internal side of the firewall to a server daemon residing on a host external to the firewall. Firewalls that are capable of stateful inspection will monitor the connection and open inbound ports if that port is associated with an established session. Application Layer Gateways (ALGs) will behave in a similar manner, proxying outbound and inbound connections for the requesting internal host. For the firewall administrator and the user, the session completes normally, and is as secure as the firewall's permissions allow.

In Figure 1.2, the request-response topology is different from the message flow shown in Figure 1.1. In this figure, an external host (IP Phone, PC softphone, etc.) attempts to place a call to an internal host. Since no session is established, stateful inspection or ALG firewalls will not allow this connection to complete. We talk about this in much more detail in Chapter 13.

Figure 1.2 Inbound VoIP Message Flow

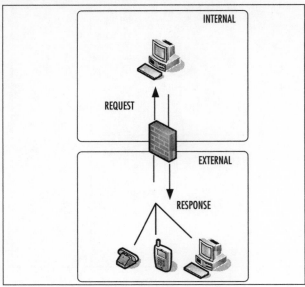

There are other differences. VoIP's sensitivity to adverse network conditions is different enough quantitatively from that of most types of data traffic that the difference is qualitative. Real-time applications, including VoIP, place requirements on the network infrastructure that go far beyond the needs of simple best-effort IP transport. Each VoIP packet represents about 20 ms of voice on average. A single lost packet may not be noticeable, but the loss of multiple packets is interpreted by the user as bad voice quality. The simple math indicates that even a short IP telephone call represents the transport of large numbers of packets. Network latency, jitter (interpacket latency variation), and packet loss critically affect the perceived quality of voice communications. If VoIP is going to work, then the network has to perform well—period.

Network engineers are accustomed to data network outages. Users, for the most part, don't suffer outages well, but they tolerate them. Users will not be as forgiving with their phone service. Even though cellular telephones seem to have the extraordinary characteristic of dropping connections at the least appropriate or convenient time, enterprise IP telephony users expect their phones to work all the time. Availability is a key VoIP performance metric.

Security Issues in Converged Networks

Convergence creates a new set of security concerns, as evidenced by the following comment by Winn Schwartau in *Network World's* November 14, 2005 edition:

> The communications world is moving toward VoIP but does not have the security expertise it needs in-house to meet the real-world stress it will encounter.

In a traditional PSTN network, the PBX or switch encompasses virtually all the intelligence in the system. It is responsible for basic call management including:

- Establishing connections (circuits) between the telephone sets of two or more users

- Maintaining such connections as long as the users require them

- Providing information for management and billing purposes.

Additionally, the PBX usually supports dozens or hundreds of ancillary call functions such as call transfer, call forwarding, voicemail, and so on.

The contemporary IP PBX functions in a similar fashion, although more functionality and intelligence is distributed to the endpoints depending upon the underlying protocols and architecture.

NOTE

Confidentiality, Integrity, and Availability: A simple but widely applicable security model is the CIA triad—standing for Confidentiality, Integrity, and Availability—three key principles that should be guaranteed in any kind of secure system. This principle is applicable across the whole security spectrum. Confidentiality refers to mechanisms that ensure that only authorized individuals may access secure information. Cryptography and Encryption are examples of methods used to ensure confidentiality of data. Integrity means that information is unchanged as it moves between endpoints. Availability characterizes the operational state of the network, and usually is expressed as "nines," or the number of nines on both sides of the decimal point (i.e., 99.999% reliability equals "5 nines"). It is critical to ensure that information is readily accessible to the authorized sender and receiver at all times. The Availability component of this triad is particularly important when securing converged networks.

One of the first security issues voiced by organizations implementing VoIP is the issue of the confidentiality of voice conversations. Unlike traditional telephone networks, which are circuit switched and relatively difficult to tap, voice traffic on converged networks is packet switched and vulnerable to interception with the same techniques used to sniff other traffic on a LAN or WAN. Even an unsophisticated attacker can intercept and decode voice conversations.

Tools & Traps...

VoIP Call Sniffers

VOIPong is a SIP, H.323, SCCP sniffer utility that can be used to detect and capture VoIP calls. With the appropriate tools, VOIPong can dump the conversation to a separate wave file. The unfortunately named vomit (Voice over Misconfigured Interenet Telephones) is an unrelated precursor to VOIPong that can translate tcp-dump files of Cisco IP telephone sessions. Other tools exist such as VoIPcrack, but these are not in the public domain.

Although this concern is real, in my view, it is not the most important security threat VoIP faces. Denial of Service (DoS) attacks, whether they are intentional or unintended, are the most difficult VoIP-related threat to defend against. Amplitude Research (www.amplituderesearch.com) reported in 2005 that:

> Companies had their share of network security problems. Virus and worm attacks led the list of intrusions as 63 percent of companies reported that they've had such problems. Trojan attacks occurred at 58 percent of companies. Backdoor viruses hit 45 percent of companies, while 35 percent say they suffered attacks from viruses or worms that were introduced internally.

Viruses and worms account for more security-related financial damage than all other security threats combined. The network traffic generated by these agents as they replicate and seek out other hosts to infect has been shown to wreck havoc with even relatively well-secured data networks. Although these data were derived from reports on data networks, VoIP networks, by their nature, are exquisitely sensitive to these types of attacks and should be expected to be affected similarly.

Security administrators can ensure confidentiality using one or several familiar tools. Conversations can be encrypted between endpoints or indirectly by tunneling conversations over VPNs. A PKI or certificate infrastructure, when implemented correctly, guarantees the identities of the two parties involved in a conversation and validates message integrity. But how does this same administrator guarantee availability when the network is under assault from the next incarnation of the Slammer worm? The answer, as it turns out, is that through careful planning and judicious use of networked controls, the physically converged network can be logically separated into compartments much like the bulkheads in a submarine, so that damage to one network compartment is limited to only that compartment. Data network problems can be segregated from the VoIP network and vice versa. We will talk about this approach in much more detail later in the book.

VoIP Threats

There are a number of ways to classify threats. The most comprehensive list of VoIP threats is maintained by VOIPSA at www.voipsa.com/Activities/taxonomy.php. The threat taxonomy is an excellent introduction to related terminology as well as the technical and social security issues surrounding VoIP. Rather than repeat their results, I've listed VoIP-specific threats based upon a simplified classification: VoIP Data and Service Disruption and VoIP Data and Service Theft. Table 1.3 lists those threats. Some of the more critical threats are explained in more detail in Chapter 9.

Table 1.3 VoIP-Specific Threats

Type of Risk	Threats
VoIP Data and Service Disruption	VoIP Control Packet Flood
	VoIP Call Data Flood
	TCP/UDP/ICMP Packet Flood
	VoIP Implementation DoS Exploit
	OS/Protocol Implementation DoS Exploit
	VoIP Protocol DoS Exploit
	Wireless DoS Attack
	Network Service DoS Attacks
	VoIP Application Dos Attacks
	VoIP Endpoint PIN Change
	VoIP Packet Replay

Continued

www.syngress.com

Table 1.3 continued VoIP-Specific Threats

Type of Risk	Threats
	VoIP Packet Injection
	VoIP Packet Modification
	QoS Modification
	VLAN Modification
VoIP Data and	VoIP Social Engineering
Service Theft	Rogue VoIP Device Connection
	ARP Cache Poisoning
	VoIP Call Hijacking
	Network Eavesdropping
	VoIP Application Data Theft
	Address Spoofing
	VoIP Call Eavesdropping
	VoIP Control Eavesdropping
	VoIP Toll Fraud
	VoIP Voicemail Hacks

A New Security Model

Access to network services is now more important than ever. The growing availability and maturity of Web services combined with advanced directory integration makes it easier to integrate information systems between business partners. Companies are moving their applications out from behind the firewall and onto the edges of their networks, where they can participate in dynamic, Internet-based transactions with customers and business partners. The network perimeter is becoming impossible to define as Intranets, extranets, business partner connections, VPN (Virtual Private Networks), and other RAS (Remote Access Services) services blur the definition of a trusted internal user; and critical corporate data may be located on handhelds, laptops, phones—anywhere.

VoIP distributes applications and services throughout the network. In a VoIP environment, IP phones (obviously) are distributed throughout the infrastructure as well. These devices incorporate microcontrollers and digital signal processors in order to perform voice compression and decompression, line and acoustic echo cancellation, DTMF (Dual Tone, Multi-Frequency—Tone Dial) detection, and network management and signaling. IP phones are smart, and depending upon the vendor, IP phones act as clients for a number of network protocols. This means that the number of network ingress/egress points will increase, and that processor cycles and memory—intelligence—are shifted to the logical edge of the network. This is a reversal of the traditional security model, where critical data is centralized, bounded, and protected.

This means that from a strategic viewpoint, converged networks, regardless of whether they are based upon H.323, SIP, or some other protocol, require a new way of thinking about information security (see Figure 1.3).

Figure 1.3 The New Security Paradigm

Old Paradigm
Trust internal users
Authenticate external users (perhaps)
Firewall internal data and users

New Paradigm
Trust no one
Authenticate everyone
Protect important data wherever it is!

"Trust no one" is an obvious bit of overstatement since every functioning system has to trust someone at some point or it won't work at all. A more concise (but not as catchy) axiom might be: "Don't assume you can trust anyone." The point here is this—Any system administrator, user, or device must be authenticated and authorized, regardless of its location, before it is able to access any network resources. Period.

Summary

We have all heard "Consultant-speak." Many of us practice it as well. I have done my best in this book to stay away from empty, jargon-laden speech, but I am sure that it creeps in at times. Here is my favorite example:

> **Consultant-speak**: VoIP Security is dependent on management of Process.

> **What this really means**: Processes define how individuals perform their duties within an organization. For securing VoIP networks, the processes include proactive ones such as formulation of security policies, identity verification management, hardening of operating systems, firewall deployment and configuration, system backup procedures, and penetration testing; and reactive processes such as log analyses, network monitoring, forensics, and incident response. If a process doesn't exist (e.g., if a task is performed in an ad hoc fashion), then one should be created. The security policies, processes, and standard operating procedures (SOPs) that have already proven successful in securing your data networks need to reused and extended. The ones that don't work should be discarded.

Organizations that deploy or plan to deploy VoIP networks will have to work harder at security than before. Security will cost more and it will require better trained administrators. We are getting to the point in networking where naïve system administration is not just bad practice, it may also be criminal. Regulations such as Sarbanes-Oxley (SOX), GLBA, and CALEA in the United States, as well as DPEC in Europe, have been interpreted to mean that privacy violations will be treated as a criminal acts. In Chapter 15, VoIP-related regulatory compliance is discussed in detail.

I've said earlier that the purpose of converging voice and data is to save money by running both types of traffic over the same physical infrastructure and to expand the spectrum of applications that can run over this infrastructure. In this architecture, packetized voice is subject to the same networking and security issues that exist on data-only networks. It seems to me that as organizations transition to this contemporary architecture there exists an unvocalized assumption: Users who have come to expect and accept short outages and sometimes erratic data network performance will *not* accept this same type of performance when it comes to voice communications. Perhaps this is true, or perhaps not. Cellular telephony come to mind here.

Traditional telephone systems have an excellent track record for reliability, and most people never question whether they will receive a dial tone when they pick up the receiver on their handsets. Contrast this with the reliability of most traditional IP networks. These same people who would never question the reliability of their telephone systems are accustomed to IP network outages and outages of systems that connect to the IP network. In a converged network, the loss of availability of the underlying IP network or the loss of availability of the IP telephony equipment (call management and adjunct servers) means the loss of availability of the telephone system.

Many organizations have reasonably well-secured logical perimeters (in so far as they can define those perimeters); however, their overall security environment offers no real defense in depth. Ideally, an enterprise network should offer multiple layers of defense—an intruder who manages to bypass one layer should then be confronted with additional layers, thereby denying the intruder quick access. On most of these networks, an unauthorized user who manages to bypass the logical (and/or physical) perimeter security controls has essentially unlimited access to all of internal assets on the internal IP network.

Authorized users are also assumed trustworthy; they have essentially unlimited access to all assets on the network as well. The lack of network-level security controls on the internal IP network exacerbates the risk of either malicious or accidental network activity, including propagation of worms and viruses.

Most people associate security attacks with the image of the lone hacker, a highly intelligent and motivated individual who attempts to penetrate an organization's IT infrastructure using a public network such as the Internet. Although remote unauthorized users do pose some risk to an organization's IT assets, the most significant IT-related risk to most enterprise organizations is potential financial loss due to direct or collateral damage from a worm or virus.

This point cannot be emphasized enough. The introduction of VoIP into an organization's IP network exacerbates the potential financial losses from a virus or worm outbreak.

The key to securing these networks—as we will see throughout this book— is to:

1. Communicate and enforce security policies.

2. Practice rigorous physical security.

3. Verify user identities.

4. Actively monitor logs, firewalls, and IDSes (Intrusion Detection Systems).

5. Logically segregate data and voice traffic.

6. Harden operating systems.

7. Encrypt whenever and wherever you can.

Solutions Fast Track

The Switch Leaves the Basement

- ☑ Converged networks offer an array of new vectors for traditional exploits and malware.

- ☑ VoIP is difficult to firewall primarily because of media stream requirements and embedded IP address information.

- ☑ Converged VoIP and data networks inherit all the security weaknesses of the IP protocol.

What Is VoIP?

- ☑ VoIP results from implementation of a common networking infrastructure to carry data and voice traffic over TCP/IP.

- ☑ Two major VoIP and multimedia suites dominate today: SIP and H.323.

- ☑ SIP is a signaling protocol for Internet conferencing, telephony, presence, events notification, and instant messaging.

- ☑ H.323 provides a foundation for audio, video, and data communications across IP-based networks.

VoIP Isn't Just Another Data Protocol

- ☑ The major differences between voice sessions and most types of common data sessions are that data and signaling channels are separate, sessions are often initiated from outside the firewall, and packet loss is unacceptable.

- ☑ Real-time applications, including VoIP, are extremely sensitive to network transport conditions, including delay, jitter, and packet loss.

- ☑ Availability is a key VoIP performance metric.

Security Issues in VoIP Networks

- ☑ Denial of Service (DoS) attacks are the most critical threat to VoIP networks.

☑ Physically shared VoIP and data networks can be logically separated for greater security.

☑ VoIP threats are a superset of data threats.

A New Security Model

☑ Any system administrator, user, or device must be authenticated and authorized, regardless of its location, before it is able to access any network resources.

☑ IP phones are intelligent, network–aware devices.

☑ The traditional "Walled City" approach to information security is reversed for converged networks, where intelligence is moved to the edge.

Frequently Asked Questions

The following Frequently Asked Questions, answered by the authors of this book, are designed to both measure your understanding of the concepts presented in this chapter and to assist you with real-life implementation of these concepts. To have your questions about this chapter answered by the author, browse to **www.syngress.com/solutions** and click on the **"Ask the Author"** form.

Q: Does VoIP work over an 802.11b/g wireless connection?

A: Yes, in fact many vendors are in the process of rolling out WiFi VoIP (VoWLAN—Voice over Wireless LAN) telephones.

Q: The "normal" phones we use have a bunch of features like hold, call forwarding, and the ability to select one of three lines to use to call/answer. I'd like the IP phone to be able to do the same kind of thing—is this possible?

A: Yes, IP phones and softphones have as many and oftentimes more features than traditional telephones.

Q: Is eavesdropping possible on a switched data network?

A: Yes. Many ARP spoofing tools allow an attacker to hijack sessions and capture them.

Q: Can I use my IP phone to call someone on the PSTN?

A: Not directly, but if your call goes through a gateway, then it is possible. Most organizations who implement VoIP provide gateways, and there are free gateways available.

Q: I'm using Skype. Iisn't this VoIP?

A: Yes. Skype runs over IP. Most people view Skype as a peer-to-peer protocol rather than a VoIP protocol.

Q: Can I really save money if I switch to VoIP?

A: It depends on your requirements. I save significant money, and most organizations claim this as well.

Chapter 2

Asterisk Configuration and Features

Solutions in this chapter:

- **What Functions Does a Typical PBX Perform?**
- **Voice Mail and Asterisk PBX**
- **How Is VoIP Different from Private Telephone Networks?**
- **What Functionality Is Gained, Degraded, or Enhanced on VoIP Networks?**

☑ **Summary**

☑ **Solutions Fast Track**

☑ **Frequently Asked Questions**

Introduction: What Are We Trying to Accomplish?

In this chapter we look into how the Asterisk PBX (Private Branch Exchange) plays an important role in our day-to-day lives of communication. We review some key functionality of Asterisk PBX systems and how they are being used to benefit our communication. We review some older PBX function technologies, such as analog and digital, as well as the new integrated VoIP-enabled functions. We review the benefits that IP-enabled PBX may have and its key differences from traditional voice technology.

In addition to providing an overview of the Asterisk PBX and examining the critical role of the PBX in our daily communications, we review the key functions of PBX systems and the multiple ways the PBX contributes to modern information exchange. The goal of this chapter is to offer solid instruction on the Asterisk PBX and underscore its significance.

Understanding the function and process of the PBX is essential to securing it successfully. After reading this chapter, you should be able to understand the Asterisk PBX system and its place of functionality in today's communication environment.

What Functions Does a Typical PBX Perform?

One of the main functions and benefits of a PBX is to reduce the number of local loops required from the PSTN central office switch. Further PBX core functions include maintain the routing information for the customer's telephone lines and to route calls accordingly. As its name delineates, PBX is used primarily as a private device owned by a solitary enterprise. The PBX system is positioned at the customer's rather than the telephone company's site.

NOTE

Do not confuse PBX routing with data routing protocols such as RIP, EIGRP, BGP, and such. PBX routes are sets of static or dynamic rules, which define routes based on Least Cost (LC). LC rules generally are decided by the destination of the number and the time of day it is dialed in order to determine the best call path with the lowest per minute charge.

The functions of the PBX have evolved since its introduction. Through a process similar to Darwin's theory of natural selection, only those functions that have proven to be the strongest and most adaptable still exist and define PBX as it is currently understood. One of the many reasons for the endurance of PBX is its ability to adapt to both emerging markets and the ever-changing needs of the consumer. It has survived its manual switchboard installations in 1896 through its analog days of the 1970s and remains relevant today as a partner to the new integrated VoIP technology.

The PBX has undergone four distinct stages of progression. The first stage was introduced in 1896 when manual switchboard PBX was installed. Operators switched calls manually by plugging wires into the PBX in order to route and connect calls. The second stage has been termed the analog stage. PBX has used analog signaling technology for communications between the PBX trunks and end-systems. The third stage arrived around 1976 when digital signaling was introduced as the newest communication method. The digital stage was accompanied by improvements such as increased PBX functionality and better overall system performance. The final and fourth and still evolving stage entered the picture in 1999 when the PBX began using the Internet Protocol (IP) for its signaling communication methods. Internet Protocol is the most common protocol used to transfer data in local area networks (LAN) and wide area networks (WAN) such as the Internet.

NOTE

In the early 1980s, Digital PBX was designed to provide all the data and voice networking in the industry. PBX was the multipurpose device through which all phones and computers were connected. Keeping in mind that in the 1980s the fastest modem capability was 9.6 Kbps and 10 Mbps and that Ethernet was yet to be created, so-called high-speed PBX data modules were introduced with rates of up to 57.6 Kbps. This new speed with digital signaling technology allowed PBX systems to interconnect computer systems at higher speeds, and introduced new advances in WAN connectivity with superior performance and flexibility of packet routing over fixed WAN circuits compared to circuit-switched alternatives. It appeared that Digital PBX had great potential and promise for its time in connecting local computers. This promise to use PBX as a hub for local computers, however, was short-lived as PBX was unable to compete after the introduction of Ethernet and cheap 10 Mbps capable hubs.

It is important to note that the three technologies described in the preceding paragraph are all used today and will be used for many years to come. Significant differences exist between analog and digital technologies. Although analog technology is relatively simple and inexpensive, it fails to offer some of the complex functions of digital.

Compare the functions of your work phone to the one in your home. At home you might have speed dial, a mute button, and redial, versus at work where you have a button for voicemail that lights up when you have new messages and buttons for transferring calls, conferencing (to connect up to four other people), operator emergency, on-hold that plays music, and other functions.

Digital signaling offers increase of sophistication in the methods used for transporting audio signal (media) across time and space. Analog signaling takes video or voice and converts it into electronic impulses. Digital signaling takes video or voice and converts it into binary format of 0s and 1s. Binary format takes less line resource than electronic impulses in analog signaling. By using this increased complexity of signaling in digital lines, more functions can be passed down to end-users from the PBX system.

The third and final stage of PBX evolution, known as VoIP, produced increased user capability. An IP-enabled PBX system taps into WAN/LAN networks, allowing them to communicate with IP-enabled devices all over the world. Our phone systems are no longer restrained to the cable distance and bandwidth limitations of traditional PBX connectivity. IP-PBX systems truly deliver on-demand remote workplace functionality, where your phone number is attached to your devices' dynamically changing IP addresses anywhere in the world. We will concentrate on describing VoIP-enabled PBX and comparing them to traditional digital PBX systems later in this chapter, and review details in Chapter 3.

Many new commercial and open source PBX systems have emerged with this new IP-based stage. One such IP-enabled PBX called the Asterisk™ has introduced this VoIP technology and graciously offers its services to the community free of charge. We will be reviewing some of Asterisk™ functionality within this chapter.

Asterisk is software running a PBX system that is freely available to anyone under GNU General Public License (GPL). Asterisk can be installed and run on a variety of different operating system (OS) platforms, such as Linux, BSD, and Mac OS X. Some of Asterisk's features include Call conferencing, Call monitoring, Call forwarding, Call parking, Call routing, Caller ID, Caller ID blocking, Calling cards, E911, IVR, Music on hold, Voicemail, and many more. It supports codecs such as ADPCM, G.711, G.723, G.726, G.729, GSM, Speex, and others. Protocols supported include IAX, H.323, SIP, MGCP, and SCCP. Its support for traditional telephony interoperability includes E&M, FXS, FXO, Loopstart, Groundstart, DTMF, and others. To find out more about Asterisk™ open source PBX visit its Web site at www.asterisk.org.

PBX Administration

Programs used for management of calls, and overall functionality of the PBX system, allows administrators to keep the PBX system healthy and running. Management interfaces handle calls by adding and deleting new extensions, updating routing plans, enabling Call parking feature, monitoring conference calls, and much more. User-friendly administration programs for complex PBX systems allow better overall support.

Asterisk Gateway Interface

Asterisk Gateway Interface (AGI) allows developers from all programming backgrounds to create custom interfaces between Asterisk's dial plan and outside programs. Developers choose their own programming languages such as Perl, Pascal, C, and PHP to manage the PBX system and its connected users. Unlike in proprietary PBX systems such as Nortel, Avaya, or Cisco, this AGI functionality in Asterisk's open-sourced PBX system invites users who want to write their own custom-built telephony management applications. For further information on AGI and available applications visit www.voip-info.org and search for AGI.

Asterisk Manager API

Asterisk provides application programming interface (API) for its PBX system to further manage overall performance and add feature functionality. Unlike the AGI, the API is used to control functionality of a PBX system from remote external application over a TCP/IP socket. API allows external programs to monitor call activity, build remote extensions, and perform basic call controls such as hanging up channels and transferring calls. Access to this socket API functionality is managed with the *manager.conf* file inside the */etc/asterisk/* directory. Figure 2.1 displays an example of the *manager.conf* file configured to allow sockets on TCP port 5038. As with every administrative application, the firewall should restrict access to administration ports. Further administrative restrictions to the administration port can be applied with **deny** and **permit** syntax lines defined in the *manager.conf* file as shown in Figure 2.1.

Figure 2.1 *manager.conf* Configuration File

```
Asterisk - PBX                                                    _ □ ×
[root@asterisk1 asterisk]# cat manager.conf
;
; Asterisk Call Management support
;
[general]
enabled = yes
port = 5038
bindaddr = 0.0.0.0

[admin]
secret = amp111
deny=0.0.0.0/0.0.0.0
permit=127.0.0.1/255.255.255.0
read = system,call,log,verbose,command,agent,user
write = system,call,log,verbose,command,agent,user

#include manager_custom.conf
```

Dial Plans

Dial plans are key to the routing function of PBX systems; they control how incoming and outgoing calls should be processed within the PBX. Dial plans consist of a set of programmed rules defined by the administrator that directs PBX on how to handle a specific call and its functions. When a call comes into the PBX system from the analog line, digital line, or VoIP, the system determines its proper destination based on extension number and dial plan properties.

Figure 2.2 illustrates the following example of a dial plan's function. When an employee with a 55xx extension inside the headquarters network dials a 7551 extension to reach one of his associates in the remote branch office A, his first stop will be PBX 1. PBX 1 receives this call and immediately looks up its Dial Plan procedures. PBX 1 looks up directions on how to handle calls going into 7551 destination and forwards it accordingly. PBX 2 will receive this call and go through a process similar to that of PBX 1. It will look up its Dialer Plan, recognize the destination 7551 as one of its own, and start the signaling/forwarding according to its final telephone equipment destination. In this scenario, a dialer plan was used in both PBX systems 1 and 2 to determine the proper procedure for incoming and outgoing calls.

Dialer plans could combine multiple call procedures. What happens when a user tries to dial 8551 extension in Branch B from the headquarters? Which path will the call most likely take? Again as explained in the previous paragraph, PBX 1 will look up its dialer plan upon receiving this call and search for 8551 destination procedures. It is likely that there will be multiple defined procedures for this destination in PBX

1. A dial plan in this example could be configured to forward this specific voice call via the IP-Internet as VoIP or it can forward this voice call through a Public Switched Telephone Network (PSTN). Decision on forwarding a call over VoIP versus PSTN could be made based on the time of day or based on call capacity. During peak hours the dial plan procedures could indicate to forward this call using VoIP data links in order to save the company money on the local telephone charges that this call would cost. During off-hours when calls might be free of charge from the telephone company, the business could choose to implement a procedure in their dial plan to forward the call over PSTN. Further dial plan decisions could be made based on priority of multiple defined paths. The dial plan can place priority on multiple paths so that multiple paths can coexist, and when trunks for the preferred path are full or otherwise unavailable, the calls can be sent on another path via another trunk group.

Figure 2.2 Dial Plan Effect

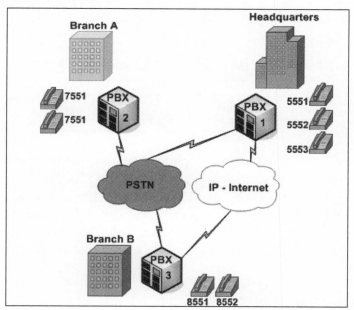

Numbering Plans

Dial plans use the numbers entered by users to identify commands and perform functions. The three most basic numbering plans that exist are the International Numbering Plan (E.164), Country Numbering Plans, and Private Numbering Plans.

The E.164 International Numbering Plan allows telephone companies to route calls across national borders. Standards developed by The International Telecommunications Union–Telecommunication Standardization Committee (ITU–T) must be closely followed and are accepted globally in the PSTN network to achieve interoperability between systems. Figure 2.3 presents the format of ITU–T recommended telephone numbers. Country Code (CC) represents one to three digits of the country, National Destination Code (NDC) specifies the numbering area within the country, and Subscriber Number (SN) defines the locally assigned number within the area.

NOTE

Article E.164, which replaced E.163 in 1997, is an ITU–T statute that establishes the international numbering plan used by public telecommunications. For more information on ITU and its standards visit the www.itu.int Web site.

Figure 2.3 ITU–T Format for International Dial Plan over PSTN

Country Numbering Plans allows telephone companies to route calls nationally. North America follows the North American Numbering Plan (NANP), which is shared with other North American countries. Figure 2.4 represents the format of NANP. The first three digits represent the area code within United States. Note that the first number N can be any number between 2 and 9. The next three digits represent location within an area code, and the last four digits is the actual number of the end-user.

Figure 2.4 NANP Format for Dial Plan

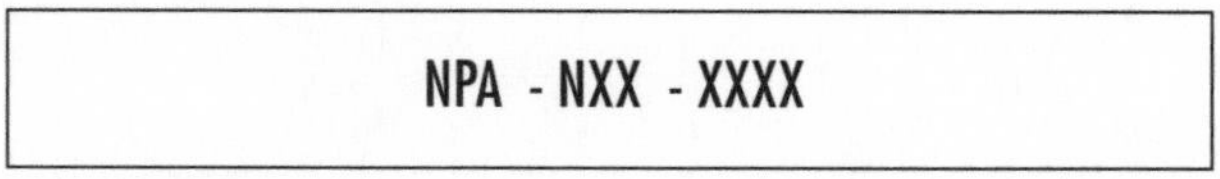

NPA - NXX - XXXX

Private Numbering Plans are used by organizations that create and use their own dial plans, which is typical of PBX systems and networks made up of such systems. Figure 2.2 is an example of a private dial plan being used on PBX systems. In Figure 2.2, employees use a four-digit number plan to reach associates in a different geographical location rather then using the NANP nine-digit numbering plan. PBX systems use their own private dialing plans, which will be our primary focus in this section. A private dial plan differs from the public PSTN network in that it is a homogeneous design maintained by private businesses.

Interconnecting an organization's branches privately, rather than using public telephone systems, allows the organization to simplify its telephone numbering plan and overall communication between members of the organization.

Choosing a Numbering Scale for Your Private Numbering Plan

One of the first steps in designing a numbering plan for your organization is to decide how many numbers you will need for your extensions in order to satisfy your overall phone environment. It is essential to keep your numbering plan user friendly. No one wants to dial a nine-digit number just to reach someone sitting in the row next to him or her.

When choosing your organization's numbering scale, three factors must be considered in order to accommodate future growth:

- Number of sites and their growth potential
- Number of employees at each site and their growth potential
- DID ranges in use at each site and potential conflicts

It is very important to anticipate future expansion when scaling your numbering plan. Your dial plan should be designed to satisfy the needs of your company for a minimum of five to10 years. By reserving enough digits for future site extensions and possible new business acquisitions, you will reduce the likelihood that you will be required to renumber your entire environment in upcoming years. For example, if your company has over 90 sites with 60 employees at each site it would not make sense to pick a four-digit numbering plan. A four-digit numbering plan in this scenario does not have any room for growth in site extensions and will require renumbering in the near future. Take care to assign enough digits to your employees' site extensions. If your sites have 60 or less employees and you are certain that they will not exceed 500 employees in five years, it is safe to assign a three-digit employee extension plan per site. Feature numbers such as "0" are reserved for the company operator and will need to be accounted for in your overall dial plan.

Assigning Dialer Plan: A Case Study

Corporation XYZ has tasked you with designing a dialer plan for its private telephone system. Corporation XYZ currently employs about 4200 employees (see Figure 2.5). Your first task is to estimate current and future site growth and any increase in the number of employees over next five to 10 years.

Figure 2.5 Corporation XYZ's Current Environment

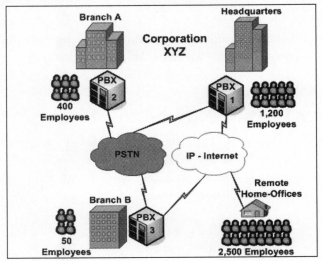

Corporation XYZ plans to increase its overall work force in the next 10 years. Corporation XYZ's major work force increase will be targeted at remote home-office employees, to which it plans to add 1400 new employees. Currently, 2500 employees work remotely. The company plans to add 700 at its headquarters. Branch A will increase by 450 employees and Branch B will increase by 10 to 20 new employees. Corporation XYZ further plans to open five to eight new branch offices similar to Branch B in the next 10 years, hosting up to 70 employees in each.

NOTE

Remember to include restricted numbers when building your private dial plan. Restricted numbers are common numbers used by your organization to reach services such as Voicemail, Operator, Emergency, Call Parking, Conferencing, and others. You must account for these extensions in your private dialer plan.

A five-digit dial plan assignment for Corporation XYZ provides for current and future growth. It will allow Corporation XYZ to double its work force and open new branch office space without having to renumber, reroute, or add a new numbering plan for the next 10 years. Table 2.1 outlines the new dialing plan. Remember that you will also need to put aside common numbers for operator, voice-mail, emergency, and such, which are not reflected in Table 2.1.

A good dial plan starts out with at least 90 percent sparse numbers on day one to accommodate growth. Anything less than five digits in this case is just asking for trouble where in few years the entire phone system may need to be renumbered.

Remote users will be required to use one of the PBX systems connected to an IP-network in order to interconnect with the company's internal phone system. Extensions will be routed to their IP addresses where IP-phones are connected. Since remote users in this case must be part of the headquarters or branch office PBX system and most likely will share the same DID number with local connected user extensions, you may just choose to expend the local PBX number extension plan rather than assigning a new number range unique just to remote users.

Table 2.1 Corporation XYZ's Number Scale

Corporate Location	Extension
Headquarters	1-xxxx to 1-9999
Remote Users	2-xxxx to 2-9999
Branch A	3-0xxx to 3-0999
Branch B	3-1xxx to 3-1999
Future Branch Use	3-2xxx to 8-9999

Extensions Based on DID

It is popular among organizations to configure dial plan extension assignments based on Direct Inward Dialing numbers (DID). DID numbers are assigned by telephone companies. For example, if the DID number for a company employee is 303-555-1212, the user's extension configured in the dialer plan on the local PBX system would be 1212. The extension matches the DID number. Extensions based on DID numbering allow for user-friendly dial plans.

Dialing Plan and Asterisk PBX

The heart of Asterisk's dial plan is sourced from the *extensions.conf* configuration file that resides in */etc/asterisk* directory by default. Asterisk's extensions configuration file defines what needs to done when an end-user signals the PBX. The extensions configuration file defines the rules for when music-on-hold is played, when to record phone conversations and at what extension, what happens when a user presses *78 (DND feature), what a caller must do in order to call an outside number (e.g., press 9 before calling), and many more PBX functions initiated by callers.

The extensions configuration file comprises four main parts: *contexts, id-extensions, priorities,* and *application-commands.* The *id-extensions* part represents extensions, a number digit that is triggered by being dialed. Each of these extensions consists of steps and *priorities,* which start from 1. Each *priority* includes an *application-command* that triggers a specific application, such as answering the call or hanging up. *Context* is used to group a number of extensions into one entity. The extensions configuration file in Asterisk consists of line codes that represent extensions, priorities, and applications that are triggered by priorities.

Figure 2.6 displays part of an *extensions.conf* file and a set of instructions that the PBX system takes when the end-user dials *78. By default in Asterisk PBX the *78 extension is used for the DND feature. Details on the DND feature will be explained later in this changer. The first line, *[app-dnd]*, represents the *context* that groups this extension together in dialing plan. The second line, *exten =>*78,1,Answer*, represents *id-extension* as *78, *priority* as 1, and *application-command* as Answer. In this case when someone dials *78 the first thing that will happen according to this set of instructions is the PBX will answer the call. The last line of this example, which has the highest priority, 7, of this *context* will hang up the call.

The extensions file in the Asterisk PBX system is the heart of the dial plan. It determines what to do when a user triggers the system by dialing a digit. There are many features and application syntaxes available for the Asterisk dial plan configuration file. Search the www.voip-info.org Web site using "dial plan" as the keyword string to find endless information on how to build and use the Asterisk dial plan.

Figure 2.6 *extensions.conf* File and *78 Extension

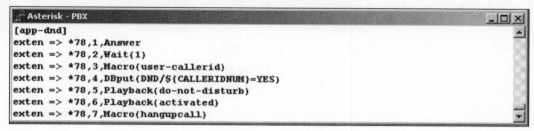

```
Asterisk - PBX                                              _ □ ×
[app-dnd]
exten => *78,1,Answer
exten => *78,2,Wait(1)
exten => *78,3,Macro(user-callerid)
exten => *78,4,DBput(DND/${CALLERIDNUM}=YES)
exten => *78,5,Playback(do-not-disturb)
exten => *78,6,Playback(activated)
exten => *78,7,Macro(hangupcall)
```

Billing

The billing feature allows you to properly bill and collect money (or cross-charge) for the use of your PBX system and its telephone services. Billing accounting allows you to bill based on the number called and the amount of service time. In addition, billing accounting allows the customer to know not only the amount that is owed but the big-three variables (who, where, and how-long) of each service call made.

Billing Accounting with Asterisk PBX System

By default Asterisk PBX generates a Call Detail Record (CDR) for each call and is configured to store call details into a Comma Separated Values (CSV) file. This file is located in the /var/log/asterisk/cdr-csv directory on the Asterisk PBX system. The CDR accounting file name is *Master.csv*. Table 2.2 lists fields stored in the CDR filename.

Table 2.2 Billing Fields and Functions Recorded

Field	Function
Accouncode	Manually assigned account code tag per extension or channel (string 20 chars)
Src	Caller ID number (string 80 char)
Dst	Destination number (string 80 char)
Cdcontext	Destination context (string 80 char)
Clid	Caller ID with text (80 char)
Channel	Channel used (80 char)
Dstchannel	Destination channel if appropriate (80 char)
Lastapp	Last application if appropriate (80 char)
Lastdata	Last application data (arguments) (80 char)

Continued

Table 2.2 continued Billing Fields and Functions Recorded

Field	Function
Start	Start of phone call (date/time)
Answer	Answer of phone call (date/time)
End	End of phone call (date/time)
Duration	Duration of phone call from dial to hang-up in seconds (integer)
Billsec	Duration of phone call from answer to hang-up in seconds (integer)
Disposition	What happened to the call dialed (e.g., busy, failed, answered)
Amaflags	What flags to use (e.g., billing, ignore) specified on per-channel basis
User field	User-defined field (255 chars)
Uniqueid	Unique channel identifier (32 chars)

Figure 2.7 displays a sample Master.csv file in Microsoft Excel using some of the CDR values that were defined in the previous table. You can modify the format of the CDR file and its fields to fit your needs. With this file in hand, you can query for a specific extension and the relative phone services records. You can find out who is spending the most time on the phone by looking up source and duration fields. Further you can find out which number is called most often by querying the destination fields. Accounting information in the Master.csv file allows you to create invoices for paying subscribers.

Figure 2.7 Modified *Master.csv* File and Its CDR Records

	A	B	C	D	E	F	G
75	Date / Time	Channel	Source	Clid	Destination	Disposition	Duration
76	2/4/2006 22:59	SIP/2000-acdd	2000	"Softphone1" <2000>	*78	ANSWERED	4
77	2/4/2006 22:59	SIP/2000-2170	2000	"Softphone1" <2000>	*79	ANSWERED	5
78	2/4/2006 23:01	SIP/2000-dc31	2000	"device" <2000>	*78	ANSWERED	1
79	2/6/2006 4:30	SIP/2001-5a3e	2001	3035552001	18005551212	ANSWERED	7
80	2/6/2006 4:31	SIP/2001-496a	2001	3035552001	18005551212	NO ANSWER	10
81	2/6/2006 4:31	SIP/2001-b883	2001	3035552001	15165551212	ANSWERED	118
82	2/4/2006 23:24	SIP/2000-98c7	2000	"Softphone1" <2000>	*79	ANSWERED	4
83	2/4/2006 23:44	SIP/2001-e21e	2001	"Softphone2" <2001>	3001	NO ANSWER	16
84	2/4/2006 23:46	SIP/3001-5d0b	3001	"device" <3001>	700	ANSWERED	37
85	2/4/2006 23:45	SIP/3001-3b2b	3001	"device" <3001>	700	ANSWERED	123
86	2/4/2006 23:44	SIP/2001-d010	2001	"Softphone2" <2001>	3001	ANSWERED	143
87	2/4/2006 23:46	SIP/2000-08da	2000	"device" <2000>	701	ANSWERED	9
88	2/6/2006 4:30	SIP/2001-5a3e	2001	3035552001	17205551212	ANSWERED	7
89	2/6/2006 4:31	SIP/2001-496a	2001	3035552001	15165551212	NO ANSWER	10
90	2/6/2006 4:31	SIP/2001-b883	2001	3035552001	18005551212	ANSWERED	118
91	2/6/2006 5:02	SIP/3001-f2f6	3001	"device" <3001>	700	ANSWERED	31

CSV file formats can be easily converted and imported into common databases. Many billing applications can then interconnect with these databases and create prepaid and postpaid billing solutions. Some supported CDR storage methods and databases include:

- Asterisk CDR records to text file with comma separated values
- Asterisk CDR records to SQLite database
- Asterisk CDR records to PostgreSQL database
- Asterisk CDR records to unixODBC supported databases
- Asterisk CDR records to MySQL
- Asterisk CDR records to Sybase

For further information on Asterisk PBX and its billing CDR conversions visit www.voip-info.org/wiki/view/Asterisk+billing.

Prepaid and Postpaid Billing

Prepaid billing solutions require the end-user to pay prior to using PBX phone services. Prepaid billing is commonly used by VoIP service providers: the user pays one monthly fee for unlimited calling prior to making calls. Additional services such as calling cards or conferences utilize prepaid billing. In the prepaid billing model the PBX must access the user's funds before a call is made and be able to disconnect a call when funds run out. Some prepaid billing solutions are Personal Identification

Number (PIN) based, requiring users to enter a PIN prior to making calls. PIN-based solutions are best compared to calling cards. Other prepaid solutions may make use of Automatic Number Identification (ANI) to identify callers. ANI is passed and carried from your phone to the PBX, which servers as an identifier. In prepaid solution scenarios, the caller must be identified and have sufficient funds prior to making a call.

Post-paid billing solutions bill users periodically after they use phone services. PBX accounting records such as Asterisk's CSV file can be imported into a database and queried for billing records. Sample billing database queries can be based on accounting codes, or source or destination phone numbers.

Tools & Traps…

Asterisk PBX Open Source Billing Solutions

Users can choose several types of Asterisk PBX open source billing solutions, including the following:

A2Billing http://voip-info.org/wiki/view/A2Billing

AstBill http://astbill.com/

MCC www.paskambink.lt/mcc/

Trabas www.trabas.com/opensource/

Freeside www.sisd.com/freeside/

Visit www.voip-info.org/wiki/view/Asterisk+billing for more commercial and open source billing solutions.

Routing

After looking up its dial plan for a specific call handling instruction, PBX must route calls to their desired destination. Routing the call allows the voice network to communicate with its peers and desired destinations. Calls can be routed based on lowest cost path, time of day, disaster recovery, and other criteria.

Time-of-Day Routing

Time-of-day routing influences call routing by using a time variable. Have you ever called a support line after business hours and ended up talking to someone in a different country? Your call was routed based on the time of day. This solution often is used by multiple call support centers in different geographic locations. For example, a company with support hours from 8 A.M. to 8 P.M. EST with two call centers, one in New York and one in California, may chose to start routing morning calls to its New York facility due to the time being three hours earlier in California. As the time changes, additional coverage can be offered by distributing calls to the west facility.

Day-of-Week Routing

Day-of-week routing influences call routing by the date variable. This routing functionality can be used for call centers that may alternate between 12-hour shift schedules. During designated holiday dates, calls can be routed to different countries that may not have same date holidays.

Source Number Routing

Source number routing influences call routing by source phone variable. This solution is best used with 800 number services or when a company has a central contact number. To reduce expenses, you would choose to route calls to the closest possible destination, keeping calls local when possible, in order to save on toll charges. You may also prefer for your customers to speak with a local call center rather than a call center out of state (or vice versa since some in-state toll rates exceed interstate rates).

Cost-Savings Routing

As the name implies, cost-savings routing selects the least expensive call path. A desired solution is defined as using your data VoIP networks to route all your interoffice voice calls, thereby avoiding any telephone company toll charges. Cost savings is one of the biggest advantages in VoIP technology.

Disaster Routing

Having multiple routing paths for your voice traffic allows for quick disaster recovery. In VoIP networks where one of your data connections used for voice to the local Internet provider fails, it automatically will be recovered by a secondary backup data connection to a different Internet provider, or you may chose to reroute traffic to your phone company over traditional phone lines. VoIP provides redundancy by automatically routing calls to a different destination when links fail.

Disaster routing recovery takes place not only when your data connectivity or phone connectivity goes down, but also when one of your PBX systems that decided to retire a bit early; calls must be rerouted through a different PBX or to a different call center altogether.

Call rerouting can be further initiated by the capacity of trunk lines to assure maximum voice quality. When one link is congested, rather than continuing to send calls down the congested link and decreasing the overall quality of new and existing connections, calls are sent to a new trunk with free available resource. Asterisk PBX system has the ability to limit outgoing calls per trunk to avoid possible congestion.

Skill-Based Routing

Skill-based routing allows the caller to be routed to the best support representative based on the skills required. Prior to talking with a support representative, the caller is prompted with a series of questions that are compared against the skill sets of multiple representatives. The caller will be routed to the best matching skill set agent to achieve the best possible support experience.

DUNDi Routing Protocol

Distributed Universal Number Discovery (DUNDi) is a peer-to-peer protocol used to dynamically discover how to reach users throughout the VoIP network. Asterisk PBX uses DUNDi protocol for scalability and redundancy among its peer PBX systems. Its advantage over ENUM protocol is that it is fully distributed without centralized authority. DUNDi is a proprietary protocol developed by Digium, submitted as an Internet Draft to the Internet Engineering Task Force (IETF).

According to the Internet Draft submitted in 2004, DUNDi supports overlaying multiple dial plans between PBX systems defined by private context. DUNDi also supports sharing of E.164 numbers between PBX systems and its route base. E.164 number route context in Asterisk's PBX is defined by "e164" and is reserved only for members agreeing to the General Peering Agreement (GPA). For more information on DUNDi visit the www.dundi.info Web site.

Other Functions

PBX systems offer other functions besides call routing, billing, dial plans, and call management. Some of their other functions include music on hold, conferencing, voicemail system, IVR system, call parking, and many more. In the following topics we will review a few of these functions and look at how they are configured on PBX.

Music on Hold

The music on hold feature provides music to a party waiting for its connection to be established. Music on hold can be triggered to play during call transfers, while waiting in queue for the next available representative, when a call is parked, or when the receiving party simply needs to mute the conversation. Playing music informs the waiting party that the connection is still established and prompts them to continue to wait.

There are several sources for music to interconnect into PBX systems. Some interconnected music sources that PBX systems can utilize include, but are not limited to, AM/FM connected radios, Television music channels, and MP3 music files.

Call Parking

Call Parking allows you to place (park) a call in a designated extension area where it can be retrieved later from the same or a different extension. This feature often is used in stores, where the operator may announce over a loudspeaker for an employee to dial extension XYZ in order to retrieve an incoming waiting call that is currently parked. Call parking helps the operator to keep the line clear by transferring callers to parked extensions. Music on hold usually is played for callers waiting in a parked extension area. An optional call parking feature called the call parking time wait interval can be configured. Time wait interval prevents parked users from waiting indefinitely. When the time wait interval for a parked user is reached, PBX will rering the original number dialed. Call parking allows mobility for employees and avoids unnecessary call back charges.

Call Parking with Asterisk PBX

Configured parked zones are simple extensions that are used to hold calls. Parking a caller in the designated extension is performed by transferring the call to the preestablished extension. Prior to parking a call, the end-user must know the designated parking extension.

Asterisk PBX uses the *features.conf* file to configure its Call parking feature. Three important variables in the configuration file include *parkext*, *parkpos*, and *parkingtime*.

- *parkext* represents the extension the end-user must dial in order to park a call.
- *parkpos* represents the extension range that PBX will use to park calls.
- *Parkingtime* represents the time wait interval before a call is transferred back to its original party.

Figure 2.8 displays Asterisk's *features.conf* file. In this particular example the designated extension that end-user must know in order to park calls is 700. When end-user transfers a call to parking extension 700, the PBX system will automatically park the call in any of the 701 to 720 available extensions defined by the *parkpos* variable in the *features.conf* configuration file. Figure 2.9 displays an Asterisk PBX debug log window of an actual call being parked into a 701 phone extension. The PBX system will announce the parking extension it has picked to the end-user and the caller.

Figure 2.8 Asterisk *features.conf* Call Parking

```
Asterisk - PBX                                                    _ □ ×
[root@asterisk1 asterisk]# cat features.conf
;
; Sample Parking configuration
;

[general]
parkext => 700                      ; What ext. to dial to park
parkpos => 701-720                  ; What extensions to park calls on
context => parkedcalls              ; Which context parked calls are in
parkingtime => 60                   ; Number of seconds a call can be parked
 for (default is 45 seconds)
```

Figure 2.9 Asterisk *features.conf* Call Parking in Action

```
Asterisk - PBX                                                    _ □ ×
    -- Started music on hold, class 'default', on channel 'SIP/2000-9f6a'
    -- Executing Park("SIP/3001-4e78", "") in new stack
 == Parked SIP/3001-4e78 on 701. Will timeout back to extension [from-internal]
s, 1 in 60 seconds
    -- Added extension '701' priority 1 to parkedcalls
asterisk1*CLI>
```

NOTE

Do not forget to restart or reload your Asterisk PBX after making changes to your *features.conf* file in order for the changes to take effect.

Call Pickup

The call pickup feature gives you the ability to retrieve and answer an incoming call directed at your phone using a different nearby phone station. This feature can be used in a scenario where you might be working in a nearby office and hear your phone ring. Call pickup allows you to use the nearest phone in the remote office and pull the incoming call from your phone station into the phone you picked up nearby. Group call pickup and direct call pickup are two features of call pickup. Group call pickup allows you to pull in an incoming call from a phone configured to be part of your call pickup group by simply picking up a phone. Direct call pickup allows you to pull in an incoming call by picking up a remote phone station and dialing your extension along with the pickup number.

Call Recording

Call recording provides the ability for a PBX to record call conversations. Call recording can be configured as a systemwide feature or be based on a specific extension group. Call recordings can start recording a conversation from start to finish or allow the operator to control the time by pressing a feature button (number) during the call to initiate and stop recording.

> **NOTE**
>
> Some jurisdictions do not allow monitoring of phone calls. Different jurisdictions may apply different laws and monitoring procedures. Some jurisdictions require for both parties to know that the call is being recorded. Make sure you consult your lawyer before implementing this recording feature.

Conferencing

Conferencing allows for more than two parties to participate in a call and enables all parties involved to hear each other at the same time. Typically the end-user's phone is able to conference up to four other parties using the conference feature button. Avaya PBX system capability can be configured with up to six party conferences from a single phone extension. The Asterisks PBX system uses the *meetmecount()* function to limit the number of available conference parties per phone and is defined by the capability of the system. For large-scale call-in meetings, designated conference numbers can be used to interconnect more parties than allowed by a single user's phone.

Conferencing with Asterisk PBX

Asterisk PBX makes use of its *MeetMe()* function to provide conferencing ability. Asterisk PBX function has the capacity to create password-protected conferences, conference administration options, dynamic and static conferences, and much more.

TIP

As a prerequisite to using the *MeetMe()* function, the Zaptel application must be installed and configured with Asterisk.

Configuring conferences in Asterisk requires editing of the *meetme.conf* and *extensions.conf* files. To illustrate this process, we will set up a simple conference room using extension 1001. The initial step is to edit the *meetme.conf* file, as noted in Figure 2.10. The first variable in the *meetme.conf* file represents our extension for the conference, the second optional variable is the pass code (11111) that the caller must enter in order to access the conference, and the third variable is the conference administrator pass code (232323). Once inside the conference, administrators have additional options, such as disconnecting users and muting the conference. Figure 2.11 represents the *extensions.conf* configuration. The top line directs the call to transfer to the (conf,1) line when a user dials extension 1001. The (conf,1) line starts the conference by initiating the *MeetMe()* function. Figure 2.12 shows a caller with extension 2001 calling into conference 1001 and initiating the *MeetMe()* function of the PBX.

Figure 2.10 Conferencing—*meetme.conf* Sample

```
Asterisk - PBX                                                    _ □ ×
; This is meetme.conf file
; Usage conf => confnumber[,userpin][,adminpin]
;
conf => 1001,11111,232323
```

Figure 2.11 Conferencing—*extensions.conf* Sample

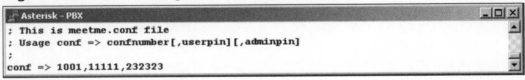

```
Asterisk - PBX                                                    _ □ ×
exten => 1001,1,Goto(conf,1)

exten => conf,1,Meetme(1001|sM)
```

Figure 2.12 Conferencing—PBX Initiating *MeetMe()* Conference Function

```
Asterisk - PBX                                                    _ |□| X|
     -- Executing Goto("SIP/2001-700f", "conf|1") in new stack
     -- Goto (from-internal,conf,1)
     -- Executing MeetMe("SIP/2001-700f", "1001|sM") in new stack
  == Parsing '/etc/asterisk/meetme.conf': Found
  == Parsing '/etc/asterisk/meetme_additional.conf': Found
     -- Created MeetMe conference 1023 for conference '1001'
     -- Playing 'conf-getpin' (language 'en')
     -- Playing 'conf-onlyperson' (language 'en')
     -- Started music on hold, class 'default', on channel 'SIP/2001-700f'
asterisk1*CLI>
```

Additional options, including recording the conference in audio format, regulating the number of participants, and permitting only one speaker can be configured. Figure 2.13 shows Asterisk's PBX Command Line Interface (CLI) and some of the **meetme** command functions available to PBX administrators. To access Asterisk's CLI, type the **asterisk −r** command within the root shell account. For a complete list of available options, visit www.voip-info.com and search for the MeetMe() feature.

Figure 2.13 Conferencing—PBX and CLI Options for Asterisk

```
Asterisk - PBX                                                    _ |□| X|
asterisk1*CLI> help meetme
Usage: meetme   (un)lock|(un)mute|kick|list <confno> <usernumber>
asterisk1*CLI> meetme list 1001
User #: 01        2001 device              Channel: SIP/2001-e4db    (unmonitored)
User #: 02        2001 device              Channel: SIP/2001-05ac    (unmonitored)
User #: 03        2000 device              Channel: SIP/2000-1ff8 (Admin)   (unmonitored)
User #: 04        3001 device              Channel: SIP/3001-cdc1    (unmonitored)
4 users in that conference.
asterisk1*CLI> meetme kick 1001 4
asterisk1*CLI> meetme list 1001
User #: 01        2001 device              Channel: SIP/2001-e4db    (unmonitored)
User #: 02        2001 device              Channel: SIP/2001-05ac    (unmonitored)
User #: 03        2000 device              Channel: SIP/2000-1ff8 (Admin)   (unmonitored)
3 users in that conference.
```

Direct Inward System Access

Direct Inward System Access (DISA) connects callers using outside phone lines to the PBX system. Callers obtain an internal dial tone as though they are connected to the inside telephone system. This feature might be used by an employee who is out of the office and needs to dial a long distance business number from his personal phone without having to pay for it himself. The caller in this scenario would dial the number allocated for the PBX DISA feature and use the PBX system as a hop to place his long distance call.

Take proper security measures when configuring the DISA feature. Pass-code authentication needs to be configured and provided by the outside caller in order to get a dial tone from the PBX system. This feature should be monitored closely by accounting reports to ensure that it is not being abused. In the interest of maintaining accountability and satisfying audits, it is important to assign and periodically change per-user codes for the DISA feature.

Unattended Transfer (or Blind Transfer)

Blind transfer exists when an end-receiver forwards a call to a different extension and hangs up without verifying that the new destination party is available. This feature is most likely to be used by an employee who has received a call by mistake. The employee then advises the caller of the error and transfers him to the correct extension.

Attended Transfer (or Consultative Transfer)

Compared to unattended transfer (blind transfer), an employee using attended transfer speaks to or notifies the receiving party before transferring the call to them. An example where attended transfer might be used is when a receptionist checks to see if a party is available before connecting a call.

Consultation Hold

Consultation hold is defined by placing an active call on hold so that a second call may be answered. This feature allows you to place a person on hold and consult with a different party without hanging up the original call. You may switch between calls as needed. Music on hold can be implemented with this feature to keep the caller notified of the line's activity.

No Answer Call Forwarding

No answer call forwarding allows calls to be forwarded to another destination, such as a different extension or voicemail, when the called party is not answering. The amount of time that it takes for a call to be forwarded can be implemented based on seconds or number of ring tones.

Busy Call Forwarding

Busy call forwarding allows calls to be forwarded when the called party is otherwise occupied. The called party could be handling another call or have initiated the Do Not Disturb (DND) feature.

Do Not Disturb (DND)

The Do Not Disturb (DND) feature gives the end-system user the ability to ignore incoming calls. The user activates the DND feature from her phone. DND functions can be implemented in Ringer Off, Ringer Mute, Busy Mode, and Mixed Mode.

- **Ringer Off/Ringer Mute** The call rings the extension without signaling the ringer. The ringer is muted at the caller extension.

- **Busy Mode** The phone extension acts as if it is off the hook. A busy signal is sent to the PBX system from the end-user's phone.

- **Mixed Mode** Allows the phone extension to act in Ringer Off/Busy Mode when standard calls come in. When priority calls come in, this mode allows the caller to overwrite the DND feature and initiate normal ringing of the phone.

NOTE

In Asterisk PBX default configuration, dialing *78 signals the PBX system to turn on the Do Not Disturb feature, and dialing *79 disables it.

Figure 2.14 shows the Asterisk PBX DND feature in the debug window. This feature is being initiated when the user dials *78. This PBX debug window shows extension 2000 initiating a database update change to enable the DND feature with DBput: family=DND, key=2000, value=YES command. Figure 2.15 shows similar debug output from the Asterisk PBX, except this time user dialed *79 to disable DND feature. The command DBdel: family=DND, key=2000 from the debug menu deletes the DND for extension 2000.

Figure 2.14 Asterisk DND Feature Enabled

```
Asterisk - PBX                                                      _ □ ×
    -- Executing DBput("SIP/2000-bcd2", "DND/2000=YES") in new stack
    -- DBput: family=DND, key=2000, value=YES
    -- Executing Playback("SIP/2000-bcd2", "do-not-disturb") in new stack
    -- Playing 'do-not-disturb' (language 'en')
    -- Executing Playback("SIP/2000-bcd2", "activated") in new stack
    -- Playing 'activated' (language 'en')
asterisk1*CLI>
```

Figure 2.15 Asterisk DND Feature Disabled

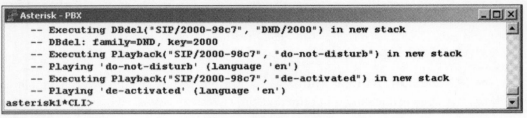

```
Asterisk - PBX                                                        _ □ X
   -- Executing DBdel("SIP/2000-98c7", "DND/2000") in new stack
   -- DBdel: family=DND, key=2000
   -- Executing Playback("SIP/2000-98c7", "do-not-disturb") in new stack
   -- Playing 'do-not-disturb' (language 'en')
   -- Executing Playback("SIP/2000-98c7", "de-activated") in new stack
   -- Playing 'de-activated' (language 'en')
asterisk1*CLI>
```

Three-Way Calling

Three-way calling, similar to conference calling, allows you to add a third party to your existing call. All three parties can hear each other at the same time.

Find-Me

The Find-Me PBX feature calls multiple outgoing destinations at the same time or in series of order at a time. The Find-Me feature allows the end-user to program multiple numbers into the PBX system so that he can be reached when he is away from his primary phone. The PBX system is configured to ring all programmed numbers at the same time. Figure 2.16 illustrates this technology by routing one inbound call to multiple destinations. This technology allows the end-user mobility and increases productivity. Routing a single incoming call to multiple destinations ensures that calls are not missed.

Figure 2.16 Find-Me Feature

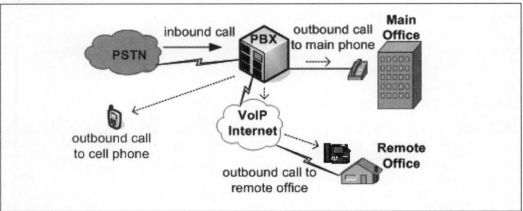

TIP

Make sure that the caller is directed to the proper voicemail system if none of the outgoing find-me destinations pick up the phone. You do not want the voicemail of the cell phone or the answering machine at home to pick up when the caller is dialing your corporate number. Measures such as limiting the number of rings per second on find-me destinations must be kept in mind to allow the main corporate voicemail system to record the missed call.

Call-Waiting Indication

The call-waiting indicator signals the end-user's station that a second incoming call is in progress. This indicator can also notify the end-user's station of a new voicemail. Some of the visual call indicator signals include a flashing light on the phone or flashing message box on video-enabled phones. An example of an audio call indicator is a periodic special ring heard by the end-user while a call is in progress that notifies the user that a second call is waiting. PBX signaling of a call indication must be supported by the end-phone station. A call indicator signals an end-user's station in order to inform of a specific message.

Voice Mail and Asterisk PBX

As the name implies, the voice-mail feature provides capability for callers to leave messages when the called party is unavailable. Asterisk PBX supports a local voice-mail (VM) system that offers many options, including password protection, system greetings, e-mail notifications, and VM forwarding.

Asterisk's *voicemail.conf* serves as the main VM configuration file that defines voice-mail boxes and their options. This voice-mail configuration file is, by default, located in the */etc/asterisk directory*. The syntax for creating a voice-mail box inside *voicemail.conf* file is as follows:

```
mailbox_num =>
voicemail_password,user_name,email_address,pager_email_address,option(s)
```

mailbox_num defines the number of the mailbox extension

voicemail_password defines the user's password to access VM options and retrieve voice messages

email_address defines the e-mail address where the new VM notifications can be sent, including the audio of the VM

pager_address defines the e-mail address where notifications of a new VM can be sent

options define additional available VM options that the user can set

Figure 2.17 displays an example of a mailbox configuration in the voicemail.conf file. In this example, mailbox 2001 and 3001 for Softphone2 and Softphone3 were created. Mailbox 2001 was configured with password 123456 and the e-mail address of **vmtest2@vmtest.com**.

Figure 2.17 Configuring *voicemail.conf* Configuration File

```
Asterisk - PBX                                                          _|□|×|
[root@asterisk1 ~]# cat voicemail.conf
[general]
#include vm_general.inc
#include vm_email.inc
[default]
2001 => 123456,Softphone2,vmtest2@vmtest.com
3001 => 112233,SoftPhone3,vmtest3@vmtest.com
```

Now that we have configured mailboxes 2001 for Softphone2 and 3001 for Softphone3 users, we must configure our dial plan to allow callers the option of leaving voice mail for these two extensions. To add voice-mail capability in our dial plan, we need to edit our *extensions.conf* file with the VoiceMail() function to extensions 2001 and 3001. Figure 2.18 displays part of the *extensions.conf* file and needed configuration. The argument inside the VoiceMail() function refers to the mailbox_num@context, which in this case is 2001@default for Softphone2 and 3001@default for Softphone3.

Figure 2.18 Configuring *extensions.conf* with VoiceMail() function

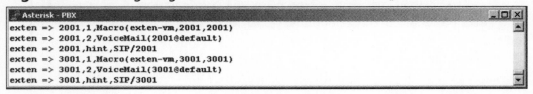

```
Asterisk - PBX                                                          _|□|×|
exten => 2001,1,Macro(exten-vm,2001,2001)
exten => 2001,2,VoiceMail(2001@default)
exten => 2001,hint,SIP/2001
exten => 3001,1,Macro(exten-vm,3001,3001)
exten => 3001,2,VoiceMail(3001@default)
exten => 3001,hint,SIP/3001
```

Now that we have created our password protected mailboxes and modified our dial plan to allow callers to leave messages, we must designate an extension number that local users can dial to gain access to and retrieve their voice messages. We accomplish this task by adding the VoiceMailMain() function to our dial plan and assigning the extension *98 that we have picked for our case study. The line added to the *extensions.conf* file will look like this: exten => *98,3,VoiceMailMain(default).

Now callers can leave VM and end-users can retrieve them by dialing *98 and their mailbox number. Figure 2.19 shows the log file from Asterisk PBX of an actual call in progress where the caller is leaving a VM for extension 3001. Notice that the VM is saved as wav and wav49 format audio file under the */var/spool/asterisk/voice-mail/default/3001/INBOX/* directory.

Figure 2.19 VoiceMail() in Action

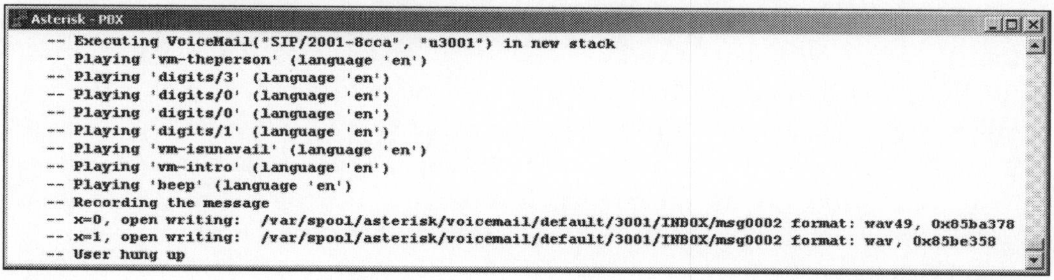

```
Asterisk - PBX                                                              _□×
    -- Executing VoiceMail("SIP/2001-8cca", "u3001") in new stack
    -- Playing 'vm-theperson' (language 'en')
    -- Playing 'digits/3' (language 'en')
    -- Playing 'digits/0' (language 'en')
    -- Playing 'digits/0' (language 'en')
    -- Playing 'digits/1' (language 'en')
    -- Playing 'vm-isunavail' (language 'en')
    -- Playing 'vm-intro' (language 'en')
    -- Playing 'beep' (language 'en')
    -- Recording the message
    -- x=0, open writing:  /var/spool/asterisk/voicemail/default/3001/INBOX/msg0002 format: wav49, 0x85ba378
    -- x=1, open writing:  /var/spool/asterisk/voicemail/default/3001/INBOX/msg0002 format: wav, 0x85be358
    -- User hung up
```

How Is VoIP Different from Private Telephone Networks?

VoIP technology brings many new capabilities to today's modern communications. The biggest difference between VoIP and traditional private telephone company networks is the transport protocol. Internet Protocol, which we identify as the transport protocol that we use for services such as viewing Web sites, playing online games, and sharing music, now is being used to carry our voice. VoIP is truly a revolutionary communication technology with rich new functionality that is being accepted by communities around the world.

Circuit-Switched and Packet-Routed Networks Compared

Packet-routed networks (such as IP networks) are designed to move data. Data is moved from source IP address to destination IP address in packets. Data from the source is dynamically broken down and encapsulated into packets before it is sent to its destination. Once the packets reach the desired destination, they are reassembled into their original data format. The Internet is constructed mainly based on packet routed technology, although many WAN links remain connected to circuit-switched networks such as Asynchronous Transfer Mode (ATM).

Circuit-switched networks (like the PSTN) are designed to move voice or data. Telephone networks that carry your traditional phone calls are circuit based. A point-to-point dedicated static connection in a circuit switched network is required prior to sending voice or data signals across multiple switches inside PSTN. Once a point-to-point static channel is allocated and nailed up in the circuit switched network, it will belong only to that one voice call and no other network traffic.

Packet-routed and switch networks both carry data, video, and voice. Packet-routed networks carry voice on top of IP. By breaking the voice, data, or video into small packets inside a packet-routed network, each packet can travel throughout the network across multiple independent paths and later be reassembled at its final destination. In circuit-switched networks voice and data travel across statically nailed-up paths. Both circuit and packet networks have the ability to carry different traffic across a network. The benefit of a packet-routed network is its dynamic approach and ability to self-recover with failed link paths because packets do not have statically allocated paths. On the other hand, the benefit of a circuit switched network is its dedicated predefined path, which assures quality for that session by not sharing with other resources.

Resource Reservation Protocol (RSVP) runs over IP and is used in packet-routed networks. RSVP is a type of QoS that signals across a packet network and allocates resources prior to making a voice call. RSVP applies circuit-switching principles to packet-routed networks but even the best RSVP guarantee cannot match the timeslot reservation guarantee inherent in circuit switched networks where a statically defined path is used by only one resource.

What Functionality Is Gained, Degraded, or Enhanced on VoIP Networks?

With every introduction of a new technology come original and improved features as well as untested problems. Several key differences in functionality are gained, lost, and enhanced between IP-enabled voice networks and traditional PSTN networks.

Gained Functionality

Two of the biggest advantages of VoIP technology are reduced costs and increased mobility.

Cost Savings

VoIP saves you money. VoIP reduces or in most cases eliminates your company's toll charges and government imposed taxes on your telephone companies that must be paid with the use of traditional voice network. By using your existing data network lines, which in most cases are underutilized by just carrying data for your voice traffic, you eliminate most of your toll charges. Further, you eliminate expensive hardware maintenance and the cable wiring charges of traditional phone equipment by consolidating your data and voice networks.

Mobility

VoIP allows greater mobility. Routing your DID number to a dynamic IP address allows you to take your phone number anywhere where you go. All your office phone functionality, such as local extension calling, is transferred with your movement.

Wiring and Scalability

Traditional phones in your office require direct connection into the PBX system and separate port allocation. With VoIP-enabled phones and PBX, you can plug into the same data-jack port as your desktop-PC and begin communicating with your PBX system. By using an already existing data port, you eliminate the need for extra phone ports and increase scalability with inexpensive LAN switches.

Open Standards

Open standards and multivendor interoperability that exists in VoIP compared with traditional proprietary phone companies' technology allows businesses and service providers to purchase hardware and phone services from multiple vendors without being dependent on one platform, one company. Open standards allows technology to grow and be developed by the community at large, leading to better functionality in the overall product.

Rich-Media Conferencing

Rich-media conferencing combines voice, video, and data. By combining the three together, participants can share presentation documents and observe each other's facial expressions, thus increasing productivity and the contribution of each participant.

Combined Functionality at Contact Centers

IP-based contact center solutions allow operators to support multiple integrated ways of communication over a single physical connection. Inbound and outbound calls can be integrated with live chat, web collaboration, and other applications, increasing an agent's productivity and caller support over single data line.

Degraded Functionality

With emerging technologies come new potential issues, which can be resolved only over time by trial and error. VoIP introduces potential degraded functionality for voice quality. The most important functionality in voice is the voice itself. It is important to hear the other party on the other end loud and clear. By using a single network for combined video, data, and voice communication, your core voice quality may be degraded by competing resources. Unlike in traditional PSTN circuit-switched networks, where dedicated channels are opened for each voice call, VoIP packet-routed network shares its channel resources between multiple applications.

Coder-Decoder codec is used to digitize analog voice. Codec has many different selections. Some codecs are highly rated such as the G.711 at 64Kbps for their speech quality but pay for higher bandwidth usage. Other codecs such as G.729 at 8Kbps offer equally good speech quality at less bandwidth usage but require higher processing power. Different codec samplers are used to encode signals into a more efficient form of transmission and are key components for the quality of voice.

Quality of Service (QoS) is a major issue in VoIP networks. When using a publicly available network such as the Internet to transfer calls, it is not easy to guarantee QoS. Three major concerns to consider when using the Internet for voice calls and QoS are:

- **Latency** Delay for packet delivery, accepted latency for voice in IP networks is less than 150ms (one way)

- **Jitter** Variations in delay of voice packet delivered

- **Packet Loss** Packets are dropped, most likely due to congestion in network

There is very little chance when you experience latency over the Internet greater than 150ms unless your own private links are saturated or you are trying to route overseas internationally or by satellite. Service level agreements (SLAs) can be negotiated with service providers to ensure your latency, jitter, or packet loss does not adversely affect your company's voice calling.

911

Emergency 911 service has been built for traditional circuit switched networks and does not integrate well with VoIP providers. VoIP providers implement E911 (Enhanced 911) that routes 911 calls over a user data link to PSTN 911 service. FCC has mandated E911 for VoIP providers, but carriers are still struggling with implementation and interconnection agreements. We discuss E911 service and its details later in Chapter 15. If your data link is down, you will lose connectivity to your 911 operator. Many VoIP service providers have agreements that each user must sign prior to the initiation of service. Many traditional phones will still allow you to call 911 even though your service has been disconnected. It is a good idea to keep an old phone line around connected to PSTN for 911 service in case an emergency occurs while your data link is down.

Enhanced Functionality

VoIP can provide redundancy to traditional PSTN networks. A company can have all its calls routed using a cost-effective VoIP solution and still have the ability to reroute calls over the PSTN during emergencies when the data network might be down.

Security for IP-enabled networks is both enhanced and in some cases degraded by VoIP. Making calls via VoIP allows you to encrypt each phone call, preventing eavesdropping, unlike over PSTN where calls are usually made in the clear. On the other hand, end-user phones and telephone equipment is now IP-enabled, which allows connectivity and attacks to come over the Internet if not protected. Viruses now have a way of connecting and potentially affecting your phone systems.

Summary

A private branch exchange (PBX) plays an important role in our day-to-day lives of communication since its first installation back in 1896 as a manual switchboard, and as today's VoIP-enabled system. One of the main functions and benefits of a PBX is to reduce the number of local loops required from the PSTN central office switch and maintain the routing information for customer's telephone extensions.

Asterisk is software running a PBX system that is freely available to anyone under the GNU General Public License (GPL). Asterisk provides all the functionality of VoIP and traditional telephony that any commercial PBX system would. Asterisk's features include conferencing, IVR, voice mail, call parking, billing solutions, and much more.

VoIP calls are transferred over packet-routed networks such as the Internet versus traditional circuit switched networks like the PSTN. Routing voice over Internet eliminates toll charges imposed by the telephone company and its PSTN network, which saves you money. Although routing voice over the Internet can increase cost savings, quality of voice could be degraded as calls share resources with other user applications.

VoIP and Asterisk PBX system are both entrepreneurs of today's technology that will keep evolving with each day. Just as with data communication over PCs, cost effective voice communication around the world will change the way we live and communicate.

Solutions Fast Track

What Functions Does a Typical PBX Perform?

☑ A PBX's main functionality is to maintain call routing information and direct calls to proper destinations using dial plan and call routing applications.

☑ The Asterisk PBX system is an open source project that supports much of the functionality of proprietary PBX systems.

☑ Find-me, Conferencing, Do Not Disturb (DND), Parking calls, Music on hold, Call recording, and Interactive Voice Response (IVR) are some of Asterisk's supported features.

☑ Asterisk's call accounting is recorded into CSV file, which can be imported into multiple database systems such as MySQL or Sybase to interact with billing solutions.

Voice Mail and Asterisk PBX

☑ Voice mail is part of PBX functionality that allows callers to leave voice messages for a missed called party.

☑ *Voicemail.conf* file sets up mailboxes and assigns passwords in the Asterisk PBX system.

☑ Asterisk PBX supports e-mail notification of new voice mails, including attaching the entire audio record inside the e-mail.

How Is VoIP Different from Private Telephone Networks?

☑ VoIP makes the use of existing data networks such as the Internet to route voice packets.

☑ VoIP runs over a packet-routed network compared to PSTN's circuit-switched network.

☑ Circuit-switched PSTN network defines a statically allocated channel prior to sending voice over it. Channels stay up for the duration of the call and are not shared with other calls.

☑ RSVP is a type of QoS that signals across packet networks and allocates resources prior to making a voice call. RSVP.

What Functionality Is Gained, Degraded, or Enhanced on VoIP Networks?

☑ VoIP saves money by running voice over packet networks to avoid toll charges.

☑ VoIP enables rich multimedia conferencing.

☑ VoIP can face QoS challenges over the Internet.

☑ VoIP QoS is affected by jitter. Differences in packet latency create jitter.

Frequently Asked Questions

The following Frequently Asked Questions, answered by the authors of this book, are designed to both measure your understanding of the concepts presented in this chapter and to assist you with real-life implementation of these concepts. To have your questions about this chapter answered by the author, browse to **www.syngress.com/solutions** and click on the **"Ask the Author"** form.

Q: Which codec should I use?

A: Different codecs exist, some with higher speach quality, others with higher processing delay and some with higher bandwidth requirements. Each network environment is different and should consider all three variables of codec prior to use.

Q: What is the maximum tolerable latency in VoIP packets?

A: Up to 150 ms one-way delay in VoIP packet is tolerable.

Q: Is a VoIP call more secure than a traditioanl PSTN call?

A: VoIP calls allow for easy encryption of your call from source to destination. PSTN calls, although sent over private switches, are unencrypted and could be intercepted.

Q: How do you prevent jitter on VoIP networks?

A: Jitter is variation delay of voice packets that can be mitigated by prioritizing time sensitive voice packets over data packets using QoS functions. Jitter cannot be eliminated without overprovisioning.

Q: In VoIP, will I lose 911 call functionality when I lose my data Internet connectivity?

A: Yes, you will not be able to dial 911 when using VoIP as it requires connectivity to your network provider to route the 911 call.

PV27

Chapter 3

The Hardware Infrastructure

Solutions in this chapter:

- Traditional PBX Systems
- PBX Alternatives
- VoIP Telephony and Infrastructure

☑ Summary

☑ Solutions Fast Track

☑ Frequently Asked Questions

Introduction

Even after the introduction of VoIP, business telephony equipment has remained focused on two areas: (1) reducing the cost of Public Switched Telephone Network (PSTN) connectivity overall and (2) adding business communications feature-functionality. Since the first private branch exchange (PBX) was introduced in 1879, business customers have sought cost savings by reducing the number of physical lines or trunks that interconnect with the PSTN. Because most calls in a large organization remain within it, cost and security benefits accrue immediately by placing a telephone switch inside the organization. And with the introduction of digital switching nearly a century later, a new wave of feature-functionality became possible. For the first time in history, the enterprise telephony capabilities would surpass that offered directly by PSTN carriers. In some respects, the latest developments in VoIP are an extension of this pattern.

NOTE

The basic architecture of the PBX over the past 100 years has evolved similarly to that of the PSTN and its switches overall. If you're interested in that evolution and how it has influenced today's PBX designs, you may want to read Chapter 4 before reading this chapter. Otherwise, consider this chapter to be a discussion of PBX architecture during the past decade and the interaction between the digital PBX and its VoIP equivalents.

From a security perspective, it's important to distinguish between several different architecture models for business and consumer telephony. On the low end, Key Telephone Systems (KTS) for up to 50 users provide a very basic means of sharing outside lines and using dedicated "intercom" lines to talk between stations, but don't provide actual switching services or advanced features (though the latest generation of such systems has blurred that distinction). The traditional PBX is likely to have an Ethernet interface for administration even if it does not support VoIP, and IP-enabled (or *hybrid*) PBX systems can support VoIP interfaces in addition to classic analog or digital stations and trunks. IP-PBX systems dispense with most analog or digital support entirely and focus exclusively on VoIP. In addition, Centrex, IP Centrex, and Hosted IP-telephony services are carrier-based alternatives that provide many of the same switching features as an on-site PBX system but place the switching equipment back into the carrier's infrastructure. Each of these alternatives has a different security profile and may interface with VoIP solutions at different levels, so let's review the critical differences between them and how they may affect your security strategy.

Traditional PBX Systems

Business telephony in large organizations has revolved around the private branch exchange (PBX) for over a century, and given that length of time, it's easy to see why VoIP often is positioned as a modern alternative to the PBX. However, this comparison is the wrong one to make, as the PBX concept itself is transport-neutral. It would be just as wrong to say "analog vs. PBX" or "digital vs. PSTN," so let's make sure we've got this basic principle down first. A PBX—or *PABX* internationally (the "A" stands for "Automated") is a communications switch that (1) replaces PSTN switching functionality for a set of associated extensions, (2) provides access trunks to carriers for routing PSTN calls, and (3) may provide additional communications feature-functionality based on configuration settings and equipment capabilities (see Figure 3.1).

Figure 3.1 A Basic PBX Diagram*

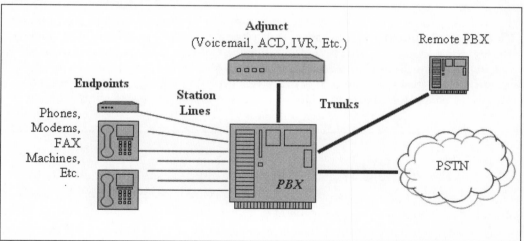

* All PBX systems provide PSTN-like switching services between endpoints and adjuncts, the PSTN, and other private PBX switches (and associated private networks). Only a few of the possible adjunct systems are mentioned here. An ACD is an Automatic Call Distribution server (for use in call centers to direct calls to groups of agents), and an IVR is an Interactive Voice Response server (also commonly used in call centers to let callers use touch tones and voice prompts to select services).

So a PBX could be all IP or all analog or anything in the middle as long as it switches calls between extensions and the PSTN as needed. In the end you will find that despite the marketing hype, most VoIP systems are just PBX systems with different combinations of support for IP lines and trunks. In some cases, the call control part of the system is split out from the gateway that handles the non–IP electrical interfaces. Or it's pushed out to a service provider. But the basic switching concept is preserved somewhere across the system as a whole. Regardless, understanding basic PBX terminology will help you understand the underlying architecture of the VoIP systems you may encounter, so let's start there.

PBX Lines

In telephony, a *line* (or *station line*) connects endpoint equipment (digital terminals, analog phones, fax machines, modems, or even an IP phone through an IP network) to the PBX (or central office) for switching. An analog line is the private equivalent of a local loop or loop transmission facility.

NOTE

A PBX is more likely than your phone company to support ground start phones and trunks on analog interfaces. Your phone at home seizes control of the line by using loop start, which involves shorting the two ends of the line together to activate the circuit. Ground start sends one of the leads to ground (typically ring) to seize the line, which is much less likely to cause glare (a condition that arises when both sides on a line or trunk simultaneously seize control of the line).

Typically, a PBX supports analog lines (and trunks) through a line card with 8, 12, 16, 24, or more lines per card, which are then wired to a patch panel for interconnection through a structured cabling system to the analog phone or device. Most of the security concerns around analog lines center on how well protected the equipment and cabling systems are from eavesdropping and tampering. Ground start loops will make theft of service less likely because a special phone is required, but otherwise the same basic rules for protecting a PSTN line from tampering apply.

Of course, *line* is also a generic term that may apply to power lines providing electricity to homes and businesses. But when we talk about an analog telephone line, we are talking specifically about the two wires involved: the tip (the first wire in a pair of phone wires, connected to the + side of the battery at the central office or PBX; it is named tip because it was the at the tip of an operator's plug) and the ring (connected to the − side of the switch battery and named because it was connected to the slip ring around the jack). Any equipment that works with Plain Old Telephone Service (POTS) lines will work with a PBX analog line configured for loop start. From a PBX, an analog line will nearly always be 2-wire although 4-wire lines with Earth & Magnet (E&M, sometimes also called Ear and Mouth) interfaces are supported from the same card for analog trunks.

TIP

If you've ever taken a peek behind the phone jacks that litter the walls of your home, you are likely to see two (or three) pairs of wires, one Green/Red, the next Yellow /Black, then White/Blue, but for our purposes only the first pair is important. The Green wire, referred to as the Tip, is the positively charged terminal. The Red terminal, the Ring, is the neutral, which completes the circuit, enabling electrical signals to flow freely. Note that newer homes may use a more recent color scheme that is also used for Ethernet cabling. The first pair is White/Blue, then White/Orange, then White/Green and finally White/Brown. This scheme is what you're most likely to see in structured cabling systems within buildings

Analog PBX systems supported only analog lines, but with the introduction of digital switching, a new class of line was developed: the digital line. In most PBX systems, a proprietary format for digital line signaling (and media) was created that requires the use of digital phones manufactured by that vendor. Some vendors, however, also support Integrated Services Digital Network (ISDN) standard phones directly (or through the PSTN) via the ITU-standardized ISDN BRI. Most proprietary digital formats use a 2-wire system with 8-wire plugs and jacks, although some are 4-wire systems. ISDN uses a 2-wire system from the CO switch, but is 8-wire to the interface used by a phone terminal, so the actual number of wires used will depend on several factors (such as whether the phone has a built-in NT-1 interface). Also, many proprietary switch features will not be supported on ISDN phones, particularly when the phone is manufactured by a different vendor. And even within a vendor product line, you may discover that newer features are supported only on newer phones or phone firmware. In any case, digital lines for proprietary digital terminals typically are supported by digital line cards with 8, 12, 16, 24, or more lines per card, and ISDN lines for ISDN phones are supported by either ISDN trunk cards or special ISDN BRI line cards, which may come in several flavors depending on the ISDN BRI type.

In the case of the modern hybrid PBX or IP-PBX, there is an equivalent concept for IP lines to IP phones, but unlike analog or digital lines the IP line isn't necessarily tied down to a single electrical interface on the PBX. In fact, the PBX can use multiple Ethernet ports to support an IP line, and IP phones can fail over to multiple IP-enabled PBX systems. The first IP line support built into most PBX systems leveraged the H.323 suite of protocols or proprietary protocols like Cisco "skinny," but almost all new development on PBX systems today uses Session Initiation Protocol (SIP). The bottom line is that the concept of an IP line exists in virtually every VoIP system out there, and understanding how the line concept is expressed in a specific VoIP system will give you an important handle with which to analyze its architecture and security.

This flexibility and versatility is a huge advantage to VoIP, but it does come at a price. Because the phones are now sharing infrastructure and bandwidth with other devices (and perhaps the entire data network), quality-of-service (QoS) guarantees for packet loss, latency (how long each packet takes to arrive from the phone to the PBX), and jitter (variability of latency across packets in a stream) now become the responsibility of the party providing the network infrastructure. Additional vectors for Denial-of-Service attacks on IP lines (either to the phone or the PBX) and Man-In-The-Middle (MITM) attacks must be considered. In my experience, the resulting loss of accountability from a single organization or vendor to multiple entities rarely is included in planning (or ROI calculations) for VoIP deployments.

PBX Trunks

A trunk is a special kind of line that connects two telephone switches. If one of the two switches is the PBX, the other could be a local or long-distance switch for PSTN access, in which case we would call these local trunks or long-distance trunks, respectively (though it's worth pointing out that even if you don't have dedicated long-distance trunks you likely are able to get long distance services through local trunks). On the other hand, if the other end of the trunk is another privately owned PBX, we would call these private trunks or tie lines, even if they happen to be routed through the PSTN (since the telephone numbers they can reach can only be dialed from within the private network). There are also trunks that can act like both types through the use of Centrex or something called a Virtual Private Network (VPN—but it's not the remote access VPN you may be familiar with from the data world—this VPN is created by a carrier to let you keep a private dial plan across many sites on the same trunks that you use for regular PSTN access).

Some say trunks are so named because in the old days, Ma Bell saw fit to use thick, lead-covered cables to connect the switches. These cables resembled an elephant's trunk. Others claim the word's origin is derived from the way the local loop network resembles the branches of a tree, with the trunks having similarity to... well, a tree trunk. Regardless, trunks are the main lines of the communications system, and the only case where a trunk is not connecting to a switch is when an adjunct server is involved (like a voice messaging server, an Automatic Call Distribution (ACD) server, an Interactive Voice Response (IVR) system, or similar system). In some cases, these servers may use station emulation instead of trunking, so you'll need to verify what actually is being used.

Trunks can be analog, digital, or VoIP-based, just like station lines. Analog trunks can be as simple as a regular 2-wire POTS line to the local CO switch, or a 4-wire analog E&M trunk that provides improved signaling response (less glare). Channelized digital T1 trunks come in two main flavors. The first and oldest type of T1 can have 24 channels of 64 kilobit per second voice with robbed-bit signaling (signaling bits are stolen from the voice stream in a way that's not noticeable to the ear). This type of T1 sends much less signaling data but cannot be used with 64 kbps switched data because of the robbed bits used for signaling, but can pass 56 kbps switched data. ISDN T1 trunks have 23 channels of voice (bearer, or B channels) and a separate 64 kbps channel for signaling (the data, or D channel) that can support ISDN User Part (ISUP) messages, including Automatic Number Identification, which allows calling and called number information to be sent (although it can be spoofed; this is discussed in Chapter 4). In Europe and internationally, the E1 is the typical digital interface, with an ISDN BRI carrying 30 bearer channels (30B+D) as opposed to the 23 channels supported by ISDN over T1 (23B+D).

VoIP trunks also come in various flavors, including H.323, SIP, and proprietary protocols like Inter-Asterisk eXchange (IAX). In some cases, IP-enabled PBX systems also use gateway control protocols with VoIP trunks, such as Simple Gateway Control Protocol (SGCP), H.248/Megaco/Media Gateway Control Protocol (MGCP), Skinny Gateway Control Protocol. One of the difficult problems with VoIP trunks, however, is feature transparency between vendors. ISUP/Q.931 or its private line equivalent (QSIG) has the most complete feature interworking capability, and standards for mapping these onto H.323 and SIP exist, but these are not evenly supported by PBX vendors at this point. Robust, reliable interworking between different PBX vendors over VoIP is not easy to find today (and is still a challenge over private tie lines).

PBX Features

PBX systems provide a plethora of features typically offered by a telephone provider, such as call waiting, three-way calling, conference calling, voicemail, additional call appearances, and many other routing features. Some vendors count 600 or more separate features among their capabilities, far more than is offered by any carrier on a central office switch as subscriber services. But often overlooked in this list are those used for access control. The PBX is effectively the firewall to the PSTN and because voice access has per-minute and geographic costs associated with each call, this aspect of PBX capability should be a critical consideration for product selection, configuration, and ongoing operations. Yet at the same time, the data security community is rarely concerned with this characteristic because it's not a ppure data security issue, yet even in a VoIP system there will be PSTN connectivity; why gamble with this?

Say a company has 200 employees, each with a phone on their desk. Without a PBX, each employee would require their own pair of copper wires from the CO, each with their own phone number that routes to their desk. However, it's a safe bet that not all 200 employees will be on the phone all the time, and it's likely that most of those calls will be to other employees. This is where a PBX really pays off. A business or campus will need many fewer lines from the Local Exchange Carrier (LEC); in the previous example, the company might require only 40 outside lines, routing those calls onto the PSTN trunk lines as necessary on a per call basis. They also could rent 200 Direct Inward Dial (DID) numbers from the LEC, which terminate though those trunk lines. The PBX will then route the inbound call based upon which DID number was dialed to reach it.

Tools & Traps...

Asterisk: The Open-Source PBX

PBX servers were notoriously expensive to justify when an organization wasn't ready for a major capital outlay, plus they tended to rely on closed or proprietary architecture, which made PBX systems more expensive than they might otherwise have been. Then along came Asterisk, from the mind of Mark Spencer. Asterisk is an open-source PBX software package that runs on many operating systems, including Linux, BSD, Mac, and even Windows. Asterisk requires very little in the way of hardware, with old Pentium 100MHz boxes with 64MB of RAM still ample enough to power a small business. Aside from the relatively low hardware horsepower requirements, Asterisk doesn't necessarily need any additional hardware, aside form what's already in your computer. Utilizing the popular Session Initiation Protocol (SIP) and the Inter-Asterisk Exchange Protocol (IAX), two

Continued

increasingly ubiquitous VoIP technologies, Asterisk can make and take calls completely over the Internet or operate with special hardware like PCI T1/E1 cards for PSTN connectivity. Users may purchase DIDs from the VoIP provider to dial in to their PBX from their normal phones, or they may dial in using a special software phone. We discuss softphones later in this chapter.

The appeal of a PBX system is obvious to not only businesses and campuses but also attackers, who have taken an increased interest in them as well, since most PBX systems can support trunk-to-trunk transfer (i.e., dial-out again from the PBX after coming in on another line). PBX security often is overlooked by enterprises until a big phone bill arrives, and oftentimes the hackers have no challenge at all when settings are never changed from the manufacturer's default. Try a Google search for "default password" and a PBX vendor and you'll see just how easy this information can be to obtain. It is important to note that because PBX vendors typically have provided detailed instructions on how to secure the PBX, the remaining security responsibility lies completely on the operator of the PBX system, and any toll charges that may be obtained by fraud are left to be paid by the PBX owner. Attackers who have compromised a PBX system may set up their own private conference room, a "party-line" where they may hang out and exchange illicit information on your dime.

Other features can be a double-edged sword as well. Many PBX systems also provide a call-monitoring feature for managers to supervise their agents (or to record calls). You know those recordings that go, "Your call may be monitored for quality assurance and training purposes"? Well, if you're not careful, they might also be monitored for humorous or larcenous purposes. And it may not be just calls to your call center that get monitored; if your monitoring system wasn't properly designed or an intruder gets access to PBX administration at a high enough level, any call can be monitored.

The bottom line when it comes to PBX features is that you need to read the associated security recommendations carefully. Some vendors have assembled detailed security guides for addressing toll fraud and feature access that are well over 100 pages, and you would be wise to find out what kind of documentation exists. And don't forget to back up your PBX regularly so that you don't lose the security policy you create! More critically, if a VoIP vendor does not have these kinds of capabilities, you would be wise to find out what can be done to reduce exposure to toll fraud. In some cases, the lack of feature-functionality in many VoIP solutions is a blessing because it reduces the opportunities for security-affecting misconfiguration. Yet at best this is a temporary benefit since VoIP solutions are becoming more sophisticated each and every year.

Notes from the Underground...

Toll Fraud

Attackers have discovered a myriad of ways to make all the long distance calls they want from your PBX system, leaving you with the hefty collect-call charges. Here are a few:

- Even with good security elsewhere, a caller can ask to transfer to extension to 9011 on a system where dialing 9 goes to an outside line and 011 is the international direct dial access code. Make sure your employees (particularly those that answer many external calls) know about this ruse and consider using your PBX's trace feature to track down the source of such calls (you can even have the call transferred to your security department as part of the trace feature).

- Attackers can read the same manuals online that your systems administrators can, and the smart ones will figure out how to get around the obvious restrictions. For instance, if trunk access codes aren't restricted, it really won't matter how well you've locked out other dial restrictions. And just because you don't use your local trunks for long distance doesn't mean an attacker won't.

- Adding support for IP softphones or WiFi phones to a PBX means that a softphone or wireless phone could be used by a remote attacker who can get onto your IP network (by wire or wireless) for toll fraud or other nefarious purposes. In this case, defense of your IP network overall is what will minimize exposure to the PBX, but it's important that the PBX not weaken overall IP security (by allowing WEP-based security on wireless networks shared by voice and data, for instance).

PBX Adjunct Servers

Most PBX systems have an adjunct server or two, providing voice messaging or call center functionality that isn't part of the core PBX switching capabilities. The larger and more complex a network gets, the more demanding traffic becomes to the underlying hardware. Given the modularity of voice networks, we can off load some of this functionality to other hardware that can be set to handle a specific task, rather than attempt to do everything itself. Of course, this also complicates the overall security model, so make sure you know how this offloading impacts security.

Voice Messaging

It's hard to remember that voicemail was once a completely optional capability for PBX systems, but it's still implemented as a separate server by most vendors using analog, digital, or IP trunks to integrate with the PBX. Some settings on that voice messaging server can open the door to fraud and abuse, so be sure to follow manufacturer recommendations for security—especially when it comes to changing default administrator passwords! Are mailboxes using strong enough PINs? Are old mailboxes closed down? Make sure you can answer these questions.

Notes from the Underground...

Voice Messaging: Swiss Army Knife for Hackers?

Voice messaging is not without its share of security considerations, though. Many vendors ship voice mail systems with default passwords installed, which some users opt to never change. These passwords are often as simple as the number of the voice mailbox itself, or a simple string of numbers like 12345. Hackers love it when it's this easy to get in. But that's only the beginning when it comes to security attacks you may need to protect against within your voice messaging systems. Here are a few other scenarios:

- When attachers gain control over a compromised PBX system that supports DID and voice-mail, they might change the outbound greeting to something like "Hello? Yes, yes, that's fine." Or just "Yes (pause) yes (pause) yes..." They then call that number collect and the operator hears what appears to be someone more than willing to accept charges! Some PBX and voice-mail systems send a special tone when a line is forwarded to voice-mail that may discourage this tactic since a savvy operator would recognize the tone. Does your organization know what's happening with old or unused mailboxes?

- Another security issue can arise when mobile phone providers offer voicemail to their subscribers, but don't require a password to access messages when the voicemail server receives the subscriber ANI (indicating that subscriber is calling from the mobile phone associated with that extension). But by offering their users the "convenience" of

Continued

quick access to their messages, these carriers may be opening the door to eavesdropping through ANI spoofing (which is discussed in more detail in Chapter 4) unless they have other means of verifying the origin of a given call.

- Eavesdropping on potentially confidential messages is certainly a threat, but an attacker may potentially hijack phone calls intended for a victim as well. This can be done by changing their outbound message greeting to say "Hi, this is Corey. Please call me at my new number at…" and leave a number that they control, performing a man-in-the-middle attack on the intended recipient.

- Another successful social engineering technique involves leaving messages within a voicemail system requesting passwords (for "testing" or "administrative purposes") on another internal extension, lulling the victim into believing that the attacker is a legitimate employee at the target company.

- The latest voice-messaging systems can be used to read e-mail using text-to-speech. Attackers know that a PIN for the voice messaging system is easy to guess, and this may be the easiest way for them to get to an e-mail system.

- And don't forget toll fraud that can happen through out-dial capabilities on voicemail systems. Consider turning off this feature if it isn't needed in your organization. Associated risks can also be mitigated through carefully crafted PBX dial policy.

Interactive Voice Response Servers

Perhaps you first ran into an IVR when you noticed an incorrect charge on your phone bill, and you decide to speak with a customer service representative to clear things up. But when you dial the toll-free number on the bill, you're greeted with a labyrinth of options allegedly to help you self-navigate to the appropriate agent. This maze of menus is brought to you through an Interactive Voice Response (IVR) system. An IVR is a series of recorded greetings and logic flows that provide a caller with a way to route through the phone system as a means of convenience. Personal feelings about speaking with a recorded voice aside, IVRs are actually a pretty clever way of providing a caller with speedy call placement, taking much of the burden away from agents or operators.

Today's latest-generation IVR systems are built on VoiceXML interpreters, and may have sophisticated development environments. IVR security is a largely unexplored topic since each IVR system is like a unique application, but we occasionally hear about poorly written IVR applications that are insecure or not sufficiently robust.

Wireless PBX Solutions

Several solutions for adding wireless extensions to PBX systems have been commercialized. Most PBX vendors have implemented proprietary 900 MHz-band solutions in the United States as well as the 1900 MHz Digital Enhanced Cordless Telecommunications (DECT) ETSI standard in Europe, which has driven widespread adoptions of vendor-neutral wireless there. More recently, a number of WiFi solutions have become available, as well as combination WiFi/GSM solutions that let a single device work with both Cellular and Enterprise PBX infrastructure. See the warnings about WEP later in this chapter.

Other PBX Solutions

Two other PBX solutions with security considerations bear some discussion: Call Detail Recording (CDR) systems and Voice Firewalls. CDR systems enable every call on a PBX to be recorded after it is complete using a standardized format. This allows special reporting software to analyze this data for forensic or diagnostic purposes. It is worth noting, however, that a CDR system will not allow you to stop a fraudulent call still in progress. For this, you would need a voice firewall such as that sold by SecureLogix. Such a firewall allows you to see current calls in real-time, apply policy based on type of call (voice, fax, or data), and set notifications, authentication requirements, or other policy based on rules very similar to those you might set for data traffic on a data firewall.

PBX Alternatives

Long before the appearance of VoIP, nonswitched alternatives to the PBX have been available. For systems of less than 50 users, Key Telephone Systems (KTS) share outside lines directly and have dedicated intercom lines to talk between stations. Current generation key systems are more PBX-like than ever, so it may be hard to find that distinction anymore. But older key systems won't support advanced switching features like trunk-to-trunk transfer that can lead to toll fraud. Still, so-called hybrid key systems should be treated like a regular PBX when it comes to security.

Centrex, IP Centrex, and Hosted IP-telephony services are carrier-based PBX alternatives that provide a private dial plan plus the more popular switching features that an on-site PBX system might. However, the switching equipment stays in the carrier's infrastructure and is managed by the carrier. This is a mixed blessing since it's likely to reduce the overall functionality and access policy tailoring available to you if your organization uses such a service, but it does mean that the carrier shoulders a larger share of the responsibility for any toll fraud that may result (and consequently won't provide high-risk services like trunk-to-trunk dialing without extra security measures).

More recently, the appearance of IP telephony has provided an opportunity for some manufacturers like Avaya to rearchitect their overall PBX approach and separate the functionality once provided in a single device into multiple devices. In particular, call control and signaling can be separated from media processing and gateway services; this approach makes possible an architecture where a few call control servers can provide redundant services across an entire organization with media gateways located in every geographic location that contains their physical presence. We'll treat this approach along with other similar VoIP architectures in the next section.

VoIP Telephony and Infrastructure

With the introduction of VoIP came a new architectural flexibility that in theory can completely distribute PBX functionality across an entire infrastructure. We'll review those concepts in this section and discuss examples of this in action, but keep in mind that few VoIP solutions take full advantage of every aspect described here (and it wouldn't surprise me to discover that none of them did, but today's VoIP market is moving so fast that it's difficult if not impossible to prove that kind of negative). Regardless, these concepts each have significant security implications.

Media Servers

The term *media server* is totally overloaded in the VoIP world (and even more so within the IT industry as a whole). If we restrict ourselves to VoIP-related definitions only, a server so named still could be any of the following:

- Interactive voice response (IVR) server or media slave, possibly running VoiceXML or MRCP
- Signaling Media Server (Media Gateway Controller) to handle call control in Voice/VoIP network
- Call distribution (ACD) for receiving and distributing calls in a contact center
- Conferencing Media Server for voice, video, and other applications
- Text-to-speech server (TTS) for listening to e-mail, for instance
- Automated voice-to-e-mail response system
- Voice or video applications server

- Streaming content server
- Fax-on-demand server

Sure, some of these are similar and can roughly be grouped together, but at best you'll get this down to semi-overlapping groups that center on two general areas: interactive media services and call or resource control. The point here is that in the VoIP world, we haven't standardized architectures and naming conventions yet so we are left with technically vague terms like *media server, media gateway*, and the worst offender, *softswitch* (a marketing term we will not spend more time on in this chapter except to note that it was intended to conjure up the image of a class 5 switch being displaced by a software blob that runs these media servers and media gateways but has become so overloaded that it has completely lost any technical meaning it once may have enjoyed).

Interactive Media Service: Media Servers

On the other hand, there is another kind of media server that actually contains DSP resources that it uses to process speech or video (and perhaps one or more additional form of media). These may be involved with generating and receiving DTMF tones, executing the logic of an IVR system, converting text-to-speech or handling streaming or document content in response to speech or DTMF input. Or it may orchestrate multiway call traffic, conference calls, handle translation between codecs, or even fax processing. Media servers of this class may provide VoiceXML interpretation for interactive, dynamic voice applications.

Call or Resource Control: Media Servers

This class of media server is responsible for managing communications resources at a higher level, such as handling call control while managing media gateways that have DSP and other gateway resources for the actual media manipulation. Most Media Servers support VoIP protocols but are likely also to support others as well, such as digital voice or video trunks, or even analog voice through media gateways. Examples of this kind of media server include call control servers from PBX vendors that control separate gateways, voice processing servers that manage and redirect DSP resources located elsewhere, and call distribution systems that manage off-board call handling resources such as switches and IVR systems.

The H.323 Gatekeeper

This gatekeeper is the manager of one or more gateways, and is responsible for providing address translation (alias to IP address) and access control to VoIP terminals and gateways. A gatekeeper acts as the central authority for other gateways, allowing an administrator to quickly and authoritatively roll out changes across a voice network. Gatekeepers limit the number of calls at a given time on a network by implementing control over a proxy. A gatekeeper works something like this: A user wants to make a call to another user at a different physical location, and his phone registers with a local gateway. The gateway then passes on his call information to the gatekeeper, which acts as a central hub to other gateways and users. The gatekeeper then passes call setup information to the gatekeeper at the other office, which in turn hands it to the appropriate destination gateway, and finally to the desktop of the called party. Many call control media servers include an H.323 gatekeeper.

Registration Servers

In a traditional PSTN or PBX switching system, where each user is at a fixed location, usually tied in place by copper wires, routing calls is (relatively speaking) simple. So-called find-me/follow-me services on PSTN or PBX switches can add PSTN mobility. Forwarding or extension-to-cellular features can increase this sense of mobility, but all these solutions require active user programming or rely on fixed forwarding algorithms and are rooted in the PSTN.

But with VoIP, a user can be geographically located virtually anywhere on the planet (as long as minimum QoS conditions are present). A registration server acts as a point of connection for mobile users. Johnny can log in to the registration server from his hotel room in Amsterdam with an unknown IP address and the registration server will let the gateways know where to route his traffic. That way, Johnny can keep the same phone number no matter where he is physically located. A similar example can be seen with instant messaging networks. A user can log in using his screen name from home and be reachable to the same users as if he had logged in from work. In the H.323 world, registration is a function of a gatekeeper; however, this can be a separate function in the SIP realm.

Redirect Servers

A SIP redirect server acts as the traffic light at the VoIP intersection. Very much like a web page with a redirect tag built in, a redirect server will inform a client if the destination the caller is trying to reach had changed. Armed with the updated information from the redirect server, the client will then rerequest the call using the new destination information. This takes some of the load off proxy servers and improves call routing robustness. In this way, a call can quickly be diverted from a proxy, rather than require the proxy to complete the connection itself.

Media Gateways

A gateway is a device that translates between protocols in general by providing logic and translation between otherwise incompatible interfaces. A voice or media gateway in particular tends to translate between PSTN (trunking) protocols and interfaces and local line protocols and interfaces (though that's not universally true). In addition, the potential protocols and interfaces that a voice gateway now might support include Ethernet and VoIP protocols as well. The voice gateway could have H.323 phones on one side and an ISDN trunk on the other (both digital) or a VoIP phone on one side and an analog loop to the carrier, or even VoIP on both sides (say, H.323 to the station and SIP trunking to the carrier). The point is that there are literally hundreds of different equipment classes that all fall under the voice gateway moniker and thousands of classes that fall under gateway to begin with.

One class of VoIP media gateway connects traditional analog or digital phone equipment or networks to VoIP equipment or networks. A simple home-user implementation of a VoIP gateway like this is an ATA, or Analog Telephone Adaptor. At a minimum a VoIP media gateway will have both a phone interface (analog or digital) and an Ethernet interface. For an ATA, a regular analog phone is connected to the adaptor, which then translates the signal to digital and passes it back over the Ethernet. Of course, media gateways can get much more complex than this. PBX vendors have split out the line-card cabinet portion of their product and recast it as a media gateway, with the gateway under the control of a media server. IP routing companies have added analog and digital voice/video interfaces to routers and recast them as media gateways. And in many respects these products do contain overlapping functionality even though they may not be equivalent.

Firewalls and Application–Layer Gateways

Within a firewall, special code for handling specific protocols (like ftp, which uses separate control and data paths just like VoIP) provides the logic required for the IP address filtering and translation that must take place for the protocol to pass safely through the firewall. One name for this is the Application Layer Gateway (ALG). Each protocol that passes embedded IP addresses or that operates with separate data (or media) and control streams will require ALG code to successfully pass through a deep-packet-inspection and filtering device. Due to the constantly changing nature of VoIP protocols, ALGs provided by firewall vendors are constantly playing a game of catch-up. And tests of real-time performance under load for ALG solutions may reveal that QoS standards cannot be met with a given ALG solution. This can cause VoIP systems to fail under load across the perimeter and has forced consideration of VoIP application proxies as an alternative.

Application Proxies

A Proxy server acts as a translator for transactions or calls of different types. If Johnny's phone speaks IAX and Jen's phone speaks only SIP, the proxy sits between them and translates the message as necessary. Even if both sides speak the same protocol, be it HTTP or SIP, there are security or NAT or other boundaries that call for either a proxy or packet manipulation in an Application Layer Gateway (ALG) within a firewall. The benefit of an application proxy is that it can be designed specifically for a protocol (or even a manufacturer's implementation of a protocol). In addition to allowing boundary traversal, a proxy can also be used as a means of access control, ensuring that a user has the rights to place a call before allowing it to proceed. And the best proxies can even guard against malformed packets and certain types of DoS attacks. Depending on the complexity of your call requirements, a proxy may be integrated into a PBX or Media Server, or it may be an entirely different piece of hardware.

Endpoints (User Agents)

In a phone system, an endpoint on the network was known as a terminal, reflecting the fact that it was a slave to the switch or call-control server. But today's endpoints may possess much more intelligence, thus in the SIP world the term User Agent is preferred. This could be a hardware IP telephone, a softphone, or any other device or service capable of originating or terminating a communication session directly or as a proxy for the end user.

Softphones

With the advent of VoIP technology, users are able to break free of classical physical restrictions of communication, namely the special-purpose telephone terminal. A softphone is a piece of software that handles voice traffic through a computer using a standard computer speaker and microphone (or improved audio equipment that is connected through an audio or multimedia card). Softphones can emulate the look and feel of a traditional phone, using the familiar key layout of a traditional phone and often even emulating the DTMF sounds you hear when you dial a call. Or it may look more like an instant messaging (IM) client, and act like audio chat added to IM.

In fact, a softphone doesn't even need a computer microphone or speaker: my favorite doesn't need to send media through the computer at all in telecommuter mode—it just uses H.323 signaling to tell my media server which PSTN number (or extension) to dial for sending and receiving the audio. This lets me turn any phone into a fully featured clone of my work extension without regard to QoS available to me on my Internet connection.

Because a soft phone resides on a PC, the principle of logically separating voice and data networks is defeated as the PC must reside in both domains. You will need to consider this trade-off as you design appropriate security policy for your VoIP network, although the long-term trends favor voice-data integration, so at best maintaining physical separation can be only a temporary strategy.

Consumer softphones have exploded over the past few years and nothing is hotter than Skype in that space. Skype is the brainchild of the people who brought us the Kazaa file sharing framework. Utilizing peer-to-peer technology and an encrypted signaling and media channel, Skype has proven to be both easy to set up and use securely by end users, while simultaneously being a thorn in the side of network administrators. Because it aggressively jumps past firewalls to create call traffic, it is considered to be a threat by many enterprise security groups.

One of Skype's major enhancements over instant-messaging-based voice is its superb codec, which is actually better than that used within traditional telephone infrastructure. This provides superior call quality when contacting other Skype users. Another major benefit of Skype is the ability to reach any phone in the PSTN by way of SkypeOut gateways. With its PSTN gateway, Skype has become an attractive alternative for small overseas call centers and other Internet businesses.

Are You 0wned?

Consumer Softphone Gotchas

Many consumer-oriented softphones contain advertising software that "phones home" with private user information. Several popular softphones (such as X-Lite) store credentials unencrypted in the Window's registry even after uninstallation of the program. Softphones require that PC-based firewalls open a number of high UDP ports as part of the media stream transaction. Additionally, any special permissions that the VoIP application has within the host-based firewall rule set will apply to all applications on that desktop (e.g., peer-to-peer software may use SIP for bypassing security policy prohibitions).

Also consider that malware affecting any other application software on the PC can also interfere with voice communications. The flip-side is also true—malware that affects the VoIP software will affect all other applications on the PC and the data services available to that PC (a separate VoIP phone would not require access to file services, databases, etc.).

IM Clients

Instant messaging is perhaps the dominant means of real-time communication on the Internet today. IM's roots can be traced back to the Internet Relay Chat (IRC) networks, which introduced the chat room concept but did not track online presence and never reached the popularity of IM. Just as IM is the next logical step from IRC, voice chat is the next leap from text-based chat. Most of today's most popular IM clients have included voice functionality, including AOL's Instant Messenger, Yahoo! Messenger, and MSN Messenger. Skype took the opposite approach and created a chat client that focuses on voice as the star and text chat as an afterthought. Even Google jumped aboard the IM bandwagon, releasing Google Talk. Let's take a look at these clients to see what makes them similar, and what makes them different.

AIM, AOL's IM service, surely wasn't the first on the scene, but it has the largest base of users. Initially AIM was limited to users of the AOL Internet service, but eventually it was opened up to the Internet as a whole. With the addition of a proprietary voice capability in late 1999, AOL was a VoIP pioneer of sorts. (although voice chat was first available through Mirablis's ICQ). Yahoo! Chat jumped aboard the voice bandwagon soon after, and Google's more recent client has included voice from the beginning. In 2005, Yahoo announced interoperability with Google and MSN (who also has a voice chat plug-in for messenger that is also used with its Live Communication Server product). In addition, Microsoft's popular Outlook e-mail client (and entire Office suite in the case of LCS) can be linked to Microsoft Messenger. Also worth mentioning is the Lotus Domino IM client that competes with Microsoft LCS in the enterprise instant messaging (and presence) space, as well as Jabber, which can be used to tie together both public and private IM services using the XMPP protocol.

Google Talk is the newest comer to the IM game. Though Google Talk is still in its infancy, it stands to succeed due largely to a philosophical stand point, embracing open standards over proprietary voice chat. Google Talk aims to connect many different voice networks over a series of peering arrangements, allowing users to minimize their need to run several IM clients. Like Skype, Google seeks to bridge traditional phone calls with Internet telephony, promising to federate with SIP networks that provide access to an ordinary telephone dial tone. Google recently released a library called libjingle to programmers, allowing them to hack new functionality into Google Talk. It will be interesting to see where Google takes Google Talk in the future.

Video Clients

Most of us can probably think back and recall seeing episodes of *The Jetsons* when we were younger. Or pictures of the AT&T PicturePhone from the 1964 World's Fair. Movies have all but promised these devices to be a staple of every day life in the future. And for decades, the video conference has been pushed by enterprises seeking to save money on travel (though investments in video conferencing equipment tend to sit around gathering dust). Live video on the Internet has its adherents, and today we see yet another wave of marketing aimed at the business use of video. So, will video finally take off around VoIP just like audio, or is there something different going on here?

The video phone has been tomorrow's next big technology for 50 years but the issue has been more sociological than technological. Certainly, popular instant messaging clients have included video chat capabilities for some time now, although each client typically supports only video between other users of the same client or messaging network. And although it always gives me a kick to see someone else announcing that they've solved the gap with technology, the point is well taken that video is here to stay in VoIP systems—even if it doesn't get as much use as VoIP.

The latest on the video bandwagon is the Skype 2.0 release. At only 15 frames per second and 40 to 75 kbps upload and download, Skype Video works well on a standard home DSL line or better. Other popular IM clients with video include Microsoft's Messenger and Yahoo Instant Messenger. AIM now offers video as well.

H.323-based IP videoconferencing systems have been available in hardware and software from many sources for almost a decade at this point, so there's no shortage of vendors in this space. And SIP video phones are available from many of these same vendors and from startup companies in the SIP space.

Wireless VoIP Clients

Over the past few years, an explosion of wireless VoIP solutions has hit the marketplace. Most of these solutions are immature and if broadly deployed can completely overrun the available bandwidth on 802.11b (or g) networks that were not engineered for high-density voice, even with QoS prioritization. And although 802.11a networks can handle higher wireless VoIP densities, they present other backward-compatibility issues of their own. And we haven't even gotten to the security issues yet! Still, the promise of WiFi VoIP is tantalizing, and most enterprises that have deployed VoIP solutions seem to have experimented with it. The idea of a combined cellphone/WiFi phone (and maybe PDA too) seems just too compelling to ignore, even if power consumption issues sideline keep the concept sidelined in the short term.

IP Switches and Routers

Although their position is defined by a standard data network rather than VoIP, a router's purpose in life is to connect two or more IP subnetworks at layer 3. An IP switch performs a similar function at layer 2. Routers and switches operate on the network and data-link layers, respectively, investigating the IP address or MAC address for each packet to determine its final destination and then forwarding that packet to its recipient. For VoIP, the biggest consideration at these levels are QoS markings and treatment such as DiffServ and RSVP, which should be supported by this infrastructure in a way that allows legitimate voice packets through with high priority and shuts out malicious packets, particularly those aimed at causing DoS attacks. This may be easier said than done in some cases. If an attacker can inject QoS-marked packets into your network, will your QoS scheme create a DoS condition for both voice and data?

Wireless Infrastructure

Wireless access points and associated infrastructure are similarly considered an extension of the data network. However, the increasing use of VoIP clients within this infrastructure creates several unique security considerations (particularly DoS given that wireless is a shared medium). In addition, wireless VoIP devices in the marketplace have lagged in implementation of the most current wireless encryption recommendations. All this should be taken into consideration in the design and operation of wireless VoIP.

Wireless Encryption: WEP

When wireless networking was first designed, its primary focus was ease of implementation, and certainly not security. As any security expert will tell you, it's extremely difficult to secure a system after the fact. WEP, the Wired Equivalent Privacy encryption scheme, initially was targeted at preventing theft-of-service and eavesdropping attacks. WEP comes in two major varieties, standard 64-bit and 128-bit encryption. 256-bit and 512-bit implementations exist, but they are not nearly as supported by most vendors. 64-bit WEP uses a 24-bit initialization vector that is added to the 40-bit key itself; combined, they form an RC4 key. 128-bit WEP uses a 104-bit key, added to the 24 bit initialization vector. 128-bit WEP was implemented by vendors once a U.S. government restriction limiting cryptographic technology was lifted.

In August of 2001, Fluhrer, Mantin, and Shamir released a paper dissecting cryptographic weaknesses in WEP's RC4 algorithm. They had discovered that WEP's 24-bit initialization vectors were not long enough, and repetition in the cipher text existed on busy networks. These so-called weak IVs leaked information about the private key. An attacker monitoring encrypted traffic long enough was able to recreate the private key, provided enough packets were gathered. Access Point Vendors responded by releasing hardware that filtered out the weak IVs.

However, in 2004 a hacker named Korek released a new statistical-analysis attack on WEP, which led the way to a whole new series of tools. These new wireless weapons broke WEP using merely IVs, and no longer just IVs were considered weak. On a 64-bit WEP encrypted network, an attacker need gather only around 100,000 IVs to crack in (although more certainly increases the chance of penetration) and only 500,000 to 700,000 for 128-bit WEP. On a home network, it can take days, even weeks to see enough traffic to make cracking the key possible. However, clever attackers discovered a way to stimulate network traffic by replaying encrypted network level packets at the target. By mimicking legitimate network traffic, the target network would respond over and over, causing a flood of network traffic and creating IVs at an accelerated rate. With this new attack, a 128-bit WEP network can be broken in as little as 10 minutes.

Wireless Encryption: WPA2

WPA, WiFi Protected Access, was created to address overwhelming concerns with WEP's inadequacy. WPA uses RC4; however, it uses a 128-bit key appended to a 48-bit initialization vector. This longer key defeats the key recovery attacks made popular against WEP using the Temporal Key Integrity Protocol (TKIP), which changes keys mid-session, on the fly. Additionally, the Message Integrity Code (MIC) includes a frame counter in the packet, which prevents the replay attacks that cripple WEP.

WPA2 was the child of the IEEE group, their certified form of 802.11i. RC4 was replaced by the favorable AES encryption scheme, which is still considered secure. WPA's MIC is replaced by CCMP, the Counter Mode with Cipher Block Chaining Message Authentication Code Protocol. CCMP checks to see if the MIC sum has been altered, and if it has, will not allow the message through.

Perhaps the most beneficial attribute of WPA2 is its ease of implementation. In most cases, hardware vendors needed only reflash the firmware of their Access Points to allow for WPA2 compatibility.

Although considerably stronger than its older brother, WEP, WPA2 is not without guilt. WPA2 encrypted traffic is still susceptible to dictionary attacks since WPA2 uses a hashing algorithm that can be reproduced. Joshua Wright released a tool called coWPAtty, which is a brute-force cracking tool that takes a list of dictionary words and encrypts them using WPA2s algorithms, one at a time. The encrypted value of each word then is compared against the encrypted value of captured traffic, and if the right password is found, POOF! The packet becomes intelligible.

Although brute-force cracking is not guaranteed to yield results, it leverages a weakness found in almost all security mechanisms—the user. If a user chooses a password that is not strong enough, or uses semipredictable modifications (the use of the number 3 instead of "e"), the network will fall. It is recommended that users install a pass-phrase instead of a traditional password. A pass-phrase longer than eight characters, which includes nonalphanumeric characters, is much less likely to be discovered by brute-forcing methods. And never, ever, use a dictionary word as a password, as these will often be discovered within minutes using freely available software from the Internet.

When implementing wireless VoIP, always use WPA2 or use an alternative means for protecting the VoIP stream (i.e., media and signaling encryption or IPSEC tunneling). Given the speed with which WEP can be cracked, it's almost pointless to use it since it adds encryption latency and creates a false sense of security.

Authentication: 802.1x

802.1x is an authentication (and to a lesser extent, authorization) protocol, whereas WEP/WPA are encryption protocols. And although 802.1x can be used on wired networks as well, it is most common today on wireless networks. It acts as an added layer of protection for existing wireless security implementations like WEP or WPA2 by requiring additional authentication to join a network beyond the shared secret associated with the encryption key.

802.1x works by forcing users (or devices) to identify themselves before their traffic is ever allowed onto the network. This happens through the use of the Extensible Authentication Protocol (EAP) framework. EAP orchestrates password negotiation and challenge-response tokens, coordinating the user with the authentication server. 802.1x sticks the EAP traffic inside of Ethernet, instead of over PPP, a much older authentication protocol used all over the Internet. Keep in mind that there are a lot of different EAP methods available, so when you are comparing vendor support for 802.1x in infrastructure and VoIP devices you need to pay careful attention to the specific methods supported.

As soon as the access point, called an *authenticator*, detects that the link is active, it sends an EAP Request Identity packet to the user requesting access, known as the *supplicant*. The user then responds with an EAP Response Identity packet, which the authenticator passes to the authentication server, who grants or denies access (see Figure 3.2).

Think of the supplicant as the guy trying to get into "Club WLAN," who asks the guy at the door if he's on the list. The authenticator then flags down the bouncer (authentication server) to see if he's "on the list." If he is, the bouncer lets him in to party with the rest of the party-packets. If not, it's to the curb he goes!

Figure 3.2 A Basic 802.1x Implementation for a Wireless Network*

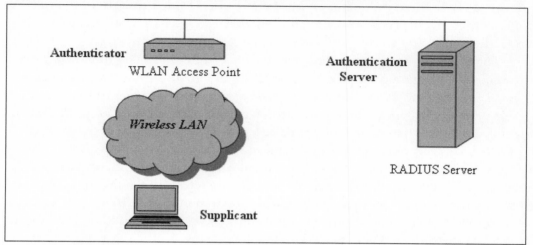

* If this were a wired 802.1x solution, the supplicant would be connected directly to the authenticator (typically a LAN switch).

Because of its moderately complex nature, 802.1x is not as quick to catch on with home users. The involvement of an authentication server (such as a RADIUS server) puts this technology just out of reach for most. However, 802.1x is ideal for businesses and public hot spots looking for more security than WEP or WPA2 alone provide.

Power-Supply Infrastructure

Often overlooked as part of the infrastructure required for secure VoIP is how power issues will be addressed. PBX and PSTN phones run on a common battery system that provides availability for free in the face of a power outage, but VoIP phones and the infrastructure that powers them must be carefully designed to meet equivalent requirements.

Power-over-Ethernet (IEEE 802.3af)

Like the name implies, Power-over-Ethernet (POE) eliminates the need to run a separate power supply to common networking appliances. POE works by injecting power using a switch or special power injector that pushes Direct Current (DC) voltage into the CAT5 cable. POE can be used directly with devices specifically designed for POE or with other DC-powered devices with a converter installed. This converter, called a picker or a tap, diverts the extra voltage from the CAT5 cable and redirects it to a regular power jack.

The major advantage of POE is that it allows greater flexibility in installing networking equipment. Access points can be set up in remote locations that normally would be limited to its proximity to a power outlet. It's often easier to route cat5 cable outdoors (on an antenna or in a tree, for instance) when only network cable is required. POE is also very popular with supplementary low-power devices, such as IP telephones and webcams, even computers!

POE is regulated by the IEEE 802.3af standard. This standard dictates the device must provide 48 volts of direct current, split over two pairs of a four-pair cable. The maximum current is limited at 350 mA and a maximum load of 16.8 watts. Several vendors have created proprietary (prestandard) implementations of POE, however in most cases newer equipment from these vendors is now available that is compliant with the IEEE standard (although at least one of these vendors now advertises an ability for the client to request a lower or higher amount of current through a proprietary process of negotiation above and beyond specifications within the standard).

To properly address VoIP phone availability concerns using POE, be sure that the power injector, network equipment, and voice servers (and gateways) can all operate on battery power for a sufficient length of time, and consider use of a generator when appropriate.

POE in action is pretty simple. The power source checks to see if the device on the other end of the wire is capable of receiving POE. If it is, the source then checks to see on which pairs of wires the device will accept power. If the device is capable, it will operate in one of two modes, A or B. In mode A, power is sent one way over pins 1 and 2, and is received over pins 3 and 6. In mode B, power is sent over pins 4 and 5 and is received over pins 7 and 8. Although only one mode will be used at a time, a device must be able to use both A or B to be IEEE 802.3af compliant.

UPS

No availability strategy can be considered complete without appropriate use of Uninterruptible Power Supply (UPS) technology. Mission critical equipment such as PBX systems and servers need to be protected from unscheduled power outages and other electrical maladies. Because of the sensitive nature of electronic equipment, safeguards need to be put in place to ensure the safety of this equipment. A UPS protects against several availability threats:

- **Power surges** When the power on the line is greater than it should be, the UPS acts as a buffer, ensuring that no more power reaches the machine than is supposed to. If a power surge were to occur without a UPS inline, sensitive electronics literally could be zapped out of life.

- **Partial loss of power** A brownout occurs when the power on the line is less than is required to run an appliance. In many cases a brown out is considered to be more dangerous than a total power failure, as electrical circuitry is very sensitive to power requirements.

- **Complete loss of power** A blackout occurs when power is completely lost to an area. This is very common during natural disasters, where severe weather may topple the electrical infrastructure of an area. Gas or battery powered UPS systems allow for equipment to continue functioning for a set period of time after the lights have gone out. This is ideal for finicky gear that needs to be completely shut down before going dark, lest system integrity be compromised.

In a call-center environment, downtime to the phone system can be fatal to business. With a properly implemented disaster recovery plan including a network of UPS devices, the phones can continue to work when standard computer systems might not be able to. This may mean the difference between success and doom for some companies.

Energy and Heat Budget Considerations

Given the heat and energy crisis being faced in many data centers due to the rapid increase in equipment densities (without a corresponding decrease in energy efficiency), planning for VoIP availability must include consideration for heat and power capacities in the room where VoIP servers and gateways will be housed. Don't omit this step only to discover after you've deployed that you have no power or cooling headroom for the additional equipment!

Summary

VoIP hardware infrastructure reflects the hybridization of two worlds that are colliding:

- A specialized voice infrastructure based on the PBX and central office circuit-switching paradigm
- A general-purpose data infrastructure based on large-scale proliferation of software-based communication solutions running over packet data networks

In order to address VoIP security, a detailed knowledge of both models is essential. As more people and organizations deploy VoIP solutions, securing that infrastructure will become more crucial than ever before. Security must be considered from the design phase in every component.

Solutions Fast Track

Traditional PBX Systems

- ☑ Know the PBX architecture model: PSTN over trunks to PBX (or gateway) to lines connecting stations and other devices. VoIP solutions may not be as far away from this architecture as you think and you need to understand the architecture to assess risk.

- ☑ Features are the value-add for a PBX; the way your organization uses them will either add risks or mitigate risks. Know your features.

- ☑ Change the default settings. Most PBX or adjunct systems that are compromised are exploited by weak or default passwords

- ☑ Make backups! Keeping up-to-date backups of your phone system are just as important as it is on your computer network.

- ☑ Audit your security! PBX systems often are overlooked when security is considered, especially if it's not in the budget. That can change quickly after a weekend of toll fraud that can create a bill of $100K or more in international long-distance charges.

PBX Alternatives

☑ Key Telephone Systems, Centrex, IP Centrex, and Host IP solutions are alternatives to PBX systems that send more of the switching intelligence offsite.

☑ These alternatives can simplify deployment and security considerations but at the cost of flexibility and overall capability.

VoIP Telephony and Infrastructure

☑ Huge differences exist between media servers and media gateways from different vendors. Know what class of device your organization plans to deploy so you can help develop an appropriate risk profile and mitigation plan.

☑ Boundary traversal for VoIP will require special attention and can be handled through proxies or application-layer gateways within firewalls.

☑ Enable WPA2 security on wireless access points and VoIP devices and consider 802.1x authentication. These devices will not have encryption or authentication turned on by default and you will need to set up supporting infrastructure.

☑ Make sure you've got enough raw power, cooling, and UPS systems in place to safe guard mission-critical systems. Don't forget that availability is a security concern!

Frequently Asked Questions

The following Frequently Asked Questions, answered by the authors of this book, are designed to both measure your understanding of the concepts presented in this chapter and to assist you with real-life implementation of these concepts. To have your questions about this chapter answered by the author, browse to **www.syngress.com/solutions** and click on the **"Ask the Author"** form.

Q: How is a PBX different from a switch in a telephone central office?

A: In many ways, the two switches serve the same basic function, but with differnt target customers. PBX systems are usually smaller-scale systems with more enterprise-specific feature functionality, and tend to interconnect a larger percentage of digital and IP phones than a PSTN switch would.

Q: Do I need an analog PBX to use an analog phone or trunk? Or a digital PBX to use a digital phone or trunk?

A: No, a digital PBX or VoIP gateway can handle analog lines and trunks just fine. These signals are converted to digital signals before bing switched on a digital PBX's Time Division Multiplexing (TDM) bus or Gateway VoIP media stream. A digital phone does require a digital PBX, but digital trunks can be split out on a channel bank for an analog switch if the signaling also is converted to an analog format.

Q: Where do the names "ring" and "tip" come from? What do they mean?

A: In the old days of telephones, operators connected calls using quarter-inch phone plugs (the same plugs that later were used with stereo headphones before the mini-phone plug became commonplace). The tip of the plug was the positive side of the circuit. The ring (or slip-ring) was a conductive circle around the plug above the tip and was the negative side of the ciruit. Sometimes another conductor was present on the plug after the ring—this was called the sleeve.

Q: What does "codec" mean, and what common codecs should I consider using? Is any kind of codec more secure than another?

A: Codec is short for COder/DECoder (and in more modern usage, COmpressor-DECompressor—though the first PCM codec was not compressed). In audio, a codec like the name implies, compresses audio before transmitting it, and decompresses the received audio. This helps pack more traffic in the same bandwidth. G.711 is standard PCM encoding, G.721 uses Adaptive Differential PCM (ADPCM) to cut the bandwidth required in half, and G.729 can compress a 64 kbps speech channeld down to 8 kbps, but with significant loss of quality (and it won't work for fax or data connections). In general, your choice of codec will not affect the security of your VoIP system one way or the other.

Q: Why do regular firewalls have so many problems with VoIP traffic?

A: There are several reasons for this. First, VoIP packets have three characteristics that make traversal more difficult: separate signaling streams from media streams, broad ranges of port numbers for media, and embedded IP addresses. Second, VoIP standards are always changing and firewall vendors have a hard time keeping up. Finally, VoIP packets are real-time by nature and firewalls aren't friendly to real-time packets under load.

Q: What is a WEP initialization vector and how is it used? Why is it not enough to protect me?

A: WEP is a stream cipher, which uses a value known as an initialization vector to ensure every signal is a unique signal, despite being encrypted by the same key. WEP's fatal flaw is that its IVs are too short, and duplication occurs

Q: Can I use WPA2 with any access point?

A: Most access points, but not all, now support WPA2 encryption. To be sure, consult the manual that came with your router (or they can usually be downloaded from the manufacturer's site) and look up the encryption they support. Some routers can be upgraded by uploading a special firmware to the device. Check the manufacturer's Web site, just to be sure.

Q: Can I run my own RADIUS server?

A: RADIUS, which stands for Remote Authentication Dial in User Service, has many free implementations for Linux and other operating systems. For a typical list of commercial and open source options, visit the VoIP-Info wiki at www.voip-info.org/wiki-Radius+Servers.

Q: What are some of the security concerns involved with using the popular instant messaging clients?

A: The same vulnerabilities that exist on the desktop are found in IM clients. This includes man-in-the-middle attacks, keylogging, and even audio capture and reconstruction with freely available tools on the Internet. And just as we've seen in the operating system world, the more widespread an IM client becomes, the more attractive a target it is to the hacking community.

Chapter 4

PSTN Architecture

Solutions in this chapter:

- **PSTN: What Is It, and How Does It Work?**
- **PSTN Call Flow**
- **PSTN Protocol Security**

☑ **Summary**

☑ **Solutions Fast Track**

☑ **Frequently Asked Questions**

Introduction

In 1876, Alexander Graham Bell patented the telephone and envisioned telephony's eventual triumph over the dominant communications network of his day: the telegraph network. Over the past decade, similar pronouncements have been made about VoIP and the Public Switched Telephone Network (PSTN) as IP-based communication becomes more pervasive. In both cases, the overall prediction has proven correct, even if the path for each was far more gradual and the result more integrated than originally anticipated. Case in point: Western Union (as a unit of First Data Corp.) did not discontinue its telegram service in the United States until January 27, 2006, even as numerous phone-to-telegram and web-to-telegram gateways continue to operate in conjunction with telegraph, cable, telex, and radio messaging networks worldwide.

With that in mind, it's essential to include the PSTN and its associated risks when examining VoIP security. Don't forget that today's Internet hacking community can trace its roots directly to the "phone phreak" subculture of the 1970s that first broadly exposed and exploited weaknesses in switch signaling protocols. Ever since automated long-distance switches were introduced by AT&T in the 1950s, people have been trying to figure out ways to bypass the toll services and get voice services for free. And the first known instances of eavesdropping by phone predate even the Bell System itself. The PSTN has evolved considerably in recent years, but the addition of VoIP services also has created new and novel vulnerabilities for both data and voice.

PSTN: What Is It, and How Does It Work?

Today, the PSTN is the most broadly interconnected communications system in the world, and is likely to remain so for at least another decade or more. For voice, it has no equal. VoIP services like Skype have banked on this fact; their business model depends on a steady flow of PSTN interconnect charges. But the PSTN provides FAX, data, telex, video, and hundreds of other multimedia services as well. And for many decades, the PSTN has enjoyed a universal numbering scheme called E.164. When you see a number that begins with "+" and a country code, you are seeing an E.164 number. In most of the world, connectivity to the PSTN is considered as essential as electricity or running water. Even the Internet itself depends on the PSTN to deliver dedicated access circuits as well as dial-up.

In the early days following Bell's invention, wired communications at its most advanced meant two (or more) devices sharing a single iron wire, whether you were using a telegraph or telephone. A grounded wire to earth completed the circuit running between phones, each with its own battery to generate the current necessary to transmit. It was noisy and lines couldn't run very far, and it would be many decades before it could truly be called a global network, much less a national one.

To fully define today's PSTN, we'll need to focus on several areas in turn. First, the physical "cable plant" required for signal distribution, from twisted-pair copper and coaxial electric to the latest fiber-optic cabling. Second, its signal transmission models, combining analog and digital signal processing and transmission over electrical, optical, and radio interfaces. This directly affects the kinds of content it can carry. Third, the increasing sophistication of associated signaling (control) protocols and "intelligent network" design introduced with the Integrated Services Digital Network (ISDN). And finally, its associated operational and regulatory infrastructure on international, national, state, and local levels.

PSTN: Outside Plant

The original premise behind the telephone exchange or Central Office (CO) was to run only one wire or set of wires into each house and have a centrally located facility for switching connections via operator (or automated equipment). Even though new homes today may see six or more wire pairs, plus a coaxial cable for broadband cable television, the basic principle remains the same: each line to the customer forms a loop that passes through to the CO.

The collection of cabling and facilities that support all local loops outside the CO (or "wire center") is known as the "loop distribution plant" and is owned by the Local Exchange Carrier (LEC). It starts out from the CO in a large underground cable vault with primary feeder cable (F1) to reach out over copper (or fiber) to the Serving Area Interface (SAI) for that area (look for a large grey or green box with doors mounted on a concrete pedestal in most areas of the United States). F1 cable is typically 600 to 2000 or more pairs and usually must be buried because of its weight (although fiber-optic F1 cable can be aerial if needed). It often is armored or pressurized and generally is enclosed in a concrete trench all the way to the CO, with manholes or other access points at least every 750 feet to allow for installation of repeaters (for digital trunks like the T1), loading coils, and other necessary equipment. In most of the world, the LEC is able to keep F1 and SAI fairly secure through physical locks, alarms, and so on.

At the SAI, F1 feeds are cross-connected to secondary feeder cable (F2) that goes out over copper underground to pedestal boxes where the distribution cable is split out or on poles to aerial drop splitters. Subscriber drop wires are then cross-connected to the F2 at that point. In rural areas, even lower-level cable facilities (F3,

F4, F5) may exist before a drop wire is terminated. A box is installed where the drop wire is terminated outside the subscriber's premises and this box is considered the demarcation point for the LEC. All wiring from there to the CO is the responsibility of the LEC, and from there to the phone devices themselves is the subscriber's responsibility (or that of the landlord). Physical security of that inside wiring—particularly in shared facilities—can be an issue in some cases. And F2 or lower feeds and pedestals are not well secured in general (and present the biggest opportunity to an eavesdropper).

Where growth or other planning challenges have exhausted the supply of F1 or F2 pairs, it's sometimes necessary for the LEC to install Remote Terminal (RT) equipment (sometimes called "pair gain" systems) that can multiplex multiple local loops on to a digital T-carrier (using Time-Division Multiplexing (TDM) over a 4-wire copper or pair of fiber-optic cables), or via older Frequency-Division Multiplexing (FDM) systems. RT units generally are locked and alarmed, however. And it is much more difficult to eavesdrop on a digital trunk (such as a T-carrier) or FDM system because of the costly equipment required. Figure 4.1 shows a diagram of a central office equipped with outside distribution plant (ODP).

Figure 4.1 The Central Office with ODP*

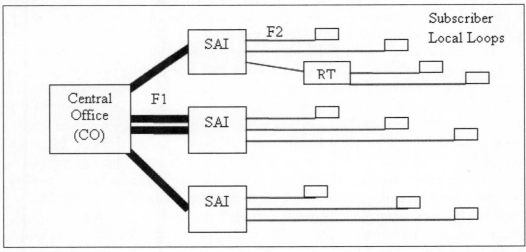

* This classic example assumes no fiber is in use to these SAIs within the CO (see SONET example in Figure 4.2).

In addition to the loop distribution plant, the LEC will have outside plant for trunking between central offices, and the LEC and other Inter-exchange Carriers (IXCs) will have outside plant for long distance connections between COs and other switching centers such as toll centers. And the LEC or other Competitive Local Exchange Carriers (CLECs) may run fiber for SONET (or SDH) rings (see Figure 4.2).

Figure 4.2 A Modern SONET Ring Example

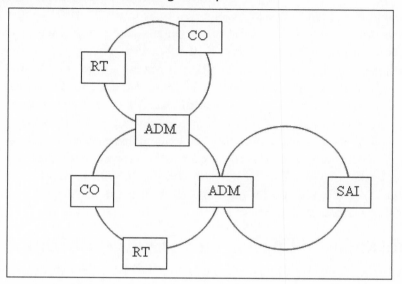

The diagram in Figure 4.2 shows that by using path diversity for fiber-optic routes along with SONET rings with Add-Drop Multiplexers, several self-healing SONET rings provide F1 and some F2 subscriber loop feeds as well as trunking between two central offices. Large business customers can also connect to this SONET ring for high-capacity voice and data services if they are located close enough to the buried fiber.

PSTN: Signal Transmission

In the old days, the path an analog voice signal took from your phone to the CO switch (or switchboard) was simple. With the appropriate cross-connects, each local loop was half of the analog circuit required for a phone conversation, and the switch (or operator) simply connected you with a calling or called party that represented the other half of that circuit. Although loading coils might have been used to reduce signal attenuation on the circuit, no amplification or signal processing was used.

Since Bell's original invention, several improvements had been added. Common battery from the CO with a separate return path instead of the earth eliminated the need for a battery in each phone and made the phone less noisy. Ringing was accomplished through magnetos, first added to the phones themselves and later pulled in to the CO and standardized as 90 Volts of Alternating Current (AC)—all other phone/PSTN functions on the line use Direct Current (DC). And eventually, automated electromechanical switching eliminated much of the need for an operator within the PSTN.

Still, analog transmission and switching had their limits. Until 1915, it wasn't possible to go much further than 1,500 miles on an analog long-distance circuit. And even when that limit was broken thanks to the vacuum-tube amplifier, these long-distance calls were very noisy. Radio telephony overseas and to ships further expanded the reach of analog telephony in 1927. And Frequency Division Multiplexing techniques were developed in the late 1930s that allowed many calls to pass over a single voice circuit by using frequency shifting techniques equivalent to those used by FM radio. Each 4 kHz band of voice conversation would be shifted up or down to a specific slot, allowing many calls to be carried simultaneously over a single coaxial cable or radio interface. By the 1950s, 79% of the inner-city CO trunks in the United States were using FDM. But even the microwave systems in use since the 1950s were analog systems.

T1 Transmission: Digital Time Division Multiplexing

Even though Alec Reeves of Britain had developed Pulse Code Modulation (PCM) techniques in 1937 for digitizing audio signals, and Bell labs had invented the transistor in 1948, which was required for the large-scale implementation of digital techniques, it would take more than a decade to make digital transmission a reality (and longer still before the advent of digital switching could make the full signal path digital outside the local loop). 1963 brought the introduction of the T1 or Transmission One digital carrier using revolutionary signal manipulation techniques that would forever change telephony.

Unlike all previous carriers, the T1 started in an all-digital format, meaning that it was structured as a series of bits (193 per frame to be exact, 8 bits per channel, 24 channels, plus the framing bit—moving at the rate of 8,000 frames, or 1,544 Megabits per second) that by design could be completely regenerated again without data loss over long distances (see Figures 4.3 and 4.4). This provides a 64-kilobit-per-second digital bitstream for each of the 24 channels, using Time Division Multiplexing (TDM).

Figure 4.3 A T1 Frame*

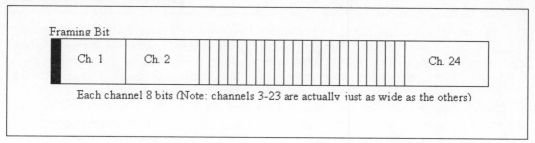

* Eight bits in each channel capture a 125μs slice of each associated analog audio signal.

Figure 4.4 Time Division Multiplexing

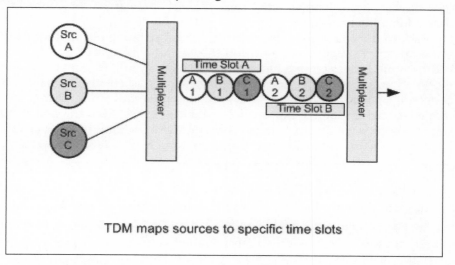

TDM maps sources to specific time slots

TDM as introduced in the T1 is the multiplexing workhorse of the telecommunications world and will be the base multiplexing environment for the rest of our discussion of the PSTN. Yet for the T1 to be successful, it is just as important to have a foolproof way of converting an analog signal to digital bits that would make or break the new form of digital transmission. This is the job of a codec. Although today in the era of digital media we take for granted the engineering required to create the first effective PCM codec—now commonly known as G.711—it was no small feat in its day. Yet, even today as debate rages over what codec is best to use for VoIP, G.711 is still considered the "toll quality" standard that others must beat, and is especially good at preserving modem and FAX signals that low-bandwidth codecs can break.

> **NOTE**
>
> Although we're not going to do a deep dive on digital/analog conversion here, it is worth pointing out that slight differences between U.S. and European standards will mean that some conversion needs to take place even *within* a standard G.711-encoded channel in order for that channel to move from a T1 to an E1 or vice versa. Specifically, slight differences in PCM encoding algorithm (μ-law vs. A-law) may require conversion when voice or VoIP streams cross international boundaries. Of course, on a data circuit, that conversion is not going to happen automatically (if it did, it would scramble the data). But it can cause problems across a VoIP if you're not careful.
>
> Similarly, when using a T1 circuit for data, it's important to make sure the circuit is properly configured since some signaling modes can use what's called "robbed-bit" signaling, which is fine for circuit-based voice but will corrupt data running on it. For this reason, only 56K of the 64K channel could be used for data on early data circuits. Today, clear channel data can be provisioned that uses a full 64K channel.
>
> Back to the codec issue, however. It's worth pointing out that very complex trade-offs exist in codec selection and they're not as simple as quality vs. bandwidth. Some codecs require much more processing, others work poorly with modems, faxes, and other nonvoice applications (particularly low bandwidth codecs: it's not hard to imagine the problems inherent with sending a 56 Kbps modem signal through a 4Kbps voice-optimized codec. Even the best compression algorithms would struggle to represent that much information in so few bits, not to mention the inherent distortion present in D/A-A/D conversion.

Starting with the introduction of the T1, timing became an important consideration for the PSTN. Digital circuits like the T1 must be plesiochronous, meaning that their bit rate must vary only within a fairly limited range or other problems can be created within the PSTN. In comparison, analog circuits are completely asynchronous. This requirement has forced a hierarchy of master clocks to be incorporated into its infrastructure.

With the advent of SONET, a fully synchronous solution to the timing problem has arrived, along with massive bandwidth that can be further enhanced with Wavelength Division Multiplexing (WDM—basically the use of different colored light on a single optical fiber to increase capacity). Pointers and bit-stuffing in SONET and SDH are used to minimize the impact of clock drift between digital circuits, though the advent of VoIP has created some challenges because VoIP is asynchronous. VoIP is also a packet technology (since it runs on packet networks), so it is subject to variations in latency and jitter and packet loss that are simply not significant issues in circuit networks because timeslots are guaranteed. On the other hand, the PSTN's circuit network is far less efficient overall than any packet network because of the excess capacity it reserves.

As T1 and other digital trunks were deployed in the PSTN, digitized voice services in 64Kbps increments, each called a *Digital Signal 0* (DS0) —became the basic switchable unit of the PSTN. A single DS0 is a 64Kbps channel equivalent to an analog line converted to digital via G.711. With the advent of TDM-based digital switching, the DS0s were aggregated by digital access and cross-connect systems (DACS) for transport or presentation to the switch via DS1 (1.5 Mbps) or DS3 (45 Mbps) interfaces. These digital switches communicate over T1 and other digital trunks to access and toll tandem switches, sending calls across the telephone network to destination switches. The DS0 voice channels are then split back out to their original 64Kbps state and converted back to analog signals sent onward to the destination local loop.

In fact, there is now a full hierarchy to the T carrier system in North American and the E carrier system in Europe (as well as the more recent SONET/SDH optical carrier system). Aggregation of voice and data channels at many levels can take place, and knowing how these systems can interact is essential. Table 4.1 roughly defines the capacity and equivalency of the various North American, Japanese, and European digital signal hierarchies in a single chart. I've never been able to find this information in one place, so I created a single chart to cover the whole range of PSTN transport solutions in use today.

Table 4.1 Digital Signal Hierarchy (North America and Europe)

Speed Mbps	Max 64k Channels	SONET	North America	Europe	SDH	Equivalency
64 kbps	1		DS0	E0		DS0 = E0
144 kbps	2B+D		ISDN BRI	ISDN BRI		2 DS0 or E0
1.544 1.728*	23B+D	VT 1.5*	ISDN PRI (NA)		VC-11*	23 DS0
	24		DS1 (T1)			24 DS0 [Japan: J1]
2.048 2.304*	30 B+D	VT 2.0*		ISDN PRI	VC-12*	30 E0
	31			E1		31 E0
3.152 3.456*	48	VT 3.0*	DS1C (T1C)			2 T1
6.312 6.912*	96	VT 6.0* [VTG*]	DS2 (T2)		VC-21* [TUG-2*]	4 T1 or 3 E1 VTG = TUG-2 [J2]
8.448	124			E2	VC-22	4 E1
32.06* 34.37	480* 496			E3	VC-3* [TUG-3]*	[J3* = 5x J2] 16 E1 via 4 E2 [VC-31]
44.74 48.96* 51.84**	672	STS-1** (OC-1)	DS3 (T3)			28 T1 or 7 T2 or 21 E1 TUG-3 = 7 TUG-2 7 VTG [VC-32]
97.73† 100.0‡ 135.0* 139.3 155.5**	1440**** 1488 1984 2016	STS-3** (OC-3)	DS3D* (T3D)	E4	VC-4** STM-1**	[J4† = 3x J3] 48 E1 via 3 E3 via 3 VC-3 64 E1 via 1 E4 via VC-4 84 T1 or 63 E1 via 3 T3 Fast Ethernet ‡, FDDI ‡
274.2 311.0**	4032	STS-6** (OC-6)	DS4 (T4)		STM-2**	168 T1 (or 126 E1) via 6 T3 128 E1 via 2 E4 or 2 VC-4
400.4 466.6**	5760 6048	STS-9** (OC-9)	DS5 (T5)		STM-3**	T5 = 240 T1 via 60 T2 [J5] 252 T1 (or 189 E1) via 9 T3
565.6 622.1**	7936 8064	STS-12** (OC-12)		E5	STM-4**	4 E4 via 4 VC-4 or 4 OC-3 336 T1 via 12 T3
1 Gbps ‡ 2.5 Gbps	32,256	STS-48 (OC-48)			STM-16	48 T3 or 16 E4 or 16 VC-4 2x Gigabit Ethernet ‡
10 Gbps	129,024	STS-192 (OC-192)			STM-64	192 T3 or 64 E4 or 64 VC-4 10 Gigabit Ethernet
40 Gbps	516,096	STS-768 (OC-768)			STM-256	21,504 T1 or 768 T3 or 256 E4 or 256 VC-4
160 Gbps	2,064,384	STS-3072 (OC-3072)			STM-1024	86,016 T1 or 3072 T3 or 1024 E4 or 1024 VC-4

In Table 4.1, dark bands are for the circuits most commonly provisioned for business customers. Bolded items are used most commonly in wide area networks overall. Note: Although SONET and SDH are directly equivalent to each other, the process of mapping between them and their T or E-carrier counterparts requires the use of SONET Virtual Tributaries (VTs) and Virtual Tributary Groups (VTGs) or SDH Virtual Containers (VCs).

As you can see from Table 4.1, 24 DS0 channels make up a T1 circuit, 28 T1 circuits make up a T3 or OC-1 link, and so forth. An OC-12 link can support up to 7936 DS0 channels if it's broken out into E4 circuits or 8064 if it's broken out by T3 circuits through a DACS or Add Drop Multiplexer (ADM). 10 Gigabit Ethernet can run over an OC-192 SONET ring, and so on. These mappings are essential to understanding capacities for Internet access circuits as well when sizing for VoIP, since upper limits on Speed (left column) cannot be physically exceeded (note that actual throughput will be at least 10% lower because of overhead).

Perhaps you have ordered and provisioned a voice or data T1 for your company or clients. Have you ever thought why only one voice T1 is needed for a company of 100 employees with a PBX, knowing that only 24 channels can be used at any one time? The answer is that not everyone will be on the phone, receiving a fax, or otherwise using an available channel at once. Normally you can count on a six-to-ten ratio when calculating how many DS0s are needed. Those in the sales and service industry may go as low as four-to-one because they are on the phone more and need higher channel availability. Even with VoIP, sizing access circuits is important, since there are hard limits on the amount of data that can be pushed through that circuit network, even if the number of channels isn't so important. Less bandwidth might be required if G.729 was used in place of G.711, but more would be required if the link also supported Internet access, especially if Quality of Service (QoS) limitations weren't set up on the corresponding routers.

In Figure 4.5 we see that the DACS can be used to combine a wide variety of digital signal inputs and present them through a single interface to the next hop, which might be a switch, SONET multiplexing equipment, enterprise routing equipment, or something else. Keep in mind that although both voice and data traffic of any flavor can run over SONET, timing requirements won't allow something like a T1 to run over something asynchronous like Gigabit Ethernet.

Figure 4.5 DACS Channel Aggregation

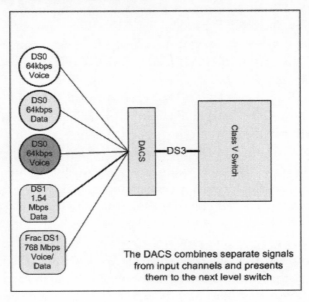

The DACS combines separate signals
from input channels and presents
them to the next level switch

NOTE

T1 links in particular have a lot of nuances not discussed here in detail, from different framing and superframing formats like D4 and Extended Super Frame (ESF) to special line coding like Bipolar 8 Zero Substitution (B8ZS) used to ensure byte synchronization without losing data or bandwidth.

Other framing considerations come into play for different digital carriers such as E1, T2, T3, STS-1, STM-2, and so on. There are excellent books on the topic for those that need more details, but in general none of these formatting issues require any security consideration.

PSTN: Switching and Signaling

As the PSTN's global reach and capabilities become more extensive, signaling became the most significant security concern within the PSTN. In its early days, signaling was no more complicated than taking the phone off-hook to let an operator know you wanted to make a call. Dialing gradually became more automatic, first for operators, then later for subscribers. Today's direct–dial networks, VoIP gateways, and myriad protocols only serve to increase the complexities and risks when it comes to signaling.

Notes from the Underground…

Blueboxing and the Original Phone Phreaks

Named for the color of the first one found in 1961, *blueboxing* was the name given to the first automated toll fraud technique to be employed by U.S. "phone phreaks." Author Ron Rosenbaum gave critical mass to the budding movement in October 1971 through a sensational article in *Esquire* magazine that attracted the attention other hobbyists, including Steve Wozniak and Steve Jobs (who for a short time produced and sold a blue box of their own before moving on to found Apple Computer). Prior to that point, independent phreaks who would later form the Internet hacking community consisted of a handful of disconnected hobbyists that had independently stumbled onto the fact that sending a 2600 Hertz tone down a long-distance trunk of that era (i.e., one using in-band ITU-T 5 signaling) would terminate the call, then seize a trunk for reuse once the tone was removed, allowing free long-distance calling and more. Ironically, the movement might never have started save for a tiny whistle included in boxes of Cap'n Crunch cereal during the 1960s that could reproduce a perfect 2600 Hertz tone.

Starring in the *Esquire* article were John Draper (known as "Cap'n Crunch" and technical mentor to Steve Wozniak and hundreds of other phreakers), Joe Engressia (a.k.a. "Joybubbles," the most prominent of a group of blind phreakers—and one who could whistle a 2600 Hertz tone thanks to perfect pitch), and Mark Bernay (another pseudonym for "The Midnight Skulker," a tireless missionary of phreaking who spread the word to hundreds along the West coast but has never been publicly identified to this day). Within a few years, the community had amassed an enormous knowledge of the phone network and gathered regularly over voice conferences to share that knowledge. Furthergrowth and sophistication followed the advent of the personal computer, the modem-based Bulletin-Board Service (BBS), dedicated hack/phreak magazines like 2600 and Phrack, and annual conferences like DefCon, each founded in the early 1980s by the phreaking community.

At its height, the phreaking community had developed dozens of specialized electronic gizmos designed to defeat PSTN billing or security mechanisms. Here are the most commonly used "colored boxes' of that era:

- Black Box—applies extra voltage to the line to enable free incoming calls (billing equipment thinks the phone was never answered, though it does look to the CO like someone was ringing the line for a long time).

Continued

- Beige Box—Lineman's handset for eavesdropping and all blueboxing functionality.

- Blue Box—2600 Hz tone generator with full Multi-Frequency Code (MFC) generator to generate dialing strings used by an operator. MFC is like Dual Tone Multi-Frequency (DTMF, a.k.a. "Touch-Tones") but uses different frequencies and includes several keys (codes) not available to DTMF.

- Red Box—Generates tones corresponding to those used by AT&T's Automated Coin Toll System (ACTS) payphones that send specific tones used when a coin is accepted (still works in many areas).

- Gold Box—Placed across two phone lines to allow call out on the other line when one is dialed (makes tracing more difficult).

Among the most notorious phreakers was Kevin Poulsen, who in 1990 decided that he wanted the Porsche 944 S2 being given away by KIIS-FM in Los Angeles to the 102nd caller on a particular Friday. Taking control of the radio station's 25 trunks through Pacific Bell's maintenance system, he blocked out all calls but his own (a stunt he's suspected of repeating to block calls into the Unsolved Mysteries tip line after he was profiled for other cybercrimes, though in the end it wasn't enough to prevent his arrest). Kevin apparently became the first person banned by the U.S. Government from using the Internet (a sentence also imposed on notorious hacker Kevin Mitnick, who was skilled in PSTN manipulation as well).

Today the in-band Channel Associated Signaling (CAS) analog switching equipment loved by phreakers has been replaced by digital switching with out-of-band Common Channel Interface Signaling (CCIS) in most of the world, and a given instance of toll fraud is more likely to occur by other means (typically through an enterprise PBX or voicemail system) and with less risk to the perpetrator.

Electromechanical automated switching equipment first appeared in 1891 following Almon Strowger's patented Step by Step (SXS) system, although Bell System resistance to it would postpone its adoption for decades. The classic rotary dial phone was another Strowger invention that was finally adopted by the Bell System in 1919 along with SXS switches. Yet it would take until 1938 for Western Electric (the equipment R&D arm of the Bell system) to develop a superior automatic switching system, namely the crossbar switch. And not until the 1950s did Bell Labs embark on a computer–controlled switch project, but the 101 ESS PBX that resulted in 1963 was only partially digital. Also introduced that year was the T1 circuit and Touch Tones, the Dual–Tone Multi-Frequency (DTMF) dialing scheme that is still with us today. Despite the fact that switching itself was analog, digital T1 circuits quickly replaced analog backbone toll circuits and most analog CO interconnect trunks. By 1965 Bell had released the first central office switch with computerized stored program control, the 1ESS that offered new features like speed dialing and call for-warding. Yet the 1ESS was still an analog switch at its core. Thanks to T1 "robbed bit" signaling, however, all signaling was out of band, at least from the phone phreaker's perspective.

Insiders suggest that AT&T was prepared to postpone true digital switching until the 1990s, but Northern Telecom changed their plans with the DMS-10 all-digital switch, introduced in the late 1970s. The need for an all-digital AT&T alternative drove development of the 5ESS and accelerated implementation of ISDN. Today, the most common Class 5 (central office) switches in North America are the Nortel DMS-100 and Lucent 5ESS, running ITU-T Signaling System Number 7 (SS7) with full ISDN support.

The Class 5 switch is the first point where we can find the full suite of tele-phone services being handled in one place as part of the Intelligent Network model. A typical Class 5 can handle operator services, call waiting, long distance, ISDN, and other data services. The Class 5 will have tables that are queried for every service and will send the appropriate request to the right place. For instance, when you pick up the phone in your house to make a long distance phone call, the Class 5 switch detects the line is open and provides a timeslot in the switch for your call (this is when you hear the dial tone), then based on the buttons pushed (dialed) the switch will send the call either to the local carrier or to the long distance provider. If you dial a long distance call from a provider who is not your local provider, the switch will deliver the request to the closest switch that handles calls for that particular car-rier. Class 5 switches act on demand (i.e., they set up, sustain, and tear down connec-tions as needed). This helps to reduce the amount of traffic over the lines when not needed, thus expanding the overall capacity of the system. These switches are a real workhorse for telephone companies (LECs, CLECs, and even IXCs, though they can use a Class 4 switch in most cases). A Class 5 switch can handle thousands of con-nections per minute.

The Intelligent Network (IN), Private Integrated Services, ISDN, and QSIG

The model drawn up in the 1980s and 1990s for advanced network functionality is called the Intelligent Network (IN). Services such as 8XX-number lookups as well as Calling Cards, Private Integrated Services Network (PISNs), and many other advanced services are all made possible through SS7, ISDN, and IN capabilities. PISNs are geographically disparate networks that are connected via leased lines that allow for enhanced services such as multivendor PBX deployments, Voice VPNs (don't get these confused with data VPNs, they are a true private network for voice, just like that provided by a PBX), and even certain kinds of VoIP. A Private Integrated service Network Exchange (PINX) lives within a PISN. Another application is integration with the QSIG protocol, which allows PBX products from other vendors be able to be used transparently to integrate all voice networks.

QSIG (a Q.931 ISDN extension) as a protocol has been around since the early to mid 1990s. We will talk about ISDN in the next section, but QSIG can be used to integrate systems even without ISDN. QSIG also leverages DPNSS, which was developed prior to when the final QSIG protocol was agreed upon. Not used much in U.S. networks, DPNSS had much of its life in the United Kingdom. Modern networks are using QSIG as the means to interconnect voice channels between PBXs while preserving critical information about caller and call state in the process.

ISDN is a common-channel signaling (CCS) solution that works with media or data traveling down one pair of wires while signaling control is handled over another. Remembering back to our earlier discussions of the channels of 64 kbps in size, a typical ISDN will hold 23 bearer (B) channels that carry voice and data and one data (D) channel that carries signaling information. All channels are 64kbps, so we have 24, 64-kbps channels totaling 1536 Mbps, or equivalent to a T1 and 30 B channels plus a D channel on an E-1, but in each case we lose one channel for signaling. Not only was distance from the central office a new issue with ISDN trunks, but the customer also had to implement new equipment. This Customer Premise Equipment (CPE) required ISDN terminators in order to access the network. Today the use of ISDN in the provisioning and delivery of broadband Internet access via DSL and cable services keep pricing competitive and affordable. Besides its use in the DSL services, ISDN still has an active share in providing redundant and emergency data network access to critical servers and services when higher speed lines or primary access has been disrupted.

Over the last 100 years, signaling has moved from operator-assisted modes to loop and disconnect modes, from single frequency to multifrequency signaling, and now to common channel signaling using the ISDN signaling channel.

ITU-T Signaling System Number 7 (SS7)

SS7 (or C7) is an ITU-T (formerly CCITT) standard that defines how equipment in the PSTN digitally exchange data regarding call setup and routing. Other ITU-T signaling systems are still in use throughout the world, particularly:

- ITU-T 4, Channel-Associated Signaling (CAS) with a 2VF (voice frequency) code in the voice band and a 2040/2400 Hz supervisory tone

- ITU-T 5 CAS with 2VF and a 2400/2600 Hz supervisory tone, plus inter-register codes with Multi-Frequency (MF) tones
- ITU-T [5] R2 is a revision of ITU-T 5 but uses different frequencies

What sets SS7 apart above all is the fact that it is Common Channel Signaling (CCS), not CAS like its predecessors. Throughout the telecommunications industry the SS7 can be used for call session setup, management and tear down, call forwarding, caller identification information, toll free, LNP, and other service as implemented by carriers. Information passed through SS7 networks are communicated completely out of band meaning that signaling and media do not travel down the same path. The SS7 was loosely designed around the OSI 7-layer model. Figure 4.6 illustrates their basic similarities.

Message Transfer Parts 1, 2, and 3 (MTP)

MTP level 1 is much the same as the Physical layer (1) of the OSI. Here the electrical and physical characteristics of the digital signaling are addressed. The physical interfaces defined here are those such as our previously discussed DS0 and T1. MTP level 2 aligns with the Data Link layer of the OSI. MTP level 2 takes care of making sure transmissions are accurate from end to end, just like the Data Link layer issues such as flow control and error checking are handled in the MTP level 2 area. MTP level 3 aligns itself with the Network layer of the OSI. MTP level 3 reroutes calls away from failed links and controls signaling when congestion is present.

Telephone User Part (TUP)

This is an analog system component. Prior to digital signaling the TUP was used to set up and tear down calls. Today most countries are using the ISDN User Part (ISUP) to handle this requirement.

ISDN User Part (ISUP)

Most countries are using ISUP to handle basic call components. ISUP works by defining the protocols used to manage calls between calling and called parties.

Automatic Number Identification (ANI), or—when it's passed on to a subscriber, known as Calling Party Identification Presentation (CLIP)—caller ID is passed to the PSTN (or back again) through ISDN trunks and displays the calling party's telephone number at the called party's telephone set during the ring cycle. ANI is used for all Custom Local Area Signaling Services (CLASS) such as custom ringing, selective call forwarding, call blocking, and so on.

Notes from the Underground…

ANI Spoofing Services: Think You Can Trust Caller ID?…Think Again!

A number of services aimed at private investigators, collections agencies, or law enforcement have sprung up since 2000 to provide pay-per-call ANI spoofing. The service works like this: After setting up payment, you choose the 10-digit ANI you want Caller ID to show (the LEC will typically add the business or individual associated with the ANI number), plus the target number you want to call, then the service calls you and initiates the spoofed ANI call to the target number you've selected. Your target thinks you're Pizza Hut calling back, or their mother, or whoever you're spoofing and you've just fooled them into picking up.

What you may not know is that this can be done from any PBX with ISDN trunks that can support ANI. Most LECs have no way of validating the ANI you present to them and happily pass that information along via CallerID, whether it's accurate or not. Note that this is different from the "Caller ID spoofing" that can be done after a caller picks up on some CallerID equipment (fun with friends, but not very useful if the caller decides not to answer). Effectively, ANI spoofing "poisons the well" from which Caller ID gets its data.

Some carriers have suggested that they will crack down on this practice, but since no comprehensive DID ownership database is kept across all LECs and CLECs there is no current method to verify an ANI in real-time when it's been presented.

Signaling Connection Control Part (SCCP)

The SCCP is used mainly for translating 800, calling card, and mobile telephone numbers into a set single point destination code.

Transaction Capabilities Applications Part (TCAP)

TCAP supports the passing and exchange of data within noncircuit-related communications. An example of noncircuit-related data is authentication of a user to a calling card plan.

Communication within an SS7 network and its equipment are called signaling points, of which there are three; Service Switching Points (SSP), Service Transfer Points (STP), and Service Control Points (SCP).

Service Switching Points (SSPs) are the primary calling switches; they set up, manage, and terminate calls. When calls need to be routed outside of the SSP's trunk group a request may be sent to a Service Control Point (SCP), which is a database that responds to queries and sends routing information to requesting switches that delivery the appropriate route for the type of call placed. A Service Transport Point (STP) is a packet switch that forwards messages down the appropriate link depending on the information contained within the packet.

Figure 4.6 shows basic OSI and SS7 stacks. Links between the SS7 network are broken down into six different types, lettered A through F. Figure 4.7 illustrates a typical SS7 network topology with specific link type labeled. Table 4.2 describes each link.

Figure 4.6 Basic OSI and SS7 Stacks

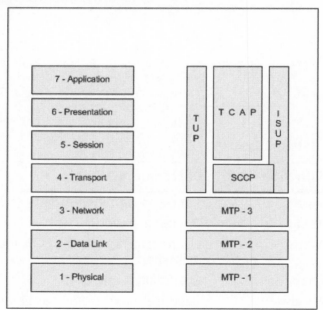

SS7 can also be run on IP networks using SCTP, using a slightly different stack that includes SCTP transport (instead of TCP or UDP).

SS7 has important security considerations, particularly between carriers where misconfigured implementations with unverified data can open the door to large scale fraud and other risks. This will be discussed in detail in this chapter's final section on PSTN Protocol Security, but the bottom line is that SS7 is a peer-to-peer protocol that may be out-of-band for phone phreaks, but carries significant risk from other sources, especially if it's running unencrypted over IP through SIGTRAN (SCTP).

Figure 4.7 An SS7 Network Topology and Link Types

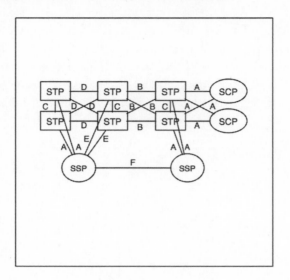

Table 4.2 SS7 Network Links

Link Name	Function	Description
A	Access	Connects signal endpoints to an STP
B	Bridge	Connects peering STPs
C	Cross	Connects STPs into pairs to improve reliability
D	Diagonal	Essentially same as B
E	Extended	Used if A links are not available
F	Fully Associated	Direct connection of two endpoints (SSPs)

PSTN: Operational and Regulatory Issues

Public Telephone and Telegraph (PTT) organizations are the highest-level monopoly (or ex-monopoly) in each country, and generally are expected to comply with ITU-T standards for interoperability. Each PTT is regulated by its country of origin. In the United States, AT&T was broken up in 1982 into a long distance unit (AT&T as the Inter-exchange carrier (IXC) was authorized only to carry long distance traffic), and reorganized groups of regional Bell Operating Companies were given a limited Local Exchange Carrier (LEC) role that until recently prevented them from selling interstate (or interLATA) long distance services. Competitive LECs (CLECs), in spite of regulatory advantages, hold less than 10% of local lines.

WARNING

VoIP used for toll bypass is illegal in certain countries. Be sure you understand associated laws before implementing a VoIP system internationally.

As part of the AT&T breakup, 160 local access and transport areas (LATAs) were created around area code boundaries. Initially, LECs could not provide long distance service across and long distance companies could not provide local service, and some states have not removed these restrictions. Similar attempts to promote competitive services within specific countries are underway in various parts of the world.

PSTN Call Flow

Now that we have discussed what makes up the PSTN, let's put it all together and walk through a messaging sequence. Here we will start from a caller picking up the phone attempting to make a call. The flow will be broken down into off-hook, digit receipt, ring down, conversation, and on-hook sections. We will start by imagining someone (Party B) picking up the phone to make the call (to Party A, on the same CO switch). The following list outlines, in order, the actions performed by the network:

Party B picks up the phone, and the off-hook sequence begins:

1. The off-hook state is detected by the switch (loop or ground start).
2. The switch establishes the time slot and sends a dial tone on the voice path.
3. The switch awaits digits pressed by Party B.

The digit receipt sequence is as follows:

1. Party B dials digits on the touch pad.
2. Each digit is received by the switch and sends a silence tone and starts Inter Digit Timer (IDT).

3. IDT starts when the switch is awaiting a dialed digit and stops when the digit is pressed.

After Party B dials the last number, the ring down sequence begins:

1. When the digit receipt stops (or when the maximum dialed digits are pressed), the switch sends the request to the called number to allocate a time slot.

2. When the called switch allocates a time slot the path is switched to the call handler.

3. Party A's phone rings (unless it is already off-hook).

Parties A and B can begin their conversation after the following sequence of steps is completed:

1. Party A picks up the phone.

2. The switch receives an answered call indication (off-hook).

3. The ring-down signals stop.

4. Parties A and B are able to speak on the established voice path.

After the two parties finish their conversation, the on-hook sequence of steps begins:

1. The conversation ends with either party hanging up the phone.

2. The on-hook indication is received by switches on access networks.

3. The switches release established paths (termination).

4. The call is ended.

During each of these sections there is traffic traveling in both directions to keep the signal alive. There are numerous acknowledgement requests between the caller and their access network, and the two access networks and the called party and their network, to keep this communication path alive. Most of this traffic is happening along the voice path.

This book is about securing voice over Internet networks, so later in the book you will be introduced to a protocol called Session Initiation Protocol (SIP). Though it is early on in the text we will now walk through a SIP to PSTN call. Remember that PSTN is a voice network and the SIP is originating from a data-only network. We will follow the sections of off-hook, digit receipt, ring down, conversation, and on-hook. To better visualize this call sequence we will use the following illustration (see Figure 4.8) to help us. Party A will be the SIP user and Party B will be the PSTN user.

Figure 4.8 SIP-to-PSTN Call Flow

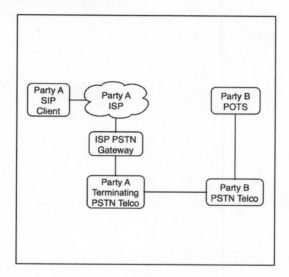

Party A picks up the phone, and the off-hook sequence begins:

1. Party A picks up the phone and dials the number.
2. An off-hook state is noticed by the SIP client.
3. The SIP client sends a request to the SIP proxy (at ISP).
4. The SIP client sends the SIP tel URL with the request.
5. ISUP message is prepared by the ISP PSTN Gateway.
6. The ISP Proxy finds the local terminating PSTN to send the call through (Network PSTN Gateway NGW).

The digit receipt sequence of steps begins:

1. Since Party A already sent the entire dialed number through the SIP phone prior to the call being sent through the Network PSTN Gateway, all the dial information is already there, so when the call is sent to the PSTN the switches already have all the information they need to process and route the call (i.e., no overlap sending is required).
2. This is sent through ISUP Messaging by the ISP PSTN Gateway.

Now, the ring down sequence begins:

1. Party A's switch establishes a one-way voice path.

2. Party A's switch sends a ringing tone.

3. At the same time, Party B's switch is establishing its voice path.

4. Party B's switch completes the set up.

5. Party B's phone rings.

Parties A and B can begin their conversation after the following sequence of steps is completed:

1. Party B picks up the phone.

2. Switches receive an answered call indication.

3. Party A's switch sets communication to bidirectional.

4. Parties A and B are able to speak on the established voice path.

When the two parties end their conversation, the on-hook sequence of steps begins:

1. The conversation ends with Party A hanging up the phone.

2. The SIP client sends a BYE message to Proxy at ISP.

3. The ISP Proxy sends a BYE signal to NGW.

4. Switches release established paths (termination).

5. The call is ended.

PSTN Protocol Security

If you thought that PSTN protocols are more secure than the IP protocols riding on PSTN access circuits, then prepare to be shocked. In some respects, one of the greatest threats to the Internet is the PSTN itself.

SS7 and Other ITU-T Signaling Security

Despite the fact that ITU-T signaling protocols prior to SS7 are notoriously insecure (see the sidebar on Blueboxing and the Phone Phreaking community earlier in the chapter), they continue to be deployed around the world along with older switching equipment that is vulnerable to toll fraud, eavesdropping, and other risks. If your VoIP system will be interfacing with such equipment, take countermeasures to reduce potential exposure and liability, set alarms, and review logs.

That is not to suggest that SS7 is particularly secure, but it is much harder for a subscriber to inject signaling into an SS7 network. That being said, the primary threat for SS7 networks are the peering arrangements (particularly among CLEC partners) for injection of false and/or fraudulent signaling and other messaging information. SS7 as currently defined does not have policy controls built in to address this issue. The risks and countermeasures were summarized quite well by the 3GPP SA WG3 Technical Specification Group in January 2000 for 3G TR 33.900 V1.2.0:

> The security of the global SS7 network as a transport system for signaling messages e.g. authentication and supplementary services such as call forwarding is open to major compromise.

> The problem with the current SS7 system is that messages can be altered, injected or deleted into the global SS7 networks in an uncontrolled manner. In the past, SS7 traffic was passed between major PTOs covered under treaty organization and the number of operators was relatively small and the risk of compromise was low

> Networks are getting smaller and more numerous. Opportunities for unintentional mishaps will increase, as will the opportunities for hackers and other abusers of networks. With the increase in different types of operators and the increase in the number of interconnection circuits there is an ever-growing loss of control of security of the signaling networks.

> There is also exponential growth in the use of interconnection between the telecommunication networks and the Internet. The IT community now has many protocol converters for conversion of SS7 data to IP, primarily for the transportation of voice and data over the IP networks. In addition new services such as those based on IN will lead to a growing use of the SS7 network for general data transfers.

> There have been a number of incidents from accidental action, which have damaged a network. To date, there have been very few deliberate actions. The availability of cheap PC based equipment that can be used to access networks and the ready availability of access gateways on the Internet will lead to compromise of SS7 signaling and this will affect mobile operators.

The risk of attack has been recognized in the USA at the highest level of the President's office indicating concern on SS7. It is understood that the T1, an American group is seriously considering the issue. For the network operator there is some policing of incoming signaling on most switches already, but this is dependent on the make of switch as well as on the way the switch is configured by operators.

Some engineering equipment is not substantially different from other advanced protocol analyzers in terms of its fraud potential, but is more intelligent and can be programmed more easily. The SS7 network as presently engineered is insecure. It is vitally important that network operators ensure that signaling screening of SS7 incoming messages takes place at the entry points to their networks and that operations and maintenance systems alert against unusual SS7 messages. There are a number of messages that can have a significant effect on the operation of the network and inappropriate messages should be controlled at entry point.

Network operators or network security engineers should on a regular basis carry out monitoring of signaling links for these inappropriate messages. In signing agreements with roaming partners and carrying out roaming testing, review of messages and also to seek appropriate confirmation that network operators are also screening incoming SS7 messages their networks to ensure that no rogue messages appear.

In summary there is no adequate security left in SS7. Mobile operators need to protect themselves from attack from hackers and inadvertent action that could stop a network or networks operating correctly.

Bottom line: Just because SS7 is harder for subscribers to crack doesn't mean it is secure overall. SS7 peering in the PSTN is not nearly as robust as its BGP equivalent on the Internet, and this has the potential for dire consequences if it were to be exploited maliciously. It's not yet clear if or how the ITU-T plans to address these concerns directly in a revision to SS7, although a T1S1 SS7 Security Standard was proposed at one time as part of an overall Study Group 17 (SG-17) effort. RFC 3788, Security Considerations for SIGTRAN protocols, was published by the Internet Engineering Task Force (IETF) in June 2004, and suggests the use of specific TLS and IPSEC profiles when using SS7 over IP, though it also notes that the

"Peer To Peer" challenge still exists with SS7. The Network Interconnection Interoperability Forum (NIIF) within the Alliance for Telecommunications Industry Solutions (ATIS) has published many guidelines on the topic of secure interconnections (available to members or to the public for a fee). The good news is that unlike the Internet's in-band signaling model, which is vulnerable to direct attack, the SS7 signaling network is out of band to the voice and data communication it carries.

ISUP and QSIG Security

Automatic Number Identification (ANI)-based security mechanisms can be spoofed in both directions, although some carriers claim to have clamped down on this practice (I'm not convinced this can be done). This can be used to create false Caller-ID data to subscribers. If your organization uses ANI to verify identity (as a very large credit card user has been known to do), you are asking for trouble. It's only slightly more difficult than spoofing an e-mail address if you know what you're doing, so tread carefully here.

Other ISUP and QSIG fields have similar problems, so be very careful with any trust assumptions you make with these protocols. Always assume that CLASS services like distinctive ringing, selective call acceptance, selective call forward, and so on will be fooled by ANI spoofing and similar ISUP or SSIG attacks.

Summary

Today's PSTN is more powerful than ever; it is now capable of delivering services that Alexander Bell could not have ever imagined (like dedicated Internet access and SONET-based Internet backbone links). The telecommunications industry that cares for the PSTN affects our everyday lives from our traditional telephone lines, cell phones, Internet access, wireless solutions, and even cable television. The act of making a single phone call requires instantaneous network performance. The networks that make up the PSTN always are responding to a fast-changing environment that continues to demand increased reliability and capability.

Digital multiplexing started with time division, but now includes wavelength division, having come nearly full circle with old analog frequency division multiplexing. In all these cases, increased capacity from the outside cable plant was created in response to increased demand for telecommunications bandwidth.

The design of the PSTN has changed from one centered on a human operator to one leveraging large-scale automated switches that handle thousands of calls at once. Located within each central office are the thousands of individual local loops coming in, such as the voice DS0s, plus DSL and many digital circuits from subscribers that are then collected via a DACS and presented up the network on high-speed digital interfaces to the switch. Adherence to industry-standard signaling and technological protocols, such as the SS7 and SIP is necessary but may not be sufficient as the number of interconnected carriers continues to multiply.

Solutions Fast Track

PSTN: What Is It, and How Does It Work?

☑ Outside plant represents cabling, interfaces, and other infrastructure outside of the CO. F1 feeds the SAI and F2 typically connects directly to the subscriber drop cable. SONET or SDH rings sometimes are used to feed an SAI or provide connectivity between COs.

☑ Frequency Division Multiplexing (FDM), an analog technology, was replaced with the more efficient and secure Time Division Multiplexing (TDM). TDM is used in various implementations throughout the communications industry.

☑ The SS7 stack is similar to the OSI network model and through SIGTRAN standards can also operate over IP. Security measures should be taken with all PSTN signaling protocols.

PSTN Call Flow

☑ Digital switches still need sophisticated circuit detection capabilities for call processing.

☑ When making SIP-based calls through an ISP, one's call may terminate several hundred miles away and not at the local central office.

☑ SIP-to-SIP based calls happen entirely over IP networks. SIP-to-PSTN calls start on an IP network and then get handed off to the PSTN.

PSTN Protocol Security

☑ Use extreme caution around pre-SS7 signaling protocols like ITU-T 5 or R2 (also known as CCITT 5 or R2 because of their toll fraud potential.

☑ Even with SS7, take precautions to limit potential damage from fraudulent or corrupted data that could arrive in your SS7 network from other carriers.

☑ Do not use ANI or any other ISUP or QSIG information for authentication.

Frequently Asked Questions

The following Frequently Asked Questions, answered by the authors of this book, are designed to both measure your understanding of the concepts presented in this chapter and to assist you with real-life implementation of these concepts. To have your questions about this chapter answered by the author, browse to **www.syngress.com/solutions** and click on the **"Ask the Author"** form.

Q: Is the PSTN of today able to handle the demands of the customers and technology of the future?

A: The answer is yes, since telecommunications companies are always enhancing the PSTN by providing more affordable or fully featured services to their customers. These changes often increase reliability while adding the capacity to offer more services. Tomorrow's PSTN is likely to have much more packet-based technology than ever imaged. Now communications companies are burying fiber-optic cable and installing broadband wireless antennas as additional ways to deliver rich bandwidth, and cable companies often have outside plant capabilities that rival that or the primary LEC.

Q: Why is fiber-optic cable a better delivery medium than coaxial cable or twisted pair mediums?

A: Fiber-optic cable allows carriers to deliver services farther from central offices and is not readily affected by lightning strikes like copper wire, though WDM can offer more capacity through a single fiber than a single CO could sustain in copper 15 years ago. Delivering services further from the central office allows carriers to condense network equipment, reduce service truck roll outs, and provide more service to more people for a cheaper cost. And the extra bandwidth increases the scope and range of network capabilities available to all of us.

Q: Has VoIP been used by carriers prior to end-user deployments?

A: Yes, for some time large carriers have used VoIP to deliver calls within their core networks for long distance and toll calls. Bringing the technology to the rest of us took some considerable planning, significant costs, and a vision that VoIP would be the next huge push in the delivery of voice traffic.

Q: Should I be worried about my carrier's SS7 network?

A: In general, no. But as more carriers connect and that network moves from its own dedicated, dark fiber and on to shared IP networks, there should be more attention paid to security and associated SS7 standards. It's not a problem yet, but if the standards and industry best practices aren't ready to implement in a few years we could see some disastrous consequences.

Q: Can I really trust my caller ID?

A: Sure, about as much as you can trust your e-mail. It won't lie to you every day but it's not hard to fool if you're determined.

Q: I'd like to try phone phreaking or blueboxing sometime. Where can I go to find out more?

A: First of all, just don't do it. It's way too easy to get caught, and most of the old techniques won't work. If you're determined, you won't find it hard to get the information you're looking for if you Google the right names in this chapter. Personally, I think it's more fun reading the history anyway.

Q: I heard that Kevin Poulsen still drives the Porsche 944 he nabbed from KIIS. Is that true?

A: According to several reports, he's been spotted in a red Porsche from time to time.

Q: People that sell me network equipment are always telling me that "circuit" is dead. Is that really true?

A: Let's put it this way: without a live circuit to run on, the Internet is dead. Any questions?

P.S. Anyone who really knows about packet and circuit knows that they both need each other in the end.

Chapter 5

H.323 Architecture

Solutions in this chapter:

- The H.323 Protocol Specification
- The Primary H.323 VoIP-Related Protocols
- H.235 Security Mechanisms

☑ Summary

☑ Solutions Fast Track

☑ Frequently Asked Questions

Introduction

VoIP protocols can be classified according to their role during message transmission. H.323 and SIP are signaling protocols—that is, they are involved in call setup, teardown, and modification. RTP and RTCP are media transport protocols, and are involved in end-to-end transport of voice and multimedia data. TRIP, SAP, STUN, TURN, and so on comprise a group of VoIP-related support protocols. Finally, because H.323 mediated VoIP relies upon the underlying transport layer to move data, more traditional protocols such as TCP/IP, DNS, DHCP, SNMP, RSVP, and TFTP are required.

The H.323 Protocol Specification

The H.323 protocol suite allows dissimilar communication devices to communicate with each other. H.323 (which is implemented primarily at versions 4 and 5 as of the time of this writing) is a sometimes Byzantine international protocol published by the ITU that supports interoperability between differing vendor implementations of telephony and multimedia products across IP-based networks. H.323 entities provide for real-time audio, video, and/or data communications. Support for audio is mandatory; support for data and video is optional.

The H.323 specification defines four different H.323 entities as the functional units of a complete H.323 network (see Figure 5.1). These components of an H.323 system include endpoints (terminals), gateways, gatekeepers, and multipoint control units (MCUs).

Figure 5.1 H.323 Entities

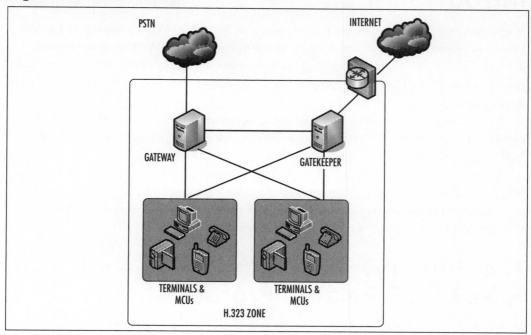

Endpoints (telephones, softphones, IVRs, voice mail, video cameras, etc.) are typically devices that end-users interact with. MS Netmeeting is an example of an H.323 endpoint. Endpoints provide voice-only and/or multimedia such as video and real-time application collaboration.

Gateways handle signaling and media transport, and are optional components. Gateways typically serve as the interface to other types of networks such as ISDN, PSTN, or other H.323 systems. You can think of a gateway as providing "translation" functions. For example, an H.323 gateway will handle conversion of H.323 to SIP or H.323 to ISUP (ISUP (ISDN User Part) defines the interexchange signaling procedures for the trunk call control). Another way to think of this is that a gateway provides the interface between a packet-based network (e.g., a VoIP network) and a circuit-switched network (e.g., the PSTN). If a gatekeeper exists, VoIP gateways register with the gatekeeper and the gatekeeper finds the "best" gateway for a particular session.

Gatekeepers, which are also optional, handle address resolution and admission to the H.323 network. Its most important function is address translation between symbolic alias addresses and IP addresses. For example, in the presence of a gatekeeper, it is possible to call "Tom," rather than 192.168.10.10. Gatekeepers also manage endpoints' access to services, network resources, and optionally can provide additional services. They also monitor service usage and provide limited network bandwidth management. A gatekeeper is not required in an H.323 system. However, if a gate-keeper is present, terminals must make use of the services offered by gatekeepers. RAS defines these as address translation, admissions control, bandwidth control, and zone management. The gatekeeper and gateway functionalities are often present on a single physical device.

MCUs support multiparty conferencing between three or more endpoints. The H.323 standard allows for a variety of ad hoc conferencing scenarios, either central-ized or decentralized.

Back-end servers (BES) are an important supplementary function in an H.323-based environment. BES may provide services for user authentication, service autho-rization, accounting, charging and billing, and other services. In a simple network, the gatekeeper or gateway provides such services.

The Primary H.323 VoIP-Related Protocols

H.323 is an umbrella-like specification that encompasses a large number of state machines that interact in different ways depending upon the presence, absence, and topological relationship of participating entities and the type of session (for example, audio or video). There are many subprotocols within the H.323 specification. In order to understand the overall message flows within an H.323 VoIP transaction, we will concern ourselves with the most common ones that relate to VoIP. Figure 5.2 shows the relevant protocols and their relationships.

Figure 5.2 VoIP-Related H.323 Protocol Stack

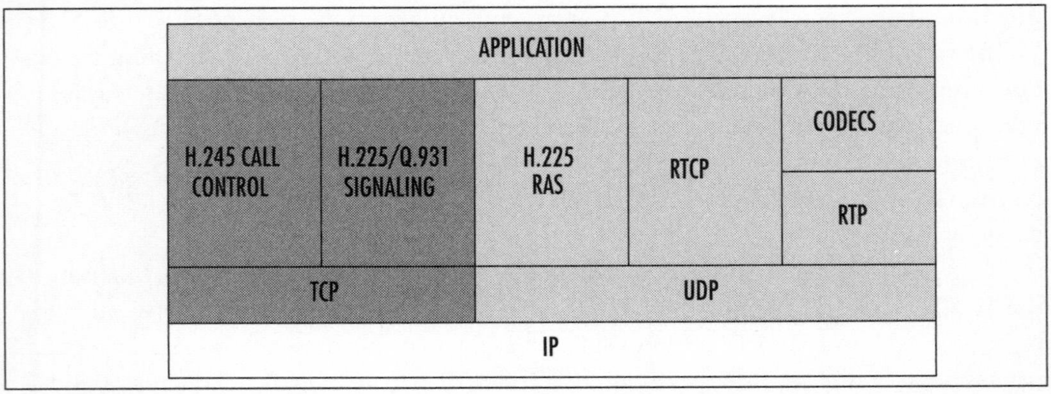

H.323 defines a general set of call setup and negotiating procedures—the most important in VoIP applications being H.225, H.235, H.245, and members of the Q.900 signaling series. Basic data-transport methods are defined by the real-time protocols RTP and RTCP. H.323 also specifies a group of audio codecs for VoIP communications, the G.700 series:

- **H.225/Q.931** Defines signaling for call setup and teardown, including source and destination IP addresses, ports, country code, and H.245 port information.

- **H.225.0/RAS** Specifies messages that describe signaling, Registration Admission and Status (RAS), and media stream information.

- **H.245** Specifies messages that negotiate the terminal capabilities set, the master/slave relationship, and logical channel information for the media streams.

- **Real Time Protocol (RTP)** Describes the end-to-end transport of real-time data.

- **Real Time Control Protocol (RTCP)** Describes the end-to-end monitoring of data delivery and QoS by providing information such as jitter and average packet loss.

- **Codecs The G.700 series of codecs used for VoIP includes:**

  1. **G.711** One of the oldest codecs, G.711 does not use compression, so voice quality is excellent. This codec consumes the most bandwidth. This is the same codec used by PSTN and ISDN.

  2. **G.723.1** This codec was designed for videoconferencing/telephony over standard phone lines and is optimized for fast encode and decode. It has medium voice quality.

  3. **G.729** This codec is used primarily in VoIP applications because of its low bandwidth requirements.

H.323 signaling exchanges typically are routed via gatekeeper or directly between the participants as chosen by the gatekeeper. Media exchanges normally are routed directly between the participants of a call. H.323 data communications utilizes both TCP and UDP. TCP ensures reliable transport for control signals and data, because these signals must be received in proper order and cannot be lost. UDP is used for audio and video streams, which are time-sensitive but are not as sensitive to an occasional dropped packet. Consequently, the H.225 call signaling channel and the H.245 call control channel typically run over TCP, whereas audio, video, and

RAS channel exchanges rely on UDP for transport. Table 5.1 shows H.323 VoIP ports and protocols.

Table 5.1 H.323 VoIP Ports and Protocols

Protocol	Function	Port(s)	Layer 4
H.225	(Q.931) Call Setup	1720	TCP
H.225	RAS	1719	UDP
H.245	Call Capabilities Negotiation	DYNAMIC	TCP
RTP/RTCP	Media Transport	DYNAMIC	UDP

In addition, H.235 recommends an assortment of messages, procedures, structures, and algorithms for securing signaling, control, and multimedia communications under the H.323 architecture. We will now look at each of these major VoIP-related protocols in more detail. Figure 5.3 shows the major signaling paths in an H.323 VoIP environment, and illustrates the several paths that signaling can take. In order to simplify the messaging sequence discussion we will ignore Fast Connect and Extended Fast Connect. There are two types of gatekeeper call signaling methods: Direct Endpoint signaling, where the terminating gateways or endpoints transfer call signaling information directly between themselves; and Gatekeeper-Routed call signaling, where setup signaling information is mediated by a gatekeeper.

Figure 5.3 Typical H.323 Channels

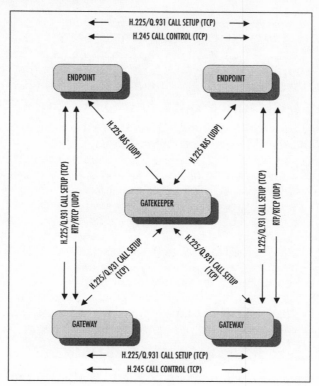

H.225/Q.931 Call Signaling

Assuming a slow start connection procedure, the H.225 protocol defines the two important stages of call setup: Call signaling and RAS. Call signaling describes standards for call setup, maintenance and control, and teardown. A subset of Q.931 call signaling messages are used to initiate connections between H.323 endpoints, over which real-time data can be transported. The signaling channel is opened between an endpoint-gateway, a gateway-gateway, or gateway-gatekeeper prior to the establishment of any other channels. If no gateway or gatekeeper is present, H.225 messages are exchanged directly between the endpoints.

Tools & Traps…

What Is the Difference Between QSIG and Q.931?

Initially, PBXs only connected via trunk lines to the PSTN. Then, people begin connecting PBXs with other PBXs over private leased lines (tie-lines) in order to save toll charges. This worked so well that these same people decided to form a single logical PBX out of a number of smaller switches. In order to provide all the extra features that callers had come to expect, supplementary signaling functionality was added to the protocols used to connect the switches. DPNSS describes this signaling. DPNSS is an industry standard interface defined between PBXs.

Q.931, also a standard, is designed to work between the PSTN and a PBX. It does not support the same features and services as DPNSS. QSIG (Q Signaling) is the European Computer Manufacturers' Association standard for PBX-to-PBX connections based on ISDN PRI. It's largely Q.931, with extensions for additional PBX features. QSIG is based on, and also supports many of the same features and services as DPNSS. QSIG is used to tunnel PSTN signaling messages over H.323 to another PSTN network transparently, as if the two PSTN networks were one and the same.

H.225 messages are encoded in binary ASN.1 PER (Packed Encoding Rules) format. Although the H.225.0 signaling channel may be implemented on top of UDP, all entities must support signaling over TCP port 1720.

NOTE

Signaling traffic is binary encoded using ASN.1 (Abstract Syntax Notation One) syntax and per encoding rules. ASN.1 is not a programming language. It is a flexible notation that allows one to define a variety of data types. ASN.1 theoretically allows two or more dissimilar systems to communicate in an unambiguous manner. Frankly, this aim is more difficult than it might seem at first.

ASN.1 encoding rules are sets of rules used to transform data specified in the ASN.1 language into a standard format that can be decoded on any system that has a decoder based on the same set of rules. The H.323 family of protocols is compiled into a wire-line protocol using PER. PER (Packed Encoding Rules), a subset of BER, is a compact binary encoding that is used on limited-bandwidth networks. PER is designed to optimize the use of bandwidth, but the tradeoff is complexity—decoding PER PDUs has led to problems due to a number of factors including issues with octet alignment (PER encoding can be aligned or unaligned), integer precision (at times, a PER value may not contain a length field), and unconstrained character strings.

The H.225 protocol also defines messages used for endpoint-gatekeeper and gatekeeper-gatekeeper communication—this part of H.225 is known as RAS (Registration, Admission, Status), and unlike call signaling, runs over UDP. RAS is used to perform registration, admission control, bandwidth status changes, and tear-down procedures between endpoints and gatekeepers. A RAS channel, separate from the call setup signaling channel, is used to exchange RAS messages. This second signaling channel is opened between an endpoint and a gatekeeper prior to the establishment of additional channels.

Establishing a call between two endpoints requires a different connection schedule depending upon what entities are involved in the session. For direct connections between endpoints, two TCP channels are set up between the endpoints: one for call setup (Q.931/H.225 messages) and one for capabilities exchange and call control (H.245 messages). First, an endpoint initiates an H.225/Q931 exchange on a TCP well-known port (TCP 1720) with another endpoint. Several H.225/Q.931 messages are exchanged, during which time the called phone rings. Successful completion of the call results in an end-to-end reliable channel that supports the first of a number of H.245 messages. At the end of this exchange the called party picks up the receiver.

Note that the first of these signaling messages, the H.225.Q.931 Call Setup message (see Figure 5.4), has been the focus of extensive security vulnerability studies by the Oulu Secure Programming Group.

Figure 5.4 H.225/Q.931 Signaling

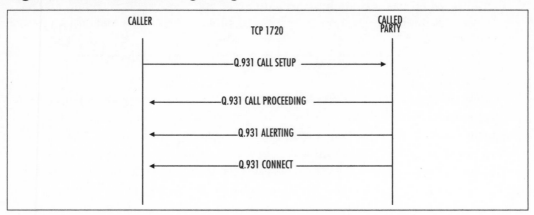

Notes from the Underground…

PROTOS Suite

In 2001–2002, The University of Oulu Secure Programming Group (OUSPG) tested the effects of sending modified Setup-PDUs to a number of differing vendor H.323 implementations. The H.225 Setup-PDU is an excellent test candidate for several reasons. The Setup-PDU contains many information elements, whose length and type are variable; the Setup PDU is normally the first packet exchanged during H.323 communication; and affected systems can be quickly rebooted for additional testing. OUSPG prepared a test suite containing approximately 4500 modified Setup-PDUs, and fed these to each tested H.323 device. They found that many systems that implement H.323 are vulnerable to one or more of these malformed PDUs.

These failures result from insufficient bounds checking of H.225 messages as they are parsed and processed by affected systems. These errors are due primarily to problems in low-level byte operations with vendor ASN.1 PER/BER PDU decoders, as mentioned earlier. Depending upon the affected system and implementation, these attacks result in system crash and reload (DoS), or in the case of systems that filter these data (such as Microsoft ISA server), execution of code within the context of the security service. The developers of the PROTOS suite have moved on to form a company called Codenomicon and have expanded their suite to cover more use cases and more protocols.

If a gatekeeper is present between the endpoints (a more common scenario), then H.225 RAS signaling precedes the Q.931 signaling and abides by the sequence diagram shown in Figure 5.5.

Figure 5.5 H.225/Q.931 RAS

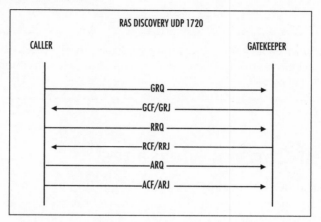

These messages are used to register with a gatekeeper and to request permission to initiate the call:

- **Gatekeeper Request (GRQ)** The GRQ packet is unicast in order to discover whether any gatekeepers exist. This requires that the gatekeepers IP address is configured on the endpoint. If this is not configured, the endpoint can fall back to multicast discovery of the gatekeeper.

- **Gatekeeper Confirm or Reject (GCF/GRJ)** Reply from the gatekeeper to endpoint that rejects the endpoint's registration request. Often due to configuration problems.

- **Registration Request (RRQ)** Request from a terminal or gateway to register with a gatekeeper.

- **Registration Confirm or Reject (RCF/RRJ)** Gatekeeper either confirms or rejects.

- **Admission Request (ARQ)** Request for access to packet network from terminal to gatekeeper.

- **Admission Confirm or Reject (ACF/ARJ)** Gatekeeper either confirms or rejects. If confirmed, the transport address and port to use for call signaling are included in the reply.

There are supplementary messages defined in the H.225/RAS specification that are used to request changes in bandwidth allocation, to reset timers, and for informational purposes. After the gatekeeper confirms the admission request, call signaling can begin. Signaling proceeds in the same manner as in Figure 5.3.

> **NOTE**
>
> We have found privately that flooding multiple, malformed GRQ (Gatekeeper Request) packets to the gatekeeper results in the disconnection of a number of vendor's IP phones.

H.245 Call Control Messages

After a connection has been set up via the call signaling procedure, H.245 messages (there are many of these) are used to resolve the call media type, to exchange terminal capabilities, and to establish the media flow before the call can be established. H.245 also manages call parameters after call establishment. H.245 messages also are encoded in ASN.1 PER syntax. The messages carried include notification of terminal capabilities, and commands to open and close logical channels. The H.245 control channel is permanently open, unlike the media channels.

> **NOTE**
>
> Table 5.2 lists various types of messages and the H.323 ports used to transport them.

Table 5.2 H.323 Ports

Message	Protocol/Port
H.245 messages	Dynamically assigned ports
RTP messages	Dynamically assigned ports
Gatekeeper	UDP Discovery Port 1718
Gatekeeper	UDP Registration and Status Port 1719
Endpoint	TCP Call Signaling Port 1720
Gatekeeper	Multicast 224.0.1.41
DNS	UDP 53
TFTP	UDP 69
SNMP	UDP 161, 162

H.245 negotiations usually take place on a separate channel from the one used for H.225 exchanges, but newer applications support tunneling of H.245 PDUs within the H.225 signaling channel. There is no well-known port for H.245. The H.245 transport address always is passed in the call-signaling message. In other words, port information is passed within the payload of the preceding H.225/Q.931 signaling packets. The media channels (those used to transport voice and video) are similarly dynamically allocated. Figure 5.6 is an example of H.245 call control.

Figure 5.6 H.245 Call Control

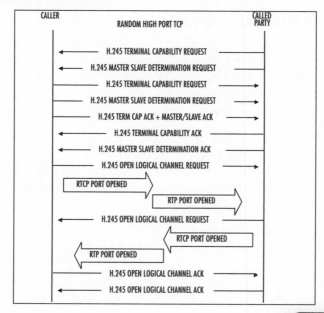

The called party opens the TCP port for establishing the control channel after extracting the port information from the H.225/Q.931 signaling packet. During this exchange, terminal capabilities such as codec choice and master/slave determination are negotiated. Media channel negotiations begin with the *OpenLogicalChannel* Request packet. When the called party is ready to talk, it responds with an *OpenLogicalChannel* Ack, which contains the dynamic port information in the payload. As an aside, this use of dynamic ports makes it difficult to implement security policy on firewalls, NAT, and traffic shaping. In some cases, a special H.323-aware firewall or firewall component called an Application Layer Gateway (ALG) is required to reliably pass H.323 signaling and associated media. Once both RTP/RTCP channels are opened, communications proceeds (see Figure 5.7).

Figure 5.7 RTP/RTCP Media Streams

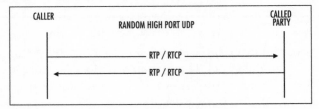

Real-Time Transport Protocol

Real-time transport protocol (RTP) is an application layer protocol that provides end-to-end delivery services of real-time audio and video. RTP provides payload identification, sequencing, time-stamping, and delivery monitoring. UDP provides multiplexing and checksum services. RTP can also be used with other transport protocols like TCP, and in conjunction with other signaling protocols like SIP or H.248.

The actual media (e.g., the voice packets) first is encoded by using an appropriate codec. The encoded audio stream is then passed via RTP, which is used to transfer the real-time audio/video streams over the Internet. Real-time transport control protocol (RTCP) is a required counterpart of RTP that provides control services for RTP streams. The primary function of RTCP is to provide feedback on the quality of the data distribution. Other RTCP functions include carrying a transport-level identifier for an RTP source, called a canonical name, which can be used by receivers to synchronize audio and video.

NOTE

RTP runs on dynamic, even-numbered, high ports (ports > 1024), whereas RTCP runs on the next corresponding odd numbered, high port.

H.235 Security Mechanisms

H.235 is expected to operate in conjunction with other H-series protocols that utilize H.245 as their control protocol and/or use the H.225.0 RAS and/or Call Signaling Protocol. H.235's major premise is that the principal security threat to communications is assumed to be eavesdropping on the network, or some other method of diverting media streams. The security issues related to DoS attacks are not addressed.

This family of threats relies on the absence of cryptographic assurance of a request's originator. Attacks in this category seek to compromise the message integrity of a conversation. This threat demonstrates the need for security services that enable entities to authenticate the originators of requests and to verify that the contents of the message and control streams have not been altered in transit.

Authentication is, in general, based either on using a shared secret (you are authenticated properly if you know the secret) or on public key-based methods with certifications (you prove your identity by possessing the correct private key). The basis for authentication (trust) and privacy is defined by the endpoints of the communications channel. For a connection establishment channel, this may be between the caller (such as a gateway or IP telephone endpoint) and a hosting network component (a gateway or gatekeeper). For example, a telephone "trusts" that the gatekeeper will connect it with the telephone whose number has been dialed. The result of trusting an element is the confidence to reveal the privacy mechanism (algorithm and key) to that element. Given the aforementioned information, all participants in the communications path should authenticate any and all trusted elements.

Encryption methods are defined as DES, 3DES, and AES. TLS (Transport Layer Security) and IPSec (IP Security) are recommended to secure layer 4 and layer 3 protocol messages, respectively. IPsec and TLS provide solutions at different levels of the ISO model—IPSec in the Network Layer, and TLS in the Transport Layer. Both use the same type of negotiation to set up tunnels, but IPSec often encrypts crucial header information, and TLS encrypts only the application payload of packet, thus TLS encryption retains IP addressing.

The scope of the H.235 specification is shown in Figure 5.8. H.235 addresses the protocols that are shaded in gray.

Figure 5.8 H.235 Scope

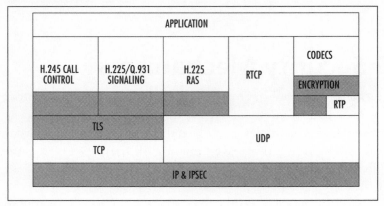

Let's look at how the H.235 specification interacts with each protocol.

- **H.245** The call signaling channel may be secured using TLS. Users may be authenticated either during the initial call connection, in the process of securing the H.245 channel, and/or by exchanging certificates on the H.245 channel. Media encryption details often are negotiated in private control channels determined by information carried in the OpenLogicalChannel connection.

- **H.225.0/Q.931** Q.931 can be secured via transport-layer security (TLS) or IPSec prior to any H.225.0 message exchange.

- **H.225.0/RAS** During the RAS phase of registering, the endpoint and the gatekeeper can exchange security policies and capabilities to define the security methods to be used in the initiated call session.

- **RTP/RTCP** H.245 signaling messages are used to provide confidentiality for a secured RTP channel. The method uses H.245 capability exchange for opening secured logical channels as part of the H.245 capability exchange phase, DES, 3DES or AES. The security capability is exchanged per media stream (RTP channel). The security mechanisms protect media streams and any control channels to operate in a completely independent manner.

H.235 specifies a number of security profiles. You can think of each security profile as a module consisting of a set of terms, definitions, requirements, procedures, and a profile overview that describe a particular instantiation of security methods. Security profiles, which are optional, may be implemented either selectively or in almost any combination. Endpoints may initially offer multiple security profiles simultaneously using the aforementioned RRQ/GRQ messages. H.235 also explicitly defines particular combinations of profiles that are useful or possible. For example, H.323 shows that the baseline security profile can be combined with SP4–Direct and selective routed call security, SP6–Voice encryption profile with native H.235/H.245 key management, and SP9–Security gateway support for H.323.

Profiles can be differentiated by the spectrum of security services each particular profile supports. The following security services are defined: Authentication, Nonrepudiation, Integrity, Confidentiality, Access Control, and Key Management. For example, the baseline security profile supports the security services shown in Figure 5.9.

Figure 5.9 Baseline Security Profile Security Services (H.235.1)

SECURITY SERVICES	CALL FUNCTIONS			
	H.245 CALL CONTROL	H.225/Q.931 SIGNALING	H.225 RAS	RTP
AUTHENTICATION	PASSWORD HMAC-SHA1-96	PASSWORD HMAC-SHA1-96	PASSWORD HMAC-SHA1-96	
NONREPUDIATION				
INTEGRITY	PASSWORD HMAC-SHA1-96	PASSWORD HMAC-SHA1-96	PASSWORD HMAC-SHA1-96	
CONFIDENTIALITY				
ACCESS CONTROL				
KEY MANAGEMENT		SUBSCRIPTION BASED	SUBSCRIPTION BASED	

You can see that this profile provides for authentication and integrity of the signaling streams but does not provide support for encryption, nonrepudiation, or access control of these streams. The baseline security profile (H.235.1) specifies the following: Authentication and integrity protection, or authentication-only for H.225/RAS, H.225/Q.931 messages, and tunneled H.245 messages using password-based protection. The security profile is applicable to communications between H.323 terminal to gatekeeper, gatekeeper to gatekeeper, and H.323 gateway to gatekeeper.

The following Security Profiles are defined:

- **235.1** Baseline security profile
- **235.2** Signature security profile
- **235.3** Hybrid security profile
- **235.4** Direct and selective routed call security
- **235.5** Framework for secure authentication in RAS using weak shared secrets
- **235.6** Voice encryption profile with native H.235/H.245 key management
- **235.7** Usage of the MIKEY key management protocol for the Secure Real Time Transport Protocol
- **235.8** Key exchange for SRTP using secure signaling channels
- **235.9** Security gateway support for H.323

Each security profile defines security services in the context of the generic classes of attacks that can be prevented by implementing that particular profile. In the case of the baseline security profile, the following attacks are thwarted.

- **Man-in-the-middle attacks** Application level hop-by-hop message authentication and integrity protects against such attacks when the man in the middle is between an application level hop.
- **Replay attacks** Use of time stamps and sequence numbers prevent such attacks.
- **Spoofing** User authentication prevents such attacks.
- **Connection hijacking** Use of authentication/integrity for each signaling message prevents such attacks.

Other threats are not addressed in this profile. For example, the issue of confidentiality via encryption is left to other security profiles. Thus, any H.323 system that uses only this profile will be subject to attacks that rely upon data interception by sniffing traffic. If however, the endpoints that specify the security profiles available to the system indicate that they support SP6–Voice encryption profile with native H.235/H.245 key management, as well as the baseline security profile, then the threat posed by eavesdropping attacks will be minimized.

The matrix describing the security services provided by security profile H.235.6 is shown in Figure 5.10.

Figure 5.10 Voice Encryption Profile with Native H.235/H.245 Key Management

SECURITY SERVICES	CALL FUNCTIONS			
	H.245 CALL CONTROL	H.225/Q.931 SIGNALING	H.225 RAS	RTP
AUTHENTICATION				
NONREPUDIATION				
INTEGRITY				
CONFIDENTIALITY				AES, 3DES, DES, RC-2
ACCESS CONTROL				
KEY MANAGEMENT	AUTHENTICATED DIFFIE-HELLMAN	AUTHENTICATED DIFFIE-HELLMAN		

In Figure 5.10 you can see that the addition of security profile H.235.6 to the baseline security profile adds methods for Diffie-Hellman key management and encryption of the media streams. In this fashion, security profiles can be added to the H.323 entities within your environment so as to provide only the security controls dictated by your security requirements. This approach allows some customization of the H.323 security controls so that, for example, they can be configured to work with your particular existing firewall infrastructure. We'll discuss H.323 firewall issues in Chapter 13.

Are You 0wned?

2005 Was a Bad Year for the Microsoft ASN Parser

CERT Advisories VU#216324 and VU#583108 warned that any application that loads the ASN.1 library could serve as an attack vector. In particular, ASN.1 is used by a number of cryptographic and authentication services such as X.509 certificates (SSL/TLS, S/MIME, IKE), Kerberos, and NTLMv2. The Local Security Authority Subsystem (lsass.exe) and a component of the CryptoAPI (crypt32.dll) use the vulnerable ASN.1 library. Both client and server systems are affected. An unauthenticated, remote attacker could execute arbitrary code with SYSTEM privileges.

Summary

As you have seen, H.323 is a complex protocol suite. A number of H.323 VoIP-related protocols create channels made up of dynamic IP address/port combinations. Each terminal-terminal conversation requires, at a minimum, four channels to be opened—two control channels per endpoint (one H.225 and one H.245), and two unidirectional voice channels. Three of these (excepting the H.225 signaling traffic) will be on dynamically allocated ports. In addition, users naturally expect to be able to make both inbound and outbound calls. Since H.323 relies heavily on dynamic ports, traditional packet filtering or stateful inspection firewalls are not a viable solution, as every port greater than 1024 would have to be opened to everyone on the Internet. Additionally, H.323 contains embedded addressing information (port numbers) that is not rewritten by most NAT implementations.

Therefore, most firewall solutions supporting H.323 must at least disassemble the control stream packets (H.245, H.225.0) and dynamically open up the firewall as needed. All these features make the implementation of H.323 security complex. As if this is not enough complexity, signaling and control messages are binary encoded according to ASN.1 rules. ASN.1 parsers have been exploited in a variety of implementations, and parsing takes time—adding latency to an already latency-sensitive application. H.323-aware firewalls, ALGs, and session border controllers (SBCs) have proven to be up to the task of effectively securing H.323 traffic without exposing internal networks to external attack.

Solutions Fast Track

The H.323 Protocol Specification

☑ H.323 explicitly specifies protocols for transport and processing of audio, video, and multimedia messages.

☑ H.323 entities include endpoints, gateways, gatekeepers, and MCUs.

☑ Gatekeepers, gateways, and MCUs are all optional.

The Primary H.323 VoIP–Related Protocols

☑ H.225/Q.931 is the signaling protocol.

☑ H.225/RAS is used to locate and register with gatekeepers.

- ☑ H.245 is the call control channel.

- ☑ Two bidirectional RTP/RTCP channels are created to transport media.

- ☑ Addressing information is cascaded in the preceding message stream for H.225, H.245, and RTP/RTCP.

H.235 Security Mechanisms

- ☑ H.235 and related protocols and annexes define security methods for H.323 traffic.

- ☑ Nine security profiles define specific methods for ensuring that one or more security services are applied to the H.225, H.245, and RTP message streams.

- ☑ Security services are defined as authentication, nonrepudiation, integrity, confidentiality, access control, and key management.

- ☑ Security profiles are optional and can be used alone or in many different combinations.

Frequently Asked Questions

The following Frequently Asked Questions, answered by the authors of this book, are designed to both measure your understanding of the concepts presented in this chapter and to assist you with real-life implementation of these concepts. To have your questions about this chapter answered by the author, browse to **www.syngress.com/solutions** and click on the **"Ask the Author"** form.

Q: I've never heard of H.323. What applications do I use that rely on this?

A: Microsoft Netmeeting for one. Polycom and Tandberg videoconferencing clients are another.

Q: Do H.323 terminals have to explicitly send the H.225 call setup messages to the IP address of the gateway?

A: Yes, an H.323 endpoint must know the transport address—for example, the IP address and port number—for the Q.931 dialogue. Q.931 then provides the transport address for the H.245 control channel. This is how addresses are bootstrapped in H.323.

Q: In what layer of ISO you can put H.323 standard?

A: H.323 doesn't map to just one layer, but is primarily implemented at layers 3 and 4.

Q: I've heard that H.323 uses more than one TCP/UDP port in order to transmit voice, video, and data. Are these ports fixed, or do they vary for each connection?

A: H.323 uses several ports and both TCP and UDP to signal and transport voice. H.225/Q.931 and H.245 use TCP and H.225/RAS and RTP/RTCP use UDP. Ports 1718–1720 are dedicated to H.323 traffic. Several dynamic port combinations are used per session as well.

Q: What is the best VoIP codec?

A: There are a number of factors to make that kind of determination. Probably most important is the nature of the network between the two ends. If you are connected of a LAN (high bandwidth, minimal delays, etc.), then G.711 generally provides the best voice quality.

Q: What's an Application Layer Gateway?

A: ALGs peer more deeply into the packet than packet filtering firewalls but normally do not scan the entire payload. Unlike packet filtering or stateful inspection firewalls, ALGs do not route packets; rather the ALG accepts a connection on one network interface and establishes the cognate connection on another network interface. An ALG provides intermediary services for hosts that reside on different networks, while maintaining complete details of the TCP connection state and sequencing.

Q: What's better, H.323 or SIP?

A: What's better, an apple or an orange? Seriously, H.323 is based on SS7 and was designed to internetwork efficiently with the PSTN. SIP is based on HTTP and was not designed with interconnecting to the PSTN in mind. So, major carriers tend to use H.323 because it translates ISDN and SS7 signaling to H.323 VoIP signaling easily. SIP does not. On the other hand, SIP supports IM, is text-based, and is implemented more cheaply than H.323.

Chapter 6

SIP Architecture

Solutions in this chapter:

- **Understanding SIP**
- **SIP Functions and Features**
- **SIP Architecture**
- **Instant Messaging and SIMPLE**

☑ **Summary**

☑ **Solutions Fast Track**

☑ **Frequently Asked Questions**

Introduction

As the Internet became more popular in the 1990s, network programs that allowed communication with other Internet users also became more common. Over the years, a need was seen for a standard protocol that could allow participants in a chat, videoconference, interactive gaming, or other media to initiate user sessions with one another. In other words, a standard set of rules and services was needed that defined how computers would connect to one another so that they could share media and communicate. The Session Initiation Protocol (SIP) was developed to set up, maintain, and tear down these sessions between computers.

By working in conjunction with a variety of other protocols and specialized servers, SIP provides a number of important functions that are necessary in allowing communications between participants. SIP provides methods of sharing the location and availability of users and explains the capabilities of the software or device being used. SIP then makes it possible to set up and manage the session between the parties. Without these tasks being performed, communication over a large network like the Internet would be impossible. It would be like a message in a bottle being thrown in the ocean; you would have no way of knowing how to reach someone directly or whether the person even could receive the message.

Beyond communicating with voice and video, SIP has also been extended to support instant messaging and is becoming a popular choice that's incorporated in many of the instant messaging applications being produced. This extension, called SIMPLE, provides the means of setting up a session in much the same way as SIP. SIMPLE also provides information on the status of users, showing whether they are online, busy, or in some other state of presence. Because SIP is being used in these various methods of communications, it has become a widely used and important component of today's communications.

Understanding SIP

SIP was designed to initiate interactive sessions on an IP network. Programs that provide real-time communication between participants can use SIP to set up, modify, and terminate a connection between two or more computers, allowing them to interact and exchange data. The programs that can use SIP include instant messaging, voice over IP (VoIP), video teleconferencing, virtual reality, multiplayer games, and other applications that employ single-media or multimedia. SIP doesn't provide all the functions that enable these programs to communicate, but it is an important component that facilitates communication between two or more endpoints.

You could compare SIP to a telephone switchboard operator, who uses other technology to connect you to another party, set up conference calls or other operations on your behalf, and disconnect you when you're done. SIP is a type of signaling protocol that is responsible for sending commands to start and stop transmissions or other operations used by a program. The commands sent between computers are codes that do such things as open a connection to make a phone call over the Internet or disconnect that call later on. SIP supports additional functions, such as call waiting, call transfer, and conference calling, by sending out the necessary signals to enable and disable these functions. Just as the telephone operator isn't concerned with how communication occurs, SIP works with a number of components and can run on top of several different transport protocols to transfer media between the participants.

Overview of SIP

One of the major reasons that SIP is necessary is found in the nature of programs that involve messaging, voice communication, and exchange of other media. The people who use these programs may change locations and use different computers, have several usernames or accounts, or communicate using a combination of voice, text, or other media (requiring different protocols). This creates a situation that's similar to trying to mail a letter to someone who has several aliases, speaks different languages, and could change addresses at any particular moment.

SIP works with various network components to identify and locate these endpoints. Information is passed through proxy servers, which are used to register and route requests to the user's location, invite another user(s) into a session, and make other requests to connect these endpoints. Because there are a number of different protocols available that may be used to transfer voice, text, or other media, SIP runs on top of other protocols that transport data and perform other functions. By working with other components of the network, data can be exchanged between these user agents regardless of where they are at any given point.

It is the simplicity of SIP that makes it so versatile. SIP is an ASCII- or text-based protocol, similar to HTTP or SMTP, which makes it more lightweight and flexible than other signaling protocols (such as H.323). Like HTTP and SMTP, SIP is a request-response protocol, meaning that it makes a request of a server, and awaits a response. Once it has established a session, other protocols handle such tasks as negotiating the type of media to be exchanged, and transporting it between the endpoints. The reusing of existing protocols and their functions means that fewer resources are used, and minimizes the complexity of SIP. By keeping the functionality of SIP simple, it allows SIP to work with a wider variety of applications.

The similarities to HTTP and SMTP are no accident. SIP was modeled after these text-based protocols, which work in conjunction with other protocols to perform specific tasks. As we'll see later in this chapter, SIP is also similar to these other protocols in that it uses Universal Resource Identifiers (URIs) for identifying users. A URI identifies resources on the Internet, just as a Uniform Resource Locator (URL) is used to identify Web sites. The URI used by SIP incorporates a phone number or name, such as SIP: user@syngress.com, which makes reading SIP addresses easier. Rather than reinventing the wheel, the development of SIP incorporated familiar aspects of existing protocols that have long been used on IP networks. The modular design allows SIP to be easily incorporated into Internet and network applications, and its similarities to other protocols make it easier to use.

RFC 2543 / RFC 3261

The Session Initiation Protocol is a standard that was developed by the Internet Engineering Task Force (IETF). The IETF is a body of network designers, researchers, and vendors that are members of the Internet Society Architecture Board for the purpose of developing Internet communication standards. The standards they create are important because they establish consistent methods and functionality. Unlike proprietary technology, which may or may not work outside of a specific program, standardization allows a protocol or other technology to function the same way in any application or environment. In other words, because SIP is a standard, it can work on any system, regardless of the communication program, operating system, or infrastructure of the IP network.

The way that IETF develops a standard is through recommendations for rules that are made through Request for Comments (RFCs). The RFC starts as a draft that is examined by members of a Working Group, and during the review process, it is developed into a finalized document. The first proposed standard for SIP was produced in 1999 as RFC 2543, but in 2002, the standard was further defined in RFC 3261. Additional documents outlining extensions and specific issues related to the SIP standard have also been released, which make RFC 2543 obsolete and update RFC 3261. The reason for these changes is that as technology changes, the development of SIP also evolves. The IETF continues developing SIP and its extensions as new products are introduced and its applications expand.

TIP

Reviewing RFCs can provide you with additional insight and information, answering specific questions you may have about SIP. The RFCs related to SIP can be reviewed by visiting the IETF Web site at www.ietf.org. Additional materials related to the Session Initiation Protocol Working Group also can be found at www.softarmor.com/sipwg/.

SIP and Mbone

Although RFC 2543 and RFC 3261 define SIP as a protocol for setting up, managing, and tearing down sessions, the original version of SIP had no mechanism for tearing down sessions and was designed for the Multicast Backbone (Mbone). Mbone originated as a method of broadcasting audio and video over the Internet. The Mbone is a broadcast channel that is overlaid on the Internet, and allowed a method of providing Internet broadcasts of things like IETF meetings, space shuttle launches, live concerts, and other meetings, seminars, and events. The ability to communicate with several hosts simultaneously needed a way of inviting users into sessions; the Session Invitation Protocol (as it was originally called) was developed in 1996.

The Session Invitation Protocol was a precursor to SIP that was defined by the IETF MMUSIC Working group, and a primitive version of the Session Initiation Protocol used today. However, as VoIP and other methods of communications became more popular, SIP evolved into the Session Initiation Protocol. With added features like the ability to tear down a session, it was a still more lightweight than more complex protocols like H.323. In 1999, the Session Initiation Protocol was defined as RFC 2543, and has become a vital part of multimedia applications used today.

OSI

In designing the SIP standard, the IETF mapped the protocol to the OSI (Open Systems Interconnect) reference model. The OSI reference model is used to associate protocols to different layers, showing their function in transferring and receiving data across a network, and their relation to other existing protocols. A protocol at one layer uses only the functions of the layer below it, while exporting the information it processes to the layer above it. It is a conceptual model that originated to promote interoperability, so that a protocol or element of a network developed by one vendor would work with others.

As seen in Figure 6.1, the OSI model contains seven layers: Application, Presentation, Session, Transport, Network, Data Link, and Physical. As seen in this figure, network communication starts at the Application layer and works its way down through the layers step by step to the Physical layer. The information then passes along the cable to the receiving computer, which starts the information at the Physical layer. From there it steps back up the OSI layers to the Application layer where the receiving computer finalizes the processing and sends back an acknowledgement if needed. Then the whole process starts over.

Figure 6.1 In the OSI Reference Model, Data is Transmitted down through the Layers, across the Medium, and Back up through the Layers

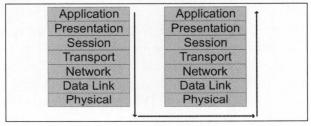

The layers of the OSI reference model have different functions that are necessary in transferring data across a network, and mapping protocols to these layers make it easier to understand how they interrelate to the network as a whole. Table 6.1 shows the seven layers of the OSI model, and briefly explains their functions.

Table 6.1 Layers of the OSI Model

Layer	Description
7: Application	The Application layer is used to identify communication partners, facilitate authentication (if necessary), and allows a program to communicate with lower layer protocols, so that in turn it can communicate across the network. Protocols that map to this layer include SIP, HTTP, and SMTP.
6: Presentation	The Presentation layer converts data from one format to another, such as converting a stream of text into a pop-up window, and handles encoding and encryption.
5: Session	The Session layer is responsible for coordinating sessions and connections.

Continued

Table 6.1 continued Layers of the OSI Model

Layer	Description
4: Transport	The Transport layer is used to transparently transfer data between computers. Protocols that map to this layer include TCP, UDP, and RTP.
3: Network	The Network Layer is used to route and forward data so that it goes to the proper destination. The most common protocol that maps to this layer is IP.
2: Data Link	The Data Link layer is used to provide error correction that may occur at the physical level, and provide physical addressing through the use of MAC addresses that are hard-coded into network cards.
1: Physical	The Physical layer defines electrical and physical specifications of network devices, and provides the means of allowing hardware to send and receive data on a particular type of media. At this level, data is passed as a bit stream across the network.

SIP and the Application Layer

Because SIP is the Session Initiation Protocol, and its purpose is to establish, modify, and terminate sessions, it would seem at face-value that this protocol maps to the Session layer of the OSI reference model. However, it is important to remember that the protocols at each layer interact only with the layers above and below it. Programs directly access the functions and supported features available through SIP, disassociating it from this layer. SIP is used to invite a user into an interactive session, and can also invite additional participants into existing sessions, such as conference calls or chats. It allows media to be added to or removed from a session, provides the ability to identify and locate a user, and also supports name mapping, redirection, and other services. When comparing these features to the OSI model, it becomes apparent that SIP is actually an Application-layer protocol.

The Application layer is used to identify communication partners, facilitate authentication (if necessary), and allows a program to communicate with lower layer protocols, so that in turn it can communicate across the network. In the case of SIP, it is setting up, maintaining, and ending interactive sessions, and providing a method of locating and inviting participants into these sessions. The software being used communicates through SIP, which passes the data down to lower layer protocols and sends it across the network.

SIP Functions and Features

When SIP was developed, it was designed to support five specific elements of setting up and tearing down communication sessions. These supported facets of the protocol are:

- User location, where the endpoint of a session can be identified and found, so that a session can be established

- User availability, where the participant that's being called has the opportunity and ability to indicate whether he or she wishes to engage in the communication

- User capabilities, where the media that will be used in the communication is established, and the parameters of that media are agreed upon

- Session setup, where the parameters of the session are negotiated and established

- Session management, where the parameters of the session are modified, data is transferred, services are invoked, and the session is terminated

Although these are only a few of the issues needed to connect parties together so they can communicate, they are important ones that SIP is designed to address. However, beyond these functions, SIP uses other protocols to perform tasks necessary that allow participants to communicate with each other, which we'll discuss later in this chapter.

User Location

The ability to find the location of a user requires being able to translate a participant's username to their current IP address of the computer being used. The reason this is so important is because the user may be using different computers, or (if DHCP is used) may have different IP addresses to identify the computer on the network. The program can use SIP to register the user with a server, providing a username and IP address to the server. Because a server now knows the current location of the user, other users can now find that user on the network. Requests are redirected through the proxy server to the user's current location. By going through the server, other potential participants in a communication can find the user, and establish a session after acquiring their IP address.

User Availability

The user availability function of SIP allows a user to control whether he or she can be contacted. Users can set themselves as being away or busy, or available for certain types of communication. If available, other users can then invite the user to join in a type of communication (e.g., voice or videoconference), depending on the capabilities of the program being used.

User Capabilities

Determining the user's capabilities involves determining what features are available on the programs being used by each of the parties, and then negotiating which can be used during the session. Because SIP can be used with different programs on different platforms, and can be used to establish a variety of single-media and multi-media communications, the type of communication and its parameters needs to be determined. For example, if you were to call a particular user, your computer might support video conferencing, but the person you're calling doesn't have a camera installed. Determining the user capabilities allows the participants to agree on which features, media types, and parameters will be used during a session.

Session Setup

Session setup is where the participants of the communication connect together. The user who is contacted to participate in a conversation will have their program "ring" or produce some other notification, and has the option of accepting or rejecting the communication. If accepted, the parameters of the session are agreed upon and established, and the two endpoints will have a session started, allowing them to communicate.

Session Management

Session management is the final function of SIP, and is used for modifying the session as it is in use. During the session, data will be transferred between the participants, and the types of media used may change. For example, during a voice conversation, the participants may decide to invoke other services available through the program, and change to a video conferencing. During communication, they may also decide to add or drop other participants, place a call on hold, have the call transferred, and finally terminate the session by ending their conversation. These are all aspects of session management, which are performed through SIP.

SIP URIs

Because SIP was based on existing standards that had already been proven on the Internet, it uses established methods for identifying and connecting endpoints together. This is particularly seen in the addressing scheme that it uses to identify different SIP accounts. SIP uses addresses that are similar to e-mail addresses. The hierarchical URI shows the domain where a user's account is located, and a host name or phone number that serves as the user's account. For example, SIP: myaccount@madeupsip.com shows that the account *myaccount* is located at the domain *madeupsip.com*. Using this method makes it simple to connect someone to a particular phone number or username.

Because the addresses of those using SIP follow a *username@domainname* format, the usernames created for accounts must be unique within the namespace. Usernames and phone numbers must be unique as they identify which account belongs to a specific person, and used when someone attempts sending a message or placing a call to someone else. Because the usernames are stored on centralized servers, the server can determine whether a particular username is available or not when a person initially sets up an account.

URIs also can contain other information that allows it to connect to a particular user, such as a port number, password, or other parameters. In addition to this, although SIP URIs will generally begin with SIP:, others will begin with SIPS:, which indicates that the information must be sent over a secure transmission. In such cases, the data and messages transmitted are transported using the Transport Layer Security (TLS) protocol, which we'll discuss later in this chapter.

SIP Architecture

Though we've discussed a number of the elements of SIP, there are still a number of essential components that make up SIP's architecture that we need to address. SIP would not be able to function on a network without the use of various devices and protocols. The essential devices are those that you and other participants would use in a conversation, allowing you to communicate with one another, and various servers may also be required to allow the participants to connect together. In addition to this, there are a number of protocols that carry your voice and other data between these computers and devices. Together, they make up the overall architecture of SIP.

SIP Components

Although SIP works in conjunction with other technologies and protocols, there are two fundamental components that are used by the Session Initiation Protocol:

- User agents, which are endpoints of a call (i.e., each of the participants in a call)
- SIP servers, which are computers on the network that service requests from clients, and send back responses

User Agents

User agents are both the computer that is being used to make a call, and the target computer that is being called. These make the two endpoints of the communication session. There are two components to a user agent: a client and a server. When a user agent makes a request (such as initiating a session), it is the User Agent Client (UAC), and the user agent responding to the request is the User Agent Server (UAS). Because the user agent will send a message, and then respond to another, it will switch back and forth between these roles throughout a session.

Even though other devices that we'll discuss are optional to various degrees, User Agents must exist for a SIP session to be established. Without them, it would be like trying to make a phone call without having another person to call. One UA will invite the other into a session, and SIP can then be used to manage and tear down the session when it is complete. During this time, the UAC will use SIP to send requests to the UAS, which will acknowledge the request and respond to it. Just as a conversation between two people on the phone consists of conveying a message or asking a question and then waiting for a response, the UAC and UAS will exchange messages and swap roles in a similar manner throughout the session. Without this interaction, communication couldn't exist.

Although a user agent is often a software application installed on a computer, it can also be a PDA, USB phone that connects to a computer, or a gateway that connects the network to the Public Switched Telephone Network. In any of these situations however, the user agent will continue to act as both a client and a server, as it sends and responds to messages.

SIP Server

The SIP server is used to resolve usernames to IP addresses, so that requests sent from one user agent to another can be directed properly. A user agent registers with the SIP server, providing it with their username and current IP address, thereby establishing their current location on the network. This also verifies that they are online, so that other user agents can see whether they're available and invite them into a session. Because the user agent probably wouldn't know the IP address of another user agent, a request is made to the SIP server to invite another user into a session. The SIP server then identifies whether the person is currently online, and if so, compares the username to their IP address to determine their location. If the user isn't part of that domain, and thereby uses a different SIP server, it will also pass on requests to other servers.

In performing these various tasks of serving client requests, the SIP server will act in any of several different roles:

- Registrar server
- Proxy server
- Redirect server

Registrar Server

Registrar servers are used to register the location of a user agent who has logged onto the network. It obtains the IP address of the user and associates it with their username on the system. This creates a directory of all those who are currently logged onto the network, and where they are located. When someone wishes to establish a session with one of these users, the Registrar server's information is referred to, thereby identifying the IP addresses of those involved in the session.

Proxy Server

Proxy servers are computers that are used to forward requests on behalf of other computers. If a SIP server receives a request from a client, it can forward the request onto another SIP server on the network. While functioning as a proxy server, the SIP server can provide such functions as network access control, security, authentication, and authorization.

Redirect Server

The Redirect servers are used by SIP to redirect clients to the user agent they are attempting to contact. If a user agent makes a request, the Redirect server can respond with the IP address of the user agent being contacted. This is different from a Proxy server, which forwards the request on your behalf, as the Redirect server essentially tells you to contact them yourself.

The Redirect server also has the ability to "fork" a call, by splitting the call to several locations. If a call was made to a particular user, it could be split to a number of different locations, so that it rang at all of them at the same time. The first of these locations to answer the call would receive it, and the other locations would stop ringing.

> **NOTE**
>
> RFC 3261 defines the different types of SIP servers as logical devices, meaning that they can be implemented as separate servers or as part of a single application that resides on a single physical server. In other words, a single physical server may act in all or one of these roles.
>
> In addition to this, the SIP servers can interact with other servers and applications on your network to provide additional services, such as authentication or billing. The SIP servers could access Lightweight Directory Access Protocol (LDAP) servers, database applications, or other applications to access back-end services.

Stateful versus Stateless

The servers used by SIP can run in one of two modes: stateful or stateless. When a server runs in stateful mode, it will keep track of all requests and responses it sends and receives. A server that operates in a stateless mode won't remember this information, but will instead forget about what it has done once it has processed a request. A server running in stateful mode generally is found in a domain where the user agents resides, whereas stateless servers are often found as part of the backbone, receiving so many requests that it would be difficult to keep track of them.

Location Service

The location service is used to keep a database of those who have registered through a SIP server, and where they are located. When a user agent registers with a Registrar server, a REGISTER request is made (which we'll discuss in the later section). If the Registrar accepts the request, it will obtain the SIP-address and IP address of the user agent, and add it to the location service for its domain. This database provides an up-to-date catalog of everyone who is online, and where they are located, which Redirect servers and Proxy servers can then use to acquire information about user agents. This allows the servers to connect user agents together or forward requests to the proper location.

Client/Server versus Peer-to-Peer Architecture

In looking at the components of SIP, you can see that requests are processed in different ways. When user agents communicate with one another, they send requests and responses to one another. In doing so, one acts as a User Agent Client, and the other fulfills the request acts as a User Agent Server. When dealing with SIP servers however, they simply send requests that are processed by a specific server. This reflects two different types of architectures used in network communications:

- Client/Server
- Peer-to-peer

Client/Server

In a client/server architecture, the relationship of the computers are separated into two roles:

- The client, which requests specific services or resources
- The server, which is dedicated to fulfilling requests by responding (or attempting to respond) with requested services or resources

An easy-to-understand example of a client/server relationship is seen when using the Internet. When using an Internet browser to access a Web site, the client would be the computer running the browser software, which would request a Web page from a Web server. The Web server receives this request and then responds to it by sending the Web page to the client computer. In VoIP, this same relationship can be seen when a client sends a request to register with a Registrar server, or makes a request to a Proxy Server or Redirect Server that allows it to connect with another user agent. In all these cases, the client's role is to request services and resources, and the server's role is to listen to the network and await requests that it can process or pass onto other servers.

The servers that are used on a network acquire their abilities to service requests by the programs installed on it. Because a server may run a number of services or have multiple server applications installed on it, a computer dedicated to the role of being a server may provide several functions on a network. For example, a Web server might also act as an e-mail server. In the same way, SIP servers also may provide different services. A Registrar can register clients and also run the location service that allows clients and other servers to locate other users who have registered on the network. In this way, a single server may provide diverse functionality to a network that would otherwise be unavailable.

Another important function of the server is that, unlike clients that may be disconnected from the Internet or shutdown on a network when the person using it is done, a server is generally active and awaiting client requests. Problems and maintenance aside, a dedicated server is up and running, so that it is accessible. The IP address of the server generally doesn't change, meaning that clients can always find it on a network, making it important for such functions as finding other computers on the network.

Peer to Peer

A peer-to-peer (P2P) architecture is different from the client/server model, as the computers involved have similar capabilities, and can initiate sessions with one another to make and service requests from one another. Each computer provides services and resources, so if one becomes unavailable, another can be contacted to exchange messages or access resources. In this way, the user agents act as both client and server, and are considered peers.

Once a user agent is able to establish a communication session with another user agent, a P2P architecture is established where each machine makes requests and responds to the other. One machine acting as the User Agent client will make a request, while the other acting as the User Agent server will respond to it. Each machine can then swap roles, allowing them to interact as equals on the network. For example, if the applications being used allowed file sharing, a UAC could request a specific file from the UAS and download it. During this time, the peers could also be exchanging messages or talking using VoIP, and once these activities are completed, one could send a request to terminate the session to end the communications between them. As seen by this, the computers act in the roles of both client and server, but are always peers by having the same functionality of making and responding to requests.

SIP Requests and Responses

Because SIP is a text-based protocol like HTTP, it is used to send information between clients and servers, and User Agent clients and User Agent servers, as a series of requests and responses. When requests are made, there are a number of possible signaling commands that might be used:

- **REGISTER** Used when a user agent first goes online and registers their SIP address and IP address with a Registrar server.

- **INVITE** Used to invite another User agent to communicate, and then establish a SIP session between them.

- **ACK** Used to accept a session and confirm reliable message exchanges.

- **OPTIONS** Used to obtain information on the capabilities of another user agent, so that a session can be established between them. When this information is provided a session isn't automatically created as a result.

- **SUBSCRIBE** Used to request updated presence information on another user agent's status. This is used to acquire updated information on whether a User agent is online, busy, offline, and so on.

- **NOTIFY** Used to send updated information on a User agent's current status. This sends presence information on whether a User agent is online, busy, offline, and so on.

- **CANCEL** Used to cancel a pending request without terminating the session.

- **BYE** Used to terminate the session. Either the user agent who initiated the session, or the one being called can use the BYE command at any time to terminate the session.

When a request is made to a SIP server or another user agent, one of a number of possible responses may be sent back. These responses are grouped into six different categories, with a three-digit numerical response code that begins with a number relating to one of these categories. The various categories and their response code prefixes are as follows:

- **Informational (1xx)** The request has been received and is being processed.

- **Success (2xx)** The request was acknowledged and accepted.

- **Redirection (3xx)** The request can't be completed and additional steps are required (such as redirecting the user agent to another IP address).

- **Client error (4xx)** The request contained errors, so the server can't process the request

- **Server error (5xx)** The request was received, but the server can't process it. Errors of this type refer to the server itself, and they don't indicate that another server won't be able to process the request.

- **Global failure (6xx)** The request was received and the server is unable to process it. Errors of this type refer to errors that would occur on any server, so the request wouldn't be forwarded to another server for processing.

There are a wide variety of responses that apply to each of the categories. The different responses, their categories, and codes are shown in Table 6.2.

Table 6.2 Listing of Responses, Response Codes, and Their Meanings

Response Code	Response Category	Response Description
100	Informational	Trying
180	Informational	Ringing
181	Informational	Call is being forwarded
182	Informational	Queued
200	Success	OK
300	Redirection	Multiple choices
301	Redirection	Moved permanently
302	Redirection	Moved temporarily
303	Redirection	See other
305	Redirection	Use proxy
380	Redirection	Alternative service
400	Client Error	Bad request
401	Client Error	Unauthorized
402	Client Error	Payment required
403	Client Error	Forbidden
404	Client Error	Not found
405	Client Error	Method not allowed
406	Client Error	Not acceptable
407	Client Error	Proxy authentication required
408	Client Error	Request timeout
409	Client Error	Conflict
410	Client Error	Gone
411	Client Error	Length required
413	Client Error	Request entity too large
414	Client Error	Request-URI too large
415	Client Error	Unsupported media type
420	Client Error	Bad extension
480	Client Error	Temporarily not available
481	Client Error	Call leg/transaction does not exist
482	Client Error	Loop detected
483	Client Error	Too many hops

Continued

Table 6.2 continued Listing of Responses, Response Codes, and Their Meanings

Response Code	Response Category	Response Description
484	Client Error	Address incomplete
485	Client Error	Ambiguous
486	Client Error	Busy here
500	Server Error	Internal server error
501	Server Error	Not implemented
502	Server Error	Bad gateway
503	Server Error	Service unavailable
504	Server Error	Gateway time-out
505	Server Error	SIP version not supported
600	Global Failures	Busy everywhere
603	Global Failures	Decline
604	Global Failures	Does not exist anywhere
606	Global Failures	Not acceptable

Protocols Used with SIP

Although SIP is a protocol in itself, it still needs to work with different protocols at different stages of communication to pass data between servers, devices, and participants. Without the use of these protocols, communication and the transport of certain types of media would either be impossible or insecure. In the sections that follow, we'll discuss a number of the common protocols that are used with SIP, and the functions they provide during a session.

UDP

The User Datagram Protocol (UDP) is part of the TCP/IP suite of protocols, and is used to transport units of data called *datagrams* over an IP network. It is similar to the Transmission Control Protocol (TCP), except that it doesn't divide messages into packets and reassembles them at the end. Because the datagrams don't support sequencing of the packets as the data arrives at the endpoint, it is up to the application to ensure that the data has arrived in the right order and has arrived completely. This may sound less beneficial than using TCP for transporting data, but it makes UDP faster because there is less processing of data. It often is used when messages with small amounts of data (which requires less reassembling) are being sent across the network, or with data that will be unaffected overall by a few units of missing data.

Although an application may have features that ensure that datagrams haven't gone missing or arrived out of order, many simply accept the potential of data loss, duplication, or errors. In the case of Voice over IP, streaming video, or interactive games, a minor loss of data or error will be a minor glitch that generally won't affect the overall quality or performance. In these cases, it is more important that the data is passed quickly from one endpoint to another. If reliability were a major issue, then the use of TCP as a transport protocol would be a better choice over hindering the application with features that check for the reliability of the data it receives.

Notes from the Underground…

UDP Denial-of-Service Attacks

Although denial-of-service (DoS) attacks are less common using UDP, data sent over this protocol can be used to bog down or even shut down a system that's victim to it. Because UDP is a connectionless protocol, it doesn't need to have a connection with another system before it transfers data. In a UDP Flood Attack, the attacker will send UDP packets to random ports on another system. When the remote host receives the UDP packets, it will do the following:

1. Determine which application is listening to the port.

2. Find that no application is waiting on that port.

3. Reply to the sender of the data (which may be a forged source address) with an ICMP packet of DESTINATION UNREACHABLE.

Although this may be a minor issue if the remote host has to send only a few of these ICMP packets, it will cause major problems if enough UDP packets are sent to the host's ports. A large number of UDP packets sent to the victim will cause the remote host to repeat these steps over and over. The victim's ports are monopolized by receiving data that isn't used by any application on the system, and ICMP packets are sent out to relay this fact to the attacker. Although other clients will find the remote host unreachable, eventually the system could even go down if enough UDP packets are sent.

To reduce the chances of falling victim to this type of attack, a number of measures can be taken. Proxy servers and firewalls can be implemented on a network to prevent UDP from being used maliciously and filter unwanted traffic. For example, if an attack appeared to come from one source previously, you could

Continued

set up a rule on the firewall that blocks UDP traffic from that IP address. In addition to this, chargen and echo services, as well as other unused UDP services, could be either disabled or filtered. Once these measures are taken, however, you should determine which applications on your network are using UDP, and monitor for signs of a UDP Flood Attack or other signs of misuse.

Transport Layer Security

Transport Layer Security (TLS) is a protocol that can be used with other protocols like UDP to provide security between applications communicating over an IP network. TLS uses encryption to ensure privacy, so that other parties can't eavesdrop or tamper with the messages being sent. Using TLS, a secure connection is established by authenticating the client and server, or User Agent Client and User Agent Server, and then encrypting the connection between them.

Transport Layer Security is a successor to Secure Sockets Layer (SSL), which was developed by Netscape. Even though it is based on SSL 3.0, TLS is a standard that has been defined in RFC 2246, and is designed to be its replacement. In this standard, TLS is designed as a multilayer protocol that consists of:

- TLS Handshake Protocol
- TLS Record Protocol

The TLS Handshake Protocol is used to authenticate the participants of the communication and negotiate an encryption algorithm. This allows the client and server to agree upon an encryption method and prove who they are using cryptographic keys before any data is sent between them. Once this has been done successfully, a secure channel is established between them.

After the TLS Handshake Protocol is used, the TLS Record Protocol ensures that the data exchanged between the parties isn't altered en route. This protocol can be used with or without encryption, but TLS Record Protocol provides enhanced security using encryption methods like the Data Encryption Standard (DES). In doing so, it provides the security of ensuring data isn't modified, and others can't access the data while in transit.

TIP

The Transport Layer Security Protocol isn't a requirement for using SIP, and generally isn't needed for standard communications. For example, if you're using VoIP or other communication software to trade recipes or talk about movies with a friend, then using encryption might be overkill. However, in the case of companies that use VoIP for business calls or to exchange information that requires privacy, then using TLS is a viable solution for ensuring that information and data files exchanged over the Internet are secure.

Tools & Traps...

Encryption versus Nonencrypted Data

When sessions are initiated using SIP, the data passed between the servers and other users is sent using UDP. As it is sent across the Internet, it can go through a number of servers and routers, and may be passed through a local network on your end or the other participant's end. During any point in this trip, it is possible that the data may be intercepted by a third party, meaning that any confidential information you transmit may be less private than you expected.

One method that third parties might use to access this data is with a *packet sniffer*. A packet sniffer is a tool that intercepts the traffic passed across a network. They are also known as *network analyzers* and *Ethernet sniffers*, and can be either software or hardware that captures the packets of data so they can be analyzed. It is a tool that can be used to identify network problems, but it is also used to eavesdrop on network users, and view the data sent to and from a specific source. This allows someone to grab the data you're sending, decode it, and view what you've sent and received.

To avoid this problem, sensitive communications should always be encrypted. When data is encrypted, the data becomes unreadable to anyone who isn't intended to receive it. If a person accessed encrypted packets of data with a packet sniffer, it would be seen as gibberish and completely unusable to them. It makes the transmission secure, preventing the wrong people from viewing what you've sent.

Other Protocols Used by SIP

As mentioned, SIP does not provide the functionality required for sending single-media or multimedia across a network, or many of the services that are found in communications programs. Instead, it is a component that works with other proto-cols to transport data, control streaming media, and access various services like caller-ID or connecting to the Public Switched Telephone Network (PSTN). These protocols include:

- Session Description Protocol, which sends information to effectively transmit data

- Real-Time Transport Protocol, which is used to transport data

- Media Gateway Control Protocol, which is used to connect to the PSTN

- Real-time Streaming Protocol, which controls the delivery of streaming media

The Session Description Protocol (SDP) and Real-time Transport Protocol (RTP) are protocols that commonly are used by SIP during a session. SDP is required to send information needed during a session where multimedia is exchanged between user agents, and RTP is to transport this data. The Media Gateway Control Protocol (MGCP) and Real-time Streaming Protocol (RTSP) commonly are used by systems that support SIP, and are discussed later for that reason.

Session Description Protocol

The Session Description Protocol (SDP) is used to send description information that is necessary when sending multimedia data across the network. During the initiation of a session, SDP provides information on what multimedia a user agent is requesting to be used, and other information that is necessary in setting up the transfer of this data.

SDP is a text-based protocol that provides information in messages that are sent in UDP packets. The text information sent in these packets is the session description, and contains such information as:

- The name and purpose of the session

- The time that the session is active

- A description of the media exchanged during the session

- Connection information (such as addresses, phone number, etc.) required to receive media

NOTE

SDP is a standard that was designed by the IETF under RFC 2327.

Real-Time Transport Protocol

The Real-Time Transport Protocol (RTP) is used to transport real-time data across a network. It manages the transmission of multimedia over an IP network, such as when it is used for audio communication or videoconferencing with SIP. Information in the header of the packets sent over RTP tells the receiving user agent how the data should be reconstructed and also provides information on the codec bit streams.

Although RTP runs on top of UDP, which doesn't ensure reliability of data, RTP does provide some reliability in the data sent between user agents. The protocol uses the Real-time Control Protocol to monitor the delivery of data that's sent between participants. This allows the user agent receiving the data to detect if there is packet loss, and allows it to compensate for any delays that might occur as data is transported across the network.

NOTE

RTP was designed by the IETF Audio-Video Transport Working Group, and origi-nally was specified as a standard under RFC 1889. Since then, this RFC has become obsolete, but RTP remains a standard and is defined under RFC 3550. In RFC 2509, Compressed Real-time Transport Protocol (CRTP) was specified as a standard, allowing the data sent between participants to be compressed, so that the size was smaller and data could be transferred quicker. However, since CRTP doesn't function well in situations without reliable, fast connections, RTP is still commonly used for communications like VoIP applications.

Media Gateway Control Protocol

The Media Gateway Control Protocol (MGCP) is used to control gateways that provide access to the Public Switched Telephone Network (PSTN), and vice versa. In doing so, this protocol provides a method for communication on a network to go out onto a normal telephone system, and for communications from the PSTN to reach computers and other devices on IP networks. A media gateway is used to convert the data from a format that's used on PSTN to one that's used by IP networks that use packets to transport data; MGCP is used to set up, manage, and tear down the calls between these endpoints.

> **NOTE**
>
> MGCP was defined in RFC 2705 as an Internet standard by the IETF. However, the Media Gateway Control Protocol is also known as H.248 and Megaco. The IETF defined Megaco as a standard in RFC 3015, and the Telecommunication Standardization Sector of the International Telecommunications Union endorsed the standard as Recommendation H.248.

Real-Time Streaming Protocol

The Real-Time Streaming Protocol (RTSP) is used to control the delivery of streaming media across the network. RTSP provides the ability to control streaming media much as you would control video running on a VCR or DVD player. Through this protocol, an application can issue commands to play, pause, or perform other actions that effect the playing of media being transferred to the application.

> **NOTE**
>
> IETF defined RTSP as a standard in RFC 2326, allowing clients to control streaming media sent to them over protocols like RTP.

Understanding SIP's Architecture

Now that we've looked at the various components that allow SIP to function on an IP network, let's look at how they work together to provide communication between two endpoints on a system. In doing so, we can see how the various elements come together to allow single and multimedia to be exchanged over a local network or the Internet.

The User agents begin by communicating with various servers to find other User agents to exchange data with. Until they can establish a session with one another, they must work in a client/server architecture, and make requests of servers and wait for these requests to be serviced. Once a session is established between the

User agents, the architecture changes. Because a User agent can act as either a client or a server in a session with another User agent, these components are part of what is called a peer-to-peer (P2P) architecture. In this architecture, the computers are equal to one another, and both make and service requests made by other machines. To understand how this occurs, let's look at several actions that a User agent may make to establish such a session with another machine.

SIP Registration

Before a User agent can even make a request to start communication with another client, each participant must register with a Registrar server. As seen in Figure 6.2, the User agent sends a REGISTER request to the SIP server in the Registrar role. Once the request is accepted, the Registrar adds the SIP-address and IP address that the User agent provides to the location service. The location service can then use this information to provide SIP-address to IP-address mappings for name resolution.

Figure 6.2 Registering with a SIP Registrar

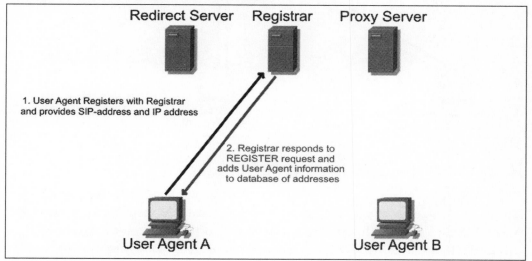

Requests through Proxy Servers

When a Proxy Server is used, requests and responses from user agents initially are made through the Proxy server. As seen in Figure 6.3, User Agent A is attempting to invite User Agent B into a session. User Agent A begins by sending an INVITE request to User Agent B through a Proxy server, which checks with the location service to determine the IP address of the client being invited. The Proxy server then passes this request to User Agent B, who answers the request by sending its response back to the Proxy server, who in turn passes this response back to User Agent A. During this time, the two User agents and the Proxy server exchange these requests and responses using SDP. However, once these steps have been completed and the Proxy server sends acknowledgements to both clients, a session can be created between the two User agents. At this point, the two User agents can use RTP to transfer media between them and communicate directly.

Figure 6.3 Request and Response Made through Proxy Server

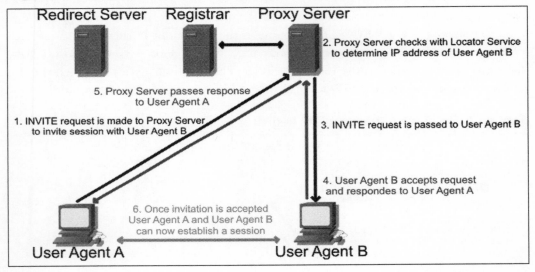

Requests through Redirect Servers

When a Redirect server is used, a request is made to the Redirect server, which returns the IP address of the User agent being contacted. As seen in Figure 6.4, User Agent A sends an INVITE request for User Agent B to the Redirect server, which checks the location service for the IP address of the client being invited. The Redirect server then returns this information to User Agent A. Now that User Agent A has this information, it can now contact User Agent B directly. The INVITE request is now sent to User Agent B, which responds directly to User Agent A. Until this point, SDP is used to exchange information. If the invitation is accepted, then the two User agents would begin communicating and exchanging media using RTP.

Figure 6.4 Request Made through Redirect Server

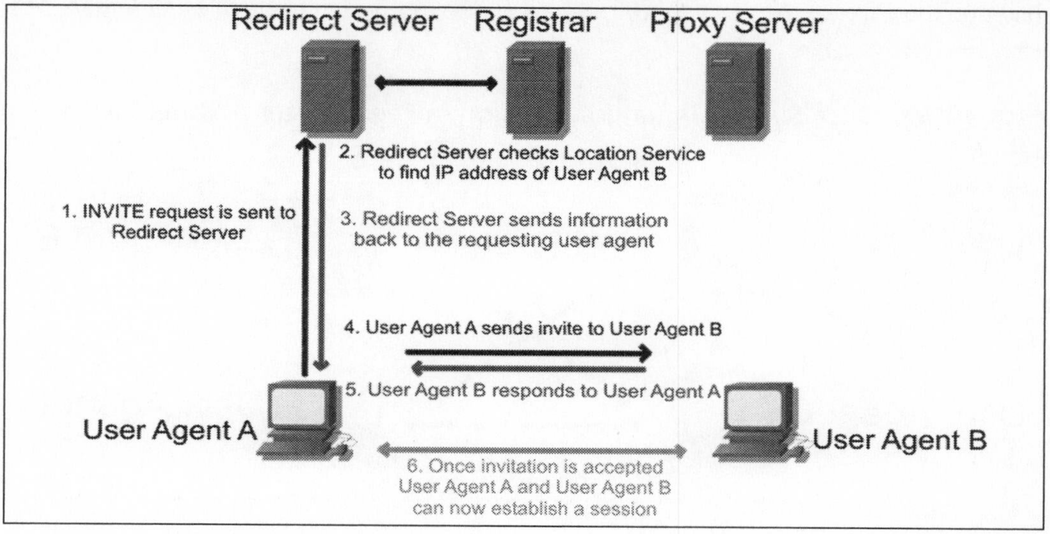

Peer to Peer

Once the user agents have completed registering themselves, and making requests and receiving responses on the location of the user agent they wish to contact, the architecture changes from one of client/server to that of peer-to-peer (P2P). In a P2P architecture, user agents act as both clients who request resources, and servers that respond to those requests and provide resources. Because resources aren't located on a single machine or a small group of machines acting as network servers, this type of network is also referred to as being *decentralized*.

When a network is decentralized P2P, it doesn't rely on costly servers to provide resources. Each computer in the network is used to provide resources, meaning that if one becomes unavailable, the ability to access files or send messages to others in the network is unaffected. For example, if one person's computer at an advertising firm crashed, you could use SIP to communicate with another person at that company, and talk to them and have files transferred to you. If one computer goes down, there are always others that can be accessed and the network remains stable.

In the same way, when user agents have initiated a session with one another, they become User agent clients and User agent servers to one another, and have the ability to invite additional participants into the session. As seen in Figure 6.5, each of these User agents can communicate with one another in an audio or videoconference. If one of these participants ends the session, or is using a device that fails during the communication, the other participants can continue as if nothing happened. This architecture makes communication between User agents stable, without having to worry about the network failing if one computer or device suddenly becomes unavailable.

Figure 6.5 Once SIP Has Initiated a Session, a Peer-to-Peer Architecture Is Used

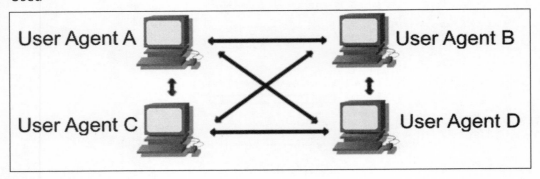

Instant Messaging and SIMPLE

Instant messaging (IM) has long been one of the most common and popular methods of communicating over IP networks. Whereas VoIP uses voice communication and videoconferencing uses live images and sound, IM simply uses text messages to allow participants to converse. These text messages are sent in real-time between the users who use the same IM application, and allows an individual to essentially create a private chat room with another individual where they can send text messages to one another. Many applications will even provide the ability to add additional participants to the chat, creating a text-based conference room of multiple users.

To manage the messages and identify whether specific users are online, an extension of SIP for instant messaging has been developed. SIMPLE is an acronym that stands for the *Session Initiation Protocol for Instant Messaging and Presence Leveraging Extensions*. Although the name is ironically less than simple to remember, it is being developed as an open standard for how individuals can determine the status of a person (i.e., whether they are online, busy, etc.), and for managing the messages that go back and forth between the participants in a chat.

Instant Messaging

In different variations, instant messaging has been around longer than the Internet has been popular. In the 1970s, the TALK command was implemented on UNIX machines, which invoked a split screen that allowed users of the system to see the messages they typed in individual screens. In the 1980s, Bulletin Board Systems (BBSes) became popular, where people would use a modem to dial into another person's computer to access various resources, such as message boards, games, and file downloads. On BBSes, the system operator (SYSOP) could invoke a chat feature that allowed the SYSOP to send messages back and forth with the caller on a similar split-screen. If the BBS had multiple phone lines, then the callers could Instant message with each other while they were online. As the Internet gained popularity, the ability to exchange messages with other users became a feature that was desired and expected.

Today there are a large number of IM applications that can be used to exchange text messages over the Internet and other IP networks. Although this is nowhere near a complete list, some of the more popular ones include:

- AIM, America Online Instant Messenger
- ICQ
- Yahoo Messenger
- MSN Messenger

In addition to these, there are also applications that allow communication using VoIP or other multimedia that also provide the ability to communicate using text messages. As seen in Figure 6.6, Skype provides a chat feature that allows two or more users to communicate in a private chat room. Each message between the participants appears on a different line, indicating who submitted which line of text and optionally the time that each message was sent. This allows participants to scroll back in the conversation to identify previously mentioned statements or topics of discussion. Although the figure depicts instant messaging in Skype, it is a common format that is used in modern IM software.

Figure 6.6 Instant Messaging through Skype

One of the important features of any IM application is the ability to keep a contact list of those with whom you routinely communicate. In many programs the contact list is also known as a *Buddy List*. However, even with this listing, it would be impossible to contact anyone if you didn't know when each contact was available. If a person had a high-speed connection and was always connected to the Internet, then they might always appear online. As such, they would need a way of indicating that they were online but not available, or whether the person was available for one form of communication but not another. The ability to display each contact's availability in a Buddy List when someone opens an IM application is called *presence*.

SIMPLE

SIMPLE is an extension of SIP, which is used for maintaining presence information and managing the messages that are exchanged between the participants using instant messaging. Just as SIP registers users with a SIP server before they can begin a session, SIMPLE registers presence information. When a user registers through SIMPLE, those with this user in their Buddy List can access information that the user is online. When the people who have the user in their lists are alerted that the user is online, they can initiate a chat. If the user needs to do some work and changes their status to busy, or goes away from their desk and changes their status to being away, then this information is updated in the IM applications that have this person as a contact. Generally, the presence of a user is indicated in these programs through icons that change based on the user's status.

Because SIMPLE is an extension of SIP, it has the same features and methods of routing messages. The users are registered, and then send text-based requests to initiate a session. The messages are sent between user agents as individual requests between User agent clients and User agent servers. Because the messages are small, they can move between the two User agents quickly with minimal time lag even during peak Internet hours.

Although the IETF IM and Presence Protocol Working Group are still developing SIMPLE as a standard, it has been implemented by a number of IM applications. Windows XP was the first operating system to include SIMPLE, and is used by Microsoft Windows Messenger, and numerous other IM applications also are using SIMPLE as a standardized method for instant messaging.

Are You 0wned?

Compromising Security with Instant Messaging

Instant messaging has become a tool that not only is used by the public for pleasure, but also one that is used by companies for business. IM software can be used as an alternative method of communicating with salespeople, customers, suppliers, and others who need to be contacted quickly. Because it is an effective communication tool, businesses have found benefits implementing it as part of their communications systems.

Unfortunately, a drawback of IM applications is that it provides a potential gap in security. Although companies will monitor outgoing e-mail for illegal or inappropriate content, IM applications available to the public don't provide a centralized method of logging conversations that can be locked down. IM applications routinely offer a method of logging conversations, but these settings can be toggled on and off by the person using the program. This means that someone could inadvertently or maliciously provide sensitive information in Instant messages without anyone at the company every realizing it.

Added to this problem is the fact that IM applications provide the ability to transfer other forms of media between participants. IM applications can be used for file sharing, where one person sends a file to another through the program.

Continued

This can result in activities like sharing music files at work, which albeit illegal is relatively harmless, but it could also cause major issues if sensitive corporate files were being sent. Imagine an employee at a hospital or doctor's office sending patient files, or a disgruntled employee sending out a secret formula to the public or competition, and its impact becomes more apparent.

Because files may contain more than you bargained for, the possibility of spyware or viruses being disseminated through instant messaging must also be considered. Some applications that have supported instant messaging include additional software that is spyware, which can obtain information about your system or track activities on your system. Even if the IM software used on a machine doesn't include spyware, the files sent between participants of a communication session can contain viruses or other malicious code. By opening these files, the person puts their computer and possibly their local network at risk.

If a company wishes to allow IM software installed on their machines, and doesn't want to block IM communications to the Internet, they need to educate users and install additional software on the computers. Just as employees should know what information should not be discussed on a telephone or sent by mail, they should know these same facts, and files should be off-limits in other communications. In addition to this, anti-virus software should be installed, and regularly updated and run. To determine if spyware is installed on the machines, they should either invest in anti-virus software that also looks for these programs or install additional software that searches for and removes them from the computer. In performing these steps, the risks associated with IM applications in a business can be decreased, making it safer for both the user and the company.

Summary

SIP works in conjunction with a variety of other protocols and specialized servers to provide communication between participants. Through SIP, a User agent is able to find the location and availability of other users, the capabilities of the software or device they're using, and then provides the functions necessary to set up, manage, and tear down sessions between participants. This allows participants to communicate directly with one another, so that data can be exchanged effectively and (if necessary) securely.

SIP is a standard of the Internet Engineering Task Force (IETF) under RFC 3261, and maps to the application layer of the OSI reference model. Because it isn't a proprietary technology, implementations of it can be used on any platform or device, and can be used on any IP network. In addition to this, SIP also makes use of other standards, such as URIs, which are used to identify the accounts used in SIP.

SIP's architecture is made up of a number of different protocols and components that allow it to function. Its architecture begins as a client/server architecture, in which requests are made to SIP servers. As the servers service these requests, they allow the participants to eventually communicate directly with one another, changing the architecture to a distributed peer-to-peer. As information is passed between these machines, a variety of different protocols are used, allowing data to be passed quickly between the computers, and securely if needed.

Instant messaging is another technology where SIP is being used. An extension of SIP called SIMPLE is used to maintain presence information and manage messages that are exchanged between the participants. Because SIMPLE provides the same features as SIP and is also an open standard, it is being used increasingly in IM software, making SIP and SIMPLE a staple in communications on IP networks.

Solutions Fast Track

Understanding SIP

☑ The Session Initiation Protocol is a signaling, application-layer protocol that is used to initiate interactive sessions on an IP network. Its purpose is to establish, maintain, and terminate sessions between two or more endpoints.

☑ SIP is a standard that was developed by the Internet Engineering Task Force (IETF). RFC 3261 is the finalized document that makes SIP a standard.

☑ SIP maps to the application layer of the OSI reference model. It is accessed by programs, to which it exports information. To make requests and access additional services, SIP uses other lower-layer protocols.

SIP Functions and Features

☑ SIP is used to determine location, availability, and capabilities of a user, and is used to set up and manage sessions.

☑ SIP's addressing system uses hierarchical URIs that are similar to e-mail addresses.

☑ SIP URIs generally begin with SIP:, but if secure transmission using the Transport Layer Security (TLS) protocol is required, then the URI will begin with SIPS:.

SIP Architecture

☑ A User agent can act in the role of a User agent client that makes requests (such as initiating a session) or a User agent server that services requests.

☑ A client/server architecture is used when the User agent communicates with various servers that may be used when establishing a session. In this architecture, the client makes requests from dedicated servers that provide specific services on the network. Such servers include Registrar servers, Proxy servers, and Redirect servers.

☑ A peer-to-peer (P2P) architecture is used when the User agents establish a session. In this architecture, the computers act as equals, and make and respond to each other's requests. In doing so, their roles change from that of User agent client to User agent server.

☑ Registrar servers are used to register the location of a User agent who has logged onto the network.

☑ Proxy servers are computers that are used to forward requests on behalf of other computers. They can also provide such functions as network access control, security, authentication, and authorization.

☑ The Redirect servers are used by SIP to redirect clients to the User agent they are attempting to contact. They also have the ability to fork a call by splitting it to several locations.

☑ User Datagram Protocol (UDP) is used to transport units of data over an IP network. It is more lightweight than TCP, requiring less processing of data and allowing data to be transported quickly.

☑ Real-time Streaming Protocol (RTSP) controls the delivery of streaming media across the network.

☑ Media Gateway Control Protocol (MGCP) controls gateways that provide access to the Public Switched Telephone Network.

☑ Real-time Transport Protocol (RTP) transports real-time data across a network.

☑ Session Description Protocol (SDP) sends description information that is necessary when sending multimedia data across the network.

Instant Messaging and SIMPLE

☑ SIMPLE is short for *Session Initiation Protocol for Instant Messaging and Presence* Leveraging *Extensions*. It is an extension of SIP, and used to determine the presence of individuals on an IP network and manage messages exchanged between participants.

☑ Instant messaging (IM) is used to communicate using text messages in a private chat room environment. IM applications can also be used to transfer files, video, and other media and data between participants.

☑ Presence technology is used to display the availability of contacts in a Buddy List.

Frequently Asked Questions

The following Frequently Asked Questions, answered by the authors of this book, are designed to both measure your understanding of the concepts presented in this chapter and to assist you with real-life implementation of these concepts. To have your questions about this chapter answered by the author, browse to **www.syngress.com/solutions** and click on the **"Ask the Author"** form.

Q: I am used to seeing users that follow the scheme *SIP: username@domain.com*, but I've also seen them with the scheme *SIPS: username@domain.com*. What's the difference?

A: SIP uses Universal Resource Identifiers (URIs) for identifying users. A URI identifies resources on the Internet, and those used by SIP incorporate phone numbers or names in the username. At the beginning of this is SIP:, which indicates the protocol being used. This is similar to Web site addresses, which begin with HTTP: to indicate the protocol to use when accessing the site. When SIP: is at the beginning of the address, the transmission is not encrypted. Those beginning with SIPS: require encryption for the session.

Q: Why do all responses to a request in SIP begin with the numbers 1 through 6?

A: This indicates the category to which the response belongs. There are six categories of responses that may be returned from a request: Informational, Success, Redirection, Client Error, Server Error, and Global Failure.

Q: I received a response that my request was met with a server error. Does this mean I can't use this feature of my VoIP program?

A: Not necessarily. When a request receives a Server Error response, it means that the server it was sent to met with the error. The request could still be forwarded to other servers. A Global Error meanns that it wouldn't be forwarded because every other server would also have the same error.

Q: I need to use a different computer for VoIP. The software is the same as the one on my computer, but I'm concerned that others won't be able to see that I'm online because I'm using a different machine.

A: When you start the program and log onto your VoIP account, SIP makes a REGISTER request that provides your SIP address and IP address to a Registrar server. This allows multiple people to use multiple computers. No matter what your location, SIP allows others to find you with this mapping of your SIP-address to the current IP address.

Q: Should I always use encryption to protect the data that I'm transmitting over the Internet?

A: Unless you expect to be discussing information or transferring files that require privacy, it shouldn't matter whether your transmission is encrypted or not. After all, if someone did eavesdrop on an average conversation, would you really care that they heard your opinion on the last movie you watched? If, however, you were concerned that the content of your conversation or other data that was transmitted might be viewed by a third party, then encryption would be a viable solution to protecting your interests. As of this writing however, there are no interoperable, nonproprietary implementations of SIP that use encrypted signaling and media, so you will need to refer to the documentation of the application(s) being used to determine if this is available.

Chapter 7

Other VoIP Communication Architectures

Solutions in this chapter:

- Skype

- H.248

- IAX

- Microsoft Live Communications Server 2005

☑ Summary

☑ Solutions Fast Track

☑ Frequently Asked Questions

Introduction

This chapter will provide an overview of three solutions that are all different in their own way. Skype has made itself into an institution for online peer-to-peer voice calls from anywhere in the world. It was even so good that eBay paid three billion dollars for this very small company. On the other hand, we have a protocol that is not new and does not have the buzz that Skype does.

H.248 is a result of the ITU and the IETF coming together on one standard. Before H.248 there was MGCP and MDCP, both of which were competing protocols. You will not hear much of H.248 in the news since it does not have the flash of Skype, but you will need it for any VOIP implementation. Last we will talk about Microsoft LCS and how Microsoft is using its new server to bring different IM providers and companies together.

Skype

Skype is a peer-to-peer VOIP client that has taken over mainstream VOIP use on the Internet. As of early 2006, Skype had claimed more than 236,799,174 downloads of the most popular voice software client on the Internet to date. Why would so many people download this client just to make a call on the Internet? Because it's free. And not only that, but it does the job better than any of its competitors that have come out with a free version in the last two years. I know what you are thinking: I still have to pay for calls to off-net users and pay for voicemail. Well as a matter of fact you do, but if you can live without those and just make calls over your computer to friends and family and elsewhere in the world, it is free.

Skype is the fastest growing communication application on the Internet. According to Australian IT, Skype has roughly 54 million users and accounts for 46 percent of all North American voice traffic carried over the Internet as of August 2005. Many refer to Skype as an instant messaging (IM) application. Think of Skype as more of a Voice Call application that also provides instant messaging features. IM allows you to type quick messages to your list of contacts instantly.

What Skype adds to IM is the ability to talk, in real-time with your contacts in addition to typical IM functions. More important, the quality of the audio, features, and options available for Skype is what gives Skype the advantage over the rest of the IM products. Skype has made Internet telephony or Voice over IP (VoIP) or Voice Calls over the Internet available to everyone, geeks and nongeeks alike. For geeks, and you know who you are, Skype is just plain cool.

Skype has grown at an incredible rate. According to Skype.com, in the approximately two years it has been available it has been downloaded over 155 million times, has approximately 54 million users, and around two million paid subscribers as of August 2005. Skype has brought Internet telephony (also known as VoIP) into the homes of just about every demographic from children to grandparents.

> **NOTE**
>
> Right now Skype is the flavor of the month, so to speak, when looking at peer-to-peer messengers. But the lack of information and recent purchase by eBay have left many diehard users wondering if they should move onto the open source Google Talk.

History

This most popular software is the brain-child of two men who brought us the free file sharing software KaZaA, Niklas Zennström and Janus Friis. Let's take a look at where and when this all started for these two gentlemen and where they have brought Skype to now.

- April 2003: Skype.com and Skype.net domain names are registered.
- August 2003: First public beta version is released.
- June 2004: Purchase of SkypeOut is available on the Skype Web site.
- July 2004: Release of a version for Windows.
- October 2004: First time one million Skype users are online at once.
- February 2005: Reached two million users.
- March 2005: SkypeIn public beta starts.
- March 2005: Skype reports one million SkypeOut users.
- April 2005: Client downloaded over 100 million times.
- May 2005: Three million Skype users are online at the same time.
- November 2005: Client downloaded over 200 million times.

One of the most important points not included in the preceding list was the purchase of Skype by the mega online auction site eBay. With the purchase of Skype, the people at eBay are banking on the fact that the buyer and seller of the online auction site will use this service as a communications tool. They bet over $3 million on this fact and are hoping for some return on investment. Was it a good move for the founders of Skype? Only time will tell but with three billion good reasons how could you go wrong?

Skype Protocol Design

Skype uses a proprietary session–establishment protocol that communicates over TCP and UDP. The purpose for using a proprietary protocol is to protect against replay, verify the peer's identity, and allow the peer to agree to a secret session key for communications purposes.

Although there have been many papers and postings on chat boards saying we think the Skype Protocol used is similar to this or that, no one knows. In the recent Skype Me Book it has been noted that the protocol used by Skype is not Session Initiation Protocol (SIP) or H.323. It has also been mentioned how similar IAX2 (the second version of the Inter-Asterisk Exchange Protocol) looks to the unknown Skype Protocol. They both can cut through a network for connectivity over a single port. But for right now the difference is that IAX2 is an open source design.

TIP

If you read on the Web that someone has solved the question of what Skype uses for its proprietary session-establishment protocol, think twice. Unless you see it on the Skype Web site, it is not true. This protocol is still a very guarded secret at Skype and is not coming out any time soon.

Skype Messaging Sequence

Skype uses P2P (point to point) technology to improve the quality of the application. P2P allows for direct communications with all parties involved, which improves performance and eliminates delays in the voice call as well as allowing for Skype to be a secure solution by connecting onlythe users involved, not running the connection through a server. Figure 7.1 is a basic Skype messaging sequence.

A P2P voice call is started first by both users connecting to the Internet (1). Users can connect many different ways, such as through a corporate LAN/WAN, cable modem, DSL, or even wirelessly.

Figure 7.1 Start of a Call

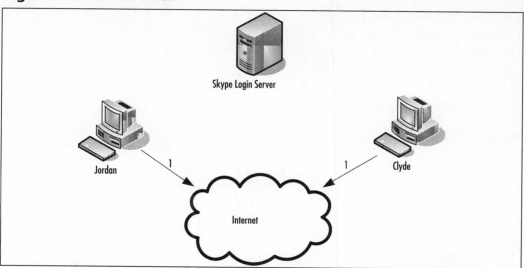

The users use TCP ports to connect to the Skype login server (2) via the Internet (see Figure 7.2). The connection is secured using 256-bit AES encryption. The symmetric AES keys that are negotiated between the server and client are handled using 1536- and 2048-bit RSA.

Figure 7.2 Users Connect via TCP

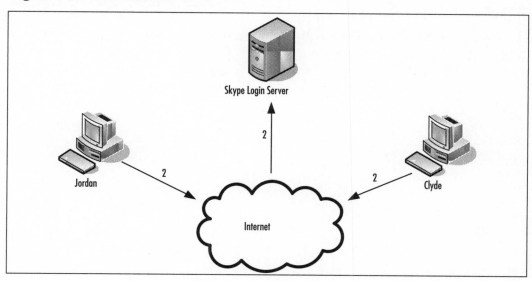

The client registers, tells the login server where the call recipient is located, and gives all other information needed to register and broadcast to other clients via the server (see Figure 7.3). For Jordan to make a connection to Clyde, his computer must search the Internet (3) using the help of intermediate Skype systems (supernodes) in the Internet "cloud," and Clyde's system also must update those same systems (3) to make Clyde's presence known. Information is passed from other clients and supernodes at this point to help complete the call.

Figure 7.3 Client Registers

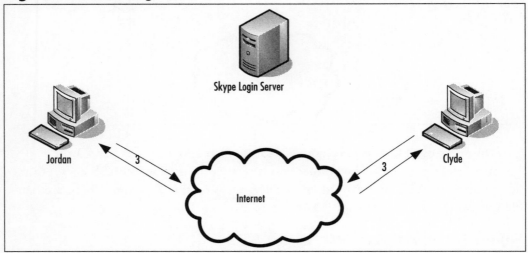

Figure 7.4 depicts the direct (P2P) connection that has been established between Jordan and Clyde (4).

Figure 7.4 Direct P2P Established

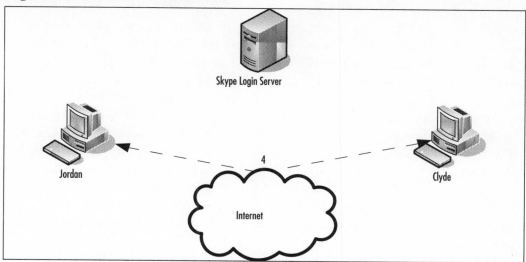

Skype Protocol Security

Since the Skype protocol is proprietary we can tell you only that it uses a 256-bit AES encrypted session to establish a connection with the Central Server. Then it will use two Central Server Key Pairs for security; one is 1536 bits and the other is 2,048 bits. As a matter of fact, all sessions are encrypted using a XORing of the plaintext and key streams generated by a 256-bit AES session running in integer count mode.

Also for those people who are paying for the extra SkypeOut service, you will be happy to know that your calls are encrypted until they reach the PSTN. If you are wondering why they are not encrypted the entire way, well, right now you just cannot do that to a regular phone. The best that you can hope for is what is being done now, which is that the call from your PC over the Internet to the PSTN gateway is totally secure. The one place you cannot use SkypeOut right now is in China.

H.248

H.248 is a protocol for control of elements in a physical multimedia gateway, which will enable separation of call control from media conversion. A Media Gateway Controller controls one or more Media Gateways. H.248 has a master–slave configuration in that a single controller is controlling a number of gateways through the use of this protocol. H.248 was also known as the Megaco Protocol

History

MGCP (RFC 3435) was first invented in 1998 to help scaling port problems that existed with service providers by the IETF, while the ITU-T was working on MDCP. Since then both have been updated and replaced with Megaco/H.248 in 2000. This standard published jointly by the ITU and the IETF primarily used to separate the call control from the media processing in a gateway. H.248 was invented by the telecommunications companies to address the issue of SS7/VoIP integration.

This was to remove the signaling control from the media gateway and move it to the gateway controller or maybe a softswitch. H.248 can support thousands of ports on a media gateway and many gateways at a time. One way to remember how to separate the two is H.248 is a Gateway Control Protocol and MGCP is a Media Gateway Control Protocol. The IETF calls the protocol Megaco and the ITU calls the protocol H.248. So now you can see why we have two different names for this protocol.

H.248 introduces several enhancements compared with MGCP, including the following:

- Support of multimedia and multipoint conferencing enhanced services

- Improved syntax for more efficient semantic message processing

- TCP and UDP transport options

- Allowance of either text or binary encoding (to support IETF and ITU-T approach)

- Formalized extension process for enhanced functionality

- Expanded definition of packages

Figure 7.5 is a history diagram of how we got to H.248 and the protocols that have come previously.

> ## WARNING
>
> Do not get caught and think MGCP is H.248 or Megaco is MGCP. The protocols are different, and the easy way to remember it is that H comes before M. So H.248 is more current than MGCP.

Figure 7.5 H.248 History

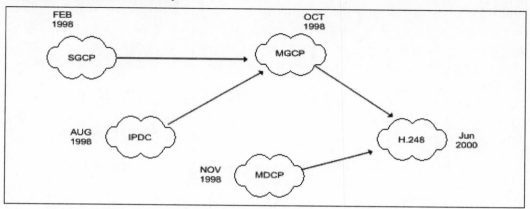

H.248 Protocol Design

As we have stated before, the use of H.248 was to remove the protocol design from the Media Gateway and move it to the Media Controller. Figure 7.6 is a diagram that shows that the protocol is used between the two in a network. But the Media Gateway Controller does control the H.248 protocol going to the Media Gateway.

Figure 7.6 A Typical H.248 Use Case

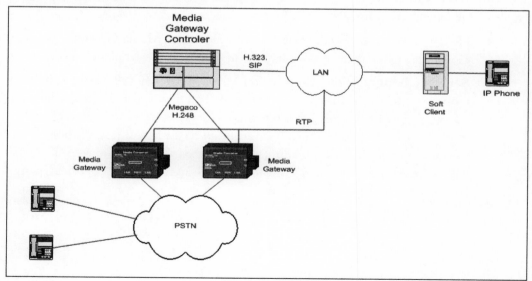

There are two basics to H.248, contexts and termination. Contexts are created and released by the gateway under command of the gateway media controller, when the context is created it is given a ContextID, and then can have terminations added and removed from it. The terminations are streams of media, either analog or digital, that enter and leave the gateway. These terminations also would be considered ports on a gateway.

The H.248 messages are in the format of ASN.1 text messages. H.248 uses a series of commands to manipulate terminations, contexts, events, and signals. The following is a list of the commands:

- **Add** Adds a Termination to a Context. On the first Termination in a Context is used to create a Context.

- **Modify** Modifies the properties, events, and signals of a Termination.

- **Subtract** Disconnects a Termination from its Context and returns statistics on the Termination's participation in the Context. The Subtract command on the last Termination in a Context deletes the Context.

- **Move** Atomatically moves a Termination to another context.

- **AuditValue** Returns the current state of properties, events, signals, and statistics of Terminations.

- **AuditCapabilities** Returns all the possible values for Termination properties, events, and signals allowed by the Media Gateway (MG).

- **Notify** Allows the Media Gateway to inform the Media Gateway Controller (MGC) of the occurrence of events in the Media Gateway.

- **ServiceChange** Allows the Media Gateway to notify the Media Gateway Controller that a Termination or group of Terminations is about to be taken out of service or has just been returned to service. ServiceChange also is used by the MG to announce its availability to an MGC (registration), and to notify the MGC of impending or completed restart of the MG. The MGC may announce a handover to the MG by sending it a ServiceChange command. The MGC may also use ServiceChange to instruct the MG to take a Termination or group of Terminations in or out of service.

H.248 Messaging Sequence

Figure 7.7 is a display call flow from when a call goes off-hook to when the call is established on the other side. As you can tell, H.248 is a very chatty protocol based on the calls' slow figures. It works very well in a master/slave model where the endpoint is something such as a simple analog phone. These would be considered "dumb" endpoints using this protocol (meaning that the phone isn't able to make call control decisions).

To put Figure 7.7 in a little better context, associate it with Figure 7.6. The following would be the association between the two figures:

- User = Soft Phone/IP Phone

- Main = Media Gateway Controller

- Encoder = Media Gateway

- Transport = PSTN

Figure 7.7 Call Flow Originator Side

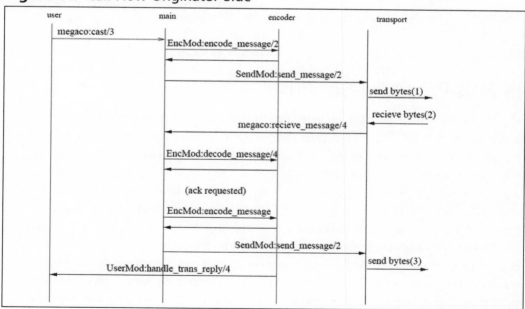

Figure 7.8 shows the message call flow from the destination side.

Figure 7.8 Call Flow Destination Side

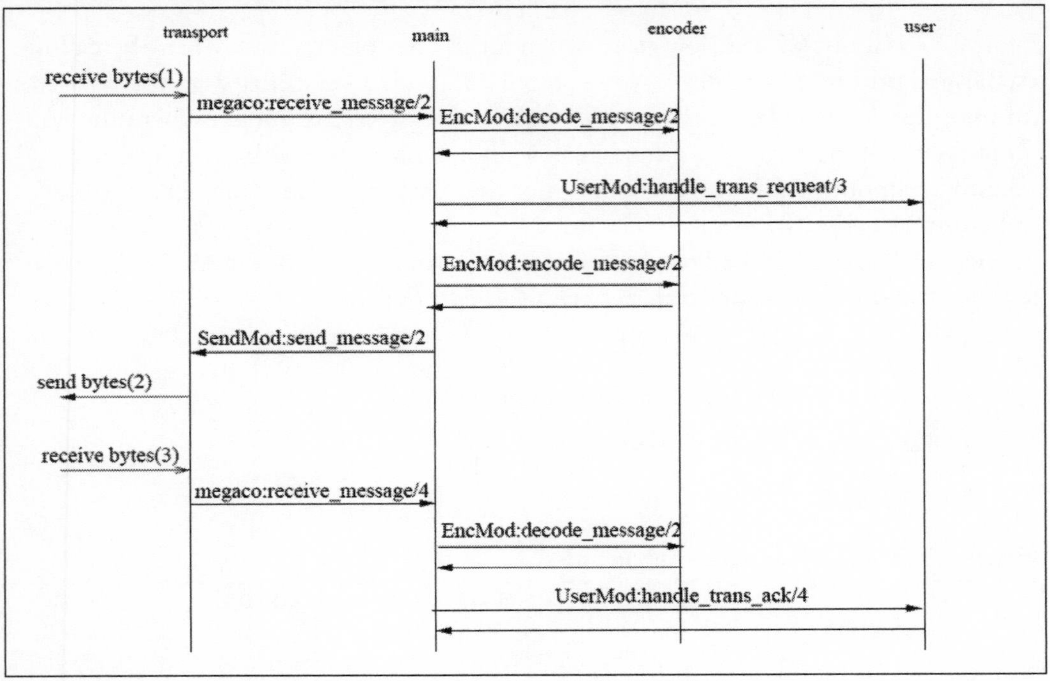

H.248 Protocol Security

H.248 standard recommends security protocols that may be in underlying transport mechanisms like IPSEC. H.248 goes further by requiring that installation of the H.248 protocol and implementing IPSEC if the underlying operating system has transport network to support IPSEC. Implementations of the protocol using IPv4 are required to implement the interim Authentication Header (AH) scheme. H.248 states that installation employing the AH header shall provide a minimum set of algorithms for integrity checking using manual keys.

Most companies do not use security between devices that use H.248 on a LAN. But when it comes to a WAN, it is recommended if not critical to use it when sending your traffic over WAN links. The security concerns are far much greater for your traffic since the WAN link most likely will not belong to your company like your LAN links will.

IAX

Inter-Asterisk Exchange (IAX) is a trunking protocol used primarily for connecting two Asterisk PBX servers or an IAX client to an Asterisk server. IAX has many benefits compared with SIP; however, it also has several shortcomings.

A short comparison: IAX traverses NAT with great ease compared with SIP. It requires only a single port to be opened on the firewall, whereas SIP requires a range of ports. There is never a situation that can be created with a firewall in which IAX can complete a call and not be able to pass audio (except, of course, for a scenario with insufficient bandwidth).

IAX Protocol Design

IAX was designed with two primary goals in mind: minimal bandwidth usage and NAT (Network Address Translation) transparency. In 1999, when IAX was first created, SIP and MGCP were still in relatively early development, and H.323 was the most popular VoIP protocol to the degree that such a thing existed. Most protocols were proprietary protocols, especially as they related to software running on a PC. Unhappy with that landscape, Mark Spencer sought to create an optimal means of transferring voice telephony data and other streaming media, including video.

Similar in function to SIP, IAX is a peer-to-peer media and signaling protocol. This means that state is maintained between two or more endpoints. Most IETF protocols use two separate means of control for the call— one for managing setup and teardown of a session, and one to manage the voice traffic itself. IAX combines both multiplexed over a single UDP stream. Because both go over a single stream, IAX avoids the NAT problems that plague its protocol brethren. When a call is established that goes through multiple IAX servers, servers in the middle will typically attempt to get the endpoints to talk directly with one another. This process is supervised, however, such that if the endpoints are unable to see each other (e.g., there is a NAT or other situation that gets in the way), the call simply continues to operate just as it was from the beginning. In this way, the IAX protocol attempts the best performing connection but falls back to always operating.

IAX Messaging Sequence

Let's take a look at how IAX handles the setup of a typical VoIP phone call. Say Bob wants to call his dear friend Alice on her Asterisk box on the East Coast.

Both Bob and Alice have opened port 4569 for UDP traffic on their firewalls, which they have pointed toward their PBX systems. It's important to note that no

Continued

specific firewall activity must take place if both servers register to a public server on the Internet.

Bob sends a NEW message to Alice, who then responds in turn with an ACCEPT message, which tells Bob, "Hey, I hear that you're trying to talk to me; I'm beginning to handle your call."

Bob sends Alice an ACK as a way of saying, "Great! Copy that, good buddy!" to inform her he got her ACCEPT message. Alice's phone then begins to ring, and her Asterisk server indicates to Bob that her phone is ringing, with a RINGING message (see Figure 7.9).

Figure 7.9 A Simple Call Setup Using the IAX Protocol

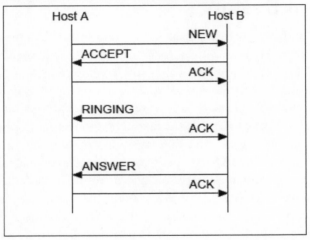

Figure 7.9 is reprinted courtesy of Mark Spencer and Frank W. Miller from *IAX Protocol Description* (March 23, 2004).

When Alice picks up her handset, her Asterisk server tells Bob "ANSWERED!" and the setup is complete. Voice traffic can now go freely between each caller.

Now let's look at how IAX tears down a session.

Bob and Alice wrap up their conversation and bid each other farewell. Bob puts his IAX phone's handset back on the hook. Bob's server sends Alice's a HANGUP message, and Alice immediately acknowledges the hangup (see Figure 7.10).

Figure 7.10 A Simple Call Teardown Using the IAX Protocol

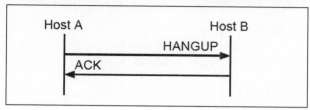

Figure 7.10 is reprinted courtesy of Mark Spencer and Frank W. Miller from *IAX Protocol Description* (March 23, 2004).

IAX Protocol Security

IAX supports MD5 and RSA authentication and can be encrypted optionally with 128-bit AES (Advanced Encryption Standard). IAX's authentication and encryption methods are extensible. IAX is built for improved security. For example, IAX does not use any text parsing, making it easier to implement IAX securely as compared with SIP. Also, because IAX uses only one port for communication, it's easier to integrate with firewalls, requiring fewer ports to be opened. By using just one port, IAX simplifies the source addresses of signaling, thereby obviating the need for the audio and signaling paths to be as promiscuous as they are in SIP.

Microsoft Live Communication Server 2005

Microsoft Office Live Communications Server 2005 (MLCS) is a manageable and extensible instant messaging server (IMS) that provides a real-time collaboration solution. MLCS is available in two configurations: a standard edition and enterprise edition. Standard edition is installed as a single server configuration using MSDE as the local database server. The enterprise edition offers scalability options using multiple front-end servers and Microsoft SQL Server 2000 as the database server. It also can be clustered for higher database server availability if needed.

The system uses the Microsoft Windows Messenger 5.1 (MWM) and Microsoft Office Communicator 2005 (MOC) as its clients for communication. The difference between the two clients is that with just Windows Messenger you get standard IM and presence. If you are asking why Microsoft offers both the Messenger and Communicator, it is because the Communicator came about from companies wanting more control over employees' access to public IM services. The MLCS also uses SIP (Session Initiation Protocol) and SIMPLE (Instant Messaging and Presence Leveraging Extensions) as the communication protocols.

There are several other components of the MLCS that we should take a look at so that you can better understand the architecture of the system. Figure 7.11 is a simple overview of the MLCS Enterprise architecture.

Figure 7.11 MLCS Architecture Enterprise Overview

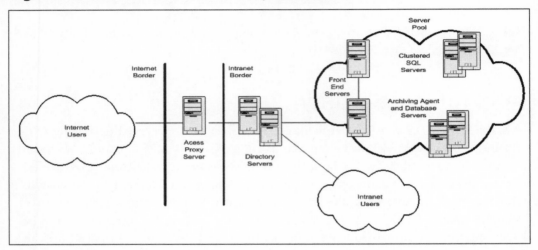

- **Access proxy servers** Used as a secure connection point for all remote users as well as other companies who have been given access to the server. It will also check the inbound message headers to make sure they are valid and mark each message as originating from outside the firewall.

- **Director servers** The first servers to receive a SIP messages from the intranet users via either the MWM or MOC. It can also receive SIP messages from remote users via the MLCS Proxy Server.

- **Front-end servers and server pool** A front-end server or servers that sit within a server pool with a single IP address.

- **Clustered SQL servers** A group of servers running Microsoft SQL Server 2000.

- **Archiving agent and database servers** Used to store information on a SAN environment network.

With the aforementioned architecture you can do many different things; one of those is to make calls outside your network or Internet. When using the MLCS to make calls to a PSTN for VOIP calling off-net, or to put it better, make a phone call using your PC client to a regular land-line phone you can accomplish this one of two ways:

- Designating a live communications server as a PSTN host
- Using a direct route to the SIP-PSTN Gateway

TIP

If you are going to use a direct route to a SIP/PSTN Gateway from the MLCS or any other SIP Proxy, it is always a best practice to use a VPN over WAN links. This will ensure your communications are kept secure.

History

Back in 1999, Microsoft deployed instant messaging services in its own network, Microsoft Exchange 2000 Server. This was to support its employees for basic presence information and instant messaging on their network. Then in 2003, Microsoft gave its employees Live Communications Server 2003. This once again was to improve the ability of the employees to find each other and communicate in real-time. It was in 2004 when Microsoft decided that it needed to update its 2003 offering because of the way IM was working internally and with other businesses.

Microsoft wanted to be able to have a MLCS that would be free of network VPN, allow real-time communications with other businesses, have a high availability deployment, and improve reporting. With all this, Microsoft then came up with MLCS 2005 for internal and external use. What Microsoft did was take things that it wanted to have in MLCS but also added support for other communications servers external to Microsoft. These would be public IM service providers like AOL, MSN, and Yahoo. Also they set up a back-end integration of MLCS so that it could communicate with a gateway/PBX to get calls to a PSTN.

MLCS Protocol Design

The MCLS, as stated earlier in this chapter, uses SIP and SIMPLE as its communication protocols. In a previous chapter the SIP protocol has been covered in much detail so we will not go back over it, but we can give you just a little more information about SIMPLE. As stated before, SIMPLE stands for SIP for instant messaging and Presence Leveraging Extensions. It is just a messaging extension added onto the SIP protocol for lack of a better term. The IETF has some parts of SIMPLE standardized like RFC 3428 but other parts like the IM sessions are still under discussion. But Microsoft is using it in their instant messenger.

MLCS Security

MLCS uses Transport Layer Security Protocol (TLS) for communication between the server and the client and it also uses Mutual Transport Layer Security Protocol between and from server to server. TLS is based on the Secure Socket Layer (SSL). The protocol is composed of two layers, first the TLS Record Protocol and then the TLS Handshake Protocol. The TLS Record Protocol provides connection security that has two basic properties, privacy and reliability, and is used for encapsulation of various higher level protocols. The TLS Handshake Protocol allows the servers and clients to authenticate to each other and also to negotiate an encryption algorithm and cryptographic keys before the application protocol transmits or receives any data.

Table 7.1 is a list of ports used for communication.

Table 7.1 Protocol and Ports

Protocol	Port
SIP/TCP Available for less secure client connection topologies	5060 (TCP)
SIP/TLS Available for more secure client connection topologies	5061 (TCP)
SIP/MTLS Used for server-to-server connections and can also be used by secure client connection topologies— this is the only recommended, secure SIP port.	5061 (TCP)

Before you can use TLS with MLCS your company must have a public key infrastructure (PKI). The reason is that certificates are used by TLS to initiate communication between the client and server. Now this part can either be good or bad for a company. The good part is if you already have a PKI established in your company you are OK, but for smaller companies it is an added cost. The cost is setting up the PKI, and having a staff to service and administer it.

If you are wondering how we secure the calls that come from the MLCS to the PSTN/Gateway, that's easy. The gateway is listed as a trusted server and will use MTLS to provide authentication to and from the MLCS and the PSTN/Gateway.

With MLCS using the aforementioned security properties to protect its clients and servers, it will no doubt help with the following threats (these are the most common type of threats you would see used against MLCS):

- Application-layer attack
- Compromised-key attack
- Denial-of-service attack
- Eavesdropping
- Identity spoofing (IP address spoofing)
- Man-in-the-middle attack
- Sniffing
- Spam
- Viruses and worms

Summary

We covered just a few very different architectures that are in use now. There are so many different architectures that perhaps we could have written a book just on the differences between them all. One that is worth note is Google Talk. Google Talk Client is Google's answer to the instant messaging services from companies such as America Online, Yahoo, Skype, and MSN.

Google Talk started off slow in beta for using an open source code but has grown due the ability of open connections and ease of use. To this day the instant messenger is fully interoperable with other communications services that support the open server-to-server XMPP (Extensible Messaging and Presence Protocol) protocol. The XMPP protocol allows the Google Talk Client to use such protocol for authentication, presence, and messaging.

If you are wondering where you have heard about XMPP protocol before, it could be from the Jabber instant messenger. Since 1999 Jabber has been using this open source protocol to run its instant messenger. Many large companies such as HP have purchased Jabber instant messenger servers to use as a corporate service.

As you can see many different ways to communicate over VoIP and IM are still emerging.

Solutions Fast Track

Skype

☑ Skype has become the peer-to-peer leader around the world in voice calls.

☑ The company has proven that is has one of the most secure clients and servers in the market today. With its proprietary protocol in use and no hints as to what it is, you are assured things will stay secure for the time being.

☑ It is yet to be seen if Skype will become more than what it is today with the recent purchase by eBay of its company.

H.248

☑ H.248 should not to be confused with MGCP; they are two different protocols.

☑ With the current advances in SIP, it is yet to be seen how long H.248 will be staying around as a protocol in VoIP.

IAX

- ☑ IAX is a lightweight protocol typically used with Asterisk, totally NAT transparentl and more efficient on the wire.

- ☑ The IETF Internet Draft is, moving towards becoming an RFC. IAX is especially well suited to "last mile" solutions and for efficient trunking.

Microsoft LCS

- ☑ The MLCS is trying to be a one-stop shop for company communications.

- ☑ With Microsoft going to the traditional way of SIP and following along with Nortel and Cisco, you really wonder where this will be heading down the road.

- ☑ Not only does the MLCS have the ability to make connections with other IM services but it can make SIP calls to a SIP/PSTN gateway.

Frequently Asked Questions

The following Frequently Asked Questions, answered by the authors of this book, are designed to both measure your understanding of the concepts presented in this chapter and to assist you with real-life implementation of these concepts. To have your questions about this chapter answered by the author, browse to **www.syngress.com/solutions** and click on the **"Ask the Author"** form.

Q: Why is it important to the MLCS to be able to connect to other IM services?

A: To be able to provide one solution that is secure, and so your company can callaborate with coworkers and friends, which is a huge advantage to any company.

Q: Why does Skype not divulge the protocol used in its clients?

A: The purpose for using a proprietary protocol is to protect against replay, verify the peer's identity, and allow the peer to agree to a secret session key for communications purposes. That's the answer you will receive from Skype.

Q: Can I have MGCP and H.248 on the same network?

A: Yes, you can, and right now I have it on my network on different equipment with SIP running across my network.

Q: With the current push by Microsoft for using SIP on the MLCS, do you think it will push others out of the space, such as Google Talk and Skype?

A: No, there will always be a place for others with different protocols and open standards.

Q: Why have I never heard of Skype until this past year?

A: It is a European software company and did not gain real momentum in the United States until this past year. Most people in the United States are on AOL, then comes Yahoo, MSN with Google, and Jabber bringing up the rear.

Q: In reading about Skype and the MLCS, I've heard that these products use encryption and are secure. Is anything really that secure these products and will never be broken into?

A: Well to say yes would be a bad bet, and to say no would be worse. But I don't think anything is totally secure.

Chapter 8

Support Protocols

Solutions in this chapter:

- DNS
- TFTP
- HTTP
- SNMP
- DHCP
- RSVP
- SDP
- SKINNY

☑ Summary

☑ Solutions Fast Track

☑ Frequently Asked Questions

Introduction

Protocols such as MGCP and SIP, or protocol umbrella groups like H.323, are usually the first things that come to mind when discussing VoIP technology. Although they are all great protocols in their own right, they depend on, and interoperate heavily with, support protocols. Many of the support protocols that are used by VoIP architectures enable services and features required for proper network operation.

This chapter will cover several of the support protocols typically found in VoIP environments and some of the security implications that they bring with them. This chapter is not intended to be an all-inclusive tutorial on these protocols. Instead, the intent is to review both their use and any security implications involving your network.

> **NOTE**
>
> It is important to keep in mind that most of these support protocols do not include any encryption or authentication mechanisms by default. For this reason, most of this traffic is susceptible to interception and/or modification. Proper network planning and configuration is thus essential.

DNS

The Domain Name System (DNS) is a static hierarchical name resolution architecture that relies on client/server communication for operation. DNS is a protocol that many use every day and may not know it. Whenever someone browses the Internet, DNS is used in the background to translate host names into IP addresses so that the proper network destinations can be found. DNS is equally important in VoIP networks for its ability to resolve destination endpoint addresses or allow gateway registration to call servers and gatekeepers by host name.

DNS was created so that no one would be required to memorize the IP addresses of every host on a private network or the Internet. Most people have a hard enough time remembering one or two passwords, let alone several billion IP addresses. With the development of DNS, the only requirement is knowledge of the target Web page name that you wish to go to. DNS resolves the target Web page name entered into one or more server IP addresses. It has also been designed to allow the reverse or "inverse" resolution of IP addresses to host names.

The DNS architecture was first discussed in detail in RFCs 881 through 883, and later updated in RFCs 1034 and 1035. Several of the newer RFCs include recommendations for how to secure the DNS architecture, including the addition of DNS security extensions (DNSSEC) beginning with RFC 4033. The next few sections detail a high-level overview of the DNS architecture and several security threats associated with DNS systems.

DNS Architecture

In order to better understand and be able to address the security concerns associated with DNS properly, it is important to have at least a high-level understanding of how DNS works. The hierarchy previously mentioned for DNS exists as a pyramid, with the highest level of the DNS architecture at the top. DNS is organized into myriad logical groupings called domains, which are further segmented into an endless number of subdomains. Figure 8.1 illustrates a sample hierarchy of the DNS system and is by no means exhaustive. The intent is to show the structure of the hierarchy.

Figure 8.1 Sample DNS Architecture

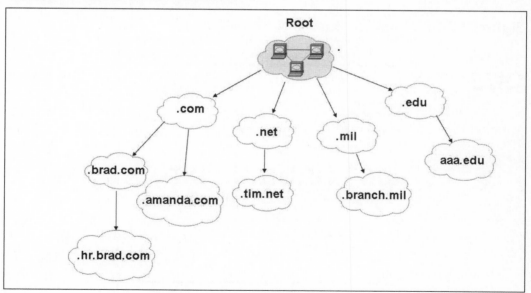

Located at the top of the DNS hierarchy are the root DNS servers. The root DNS servers are located in the root DNS zone, annotated by a single ".", and are responsible for maintaining the location of the top-level domain servers (TLD). A TLD DNS server is one that is responsible for the management of one of the commonly associated address suffix identifiers, such as .com, .net, .edu, or .org. The TLD DNS servers are assigned or "delegated" the responsibility by the root DNS servers. They are known as the authoritative server for that TLD. Likewise, the TLD DNS servers delegate the management of one of their many subdomains. The subdomain DNS servers for .brad.com would be responsible for any resource records (RR) for that subdomain as well as the location of any related subdomains (.hr.brad.com). The resource records are the entries for the host systems. This process of delegation distributes the load of the DNS system across many different servers.

Fully Qualified Domain Name (FQDN)

Each host has its own pointer for DNS, known as a fully qualified domain name (FQDN). The FQDN is used to identify the path taken through the DNS architecture to find the requested host. Figure 8.2 illustrates what path is taken through the previously discussed DNS hierarchy from Figure 8.1 to reach host pc1.

Figure 8.2 Fully Qualified Domain Names (FQDNs)

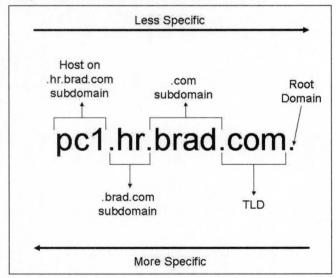

There are a couple of things to keep in mind about FQDNs. First of all, the explicit FQDN path from the top of the hierarchy (root) is read from right to left. Secondly, even though most FQDN illustrations do not include the final dot to represent the root domain, it is an implied part of the complete FQDN. Most applications, like IE, will not append a trailing "." to the end of a requested Web resource. Followed from right to left, the host pc1 follows a path out of the root domain, through the TLD .com, to the .com subdomain .brad.com, and then finally into the .brad.com subdomain of .hr.brad.com.

FQDNs are entered into the DNS tables as one of several types of RRs:

- **A** An A record is an address record, denoting a standard host entry in the DNS table. The key here is that it is used to resolve an FQDN to an IP address.

- **PTR** PTR records are used by the inverse lookup zones in DNS. The PTR record resolves an IP address to an FQDN.

- **SOA** The SOA record identifies zone information such as the zone name and serial number.

- **MX** MX records identify mail servers for the zone.

- **NS** NS records are used for name servers for the zone.

- **CNAME** CNAME records act as alias records to allow for the translation of one host name into another.

- **INFO** Provides information about hosts listed in the DNS table.

- **SRV** SRV records identify SIP servers for the zone.

DNS Client Operation

In order to locate the IP address for a host, the client's application will send a request to a resolver on the same client system. The resolver will then formulate and send out the DNS query. From a high level, the query will typically follow a path of trial and error known as a recursive lookup. Figure 8.3 illustrates what a recursive lookup from a host, pc2, would look like to find the IP address for host pc1.

Figure 8.3 Recursive Lookups Using DNS

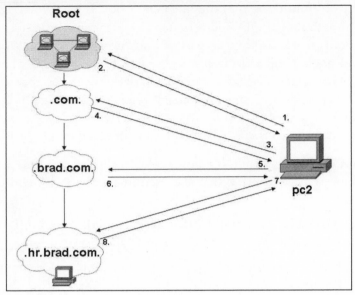

1. The client's resolver sends its DNS query, which will be sent to the root domain.

2. The root domain server does not have the RR for the host pc1, so the response is sent to redirect the resolver on pc2 to the TLD DNS server for .com since it knows where .com. is.

3. The resolver, in turn, sends a query to the TLD DNS server for .com.

4. The TLD DNS server does not have the RR for the host pc1, so the response is sent to redirect the resolver on pc2 to the .brad.com. DNS server since it knows where .brad.com. is.

5. The resolver, in turn, sends a query to the DNS server for .brad.com.

6. The .brad.com. DNS server does not have the RR for the host pc1, so the response is sent to redirect the resolver on pc2 to the .hr.brad.com. DNS server since it knows where .hr.brad.com. is.

7. The resolver, in turn, sends a query to the DNS server for .hr.brad.com.

8. The authoritative DNS server for .hr.brad.com. has the RR for the host pc1 and sends back the information to pc2. pc2 now has the IP address information for pc1, and may use it accordingly.

> **NOTE**
>
> It is not required to have a separate DNS server for each subdomain. A single DNS server may be the authoritative server for many, or all, of the subdomains in a corporation, although there are usually backup DNS servers configured for each primary DNS server.

DNS Server Operation

The DNS server is responsible for cataloging all of the RRs that belong to any of the zones that it is the authoritative DNS server for. It is also responsible for keeping track of any of the DNS servers that it has delegated subdomain responsibility to. By keeping track of the subdomains, the DNS server is able to redirect client queries to the proper location in the event that the requested host RR does not reside on that server.

DNS servers may also be configured to maintain a cache of domain names, as well as their respective IP addresses, as they are requested by clients. This configuration allows a DNS server to retrieve an IP address only once and then store the value for any subsequent queries by the same client or any other client. These entries are cached for only a short period of time, equal to the Time To Live (ttl) value applied to the record. When a client requests a particular domain name resolution, the DNS server will first attempt to find the records in its local database. If this search fails, the DNS server will attempt to contact a root name server, if it's been configured to do so, to request the value.

Another important function that the DNS servers provide is the replication of the DNS table, also known as a zone transfer. The zone transfer insures that all entries for a given zone will be available on all DNS servers in that zone. This is necessary so that DNS can provide a resilient operating architecture. Two types of zone transfers can be found between DNS servers: full and incremental. A full zone transfer is exactly as it sounds, a complete transfer of zone information between DNS servers. An incremental zone transfer, on the other hand, is one where only changed zone information is exchanged between DNS servers. Incremental zone transfers make more efficient use of bandwidth and network resources, but not all DNS server vendors support the newer implementation.

Zone transfers are based on several items, including serial numbers and refresh intervals. The secondary DNS server will request a zone transfer from the primary DNS server and there is a serial number embedded in the response. If the secondary server receives the response and the serial number is lower than or equal to the serial number of its current table version, the response will not be used to update the server's table. However, if the serial number is higher, the DNS table will be updated to what is enclosed in the response.

The refresh interval is used to identify how often the secondary server should request a zone transfer from the primary server. It is used as a polling mechanism to help ensure that the secondary server remains up-to-date with the current DNS information. NOTIFY messages may also be used by the primary DNS server to tell the secondary DNS servers when changes have been made to the DNS table. When the secondary DNS server receives the NOTIFY, they can request a zone transfer to ensure table synchronization.

Security Implications for DNS

DNS is a core component of modern networking, and as such, is a rather attractive target for many attackers. When the DNS architecture was developed, security was not included as part of the design. There was nothing designed into the architecture for peer authentication, origin authentication, or data encryption. Some recent advancements in DNS have helped to alleviate some of the current security concerns, but they have not been able to remove them altogether.

The dangers of DNS are well publicized and well documented, owing to its long life on the Internet. More information on these security threats, how they are performed, and how to protect your DNS servers can be found at *www.dnssec.net/dns-threats.php*. There is also an RFC on DNS Threats, published as RFC 3833. Several types of attacks should be kept in mind regarding your DNS deployment, and some best practices can be employed to help lessen your exposure:

- DNS footprinting (using DNS zone data to learn host names, subdomains, and subnets)
- Denial of Service (DoS)
  1. SYN flooding of DNS server
  2. Transfer of blank DNS table
- DNS cache poisoning

TFTP

The Trivial File Transfer Protocol (TFTP) is a simplified protocol used to transfer files from a server to a client. Unlike more evolved file protocols, such as FTP, TFTP was designed to work in pure simplicity, requiring less overhead and interaction. Its primary usage today is in computers and devices that do not have storage devices, commonly known as "thin client PCs." Without offline storage, especially one that can be updated, it is difficult to maintain how such devices can operate. Instead of booting off of a hard drive or flash ROM, these devices use TFTP to request data from a central server to boot from. Or, such devices can boot from internal ROM memory and use TFTP to request configuration data to use during their operation. Also, devices can use TFTP to request firmware updates which they can then flash to their ROM chips to update the built-in software code. This is especially useful since customized sets of data can be stored for individual user devices within a corporate environment.

The role of TFTP in transferring data is well used throughout the computer industry. Virtually all modern computers support the ability to boot from the network. In this mode, the computer will attempt to locate a TFTP server on its network segment once it boots. In finding one, the client requests a bootable image from the server, usually in the form of a floppy disk image. Once it has received the data, the client will then proceed to boot from the image, as if it was an actual floppy disk or CD-ROM.

In the VoIP community, TFTP has a critical role in allowing VoIP devices and telephones to obtain configuration data from centralized servers. These devices are built with internal Flash ROM memory chips that contain simplified hardware architecture that does not allow for continual write access to memory. Instead, data is only written once to the device's memory and read continuously by the internal operating system.

The TFTP protocol was first described in 1980 as IEN (Internet Experiment Note) 133. Its first formal RFC was RFC 783, which was later updated in RFC 1350. However, there are various RFCs that also describe individual actions and abilities that TFTP could be used for. These include Bootstrap loading (RFC 906) and TFTP multicasting (RFC 2090). The next few sections of the chapter detail a high-level overview of the TFTP architecture and several related security threats associated with the protocol.

TFTP

In order to better understand and be able to address the security concerns associated with TFTP properly, it is important to have at least a high-level understanding of how TFTP works. Unlike most other file transfer protocols, TFTP operates by transmitting UDP packets. While connection-less UDP packets are generally frowned upon for reliable data transmissions, they allow for a simpler implementation into the protocol, as well as faster transfer speeds. The abilities of the protocol are also very limited, allowing only for the ability to read and write data. The protocol does not have any mechanism displaying information about available files and directories on a server. The client must know the name of the file that they wish to download when connecting.

There are very strict regulations on how data is sent between computers, which allows for client applications to be written easier. Similar to the FTP protocol, TFTP allows for data to be sent as either ASCII or binary. This data is sent in individual UDP packets between the two devices. Of these packets, five types can be transmitted, each one identified by an operation code in the header of the data.

- Read Request (RRQ)
- Write Request (WRQ)
- Data
- Acknowledgement (ACK)
- Error

TFTP File Transfer Operation

When a client wishes to download a file from a TFTP server, it first sends a Read Request (RRQ) packet to the TFTP server. This packet identifies itself as an RRQ packet, and also specifies both the name of the file the client wishes to download and the data mode (binary or ASCII). Likewise, if the client wishes to upload a file to a TFTP server, it sends an identical Write Request (WRQ) packet, which also contains the file name and data mode. The sending computer then immediately starts sending data packets to the recipient computer. If the data is greater than 512 bytes in size, multiple packets will be sent. A packet that contains a data portion smaller than 512 bytes is seen as the last packet in the transfer. Following the receipt of each data packet, the receiving computer sends an acknowledgement (ACK) packet to the sender, notifying it that the transfer was successful. Figure 8.4 details this transfer of data between two computers.

Figure 8.4 TFTP Data Transferral

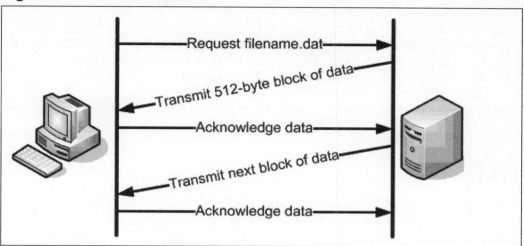

Security Implications for TFTP

Insomuch that TFTP was designed for simplicity and ease of use, any mechanisms normally used to secure data were not implemented into its protocol. It was originally planned by engineers that usernames and passwords should not ever be required for TFTP access, but this has led to many security issues. This concern is also greater because all TFTP packets are sent in the clear across a network, with no data encryption. Given there is no authentication, and no encryption, TFTP is generally not recommended for the transfer of sensitive data. However, its role as a "bootstrap protocol" could allow usernames and passwords to be transferred in the clear across a network when these aren't protected by higher-level mechanisms. Since TFTP is often used to download boot images from a remote server, which often contain sensitive data required to connect into various servers on the network, it is possible to retrieve stored account information from within these boot images. Any person who is capturing network traffic on the same network segment as the TFTP session could easily gather the transferred data and re-create the original file. If the file contains sensitive data, such as usernames and passwords, it would then be readily available to anyone capturing the traffic.

> **WARNING**
>
> The TFTP protocol sends all data in clear text across the network. As it is commonly used to transfer configuration data to devices and clients, it is important to verify that there is no sensitive data contained within transferred data. Otherwise, anyone sniffing the wire could have access to various usernames and passwords used by such devices.

HTTP

The HyperText Transfer Protocol (HTTP) is one of the most well known, and well used, protocols on the Internet. It is the protocol by which Web pages are transmitted from Web servers to clients, but it is also used by many other applications to send data between computers. For example, many peer-to-peer clients make use of the solid structure of HTTP to transfer data segments of shared files between peers. HTTP can be used to transmit both ASCII and binary data between computers.

HTTP is commonly used in the VoIP community as a way for administrators to remotely administer and configure devices. Many network management devices offer a Web-based administration panel by which the device can be altered and configured for a particular environment. Many such devices also require user authentication to be able to fully access the configuration data.

HTTP was first described in RFC 1945 at HTTP 1.0 by its founder, Tim Berners-Lee. Currently, RFC 2616 is used to describe the HTTP 1.1 protocol; however, various other RFCs describe additional extensions and uses for the HTTP protocol. These include HTTP Authentication (RFC 2617), Secure HTTP (RFC 2660), and CGI (RFC 3875).

HTTP Protocol

The function of HTTP and its protocol was designed to be very straightforward and usable by many applications. When a client wishes to request a file from an HTTP server, it simply creates a TCP session with the server and transmits a GET command with the name of the requested file and the HTTP protocol version (for example, GET /index.html HTTP/1.1). The HTTP server then responds back with the appropriate data. The response from the server will be either the data requested by the client, or an error message describing why it cannot send the data. All of the commands within the HTTP protocol are sent in regular ASCII text, with each line followed by a carriage return/line feed (CR/LF). In network logs, the CR/LF appear as hexadecimal 0x0D0A.

HTTP Client Request

For a client to retrieve data from an HTTP server, it must know the exact filename and location to construct an appropriate file request. For most purposes, this information is supplied in the form of a uniform resource locator (URL), which specifies a particular HTTP server, directory path, and file name (for example, www.digg.com/faq/index.php). When a client wishes to view this specific page, index.php, it must first make a connection to www.digg.com. This is performed by resolving the domain name to an IP through DNS, which results in the IP address of 64.191.203.30. The client then initiates a TCP connection to 64.191.203.30 and makes a request of GET /faq/index.php HTTP/1.1. This request also includes other information about the client, some of which may be required for HTTP 1.1, such as the host value. An example of a full HTTP GET request is shown next:

```
GET /download.html HTTP/1.1
Host: www.ethereal.com
User-Agent: Mozilla/5.0 (Windows; U; Windows NT 5.1; en-US; rv:1.6)
Gecko/20040113
Accept: \
text/xml,application/xml,application/xhtml+xml,text/html;q=0.9,text/plain; \
q=0.8,image/png,image/jpeg,image/gif;q=0.2,*/*;q=0.1
Accept-Language: en-us,en;q=0.5
Accept-Encoding: gzip,deflate
Accept-Charset: ISO-8859-1,utf-8;q=0.7,*;q=0.7
Keep-Alive: 300
Connection: keep-alive
Referer: http://www.ethereal.com/development.html
```

HTTP Server Response

Upon receiving a GET request from a client, a server first ensures that the file requested does exist. If it does, the data is then sent back to the requesting client. If not, an error message is sent. Regardless of the action, a specific server response is sent back to the client that includes a status code. This status code informs the client of the response type. The most common is a 200 code, which informs the client that the file was found and will be sent. It is transmitted in the form of HTTP/1.1 200 OK, which specifies the HTTP protocol version, the status code, and a brief description of the code. Other common status codes include "404 Not Found," which indicates that the requested file could not be located by the server, and "500 Internet Server Error," which indicates that there is a problem with the HTTP server. The following is an example of an HTTP response:

```
HTTP/1.1 200 OK
Date: Thu, 13 May 2004 10:17:12 GMT
Server: Apache
Last-Modified: Tue, 20 Apr 2004 13:17:00 GMT
Accept-Ranges: bytes
Content-Length: 18070
Keep-Alive: timeout=15, max=100
Connection: Keep-Alive
Content-Type: text/html; charset=ISO-8859-1
```

Security Implications for HTTP

Due to the simple design of HTTP, and the early state of the Internet when it was unveiled, security wasn't a high priority in the protocol. All data sent through HTTP was sent as clear text, which allowed any person to be able to sniff the traffic flowing across the wire and parse out sensitive data, such as usernames, passwords, and network configuration data. This is particularly dangerous since many VoIP and network management devices use HTTP as a means to allow administrators to check the status of the device and to configure additional settings. A person with malicious intent on the same network segment as the device could pick out various usernames and passwords that may work on additional computers or devices.

HTTP also supports multiple forms of authentication, which is a means by which the HTTP server can verify a user's identity. The two authentication forms currently used are basic and digest authentications. When a server supports authentication, it sends a 401 "Authentication Required" response to clients that request sensitive data. This response will also include a "realm" (a name associated with the Web site) that notifies the user what they are accessing. When a client receives such a response, it will provide a log-in window to the user to input a valid user name and password. These values will then be transmitted back to the requesting server for verification. Because of HTTP's design, though, these credentials will have to be constantly transmitted to the server for every further data transmission. Each of these transactions will transmit the user name and password in the clear.

Another form of authentication supported by modern HTTP clients and servers is digest authentication, which is described in depth in RFC 2617. Digest authentication has an advantage over basic authentication in that it does not send a clear password over the network. Instead, an MD5 (Message Digest) value of the password is transmitted to the requesting server. The server then uses this digest value for password comparisons. However, digest authentication is not fully supported in many older Web browsers. It also does not fully protect a user's credentials. The user name and other information about the user are still transmitted in the clear. And, even though the password is obfuscated, a skilled, malicious user can still capture the MD5 value and use it for future transactions with that particular server to use another person's account.

Many devices have recently provided support for HTTPS to overcome the openness of the HTTP protocol. HTTPS is a modification of HTTP wherein all data between a client and server are encrypted using the Secure Sockets Layers (SSL). In order for HTTPS to function, both the server and the client must be able to support it, and it must be specifically chosen as the form of communication in the URL. For example, instead of http://www.foo.com, a secure connection would use https://www.foo.com.

SNMP

SNMP, short for Simple Network Management Protocol, is a high-level protocol and architecture that allows for the monitoring and maintenance of network devices to detect problems, and to fine-tune the network for performance. There are two key versions of SNMP in use today, SNMPv1 and SNMPv2. While the two share many commonalities, there are some very beneficial additions made to SNMPv2. However, as many people disagreed with the security profiles implemented into SNMPv2, it has remained less popular and less used than SNMPv1. Since that time, a newer version of SNMP was released: the Community-Based SNMP, or SNMPv2c. However, the current standard, adopted in 2004, is SNMPv3. SNMP plays a useful role in maintaining and administering VoIP networks by allowing a person the ability to easily monitor the bandwidth and performance of all the major components of a network.

The SNMP protocol is defined under RFC 1157 as SNMPv1, and the characteristics of its immediate successor, SNMPv2, are defined in RFC 1902. SNMPv2c is officially detailed in RFC 1901 and in RFC 1908. SNMPv3 is defined in RFC 3411 and RFC 3418.

SNMP Architecture

An SNMP implementation on a network involves three components to be integrated: the devices to be managed, agents, and Network Management Systems (NMSes). The devices to be managed are simply computers or devices on the network that reside on the network. These are the devices that an administrator would like to monitor on the network. Each device must have an agent installed on them, which is a software application that continually monitors the device for predefined events or errors and transmits them to a centralized management server, an NMS.

The NMS collects all of the data that is routinely transferred from the various network devices and correlates it into useful information for an administrator to read and evaluate.

However, even with all of these components working together on a network, there still must be a structure to all of the individual data that can be gathered across a network by an NMS. This is implemented by the use of a Management Information Base (MIB). See Figure 8.5 for a diagram on how these components work together.

Figure 8.5 SNMP Network Components

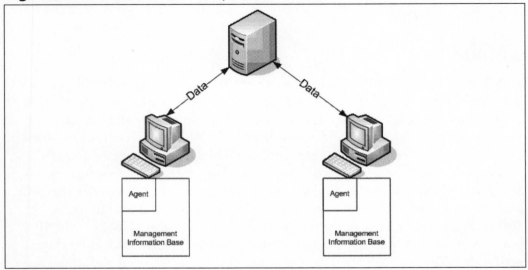

SNMP Operation

The SNMP protocol works under a very simplified model of data collection and control of the managed devices. Only a few basic commands are used in the SNMP protocol, such as GETREQUEST, GETNEXTREQUEST, SETREQUEST, and TRAP. An NMS invokes GETREQUEST to collect data from a device, and GETNEXTREQUEST to retrieve the next value in a set. An NMS can also invoke the SETREQUEST command to save data to a managed device. The TRAP command is the only one not initiated by the NMS; it is sent out by the client to report any unusual activity it has detected.

On the client side, the Management Information Base (MIB) acts as a tree that catalogs all of the various data components of the system or device. Each of these data components are known by their object identifiers (OIDs). The OID is made up of multiple sets of numbers, each separated by a period, in a structured order similar to that of an IP address. As a general rule, all OIDs begin with .1.3.6.1.2.1, except on many Cisco devices which use .1.3.6.1.4.1.9. To request a data value, an established OID must be specified. For example, to request the system up time, OID .1.3.6.1.2.1.1.2 is read.

SNMP Architecture

The SNMP protocol has many areas that require careful attention and configuration simply due to the amount of information that could be leaked out to malicious users. Since all of this data is retrievable by anyone requesting it, there must be some safeguards put in place to prevent unauthorized users from being able to read data, or modify it. This is performed by the use of a community string. A community string acts as a password to group data into either read-only or read-write areas. By default, most software is setup to use a default community string of "public" for their read-only data. Likewise, many implementations use a default community string of "private" for their read-write data. It is particularly dangerous to leave such community strings in place, as they are well known to malicious users, and an unchanged read-write community string allows an attacker the ability to modify critical data on a device.

Are You Owned?

Are You Allowing Sensitive Data to Be Leaked?

Due to the open nature of SNMP, allowing any person to easily request data, unique community strings should be defined for network components that you can administer. Proper care must also be taken in evaluating IP telephones to ensure that they do not have unsecured SNMP access available. Otherwise, all of your SNMP-enabled components, such as workstations, servers, routers, and phones, can disclose sensitive information to anyone who asks. Unless you are constantly monitoring network traffic, you may not even know that this information is being gathered by malicious people within your network environment—or, even worse, being modified to cover unauthorized actions.

This issue came to light recently when it was discovered that the Cisco 7920 Wireless IP Phone contained a fixed community string that allowed malicious users to gather and modify data on the devices. The vulnerability and its fix were given a Cisco bug ID of CSCsb75186. They can also be reviewed at http://securitytracker.com/id?1015232.

Continued

Likewise, similar SNMP vulnerabilities surfaced with the Hitachi IP5000 phone. These devices did not have a protected community string, which meant that any person could have full SNMP access to all of the data on the device, including the ability to alter and erase it.

On a lesser scale, the UTstarcom F1000 IP phone featured the default public community string, which allowed anyone to view data stored on the phone, some of which could be considered sensitive. Additionally, when using SNMP scanning software, the phone suffered from numerous SNMP issues that required a full reboot to fix.

DHCP

The Dynamic Host Configuration Protocol (DHCP) is a protocol that was designed to allow network configuration of clients and workstations. Every workstation and device that is making use of a network must be assigned a unique IP address, as well as assigned a subnet mask and gateway IP address. In a network environment where there are hundreds, or thousands, of workstations, this could become an administrative nightmare. DHCP is a popular answer to this problem, automatically assigning IP addresses and other relevant configuration information to each individual device as it comes online.

DHCP is a critical support protocol in the VoIP world because it allows VoIP phones and devices to be portable from one network to another. Instead of manually configuring the device after plugging it into each network, the device simply "pings" the network to find an existing DHCP server. The device then automatically receives an IP address and network details from the server and is then immediately useable on the network, without any interaction with the user.

The DHCP protocol was first discussed in RFC 1531 and RFC 1541 in 1993. Currently, RFC 2131 describes DHCP, and has made the previous RFCs obsolete. There are many RFCs that describe additional extensions and uses for DHCP, though—for example, DHCP for IEEE 1394 (RFC 2855) and DHCP for SIP servers (RFC 3361).

DHCP Protocol

The primary function of DHCP is to supply critical network information to clients automatically, to reduce the effort of a network administrator in manually configuring various devices on a network. For DHCP to work, there must be a DHCP server (or relay) running on the network segment where clients will be connecting. The DHCP server listens constantly for incoming UDP packets on port 67, a port reserved for DHCP usage. When a new, DHCP-enabled device is connected to the network, it sends a broadcast packet to detect any running DHCP servers. The DHCP server then responds with a DHCP offer, which contains an assigned IP address.

Eight types of packets are used within the DHCP protocol:

- Discover
- Offer
- Request
- Decline
- ACK
- NAK
- Release
- Inform

DHCP Operation

When a client first joins a network, either by being plugged into the network segment or by being powered on, it does not have an IP address assigned to it. In order to request one, it sends a DHCP Discover packet across the network. It does so by sending a packet from IP address 0.0.0.0 to the broadcast IP address 255.255.255.255, which allows the packet to reach every single device on the network segment. This packet may include information about the client itself, such as the network interface's MAC address and the computer's designated host name.

Once a server has received a DHCP Discover packet, it immediately checks its preset range (scope) of IP addresses to determine the next available number. Optionally, the DHCP server will also compare the requestor's MAC address against a local table to determine if the client is allowed to receive an IP address. After an address has been chosen, a DHCP Offer packet is transmitted back to the requesting client, targeted by its MAC address. This packet includes the assigned IP address, the lease time of the IP address, subnet mask, gateway address, and chosen DNS servers, as well as other network information that is to be implemented into the client.

Once the client has received a DHCP Offer packet, it responds with a DHCP Request packet. This packet is similar to the original DHCP Discover packet in that it is sent from 0.0.0.0 to 255.255.255.255. This packet serves to notify the server that the client has accepted the assigned IP address, and also notifies all other clients on the network segment that the assigned IP address has been taken. Finally, the server responds back to the client with a DHCP Acknowledgement (ACK) to confirm the address has Request has been received. This communication between the client and DHCP server is detailed in Figure 8.6.

Figure 8.6 The DHCP Process

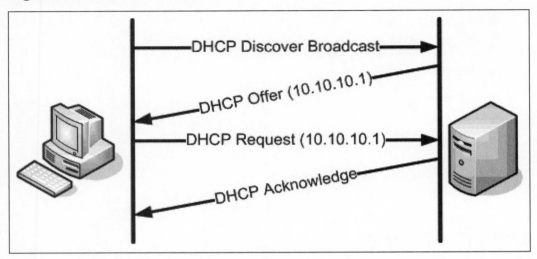

Security Implications for DHCP

A variety of security concerns come into play whenever DHCP is enabled on a network segment. These security issues don't deal so much with leaked data such as passwords. Instead, they focus more on access into a network from unauthorized clients. A basic DHCP server runs under the assumption that any DHCP Discover and Request should be honored as an authorized client. In this setup, any device that requests network information will be able to receive it, no questions asked. However, this opens the door for any person with physical access to the network to be able to plug in unauthorized devices and receive network access.

A number of ways exist to reduce this network exposure, from modifying the network switches to modifying the DHCP configuration. Most of these security implementations involve verifying the MAC address of the client device before allowing it to receive an IP address. One of the more extensive fixes is to enable port security on the implemented network switches. With port security in place, the physical connection port can be locked to allow only a single MAC address access through it. This can help prevent employees, or contractors, from installing a small network hub or wireless router, and giving multiple devices access to the network.

However, an easier method is to provide DHCP addresses just to devices that have a particular MAC address assigned to them. All network devices have a MAC address coded into them, and these addresses follow a set structure. The first six bytes of the MAC address specifies the vendor ID, or the company that manufactured the device. If you wish to restrict DHCP to just particular VoIP phones or devices on your network, this is possible by identifying the vendor ID on the devices and configuring the DHCP server to provide addresses only to devices that have the same vendor ID. For example, Grandstream Networks VoIP phones all have a vendor ID of 00:0B:82.

Another security issue that can arise with DHCP is coupled with TFTP, and the security risks associated with it. If a network uses a TFTP server to transmit bootable disk images to computers, much of the configuration material to specify where these particular disk images are located is located within the DHCP responses. When clients receive a DHCP offer, they can choose to take advantage of this information, depending on their boot states. However, a malicious user could monitor these packets to determine the location of any TFTP servers, as well as the particular files used on these servers.

TIP

To ease the installation of IP telephones, create a separate scope of IP addresses with a MAC filter to only allow IP telephones to lease an address. Collect the unique vendor IDs from the authorized telephones to create this filter.

RSVP

RSVP, short for the **R**esource Re**S**er**V**ation **P**rotocol, is a protocol designed to allow clients on networks to negotiate bandwidth to provide and maintain a high Quality of Service (QoS) for a specific connection. Normally, TCP/IP will make a best effort to route packets from one machine to another as quickly as possible. However, due to the dynamic routing of internetworking, where packets take completely different routes each time they are transmitted, this cannot be guaranteed. This creates a special issue for VoIP communication, which requires a high QoS to maintain seamless and non-interruptive communication between two people. VoIP can be an especially demanding protocol that requires long periods of high bandwidth and low latency, and without RSVP, these conditions may fall below acceptable levels which could result in a loss of quality or disconnections. RSVP allows a dedicated path across a network between each client so that packets are routed randomly around, which retains a high level of bandwidth, and less latency. RSVP is especially useful for

WAN connections within a global organization to maintain these set paths inside a network, as many Internet routers do not support the protocol.

The RSVP protocol was first described in RFC 2205 in late 1997. Further modifications were made to this RFC, and the best current practices for the RSVP protocol are now discussed in RFC 3936, created in late 2004. There are also other RFCs that describe additional extensions and uses for the RSVP protocol. These include RSVP for LSP Tunnels (RFC 3209) and RSVP security properties (RFC 4230).

RSVP Protocol

The RSVP protocol works by transferring UDP packets from the recipient of the data transfer to its sender. This allows the data recipient to control whether to use regular TCP/IP or to use a dedicated path of travel between the two clients. The connection recipient initiates this path by sending a constructed RSVP packet to the connection initiator. This packet will contain a specific Message Type that indicates the action that should be acted upon. The common Message Types for an RSVP protocol are

- Path
- Resv (Reservation Request)
- PathErr (Path Error)
- ResvErr (Reservation Error)
- PathTear (Path Teardown)
- ResvTear (Reservation Teardown)
- ResvConf (Reservation Confirmation)

The RSVP packet also carries a data payload containing specific information on how the path should be constructed. The payload contains information such as:

- Session (Destination IP, Tunnel ID, Extended Tunnel ID)
- Hop (the neighboring router's IP)
- Time Values (the refresh interval)
- Explicit Route (a list of routers between the two devices that creates the data path)
- Adspec (specifies the minimum path latency, MTU, and bandwidth requirements)

RSVP Operation

To create a dedicated path of travel, the RSVP protocol relies heavily on its Path and Resv messages. The Path message packet is used to define the path of routers to be used for communication between the two clients. This packet is sent from the receiving end of the communication towards the sender. As it passes through each individual router, the router examines the packet to determine its neighboring IP addresses, to which it must route packets to. The Resv message, or Reservation request, is equally important. The Resv message is sent from each router to its neighboring router, one hop at a time. The Resv packet helps create the reservation on each router involved in the path. The transfer of Path and Resv packets is detailed in Figure 8.7.

Figure 8.7 Creating an RSVP Path

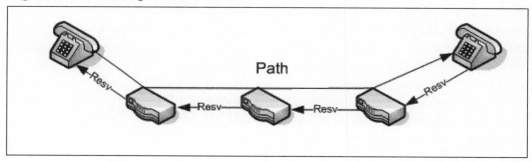

Once a path has been created, with each router maintaining a reservation for the data, it must be updated routinely to remain open. If a router has not received a Resv and Path packet before the refresh interval on the path has been exhausted, then the router will remove the reservation from itself. As Resv and Path packets arrive to maintain the reservation, they may also make changes to it. If the path between the clients is to change to substitute routers, the recipient just sends a new Path message with the updated path and it will become effective. Each router will continually update its stored information based on the packets it continually receives during the transmission.

Once the communication between the two devices has ended, they initiate a teardown of the path. Although, realistically they could just stop transmitting RSVP packets and eventually the reservations on the routers would expire, it is recommended that they formally tear down the path immediately after finishing the connection. The teardown may be initiated by either side of the communication, or from any of the routers within the communication. A PathTear packet may be sent downstream from the sender, or a ResvTear may be sent upstream from the receiver.

As each router in the path receives a teardown packet, they will immediately remove the path reservation and forward the packet onto the next hop in the path.

Security Implications for RSVP

Many of the security issues with the RSVP protocol involve actions that a person with malicious intentions could take to either disrupt traffic or capture it. For one, as the Path and Resc packets are transmitted across the network, they each include a session ID that can be used to uniquely identify a particular RSVP session. This data is also sent as clear text, where anyone who is armed with a network sniffer can capture the data. Knowing the session ID, a person could then use the same session ID and send a Path message to one of the routers in the path. This new Path could alter the path of the network, leading the network transmission to a completely different client than intended. Or, it could be used to disrupt the communication completely, preventing an RSVP connection to take place between the two devices.

There are various solutions that have come about to resolve issues like this. For one, the Session ID could be encoded into a public key that will be included in each packet, as well as a timestamp that acts as a digital signature. If the two devices are within the same localized network, a third-party server could be used to establish the identities of each device. Many such security implications and solutions were drafted by various authors, including Hannes Tschofenig, in an Internet Draft located at www.tschofenig.com/drafts/draft-ietf-nsis-rsvp-sec-properties-06.txt.

SDP

SDP, short for Session Description Protocol, is a simple protocol that allows clients to share information about a multimedia stream to clients wishing to connect. Further extensions on the protocol also allow clients to share their multimedia abilities with other devices. As its name denotes, it is used primarily to describe a client's session abilities. It plays an integral part in VoIP communications to share the fact that a communication session is taking place, and to provide information to other clients so that they have the ability to join and interact with the session, such as with a group teleconference.

SDP was first described in RFC 2327 in April 1998, and the original RFC still defines the protocol's basic abilities today. There are updates, though, to the RFC, such as RFC 3266, which adds IPv6 support to SDP. Other associated RFCs include the RTCP attribute in SDP (RFC 3605), TCP-Based Media Transport in SDP (RFC 4145) and PSTN/Internet Interworking (PINT), a set of extensions to SIP and SDP for IP Access to Telephone Call Services (RFC 2848). A fairly recent RFC, RFC 3407, allowed the clients the ability to share their multimedia abilities to other devices.

SDP Specifications

SDP is used as a specification protocol, not as an actual transport protocol (or even a session negotiation protocol, although higher-level protocols like SIP may add that capability above it). In other words, SDP does not actually transfer data between clients, it just establishes a structure for communicating the attributes for those data streams. The data must be transferred using another transport protocol, such as SAP, SIP, RTSP, or HTTP. The information contained within an SDP packet is in ASCII text, and although it was not designed for human readability, it is easy to decipher. An SDP packet is broken into multiple lines of text, where each line represents a single field and its corresponding value. Common data fields include

- **v** (Protocol Version)
- **o** (Owner of session, Session ID, Session Version, Network Type, Address type, and Owner's IP Address)
- **s** (Session name)
- **i** (Session description)
- **u** (URI of subject material)
- **e** (E-mail address of Session Point of Contact)
- **p** (Phone number of Session Point of Contact)
- **c** (Connection information: IP version and CIDR IP address)
- **k** (Encryption key as clear text, base64, uri, or prompt)
- **m** (Media type, connection port, transport method, and format list)
- **t** (Session begin and end times)
- **a** (Attribute)

The following is an example of SDP data for supplying capabilities:

```
v=0
o=bsmith 2208988800 2208988800 IN IP4 68.33.152.147
s=-
e=bsmith@foo.com
c=IN IP4 20.1.25.50
t=0 0
a=recvonly
m=audio 0 RTP/AVP 0 1 101
a=rtpmap:0 PCMU/8000
```

```
a=rtpmap:1 GSM/8000
a=rtpmap:101 telephone-event/8000
```

SDP Operation

Once a device has been queried, usually by a client sending an SIP request, it forms an SDP packet to send back. This SDP packet supplies all of the critical information about the session capabilities that the device offers. In its simplest form, this data contains the owner information, the audio and video codecs supported, and which ports connections are accepted on. In queries for particular sessions, the reply contains the session name, the session description, connection ports, and the range of time when the session will be active. All time stamps in SDP data are formed using Network Time Protocol (NTP) values. Additionally, the session ID and session version, which must be unique values, are generally created using NTP values to signify the current date and time.

Much of the current SDP usage is documented in RFC 4317, which describes the SDP Offer/Answer model. In this model, when a client wishes to communicate with another, it transmits an SDP offer packet. This packet is arranged in a structure similar to the following example, provided by RFC 4317:

```
v=0
o=alice 2890844526 2890844526 IN IP4 host.atlanta.example.com
s=
c=IN IP4 host.atlanta.example.com
t=0 0
m=audio 49170 RTP/AVP 0 8 97
a=rtpmap:0 PCMU/8000
a=rtpmap:8 PCMA/8000
a=rtpmap:97 iLBC/8000
m=video 51372 RTP/AVP 31 32
a=rtpmap:31 H261/90000
a=rtpmap:32 MPV/90000
```

Reading through this packet, you can see that the owner line describes that the packet sender is "alice," who is listening for connections on host.atlanta.example.com. This data is sent to the person with whom she wishes to communicate. Once the other person has received the data and wishes to continue the connection, an answer packet is returned. Here is an example of this answer:

```
v=0
o=bob 2808844564 2808844564 IN IP4 host.biloxi.example.com
```

```
s=
c=IN IP4 host.biloxi.example.com
t=0 0
m=audio 49174 RTP/AVP 0
a=rtpmap:0 PCMU/8000
m=video 49170 RTP/AVP 32
a=rtpmap:32 MPV/90000
```

In this example, Alice is initiating a connection with Bob. Alice's Offer packet identifies that she supports three types of audio connections (PCMU, PCMIA, and iLBC), as well as two types of video connections (H.261 and MPV). Once Bob's client has received the invitation and parsed the values, it chooses a compatible audio and video format and responds back. In the answer packet shown earlier in this chapter, Bob's client responds back wishing to communicate with PCMU audio and MPV video.

Security Implications for SDP

Similar to the security issues of RSVP, much of the security implications for SDP arise due to the fact that a person can easily read session IDs and connection information off of a network segment and then tamper with existing communications. In seeing existing connection offers, and their corresponding SDP replies, an eavesdropper could use the information to determine devices that are allowing VoIP communications, and also spoof his way into an existing communication. An attacker may also be able to collect SDP offers and replay them at a later time, overriding values for ongoing communications, with the potential to disable audio feeds. However, nearly all security issues with SDP can be solved by using protocols to handle user authentication, such as SIP.

Skinny

The Skinny protocol is the casual name for a complex, lightweight VoIP protocol signaling scheme owned by Cisco Systems, Inc., and is in use for all VoIP telephones that Cisco produces. The formal name is SCCP, for Skinny Client Control Protocol, and was originally designed by the Selsius Corporation, which Cisco acquired. Skinny is a proprietary protocol that allows "skinny clients", such as Cisco IP telephones, to communicate with each other via Cisco CallManager (CCM). The Skinny clients are small, user-friendly devices that work in conjunction with a CCM. The CCM also acts as a proxy to relay communications to H.323 clients and the PSTN.

Skinny Specifications

Skinny (SCCP) is the exclusive protocol used by Cisco brand IP telephones, as well as some phones developed by other manufacturers. Using the Skinny protocol, an IP phone will use normal TCP/IP to communicate with the Cisco CallManager. If the Cisco phone needs to communicate with a non-Skinny client, then the CCM acts as a proxy gateway, allowing the two to communicate, at which time the phones will start using UDP. However, when a Skinny phone wishes to communicate with another Skinny phone, the two will use RTP/UDP packets for communication.

Skinny Operation

The ability for Skinny clients to communicate with each other is governed by the Cisco CallManager (CCM) on the same network. When an IP phone wishes to dial another on the same network, the user takes the phone off-hook and begins dialing the necessary numbers. As the numbers are entered, they are transmitted to the CCM over TCP packets. The CCM performs a "digit analysis" to determine if they match another phone number in the database. If so, the CCM communicates with the receiving phone, causing it to start ringing and to send a ring back to the calling phone. Once the second phone goes off-hook, the CCM sends packets to both phones requesting their IP address and open UDP port on which to accept the RTP media. The CCM also checks the media capabilities of each phone to determine if they can directly communicate with each other, or if a transcoder is required to allow the communication. Once the CCM has received the connection information from each phone, it proceeds to transmit the information to the other phone, so that each phone has the connection information of its peer. At this point, the CCM creates an RTP/UDP channel for the phones to pass data through for communication. Once either of the phones goes on-hook and disconnects the line, the CCM terminates the channel. An example of this connection process is shown in Figure 8.8.

Figure 8.8 The Skinny Client Communication Process

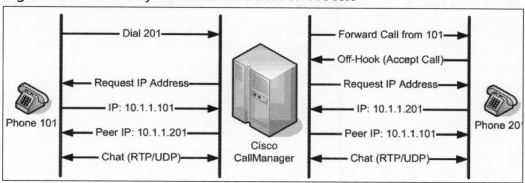

Security Implications for Skinny

Similar in implications to the other protocols discussed previously, the largest problem with the Skinny (SCCP) protocol is the fact that all traffic that uses it is sent in the clear, with no encryption taking place unless the device is capable and configured to support Transport Layer Security (TLS). Ultimately, this means that people with malicious intent on the same network segment are able to capture the traffic using a network sniffer. This allows such people to store recorded conversations, or to even capture the numbers that a particular phone dials during a time period.

NOTE

While the SCCP/Skinny protocol was not designed for the transfer of secure data, some protocols are. Cisco CallManager 4.0 introduced Secure SCCP, or simply "Secure Skinny" to add beefier security to a Cisco VoIP network. Secure SCCP encrypts all data between IP telephones and the Cisco CallManager using TLS.

Certain Cisco CallManager versions also suffer from a known vulnerability. This vulnerability takes advantage of malformed SCCP packets sent to a vulnerable Cisco IOS (internal operating system). If successful, the exploit is able to cause devices, or the entire CCM, to reboot. The issue is documented as Cisco bug ID CSCee08584, and can be fixed up upgrading or migrating the IOS of the affected hardware.

Summary

While there are more popular and interesting protocols in place to handle much of the VoIP traffic on networks and the Internet, there is also a very important set of support protocols that doesn't share as much of the limelight. These protocols are crucial in making sure VoIP networks can operate, and that individual clients can communicate with each other quickly and efficiently. However, they also all have their own specific security risks and implications when implemented.

DNS is one such protocol which is required for most usage on the Internet. As the means by which domain names are resolved to IP addresses, it has ultimate control over where to send clients that are asking for directions to a particular machine. Proper care must be taken to ensure that network clients are using appropriate DNS servers that can be trusted to direct devices properly. TFTP is mentioned as one of the primary protocols used to transfer small data files between a server and a device. Though its primary usage is in transferring bootable images to thin clients, TFTP is also critical in supplying configuration information to devices that do not have the means to store data. However, this configuration information could be sensitive in nature, if it contains authentication information, and due to the protocol design, it will be sent in the clear on the network, allowing anyone listening to gather it. HTTP is one of the most popular, and well-used, protocols in use today and is the primary means for users to download data from Web servers. It is also commonly used in other applications and areas as a way to transfer data between computers. However, if SSL is not used, the information is also sent in the clear and is thus visible to network sniffers.

SNMP is one of the more useful protocols for network administrators since it allows applications to create a central repository of data involving all networked devices on a network segment. This data can then be used to monitor network activity, improve performance, or locate and resolve issues as they occur. It is also a protocol implemented into many VoIP telephones in use today. However, as shown earlier, many implementations of SNMP were not done correctly in some IP phone models, allowing malicious users to gather, modify, or erase data contained within these devices. DHCP is another useful protocol for many network administrators across the world. DHCP allows IP addresses to be leased out to computers as they come online, abolishing the practice of manually configuring each and every network device with a unique IP address. The use of DHCP allows for a greater number of devices to use a network during a day since many components are not running continuously. However, it dangerously supplies IP addresses and network information to unauthorized clients. Various methods of protecting your network from this are available, however, as discussed in this chapter.

RSVP is an important protocol in the VoIP world since it allows for static pathways to be constructed between two VoIP telephones across a network, or the Internet. This pathway uses Quality of Service controls to maintain a high-bandwidth connection between the two devices to avoid static and dropped connections. However, due to its unencrypted design, it is also possible for unauthorized users to track the pathways, and even change them in mid-stream, severing communications between devices. SDP was also mentioned as a data format protocol used to provide information about an ongoing telephony session, or to just provide information about what protocols a particular device is capable of communicating with. Its open design allows unauthorized users to detect and track ongoing communication sessions, and to even disrupt them. Finally, the Skinny (SCCP) protocol was discussed, being Cisco Systems proprietary protocol used for their internal VoIP network implementations. The Skinny protocol uses the Cisco CallManager system to make connections to other telephones within the network segment, or to devices on other network segments.

Solutions Fast Track

DNS

☑ DNS is the network protocol responsible for translating Fully Qualified Domain Names (FQDNs) into IP addresses, and vice versa.

☑ DNS servers maintain a list of resource records (RRs) that specify how domain names are to be configured and passed along to requesting clients.

☑ DNS servers are under heavy scrutiny by network attackers due to their integral role in network communications.

TFTP

☑ TFTP was designed to transfer bootable images and data to "thin clients," devices without a primary storage device.

☑ TFTP is based off of the FTP protocol, but was made much simpler to reduce overhead and complexity.

☑ UDP packets are used to improve network speed, but because the protocol does not support encryption or user authentication, the data can be visible to users on the network.

HTTP

☑ HTTP is one of the primary methods of data transferal between computers on the Internet, and can be implemented in everything from Web browsers to P2P clients.

☑ The protocol is similar to FTP, where a client specifies a host server, directory path, and file name they wish to retrieve.

☑ HTTP is one of the primary methods by which network devices can be accessed and configured by a network administrator.

SNMP

☑ SNMP is used to monitor network components and devices for errors or performance deficiencies.

☑ Data within SNMP-enabled devices are stored in a structured, number-based hierarchy, which requires extensive documentation to understand and parse.

☑ SNMP may also be used to configure and modify data within clients.

DHCP

☑ DHCP offers the ability to automatically assign IP addresses and network information to network devices as soon as they join the network.

☑ The use of DHCP allows portable devices, such as laptops and IP telephones, to be transported between networks without any manual configuration changes.

RSVP

☑ The RSVP protocol is used to create a static route between two VoIP devices, allowing for a consistent, high-bandwidth connection.

☑ RSVP's unencrypted data allows malicious users to monitor, or disrupt, VoIP communications.

SDP

☑ SDP allows session information to be distributed to clients that request it, thus detailing an ongoing session and its subject matter.

Skinny

☑ Skinny is a Cisco proprietary protocol used for communication between Cisco telephones and a Cisco CallManager device.

☑ The Skinny protocol transmits all data in an unencrypted format, thus allowing malicious network users to capture, monitor, or disrupt communication connections, although an encrypted version of Skinny (over TLS) is supported on some devices.

Frequently Asked Questions

The following Frequently Asked Questions, answered by the authors of this book, are designed to both measure your understanding of the concepts presented in this chapter and to assist you with real-life implementation of these concepts. To have your questions about this chapter answered by the author, browse to **www.syngress.com/solutions** and click on the **"Ask the Author"** form.

Q: How can I check to see if my SNMP devices are vulnerable?

A: A variety of free tools can be used to assess the security of SNMP devices. One such tool is SNMPwalk. There is also Mirage (http://pointblanksecurity.com/mirage.php), which provides an easy-to-use GUI environment for scanning.

Q: If I use unencrypted traffic, can people really capture, and listen to, my phone conversations?

A: Yes, and quite easily, too. By using simple network capture and analysis tools, like Ethereal, communication sessions can be stripped out and saved. Additional tools can then be used to convert the raw network data into playable audio files. One such tool is the Voice Over Misconfigured Internet Telephones (VOMIT) located at http://vomit.xtdnet.nl.

Chapter 9

Threats to VoIP Communications Systems

Solutions in this chapter:

- Denial-of-Service or VoIP Service Disruption
- Call Hijacking and Interception
- H.323-Specific Attacks
- SIP-Specific Attacks

☑ Summary

☑ Solutions Fast Track

☑ Frequently Asked Questions

Introduction

Converging voice and data on the same wire, regardless of the protocols used, ups the ante for network security engineers and managers. One consequence of this convergence is that in the event of a major network attack, the organization's entire telecommunications infrastructure can be at risk. Securing the whole VoIP infrastructure requires planning, analysis, and detailed knowledge about the specifics of the implementation you choose to use.

Table 9.1 describes the general levels that can be attacked in a VoIP infrastructure.

Table 9.1 VoIP Vulnerabilities

Vulnerability	Description
IP infrastructure	Vulnerabilities on related non-VoIP systems can lead to compromise of VoIP infrastructure.
Underlying operating system	VoIP devices inherit the same vulnerabilities as the operating system or firmware they run on. Operating systems are Windows and Linux.
Configuration	In their default configuration most VoIP devices ship with a surfeit of open services. The default services running on the open ports may be vulnerable to DoS attacks, buffer overflows, or authentication bypass.
Application level	Immature technologies can be attacked to disrupt or manipulate service. Legacy applications (DNS, for example) have known problems.

Denial-of-Service or VoIP Service Disruption

Denial-of-service (DoS) attacks can affect any IP-based network service. The impact of a DoS attack can range from mild service degradation to complete loss of service. There are several classes of DoS attacks. One type of attack in which packets can simply be flooded into or at the target network from multiple external sources is called a distributed denial-of-service (DDoS) attack (see Figures 9.1 and 9.2).

Figure 9.1 Typical Internet Access

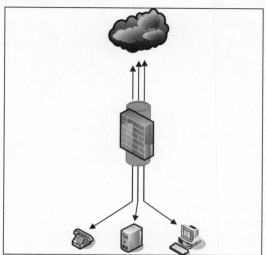

In this figure, traffic flows normally between internal and external hosts and servers. In Figure 9.2, a network of computers (e.g., a botnet) directs IP traffic at the interface of the firewall.

Figure 9.2 A Distributed Denial-of-Service Attack

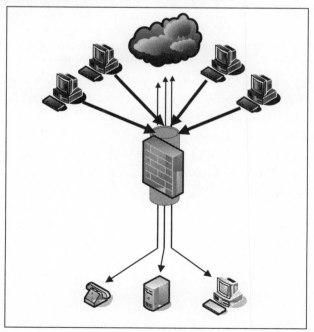

Tools & Traps...

Botnets

In June of 2004, the Google, Yahoo, and Microsoft Web sites disappeared from the Internet for several hours when their servers were swamped with hundreds of thousands of simultaneous Web page requests that swamped the available bandwidth to the servers and upstream routers, and exhausted the processing power of the server CPUs. The cause—botnets.

In a general sense, a bot is a program that acts semiautonomously in response to commands sent by human operators. Bots aren't necessarily evil. For instance, the GoogleBot scours the Web for the purpose of improving that search engine. But when an attacker initiates an assault via IRC, P2P, or HTTP commands, as many as 100,000 or more bots (most bots are installed on unwitting user PCs through some type of malware), which comprise a *botnet*, can be directed to send traffic targeted at a particular host or subnet. The resulting packet barrage incapacitates victim computers because of resource (bandwidth and CPU cycles) exhaustion.

Interestingly, some DDoS attacks are not the result of malicious intent, but rather, are caused by a sudden upsurge in traffic due to the popularity of a particular Web site. This is sometimes called "The Slashdot Effect," since oftentimes, mention of a Web site in a Slashdot article results in enough subsequent viewers of that Web site that the Web server fails under the load.

The second large class of Denial of Service (DoS) conditions occurs when devices within the internal network are targeted by a flood of packets so that they fail—taking out related parts of the infrastructure with them. As in the DdoS scenarios described earlier in this chapter, service disruption occurs to resource depletion—primarily bandwidth and CPU resource starvation (see Figure 9.3). For example, some IP telephones will stop working if they receive a UDP packet larger than 65534 bytes on port 5060.

Figure 9.3 An Internal Denial-of-Service Attack

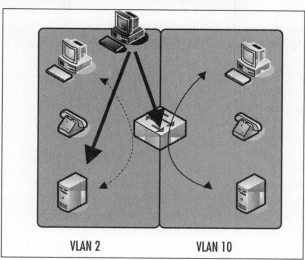

VLAN 2   VLAN 10

Neither integrity checks nor encryption can prevent these attacks. DoS or DDoS attacks are characterized simply by the volume of packets sent toward the victim computer; whether those packets are signed by a server, contain real or spoofed source IP addresses, or are encrypted with a fictitious key—none of these are relevant to the attack.

DoS attacks are difficult to defend against, and because VoIP is just another IP network service, it is just as susceptible to DoS attack as any other IP network services. Additionally, DoS attacks are particularly effective against services such as VoIP and other real-time services, because these services are most sensitive to adverse network status. Viruses and worms are included in this category as they often cause DoS or DDoS due to the increased network traffic that they generate as part of their efforts to replicate and propagate.

NOTE

Bugtraq is a mailing list hosted by Symantec SecurityFocus that serves as a vehicle for announcing new security vulnerabilities. Bugtraq is located on the Web at www.securityfocus.com/archive/1.

CERT and US-CERT are not acronyms. CERT is an organization devoted to ensuring that appropriate technology and systems management practices are used to resist attacks on networked systems and to limiting damage and ensuring continuity of critical services in spite of successful attacks, accidents, or failures. CERT is based at Carnegie Mellon University and is funded by the U.S. Department of Defense and the Department of Homeland Security. CERT's homepage is www.cert.org/.

CVE (Common Vulnerabilities and Exposures) is a list of standardized names for vulnerabilities and other information security exposures—CVE aims to standardize the names for all publicly known vulnerabilities and security exposures. The MITRE Corporation maintains CVE, and the CVE editorial board. The CVE editorial board is composed of individuals from a range of interests within the security industry including intrusion detection experts, network security analysts, security services vendors, academia, tool vendors, software providers, incident response teams, and information providers.

How do we defend against these DoS conditions (we won't use the term attack here because some DoS conditions are simply the unintended result of other unrelated actions)? Let's begin with internal DoS. Note in Figure 9.3 that VLAN 10 on the right is not affected by the service disruption on the left in VLAN 2. This illustrates one critical weapon the security administrator has in thwarting DoS conditions—logical segregation of network domains in separate compartments. Each compartment can be configured to be relatively immune to the results of DoS in the others. This is described in more detail in Chapter 13.

Point solutions will also be effective in limiting the consequences of DoS conditions. For example, because strong authentication is seldom used in VoIP environments, the message processing components must trust and process messages from possible attackers. The additional processing of bogus messages exhausts server resources and leads to a DoS. SIP or H.323 Registration Flooding is an example of this, described in the list of DoS threats, later. In that case, message processing servers can mitigate this specific threat by limiting the number of registrations it will accept per minute for a particular address (and/or from a specific IP address). An intrusion Prevention System (IPS) may be useful in fending off certain types of DoS attacks. These devices sit on the datapath and monitor passing traffic. When anomalous traffic is detected (either by matching against a database of attack signatures or by matching the results of an anomaly-detection algorithm) the IPS blocks the suspicious traffic. One problem I have seen with these devices—particularly in environments with high availability requirements—is that they sometimes block normal traffic, thus creating their own type of DoS.

Additionally, security administrators can minimize the chances of DoS by ensuring that IP telephones and servers are updated to the latest stable version and release. Typically, when a DoS warning is announced by bugtraq, the vendor quickly responds by fixing the offending software.

NOTE

VoIP endpoints can be infected with new VoIP device or protocol-specific viruses. WinCE, PalmOS, SymbianOS, and POSIX-based softphones are especially vulnerable because they typically do not run antivirus software and have less robust operating systems. Several Symbian worms already have been detected in the wild. Infected VoIP devices then create a new "weak link" vector for attacking other network resources.

Compromised devices can be used to launch attacks against other systems in the same network, particularly if the compromised device is trusted (i.e., inside the firewall). Malicious programs installed by an attacker on compromised devices can capture user input, capture traffic, and relay user data over a "back channel" to the attacker. This is especially worrisome for softphone users.

VoIP systems must meet stringent service availability requirements. Following are some example DoS threats can cause the VoIP service to be partially or entirely unavailable by preventing successful call placement (including emergency/911), disconnecting existing calls, or preventing use of related services like voicemail. Note that this list is not exhaustive but illustrates some attack scenarios.

- **TLS Connection Reset** It's not hard to force a connection reset on a TLS connection (often used for signaling security between phones and gateways)—just send the right kind of junk packet and the TLS connection will be reset, interrupting the signaling channel between the phone and call server.

- **VoIP Packet Replay Attack** Capture and resend out-of-sequence VoIP packets (e.g., RTP SSRC—SSRC is an RTP header field that stands for Synchronization Source) to endpoints, adding delay to call in progress and degrading call quality.

- **Data Tunneling** Not exactly an attack; rather tunneling data through voice calls creates, essentially, a new form of unauthorized modem. By transporting modem signals through a packet network by using pulse code modulation (PCM) encoded packets or by residing within header information, VoIP can be used to support a modem call over an IP network. This technique may be used to bypass or undermine a desktop modem policy and hide the existence of unauthorized data connections. This is similar in concept to the so-called "IP over HTTP" threat (i.e., "Firewall Enhancement Protocol" RFC 3093)—a classic problem for any ports opened on a firewall from internal sources.

- **QoS Modification Attack** Modify non-VoIP-specific protocol control information fields in VoIP data packets to and from endpoints to degrade or deny voice service. For example, if an attacker were to change 802.1Q VLAN tag or IP packet ToS bits, either as a man-in-the-middle or by compromising endpoint device configuration, the attacker could disrupt the quality of service "engineered" for a VoIP network. By subordinating voice traffic to data traffic, for example, the attacker might substantially delay delivery of voice packets.

- **VoIP Packet Injection** Send forged VoIP packets to endpoints, injecting speech or noise or gaps into active call. For example, when RTP is used without authentication of RTCP packets (and without SSRC sampling), an attacker can inject RTCP packets into a multicast group, each with a different SSRC, which can grow the group size exponentially.

- **DoS against Supplementary Services** Initiate a DoS attack against other network services upon which the VoIP service depends (e.g., DHCP, DNS, BOOTP). For example, in networks where VoIP endpoints rely on DHCP-assigned addresses, disabling the DHCP server prevents endpoints (soft- and hardphones) from acquiring addressing and routing information they need to make use of the VoIP service.

- **Control Packet Flood** Flood VoIP servers or endpoints with unauthenticated call control packets, (e.g., H.323 GRQ, RRQ, URQ packets sent to UDP/1719). The attacker's intent is to deplete/exhaust device, system, or network resources to the extent that VoIP service is unusable. Any open administrative and maintenance port on call processing and VoIP-related servers can be a target for this DoS attack.

- **Wireless DoS** Initiate a DoS attack against wireless VoIP endpoints by sending 802.11 or 802.1X frames that cause network disconnection (e.g.,

802.11 Deauthenticate flood, 802.1X EAP-Failure, WPA MIC attack, radio spectrum jamming). For example, a Message Integrity Code attack exploits a standard countermeasure whereby a wireless access point disassociates stations when it receives two invalid frames within 60 seconds, causing loss of network connectivity for 60 seconds. In a VoIP environment, a 60-second service interruption is rather extreme.

- **Bogus Message DoS** Send VoIP servers or endpoints valid-but-forged VoIP protocol packets to cause call disconnection or busy condition (e.g., RTP SSRC collision, forged RTCP BYE, forged CCMS, spoofed endpoint button push). Such attacks cause the phone to process a bogus message and incorrectly terminate a call, or mislead a calling party into believing the called party's line is busy.

- **Invalid Packet DoS** Send VoIP servers or endpoints invalid packets that exploit device OS and TCP/IP implementation denial-of-service CVEs. For example, the exploit described in CAN-2002-0880 crashes Cisco IP phones using jolt, jolt2, and other common fragmentation-based DoS attack methods. CAN-2002-0835 crashes certain VoIP phones by exploiting DHCP DoS CVEs. Avaya IP phones may be vulnerable to port zero attacks.

- **Immature Software DoS** PDA/handheld softphones and first generation VoIP hardphones are especially vulnerable because they are not as mature or intensely scrutinized. VoIP call servers and IP PBXs also run on OS platforms with many known CVEs. Any open administrative/maintenance port (e.g., HTTP, SNMP, Telnet) or vulnerable interface (e.g., XML, Java) can become an attack vector.

- **VoIP Protocol Implementation DoS** Send VoIP servers or endpoints invalid packets to exploit a VoIP protocol implementation vulnerability to a DoS attack. Several such exploits are identified in the MITRE CVE database (http://cve.mitre.org). For example, CVE-2001-00546 uses malformed H.323 packets to exploit Windows ISA memory leak and exhaust resources. CAN-2004-0056 uses malformed H.323 packets to exploit Nortel BCM DoS vulnerabilities. Lax software update practices (failure to install CVE patches) exacerbate risk.

- **Packet of Death DoS** Flood VoIP servers or endpoints with random TCP, UDP, or ICMP packets or fragments to exhaust device CPU, bandwidth, TCP sessions, and so on. For example, an attacker can initiate a TCP Out of Band DoS attack by sending a large volume of TCP packets marked "priority delivery" (the TCP Urgent flag). During any flood, increased processing load interferes with the receiving system's ability to process real traffic, initially delaying voice traffic processing but ultimately disrupting service entirely.

- **IP Phone Flood DoS** Send a very large volume of call data toward a single VoIP endpoint to exhaust that device's CPU, bandwidth, TCP sessions, and so on. Interactive voice response systems, telephony gateways, conferencing servers, and voicemail systems are able to generate more call data than a single endpoint can handle and so could be leveraged to flood an endpoint.

Notes from the Underground...

Pharming

Pharming exploits vulnerabilities in DNS—the protocol responsible for translating e-mail and Web addresses into IP addresses. By using DNS Poisoning VoIP users' calls can be redirected without their knowledge, to addresses completely different from the ones the users dialed. Essentially, pharming attacks attempt to persuade a user that he or she is viewing one site—www.yourbank.com, for example—when the user actually is viewing a bogus, criminal site. The bogus site is designed to mimic the real site, and often provides numerous means for the user to enter personal information.

Pharming against IP telephony is not only possible, it is probable. ZDNet describes how pharming may be used to redirect IP phone traffic from the intended recipient to another location. Imagine dialing your bank's number, entering your SSN and password at the voice prompts, and then a month later, realizing that you donated your personal information to a 15-year-old in Romania.

Call Hijacking and Interception

Call interception and eavesdropping are other major concerns on VoIP networks. The VOIPSA threat taxonomy (www.voipsa.org/Activities/taxonomy-wiki.php) defines eavesdropping as "a method by which an attacker is able to monitor the entire signaling and/or data stream between two or more VoIP endpoints, but cannot or does not alter the data itself." Successful call interception is akin to wiretapping in that conversations of others can be stolen, recorded, and replayed without their knowledge. Obviously, an attacker who can intercept and store these data can make use of the data in other ways as well.

Tools & Traps…

DNS Poisoning

A DNS A (or address) record is used for storing a domain or hostname mapping to an IP address. SIP makes extensive use of SRV records to locate SIP services such as SIP proxies and registrars. SRV (service) records normally begin with an underscore (_sip.tcpserver.udp.domain.com) and consist of information describing service, transport, host, and other information. SRV records allow administrators to use several servers for a single domain, to move services from host to host with little fuss, and to designate some hosts as primary servers for a service and others as backups.

An attacker's goal, when attempting a DNS Poisoning or spoofing attack, is to replace valid cached DNS A, SRV, or NS records with records that point to the attacker's server(s). This can be accomplished in a number of fairly trivial ways—the easiest being to initiate a zone transfer from the attacker's DNS server to the victim's misconfigured DNS server, by asking the victim's DNS server to resolve a networked device within the attacker's domain. The victim's DNS server accepts not only the requested record from the attacker's server, but it also accepts and caches any other records that the attacker's server includes.

Thus, in addition to the A record for www.attacker.com, the victim DNS server may receive a bogus record for www.yourbank.com. The innocent victim will then be redirected to the attacker.com Web site anytime he or she attempts to browse to the yourbank.com Web site, as long as the bogus records are cached. Substitute a SIP URL for a Web site address, and the same scenario can be repeated in a VoIP environment.

This family of threats relies on the absence of cryptographic assurance of a request's originator. Attacks in this category seek to compromise the message integrity of a conversation. This threat demonstrates the need for security services that enable entities to authenticate the originators of requests and to verify that the contents of the message and control streams have not been altered in transit.

In the past several years, as host PCs have improved their processing power and their ability to process networked information, network administrators have instituted a hierarchical access structure that consists of a single, dedicated switched link for each host PC to distribution or backbone devices. Each networked user benefits from a more reliable, secure connection with guaranteed bandwidth. The use of a switched infrastructure limits the effectiveness of packet capture tools or protocol analyzers as a means to collect VoIP traffic streams. Networks that are switched to the desktop allow normal users' computers to monitor only broadcast and unicast traffic that is destined to their particular MAC address. A user's NIC (network interface card) literally does not see unicast traffic destined for other computers on the network.

The address resolution protocol (ARP) is a method used on IPv4 Ethernet networks to map the IP address (layer 3) to the hardware or MAC (Media Access Control) layer 2 address. (Note that ARP has been replaced in IPv6 by Neighbor Discovery [ND] protocol. The ND protocol is a hybrid of ARP and ICMP.) Two classes of hardware addresses exist: the broadcast address of all ones, and a unique 6 byte identifier that is burned into the PROM of every NIC (Network Interface Card).

Figure 9.4 illustrates a typical ARP address resolution scheme. A host PC (10.1.1.1) that wishes to contact another host (10.1.1.2) on the same subnet issues an ARP broadcast packet (ARPs for the host) containing its own hardware and IP addresses. NICs contain filters that allow them to drop all packets not destined for their unique hardware address or the broadcast address, so all NICs but the query target silently discard the ARP broadcast. The target NIC responds to the query request by unicasting its IP and hardware address, completing the physical to logical mapping, and allowing communications to proceed at layer 3.

Figure 9.4 Typical ARP Request/Reply

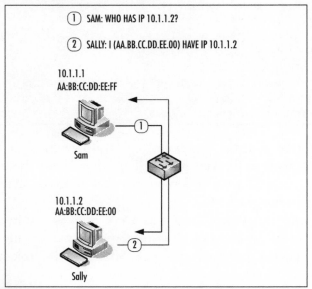

To minimize broadcast traffic, many devices cache ARP addresses for a varying amount of time: The default ARP cache timeout for Linux is one minute; for Windows NT, two minutes, and for Cisco routers, four hours. This value can be trivially modified in most systems. The ARP cache is a table structure that contains IP address, hardware address, and oftentimes, the name of the interface the MAC address is discovered on, the type of media, and the type of ARP response. Depending upon the operating system, the ARP cache may or may not contain an entry for its own addresses.

In Figure 9.4, Sam's ARP cache contains one entry prior to the ARP request/response:

Internet Address	Physical Address	
10.1.1.1	AA:BB:CC:DD:EE:FF	int0

After the ARP request/response completes, Sam's ARP cache now contains two entries:

Internet Address	Physical Address	
10.1.1.1	AA:BB:CC:DD:EE:FF	int0
10.1.1.2	AA:BB:CC:DD:EE:00	int0

Note that Sally's ARP cache, as a result of the request/response communications, is updated with the hardware:IP mappings for both workstations as well.

ARP Spoofing

ARP is a fundamental Ethernet protocol. Perhaps for this reason, manipulation of ARP packets is a potent and frequent attack mechanism on VoIP networks. Most network administrators assume that deploying a fully switched network to the desktop prevents the ability of network users to sniff network traffic and potentially capture sensitive information traversing the network. Unfortunately, several techniques and tools exist that allow any user to sniff traffic on a switched network because ARP has no provision for authenticating queries or query replies. Additionally, because ARP is a stateless protocol, most operating systems (Solaris is an exception) update their cache when receiving ARP reply, regardless of whether they have sent out an actual request.

Among these techniques, ARP redirection, ARP spoofing, ARP hijacking, and ARP cache poisoning are related methods for disrupting the normal ARP process. These terms frequently are interchanged and confused. For the purpose of this section, we'll refer to ARP cache poisoning and ARP spoofing as the same process. Using freely available tools such as ettercap, Cain, and dsniff, an evil IP device can spoof a normal IP device by sending unsolicited ARP replies to a target host. The bogus ARP reply contains the hardware address of the normal device and the IP address of the malicious device. This "poisons" the host's ARP cache.

In Figure 9.5, Ned is the attacking computer. When SAM broadcasts an ARP query for Sally's IP address, NED, the attacker, responds to the query stating that the IP address (10.1.1.2) belongs to Ned's MAC address, BA:DB:AD:BA:DB:AD. Packets sent from Sam supposedly to Sally will be sent to Ned instead. Sam will mistakenly assume that Ned's MAC address corresponds to Sally's IP address and will direct all traffic destined for that IP address to Ned's MAC. In fact, Ned can poison Sam's ARP cache without waiting for an ARP query since on Windows systems (9x/NT/2K), static ARP entries are overwritten whenever a query response is received regardless of whether or not a query was issued.

Figure 9.5 ARP Spoofing (Cache Poisoning)

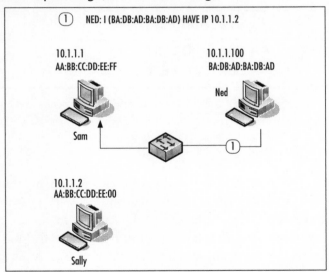

Sam's ARP cache now looks like this:

Internet Address	Physical Address	
10.1.1.1	AA:BB:CC:DD:EE:FF	int0
10.1.1.2	BA:DB:AD:BA:DB:AD	int0

This entry will remain until it ages out or a new entry replaces it.

ARP redirection can work bidirectionally, and a spoofing device can insert itself in the middle of a conversation between two IP devices on a switched network (see Figure 9.6). This is probably the most insidious ARP-related attack. By routing packets on to the devices that should truly be receiving the packets, this insertion (known as a Man/Monkey/Moron in the Middle attack) can remain undetected for some time. An attacker can route packets to /dev/null (nowhere) as well, resulting in a DoS attack.

Figure 9.6 An ARP MITM Attack

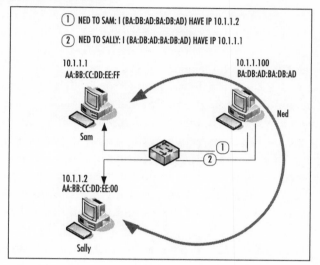

Sam's ARP cache:

Internet Address	Physical Address	
10.1.1.1	AA:BB:CC:DD:EE:FF	int0
10.1.1.2	BA:DB:AD:BA:DB:AD	int0

Sally's ARP cache:

Internet Address	Physical Address	
10.1.1.1	BA:DB:AD:BA:DB:AD	int0
10.1.1.2	AA:BB:CC:DD:EE:00	int0

As all IP traffic between the true sender and receiver now passes through the attacker's device, it is trivial for the attacker to sniff that traffic using freely available tools such as Ethereal or tcpdump. Any unencrypted information (including e-mails, usernames and passwords, and web traffic) can be intercepted and viewed.

This interception has potentially drastic implications for VoIP traffic. Freely available tools such as vomit and rtpsniff, as well as private tools such as VoipCrack, allow for the interception and decoding of VoIP traffic. Captured content can include speech, signaling and billing information, multimedia, and PIN numbers. Voice conversations traversing the internal IP network can be intercepted and recorded using this technique.

There are a number of variations of the aforementioned techniques. Instead of imitating a host, the attacker can emulate a gateway. This enables the attacker to intercept numerous packet streams. However, most ARP redirection techniques rely on stealth. The attacker in these scenarios hopes to remain undetected by the users being impersonated. Posing as a gateway may result in alerting users to the attacker's presence due to unanticipated glitches in the network, because frequently switches behave in unexpected ways when attackers manipulate ARP processes. One unintended (much of the time) consequence of these attacks, particularly when switches are heavily loaded, is that the switch CAM (Content-Addressable Memory) table—a finite-sized IP address to MAC address lookup table—becomes disrupted. This leads to the switch forwarding unicast packets out many ports in unpredictable fashion. Penetration testers may want to keep this in mind when using these techniques on production networks.

In order to limit damage due to ARP manipulation, administrators should implement software tools that monitor MAC to IP address mappings. The freeware tool, Arpwatch, monitors these pairings. At the network level, MAC/IP address mappings can be statically coded on the switch; however, this is often administratively untenable. Dynamic ARP Inspection (DAI) is available on newer Cisco Catalyst 6500 switches. DAI is part of Cisco's Integrated Security (CIS) functionality and is designed to prevent several layer two and layer three spoofing attacks, including ARP redirection attacks. Note that DAI and CIS are available only on Catalyst switches using native mode (Cisco IOS).

The potential risks of decoding intercepted VoIP traffic can be eliminated by implementing encryption. Avaya's Media Encryption feature is an example of this. Using Media Encryption, VoIP conversations between two IP endpoints are encrypted using AES encryption. In highly secure environments, organizations should ensure that Media Encryption is enabled on all IP codec sets in use.

DAI enforces authorized MAC-to-IP address mappings. Media Encryption renders traffic, even if intercepted, unintelligible to an attacker.

The following are some additional examples of call or signal interception and hijacking. This class of threats, though typically more difficult to accomplish than DoS, can result in significant loss or alteration of data. DoS attacks, whether caused by active methods or inadvertently, although important in terms of quality of service, are more often than not irritating to users and administrators. Interception and hijacking attacks, on the other hand, are almost always active attacks with theft of service, information, or money as the goal. Note that this list is not exhaustive but illustrates some attack scenarios.

- **Rogue VoIP Endpoint Attack** Rogue IP endpoint contacts VoIP server by leveraging stolen or guessed identities, credentials, and network access. For example, a rogue endpoint can use an unprotected wall jack and auto-registration of VOIP phones to get onto the network. RAS password guessing can be used to masquerade as a legitimate endpoint. Lax account maintenance (expired user accounts left active) increases risk of exploitation.

- **Registration Hijacking** Registration hijacking occurs when an attacker impersonates a valid UA to a registrar and replaces the registration with its own address. This attack causes all incoming calls to be sent to the attacker.

- **Proxy Impersonation** Proxy impersonation occurs when an attacker tricks a SIP UA or proxy into communicating with a rogue proxy. If an attacker successfully impersonates a proxy, he or she has access to all SIP messages.

- **Toll Fraud** Rogue or legitimate VoIP endpoint uses a VoIP server to place unauthorized toll calls over the PSTN. For example, inadequate access controls can let rogue devices place toll calls by sending VoIP requests to call processing applications. VoIP servers can be hacked into in order to make free calls to outside destinations. Social engineering can be used to obtain outside line prefixes.

- **Message Tampering** Capture, modify, and relay unauthenticated VoIP packets to/from endpoints. For example, a rogue 802.11 AP can exchange frames sent or received by wireless endpoints if no payload integrity check (e.g., WPA MIC, SRTP) is used. Alternatively, these attacks can occur through registration hijacking, proxy impersonation, or an attack on any component trusted to process SIP or H.323 messages, such as the proxy, registration servers, media gateways, or firewalls. These represent non–ARP-based MITM attacks.

- **VoIP Protocol Implementation Attacks** Send VoIP servers or endpoints invalid packets to exploit VoIP protocol implementation CVEs. Such attacks can lead to escalation of privileges, installation and operation of malicious programs, and system compromise. For example, CAN-2004-0054 exploits Cisco IOS H.323 implementation CVEs to execute arbitrary code. CSCed33037 uses unsecured IBM Director agent ports to gain administrative control over IBM servers running Cisco VOIP products.

Notes from the Underground...

ANI/Caller-ID Spoofing

Caller ID is a service provided by most telephone companies (for a monthly cost) that will tell you the name and number of an incoming call. Automatic Number Identification (ANI) is a system used by the telephone company to determine the number of the calling party. To spoof Caller-ID, an attacker sends modem tones over a POTS lines between rings 1 and 2. ANI spoofing is setting the ANI so as to send incorrect ANI information to the PSTN so that the resulting Caller-ID is misleading. Traditionally this has been a complicated process either requiring the assistance of a cooperative phone company operator or an expensive company PBX system.

In ANI/Caller-ID spoofing, an evildoer hijacks phone number and the identity of a trusted party, such as a bank or a government office. The identity appears on the caller ID box of an unsuspecting victim, with the caller hoping to co-opt valuable information, such as account numbers, or otherwise engage in malicious mischief. This is not a VoIP issue, per se. In fact, one of the big drawbacks about VoIP trunks is their inability to send ANI properly because of incomplete standards.

H.323-Specific Attacks

The only existing vulnerabilities that we are aware of at this time take advantage of ASN.1 parsing defects in the first phase of H.225 data exchange. More vulnerabilities can be expected for several reasons: the large number of differing vendor implementations, the complex nature of this collection of protocols, problems with the various implementations of ASN.1/PER encoding/decoding, and the fact that these protocols—alone and in concert—have not endured the same level of scrutiny that other, more common protocols have been subjected to. For example, we have unpublished data that shows that flooding a gateway or media server with GRQ request packets (RAS registration request packets) results in a DoS against certain vendor gateway implementations—basically the phones deregister.

SIP-Specific Attacks

Multiple vendors have confirmed vulnerabilities in their respective SIP (Session Initiation Protocol) implementations. The vulnerabilities have been identified in the INVITE message used by two SIP endpoints during the initial call setup. The impact of successful exploitation of the vulnerabilities has not been disclosed but potentially could result in a compromise of a vulnerable device. (CERT: CA-2003-06.) In addition, many recent examples of SIP Denial of Service attacks have been reported.

Recent issues that affect Cisco SIP Proxy Server (SPS) [Bug ID CSCec31901] demonstrate the problems SIP implementers may experience due to the highly modular architecture or this protocol. The SSL implementation in SPS (used to secure SIP sessions) is vulnerable to an ASN.1 BER decoding error similar to the one described for H.323 and other protocols. This example illustrates a general concern with SIP: As the SIP protocol links existing protocols and services together, all the classic vulnerabilities in services such as SSL, HTTP, and SMTP may resurface in the VOIP environment. We also discuss SIP security vulnerabilities in Chapter 16.

Summary

DoS attacks, whether they are intentional or unintended, are the most difficult VoIP-related threat to defend against. The packet switching nature of data networks allows multiple connections to share the same transport medium. Therefore, unlike telephones in circuit-switched networks, an IP terminal endpoint can receive and potentially participate in multiple calls at once. Thus, an endpoint can be used to amplify attacks. On VoIP networks, resources such as bandwidth must be allocated efficiently and fairly to accommodate the maximum number of callers. This property can be violated by attackers who aggressively and abusively obtain an unnecessarily large amount of resources. Alternatively, the attacker simply can flood the network with large number of packets so that resources are unavailable to all other callers.

In addition, viruses and worms create DoS conditions due to the network traffic generated by these agents as they replicate and seek out other hosts to infect. These agents are proven to wreak havoc with even relatively well-secured data networks. VoIP networks, by their nature, are exquisitely sensitive to these types of attacks. Remedies for DoS include logical network partitioning at layers 2 and 3, stateful firewalls with application inspection capabilities, policy enforcement to limit flooded packets, and out-of-band management. Out-of-band management is required so that in the event of a DoS event, system administrators are still able to monitor the network and respond to additional events.

Theft of services and information is also problematic on VoIP networks. These threats are almost always due to active attack. Many of these attacks can be thwarted by implementing additional security controls at layer 2. This includes layer 2 security features such as DHCP Snooping, Dynamic ARP Inspection, IP Source Guard, Port Security, and VLAN ACLs. The fundamental basis for this class of attacks is that the identity of one or more of the devices that participate is not legitimate.

Endpoints must be authenticated, and end users must be validated in order to ensure legitimacy. Hijacking and call interception revolves around the concept of fooling and manipulating weak or nonexistent authentication measures. We are all familiar with different forms of authentication, from the password used to login to your computer to the key that unlocks the front door. The conceptual framework for authentication is made up of three factors: "something you have" (a key or token), "something you know" (a password or secret handshake), or "something you are" (fingerprint or iris pattern). Authentication mechanisms validate users by one or a combination of these. Any type of unauthenticated access, particularly to key infrastructure components such as the IP PBX or DNS server, for example, can result in disagreeable consequences for both users and administrators.

VoIP relies upon a number of ancillary services as part of the configuration process, as a means to locate users, manage servers and phones, and to ensure favorable transport, among others. DNS, DHCP, HTTP, HTTPS, SNMP, SSH, RSVP, and TFTP services all have been the subject of successful exploitation by attackers. Potential VoIP users may defer transitioning to IP Telephony if they believe it will reduce overall network security by creating new vulnerabilities that could be used to compromise non-VoIP systems and services within the same network. Effective mitigation of these threats to common data networks and services could be considered a security baseline upon which a successful VoIP deployment depends. Firewalls, network and system intrusion detection, authentication systems, anti-virus scanners, and other security controls, which should already be in place, are required to counter attacks that might debilitate any or all IP-based services (including VoIP services).

H.323 and SIP suffer security vulnerabilities based simply upon their encoding schemes, albeit for different reasons. Because SIP is an unstructured text-based protocol, it is impossibly to test all permutations of SIP messages during development for security vulnerabilities. It's fairly straightforward to construct a malformed SIP message or message sequence that results in a DoS for a particular SIP device. This may not be significant for a single UA endpoint, but if this "packet of death" can render all the carrier-class media gateway controllers in a network useless, then this becomes a significant problem. H.323 on the other hand is encoded according to ASN.1 PER encoding rules. The implementation of H.323 message parsers, rather than the encoding rules themselves, results in security vulnerabilities in the H.323 suite.

Solutions Fast Track

Denial-of-Service or VoIP Service Disruption

- ☑ DoS attacks are particularly effective against services such as VoIP and other real-time services, because these services are most sensitive to adverse network status.

- ☑ Logical segregation of network domains can limit the damage due to DoS attacks.

- ☑ Point solutions will be effective in limiting the consequences of DoS conditions.

Call Hijacking and Interception

- ☑ Call interception and eavesdropping are major concerns on VoIP networks.

- ☑ This family of threats rely on the absence of cryptographic assurance of a request's originator.

- ☑ Endpoints must be authenticated, and end users must be validated in order to ensure legitimacy.

H.323-Specific Attacks

- ☑ The existing H.323 security vulnerabilities take advantage of differing implementation's ASN.1 parsing defects.

SIP-Specific Attacks

- ☑ SIP is an unstructured text-based protocol. It is impossible to test all permutations of SIP messages during development for security vulnerabilities.

- ☑ As the SIP protocol links existing protocols and services together, all the classic vulnerabilities in services such as SSL, HTTP, and SMTP, may resurface in the VOIP environment.

Frequently Asked Questions

The following Frequently Asked Questions, answered by the authors of this book, are designed to both measure your understanding of the concepts presented in this chapter and to assist you with real-life implementation of these concepts. To have your questions about this chapter answered by the author, browse to **www.syngress.com/solutions** and click on the **"Ask the Author"** form.

Q: What is proxy ARP?

A: Proxy ARP describes a method for a device (normally a router) to provide an ARP response on one interface that substitutes for the normal ARP responses of devices attached to another interface.

Q: Why don't I see any ARP requests from Web sites I visit?

A: ARP is a layer 2 protocol that does not cross subnets.

Q: What is a B2BUA?

A: A Back2Back User Agent acts as a proxy for both ends of a SIP session. The B2BUA translates signaling (i.e., SIP to ISUP), manages call session parameters (i.e., setup, teardown), and maintains session state. From the perspective of a SIP IP phone, the B2BUA looks like a UA server. From the point of view of a SIP UA server, the B2BUA looks like a client.

Q: I have a system exposed to the Internet that is being DoS attacked. What can I do?

A: Change the IP address and update the change in your nameservers. Talk with your ISP to determine the source of the packet flood, and try to filter it more closely to the source.

Q: How prevalent are DoS attacks in the Internet today?

A: It is difficult to determine, but data from 2001 suggested that there were over 12,000 reported attacks that year. I would expect that that number has increased significantly, but I am not aware of any data that supports or refutes this.

Q: What is SPIT?

A: Spam over IP Telephony.

Chapter 10

Validate Existing Security Infrastructure

Solutions in this chapter:

- **Security Policies and Processes**
- **Physical Security**
- **Server Hardening**
- **Supporting Services**
- **Unified Network Management**

☑ **Summary**

☑ **Solutions Fast Track**

☑ **Frequently Asked Questions**

Introduction

We begin the process of securing the VoIP infrastructure by reviewing and validating the existing security infrastructure. Addition of VoIP components to a preexisting data network is the ideal opportunity to review and bolster existing security policy, architecture, and processes.

One way of visualizing the components of a given security architecture is to use Figure 10.1, which graphically shows a number of network security interfaces.

Figure 10.1 Security Interfaces

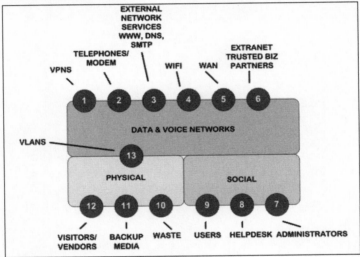

The interfaces between data and voice networks and the external world are represented by the red circles numbered 1 through 6. Additionally, data and voice networks share interfaces with the physical and social realms. Interfaces to data and networks include VPNs, telephones and modems (modems that are used to control or monitor servers or other critical systems are particularly interesting to miscreants), typical web browsing and e-mail services, intracompany WAN connections, and intranet or external connections with vendors and business partners. Technical security controls such as firewalls, IDS, and ACLs are useful at these interfaces.

Interfaces 7 through 9 portray the users, administrators, and help desk personnel that connect with the data and voice networks. In some situations, a call center for example, an additional class of users—operators—could be defined. I believe, based upon personal and anecdotal evidence, that most criminal information security incidents occur via these social interfaces. Unfortunately, technological security controls are difficult to implement and manage at these interfaces.

Interfaces 10 through 12 represent the interfaces between the physical domain and the data and voice network. Recently, problems in this area have resulted in the loss of critical data. In January 2006, a laptop stolen from an Ameriprise Financial worker resulted in the loss of personal information from more than 230,000 customers, and in the same month, an unnamed Toronto health clinic found its private patient data literally "blowing in the wind," as the clinic's waste disposal operator improperly recycled rather than shredded the clinic's data. Numerous other examples exist where discarded laptops or hard drives have been found to contain private information; and "dumpster-diving" is recognized in the security industry as a valid and often lucrative source of information.

Lastly, interface 13 describes the VLAN (Virtual LAN) interface.

This listing is not necessarily complete, but it suggests where security controls can be most effectively implemented. Traffic can oftentimes be monitored, dropped, or approved, or throttled at these synapse-like junctions.

The purpose of this chapter is to reinforce the concept that many of the components that you will require to secure a VoIP/Data network are likely to exist within your current infrastructure.

The first portion of this chapter is not designed as a "how-to" on writing security policies because there a large number of these resources available. In this section, we will argue that information security is critical to an organization, and that security policy underpins all other security efforts. Then we will review the processes required to implement a functional security policy, and we'll look at some of the critical factors that determine the value of a security policy. We have provided a worksheet that will allow you to perform a gap analysis on your existing security policies. A commented sample VoIP Security Policy module is provided for you as a template at the end of this chapter.

Security Policies and Processes

In order to reap the benefits of modern communications, we are required to secure the systems and networks that comprise the communications infrastructure.

The process of securing a converged VoIP + Data network begins with the formulation, implementation, and communication of *effective* security policies. This is true for pure data networks as well. Security policy provides metrics against which costs can be justified, drives security awareness, and provides the framework for technology and process. Once policy is in writing, less time will be spent debating security issues. Policy provides a vantage point that can be built into an organization's reporting systems in order to reassure management about the quality, reliability, and comprehensiveness of its security infrastructure. When approached in this fashion, information security becomes less an administrative and technical burden, and more of a competitive advantage.

NOTE

A competitive advantage within a vertical can be gained either by providing products or services that provide more benefits at a fixed price, or by providing the same benefits at a lower price. An organization can gain a competitive advantage by utilizing its resources (things like people, knowledge, reputation, brand) or its capabilities (processes, procedures, routines, etc.) more effectively than its competitors. Basically, a competitive advantage allows an organization to sustain profits that exceed the average for other organizations within its industry. In the context of information security, competitive advantage can be affected positively by implementing and maintaining a workable information security methodology. These processes can and should be regularly disseminated to clients and vendors, thus creating a reputation for honest and professional treatment of information. Any types of mishandling of client or vendor information—whether from hackers or from simple misuse—leads to reputation, brand, or knowledge damage, and consequently, loss of competitive advantage.

Policy formulation is an important step toward standardization of enterprise security activities. The organization's policy is management's vehicle for emphasizing its commitment to IT security and making clear the expectations for associate involvement and accountability. Policy formulation establishes standards for all information resource protection by assigning program management responsibilities and providing basic rules, guidelines, definitions, and processes for everyone within the organization. One major aim of the security policy is to prevent behavioral inconsistencies that can introduce risks. Ideally, policy will be sufficiently clear and comprehensive to be accepted and followed throughout the organization yet flexible enough to accommodate a wide range of data, activities, and resources.

There is no single best process for developing a security policy. Much of the process is dependent upon variables such as the size, age, and location of an organization, the vertical that the organization occupies, the impact of regulation on the organization, and the organization's sensitivity toward risk. Figure 10.2 shows how an approach to policy development and implementation can be organized.

Figure 10.2 Policy Development and Implementation

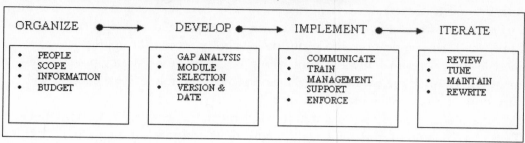

In general, the first step in policy formulation is convincing management that these policies are necessary. In today's environment, this task is simplified by regulatory requirements and by the sheer number of security-related incidents reported in the popular press (see the previous section of this chapter for recent examples). Once management commits to security policy development, the individuals responsible for policy formulation are selected to form a security steering committee.

One of the most common reasons policy efforts fail is that policy too often is developed in a vacuum or by decree, and as a result, does not reflect the security needs of the entire organization. Being inclusive from the start will make it easier to market the policy within the organization later on; in order for security policy to be appropriate and effective, it needs to have the acceptance and support of all levels of employees.

The following is a list of individuals who should be involved in the creation and review of security policy documents:

- Information or Site security officer (see the CSO discussion in the next section of this chapter)

- Information technology technical staff (network managers, system administrators, etc.)

- Help desk staff

- Business unit heads or authorized representatives

- Security emergency response team

- Representatives of the user groups affected by the security policy

- Management

- Legal counsel

- Human Resources

The previous list is not necessarily comprehensive. The idea is to bring in representation from key stakeholders, management who have budget and policy authority, technical staff who know what can and cannot be supported, and legal counsel who know the legal ramifications of various policy choices. It may be appropriate to include audit personnel. Involving this group is important if resulting policy statements are to reach the broadest possible acceptance. The role of legal counsel will vary from country to country.

After the security steering committee is formed, the next step is to write policy. These can be written from scratch although I don't recommend this as it is difficult to be comprehensive with this approach. A better method relies on modifying existing security policies or policy modules that can be found on the web (Googling "security polices" garners over 306 million hits). Policies are available for free or can be purchased, oftentimes as templates.

One approach to modifying either new or existing security policies is to perform a gap analysis—contrasting the proposed policies with existing conditions or perceptions. Using the worksheet shown in Table 10.1, you can compare an organization's inventory of policies, procedures, standards, and guidelines to a checklist that identifies the security industry's best practices.

This worksheet should be sent to a set of individuals within the organization that represent each business unit. The individuals are asked to determine in their experience, whether or not a particular policy exists as a formal document, an informal document, a draft; or does not exist, is not applicable, or is unknown. In addition, they are asked to rate, on a scale of 1–5 (with 5 equaling the highest priority), how important they felt each policy area was. They are limited to answering 5 (high priority) to only six of the 24 categories.

The questionnaires are returned, and the results are averaged. This gap analysis identifies any important security policies, procedures, standards, and guidelines that are absent, and gives some indication of the strengths and weaknesses of existing security policies.

Table 10.1 A Gap Analysis Worksheet

EXISTENCE (1–6): 1=FORMAL; 2 =INFORMAL; 3 =DRAFT; 4 =NO; 5 =NA; 6=UNKNOWN

PRIORITY (1–5): 1=NOT IMPORTANT; 5=CRITICAL

NAME	EXISTENCE	PRIORITY	DESCRIPTION
Acceptable Use Policy			Establishes computer resource usage guidelines for staff during the course of their job duties in a responsible and ethical manner. It also specifies behaviors and practices that are prohibited.
Access Control Policy			This policy defines the access rights and level of authority of each user or group of users based on their business need. Ensures that only authorized users are given access to certain data or resources.
Account Management Policies			Defines who has authority to make account modifications, and how accounts are created or disabled.
Privacy Policies			Defines reasonable expectations of privacy regarding such issues as monitoring of electronic mail, logging of keystrokes, and access to users' files.

Continued

Table 10.1 continued A Gap Analysis Worksheet

NAME	EXISTENCE	PRIORITY	DESCRIPTION
Availability Policies			Statement that sets users' expectations for the availability of resources. It should address redundancy and recovery issues, as well as specify operating hours and maintenance downtime periods. It should also include contact information for reporting system and network failures.
Technology Purchasing Guidelines			Specifies required, or preferred, security features. These typically supplement existing purchasing policies and guidelines.
Configuration Management Policies & Procedures			Defines how new hardware and software are tested and installed, defines how changes are documented.
Control of proprietary information and intellectual property			Defines policies to handle proprietary information, trade secrets, and intellectual property. It includes procedures to protect and safeguard information that is considered sensitive and proprietary.
Data Backup Procedures			Defines what gets backed up, when, how often, and how. Also covers how tapes are stored (to prevent theft).

Continued

Table 10.1 continued A Gap Analysis Worksheet

NAME	EXISTENCE	PRIORITY	DESCRIPTION
Firewall Management Policy			Describes how the firewall hardware and software is managed and configured; how changes are requested and approved; and auditing requirements and procedures.
Internet Access Control Policy			Defines the services (inbound and outbound) that will be supported when traffic travels between the Internet and company systems.
General Encryption Policy			To assure interoperability and consistency across the organization, this policy would mandate standards to which encryption systems must comply, possibly specifying algorithms and parameters to be used.
Internet Security Awareness & Education Policy			Outlines the educational and training measures that will be taken to make computer users aware of their security responsibilities.
Intrusion Detection Policy/Procedures			Defines responsibilities and scope for tools that provide for the timely detection of malicious behavior by users on the network or individual hosts. (Excludes antiviral measures.)

Continued

Table 10.1 continued A Gap Analysis Worksheet

NAME	EXISTENCE	PRIORITY	DESCRIPTION
Network Connection Policy			Describes the requirements and constraints for attaching devices to the corporate network.
Password Management Policy/Procedures			Guidelines to support operations for password management such as password assignment, reset, recovery, protection, and strength. These guidelines support privileged and nonprivileged account password assignment.
Remote Access Policy			Outlines and defines acceptable methods of remotely connecting to the internal corporate network (including Internet and VPN access).
Security Incident Handling Policies & Procedures			Procedures describing the steps to be taken in response to computer security incidents that occur within facilities or networks. This includes interfacing with law enforcement agencies, logging and documenting incidents, evidence preservation, and forensic analysis.

Continued

Table 10.1 continued A Gap Analysis Worksheet

NAME	EXISTENCE	PRIORITY	DESCRIPTION
System Security Standards (for specific OSes)			Procedures for securing specific operating systems (e.g., NT/Win2K, MVS, Linux) that are used within the organization. This document explains how a specific OS needs to be configured for corporate use.
Privileged Access Policy			Establishes requirements for the regulation and use of special access (e.g., root or Administrator) on corporate systems in a responsible and ethical manner. It also specifies behaviors and practices that are prohibited.
Remote Partner Acceptable Use & Connectivity Policy /Procedures			Provides guidelines for the use of network and computing resources associated with third-party networks. Provides a formalized method for the request, approval, and tracking of such connections.
User Account Policies			Outlines the requirements for requesting and maintaining accounts on corporate systems.
Virus Prevention Policy/Procedures			Defines actions that will be taken to detect and remove computer viruses.
IM Policy/Procedures			Defines architecture and deployment guidelines for Instant Messaging.

Continued

Table 10.1 continued A Gap Analysis Worksheet

NAME	EXISTENCE	PRIORITY	DESCRIPTION
Wireless Policy/ Procedures			Defines architecture, and deployment guidelines for 802.11a/b wireless networks.
VoIP Policy/Procedures			Defines architecture, and deployment guidelines for Voice-over IP networks.

Policies & Procedures...

What Defines a Good Security Policy?

You can begin by evaluating your organizational security policy using the criteria derived from Dr. Dan Geer's (Chief Technology Officer — @stake):

1. Has to be understandable on the first read.
2. Has to be readable—short and sweet.
3. Has to be assimilable—can a responsible person remember it?
4. Has to be practical—can a responsible person do this?
5. Define the goal states, not the mechanisms.

Regardless of the starting point, my experience has been that policy development is an iterative process—policy first is broken down into modules (see sidebar for an example listing of high-level modules), modules are assigned to the appropriate individuals, and each module then is edited by steering committee members. After several cycles through this process, a draft version 1.0 document is produced.

The draft security policy document should be evaluated by the security steering committee based upon a number of characteristics:

- Is the scope of the document appropriate?

- To whom does the policy apply (i.e., all employees, full-time employees only, contractors, consultants, customers)?

- Are the organization's information assets comprehensively defined and are the appropriate controls implemented?

- Is the policy consistent with existing corporate directives and guidelines, and with applicable legislation and regulations?

- Is the document concise? Can it be understood and remembered by all affected parties? I've seen several security policies that numbered over 100 pages. I believe that, in the case of security policy development, shorter is always better. Any policy longer than 40 to 50 pages will not be read or remembered by most users.

- Are the policy guidelines reasonable? That is, can the normal person follow the policy directives and still perform their regular duties? Are the guidelines consistent with current technology, organizational culture, and mission?

- Does the document leave room for good judgment? All relevant personnel should be responsible for exercising good judgment regarding the reasonableness of personal use of company resources. Employees should understand that effective security is a team effort involving the participation and support of all those who deal with information and/or information systems.

- Is the document extensible?

Policies & Procedures...

Sample Policies, Procedures, and Guidelines Summary

The following guidelines, polices, and procedures are necessary to effectively secure your systems and network:

1. Acceptable Use Policy
2. Access Control Policy
3. Account Management Policies
4. Availability Policies
5. Configuration Management Policies & Procedures
6. Control of Proprietary Information and Intellectual Property
7. Data Backup Procedures
8. Firewall Management Policy

Continued

9.   General Encryption Policy

10.   IM Security Policy/Procedures

11.   Internet Access Control Policy

12.   Internet Security Awareness & Education Policy

13.   Intrusion Detection Policy/Procedures

14.   Network Connection Policy

15.   Partner Connection Acceptable Use & Connectivity Policy/Procedures

16.   Password Management Policy/Procedures

17.   Privacy Policies

18.   Privileged Access Policy

19.   Remote Access Policy

20.   Security Incident Handling Policies & Procedures

21.   System Security Standards (for specific OSes)

22.   Technology Purchasing Guidelines

23.   User Account Policies

24.   Virus Prevention Policy/Procedures

25.   VoIP Security Policy/Procedures

26.   Wireless Policy/Procedures

Implementation of the resulting security policies is also a process. Policy cannot merely be pronounced by upper management in a one-time directive with high expectations of its being readily accepted and acted upon. Rather, just as formulating and drafting policy involves a process, implementation similarly involves a process, which begins with the formal issuance of policy, and continues via user awareness training, intracompany communications utilizing an intranet or other company communications vehicles, review, and update of policy and policy definitions at regular intervals.

Often there exists a lack of awareness of an organization's IT security policies, among both the general user population and the IT staff. It is imperative that an organization undertake some form of education campaign among the general user population to raise awareness of both the existence of IT security policies and their contents.

All employees should be required to read and acknowledge their understanding of parts of the IT security policy relevant to the general user population during the on-boarding process. As updates are made to the policies that affect the general user population, notices should be sent to the users so that they can acquaint themselves with the changes. It is not enough for these notices to be sent out by e-mail; the notification procedure must include some mechanism for the user to acknowledge receipt of the notice and understanding as to the changes to the policy.

The IT security staff should also consider conducting brief, in-person group trainings regarding the provisions of the IT security policy and physical security in general. These trainings are often more effective than impersonal mechanisms such as e-mail, which are often ignored or acknowledged without a full understanding of the contents of the message or notification. In-person trainings also allow the general user population to gain a fuller understanding of IT security issues, as it allows them to ask questions and voice concerns regarding the policy.

In the process of raising awareness of IT security policies, it is important that the general user population understands the sanctions associated with violating these policies. A security policy that is not enforced, or that is enforced on an arbitrary basis, will be honored more in the breach than in the practice. The policies should include mechanisms for measuring compliance, detecting noncompliance, and responding to policy violations. The general user population must be made aware of these mechanisms. These processes are necessary to make sure that users are held accountable for their actions, as well as to guard against the consequences of inappropriate actions.

A sample VoIP security policy module is included at the end of this chapter. You can use this as a starting point for your own customized VoIP security policy module.

Physical Security

Physical security is an essential part of any security plan. Physical security refers to the protection of building sites and equipment (and all other information and software contained therein) from theft, intrusion, vandalism, natural disaster, man-made catastrophes, and accidental damage (e.g., from electrical surges, extreme temperatures, and spilled coffee). It requires suitable emergency preparedness, reliable power supplies, adequate climate control, and appropriate protection from intruders.

Statistics show that 70 percent of data theft is physical theft (Computer Associates/Pinkerton, 2004). Physical security safeguards provide a first line of defense for information resources against physical damage, physical theft, and unauthorized disclosure of information.

Safeguards can be broken down into two categories: human and environmental. Human safeguard recommendations are:

- Console access should be restricted or eliminated.

- Logon, boot loader, and other passwords must be a minimum of eight characters including at least one each of alpha, numeric, and ctl characters.

- VoIP components must be located in a secure location that is locked and restricted to authorized personnel only.

- Access to these components, wiring, displays, and networks must be controlled by rules of least privilege.

- System configurations (i.e., hardware, wiring, displays, networks) must be documented. Installations and changes to those physical configurations must be governed by a formal change management process.

- A system of monitoring and auditing physical access to VoIP components, wiring, displays, and networks must be implemented (e.g., badges, cameras, access logs). From the point at which an employee enters the building, it is recommended that there be a digital record of their presence.

- The server room should be arranged in a way that people outside the room cannot see the keyboard (thus seeing users/admin passwords).

- Any unused modems must be disabled/removed.

- No password evidence (notes, sticky notes, etc.) is allowed around the system.

Environmental safeguard recommendations are:

- The CPU case should be locked and the key must be accounted for and protected. A backup key should be made and kept securely offsite (e.g., in a safety deposit box).

- USB, CD-ROM, monitor port, and floppy disks drives should be removed, disabled, or glued shut.

- Adequate temperature and humidity controls must be implemented to avoid equipment damage.

- Adequate surge protectors and UPS must be implemented, maintained, and tested.

- Cleaning and maintenance people should be prohibited from the area surrounding any electronics.

- Food, drink, or smoking is prohibited in the same areas.

Frequently, IT and security staff only considers IT security through the prism of logical (IT-related technical) security controls. However, it is often the case that lapses in physical perimeter security controls can contribute to weaknesses in IT security. Methodical testing and anecdotal evidence indicate that the physical perimeter security is insufficient to prevent unauthorized users from entering secured areas, resulting in easy access to the internal network.

> **NOTE**
>
> Choke Points: Often, the largest failing of physical security is the lack of a single choke point for the authentication and admittance of authorized visitors. Following is a real-world example.
>
> Normally visitors are authenticated in a visitor registration area and are then admitted to an elevator area in a separate part of the building using a badge issued in the visitor registration area. The badge is designed to provide a visual indication once it has expired, and is valid only for that specific day or week. However, still-valid daily badges often can be found discarded in trash receptacles. Since the elevator area is watched by a different group of people from those who authenticate the visitor, the guards at the elevator area have no idea whether a visitor is authorized or not other than the possession of a valid visitor badge.
>
> In this example, multiple choke points result in virtually unrestricted physical access to the internal infrastructure.

IP-PBX equipment should be located in a locked room with limited access. This type of access should be provided as a user authentication system with either a keycard or biometric device. The use of a keypad alone to gain access is not permitted. All methods of gaining entry into the room must provide for a list of users that have accessed the room along with a date/time stamp.

Perimeter Protection

Perimeter protection is designed as a deterrent to trespassing and to route employees, visitors, and the guests to selected entrances. Here are two useful examples.

Closed-Circuit Video Cameras

CCTV cameras are relatively inexpensive to deploy and provide a large return on investment. The typical camera should be on a pan/tilt mounting and have a zoom lens, both of which should be controllable by the operator. These features permit the monitoring of wide areas for general activity or the ability to zero in on a particular location.

It is unrealistic to expect an operator to alertly monitor for long periods of time. Therefore, the system should be programmed for periodic sweeps or augmented with intrusion devices triggered by unusual events. All video output should be recorded for future replay if necessary. The videotapes should be archived for a minimum of 30 days. A videotape should be retired and physically destroyed after three complete usage cycles.

Token System

A token is an object physically carried by the user used for authentication purposes. There are several different types of token identification methods including token cards, readers, and biometric devices. The most widely used method is a token card. The following is a sample of the different types of access cards.

Challenge/Response Tokens

This device generates a random passcode, based upon a built-in algorithm that is combined with a user pin number. This resulting number is used, in combination with the standard username and password, for user verification method. Passcode sniffing and brute force attacks are futile since the result is good only for one specific period of time.

Dumb Cards

An example of a dumb card is a photo identification badge. The photo and individual statistics supply enough information to complete the authentication process. Generally, the authentication process is a visual comparison of the ID and the face of the individual.

Smart Cards

The classic example of a smart card is an ATM card. This device combines an individual PIN with information encoded on the card itself.

Biometric Devices

All biometric devices rely upon some type of input device, such as a video camera, retinal scanner, thumb pad, or microphone. The data is than digitized and compared to a stored record. If the match is within defined parameters access is granted.

Wire Closets

Wire closets form a very important piece of the actual network as well as the data that travels on it. Many wire closets contain both network and telephone connections. Oftentimes cases exist where the wire closet is shared by many of the building occupants. The wiring closet can be a very effective launch pad for internal attacks. It is also well suited to the unobserved monitoring of a network. We recommend securing these sensitive locations. When available, they could be added to the already existing card key systems. This would automate the logging of who accessed the location and when. A recommended course of correction would also include the requirement that your organization's representative be physically present during the entire period a collocated wire closet is accessed.

What if the landlord controls access to the closet in a shared-tenant space (a common scenario)? One answer is to use the closet only for external PSTN connectivity and home-run all other wiring to a dedicated closet.

> ### Security Elements...
>
> ## Passwords: The Single Most Important Security Control
>
> You will see this axiom repeated several times in this text. **Well-chosen passwords are the single most important element of any computer security policy.** They are the front line of protection, and often the only line of protection, for user and administrative accounts. A single poorly chosen password may result in the compromise of an entire enterprise network. The first step in protecting against unauthorized access is to define, communicate, and enforce strong password policies.

Server Hardening

From a high-level point of view, all devices that participate in network communications should follow the principle of "Least Privilege." This concept is simple to understand and difficult to put into practice as it often interferes with or interrupts an individual's (particularly administrators) ability to perform routine functions. This means that anything not required should be disabled. Turn off all unneeded services. Disable any features that are not in use. Remove unnecessary applications. This maxim is particularly important when applied to critical infrastructure including servers, routers, firewalls, and so on. Adhering to this principle will reduce the number of potential attack vectors on these systems.

The potential for attack against components of the PBX system is real, and failure to secure a PBX and voice mail system can expose an organization to toll fraud, theft of proprietary information, loss of revenue, and loss of reputation. Hardening the PBX system components limits unauthorized access and use of system resources. The hardening process is OS-specific, but regardless of the OS, consists of: patching, removal of extraneous services, extending logging, removal of unnecessary administrative and user accounts, permission tightening, activation of internal security controls, and various other security tweaks.

Eliminate Unnecessary Services

Most VoIP server platforms ship today on either the Windows or Linux operating systems. Typically, these systems are delivered with many unneeded services activated. These extra services are potential security risks. There are a large number of online and hardcopy references that explain the details of hardening with Windows and Linux operating systems, so in this section we'll survey the high points.

On the Linux platform, examine the /etc/inetd.conf file. This file specifies the services for which the inetd daemon will listen. By default, /etc/inetd.conf is configured to activate a number of listening daemons. You can see these by typing:

```
grep -v "^#" /etc/inetd.conf
```

Determine the services that you require, and then comment out the unneeded services by placing a "#" sign in front of them. This is important, as several of the services run by inetd can pose security threats, such as popd, imapd, and rsh.

Next check your running services by typing:

```
ps aux | wc -l
```

This command will show you the services that normally are started by the .rc scripts. These scripts determine the services started by the init process. Under Red Hat Linux, these scripts reside in /etc/rc.d/rc3.d (or /etc/rc.d/rc5.d if you automatically boot to a GUI, such as Gnome or KDE). To stop a script from starting, replace the uppercase S with a lowercase s. You can easily start the script again just by replacing the lowercase s with an uppercase S. There are other ways to do this, such as chkconfig. The numbers in the names of the startup scripts determine the sequence of initialization. This may vary depending upon the version and Linux distribution that you are using. Scripts that start with an uppercase K instead of an uppercase S are used to kill services that are already running.

On most Windows Server platforms, the active services are listed in the Services window. This can be reached by typing:

```
services.msc
```

At a command prompt, Services simply can be stopped or started by clicking the appropriate stop/start buttons in the toolbar. Alternatively, services can be permanently stopped or started by double-clicking the particular service that you are interested in, and setting its startup type to either manual (the service may still be activated) or disabled. The choice of running services depends upon your environment, but the adage still remains—turn off any service that you don't explicitly require.

Additionally, Microsoft offers two tools that should be run on any server that is a component of critical infrastructure. These are Microsoft Baseline Security Analyzer (MBSA v.2.0) and the IIS lockdown tool. MBSA is a software tool that scans local and remote Windows machines and generates a report that lists both security vulnerabilities (missing patches, incorrect permission settings, etc) and the means to remediate those vulnerabilities. You can find it at www.microsoft.com/technet/security/tools/mbsahome.mspx. The IIS Lockdown Tool functions by turning off unnecessary features and removing particular directories. It also incorporates URLScan, which adds additional protection based upon predefined templates. All the default security-related configuration settings in IIS 6.0 (Windows 2003) meet or exceed the security configuration settings made by the IIS Lockdown tool, so it isn't necessary to run this tool on those servers. Currently, you can find the IIS lockdown tool at www.microsoft.com/technet/security/tools/locktool.mspx.

NOTE

Bastille Linux is one of the more popular tools for hardening Linux. You can find it at www.bastille-linux.org/.

Logging

Once you have turned off as many services as are consistent with proper server function, enable extended logging. On Linux platforms the system logger (syslog) is controlled by the configuration file, /etc/syslog.conf. Syslog is a system utility for tracking and logging all types of system messages from informational to critical. Each message sent to the syslog server is formatted as ASCII text, and has two descriptive labels associated with it. The first describes the function (facility) of the application that generated it. For example, applications such as kernel and cron generate messages with easily identifiable facilities named kernel and cron. The second describes the degree of severity of the message. There are eight levels of criticality ranging from emergencies to debugging with emergencies signifying the most critical messages. All system logs reside in /var/log. /etc/syslog.conf can be configured to store messages of differing severities and facilities in different files, and on different remote computers. Many references exist on the Web that describe configuring syslog on Linux. A good one is www.siliconvalleyccie.com/linux-hn/logging.htm.

Note that remote syslog messages are encapsulated as UDP packets, and until RFC3411 is updated, remote syslog messages are not encrypted. Thus, anyone on the LAN can sniff the syslog traffic. This may be an issue if extended debug messages are generated by a critical server and sent across the LAN.

Windows does not ship with a native syslog daemon; instead, Windows relies upon the System Event Notification manager to track system events such as Windows logon, network, and power events. The System Event Notification manager also notifies COM+ Event System subscribers of these events. A number of syslog addons for Windows exist—I recommend the Kiwi Syslog Daemon. The KIWI product is a full-featured syslog daemon that is free in its basic edition. The extended version can be very useful in that it allows logging to a number of ODBC-compliant databases. Additionally, Kiwi offers a free syslog generator that simplifies testing of syslog functions and connections.

Additionally, under Windows, you'll want to enable extended logging via the Domain Security Policy and Local Security Policy snap-ins. These determine which security events are logged into the Security log on the computer (successful attempts, failed attempts, or both). (The Security log is part of Event Viewer.) Under the Audit Policy tab, logging can be enabled for nine particular security-related events. You should at least enable auditing of failed logon events, successful or failed policy change events, successful or failed account management, and successful or failed privilege use. Note that if the server is in a domain, domain security policies will override local security policies.

Permission Tightening

Under Windows, permission tightening is an art. In addition, the process is significantly different depending upon whether the server version is Windows 2000 or Windows 2003. In these operating systems, Microsoft created a complex and powerful set of interrelating file, folder, and user permission controls that are, frankly, too complex for most system administrators to understand and configure. In my view, the complexity of configuring permissions leads to more security-related events than bad coding on Microsoft platforms, because most administrators rely on default permissions. I will note that with Windows 2003, Microsoft has created a more secure platform with regard to default permissions. Unfortunately, we don't have the space to cover the intricacies securing Windows permissions here. Suffice to say that if you are given the option, choose Windows 2003 as the base OS rather than Windows 2000.

Linux provides a number of accounts that likely are not required for use as a media server or PBX. The rule of thumb is: If you do not require an account, remove it. Each additional account is one more possible avenue of access to the system.

Create the "wheel" group if it doesn't already exist, and populate that group with administrators. The wheel group is a group of select individuals that can execute powerful commands, such as /bin/su. By limiting the people that can access these commands, you enhance system security.

If they exist on your system, lock down the files .rhosts, .netrc, and /etc/hosts.equiv. The r commands, which are deprecated for remote access nowadays, use these files to configure access to systems. To lock them down, touch the files, and then change the permissions to zero. This way no one but root can create or alter the files. For example:

```
/bin/touch /root/.rhosts /root/.netrc /etc/hosts.equiv
/bin/chmod 0 /root/.rhosts /root/.netrc /etc/hosts.equiv
```

This step disables any rhost-based authentication.

Change the following files (if they exist) permissions to the following more secure mode:

File	Owner	Mode
/bin/	root.root	711
/boot/	root.root	700
/dev/	root.root	711
/etc/	root.wheel	711
/etc/modules.conf	root.wheel	640
/etc/cron.daily/	root.wheel	750
/etc/cron.hourly/	root.wheel	750
/etc/cron.monthly/	root.wheel	750
/etc/cron.weekly/	root.wheel	750
/etc/crontab	root.wheel	640
/etc/ftpaccess	root.wheel	640
/etc/hosts.allow	root.wheel	640
/etc/hosts.deny	root.wheel	640

/etc/hosts.equiv	root.wheel	640
/etc/inetd.conf	root.wheel	640
/etc/rc.d/init.d/	root.wheel	750
/etc/rc.d/init.d/syslog	root.wheel	740
/etc/inittab	root.wheel	640
/etc/ld.so.conf	root.wheel	640
/etc/modules.conf	root.wheel	640
/etc/motd	root.wheel	644
/etc/printcap	root.lp	640
/etc/profile	root.root	644
/etc/rc.d/	root.wheel	640
/etc/securetty	root.wheel	640
/etc/shutdown.allow	root.root	600
/etc/ssh/ssh_config	root.root	644
/etc/ssh/ssh_host_key	root.wheel	640
/etc/ssh/ssh_host_key.pub	root.wheel	644
/etc/ssh/sshd_config	root.wheel	640
/etc/syslog.conf	root.wheel	640
/etc/updatedb.conf	root.wheel	640
/home/	root.wheel	751
/home/*	current	700
/lib/	root.wheel	751
/mnt/	root.wheel	750
/root/	root.root	700
/sbin/	root.wheel	751
/tmp/	root.root	1777
/usr/	root.wheel	751
/usr/*	root.wheel	751
/usr/bin/	root.wheel	751
/usr/sbin/	root.wheel	751
/var/	root.root	755
/var/log/	root.root	711
/var/log/*	root.root	600
/var/spool/mail/	root.mail	771
/var/tmp	root.root	1777

Additional Linux Security Tweaks

Now we'll discuss additional security tweaks for securing Linux systems.

1. Remove any files related to: audio (esp), and DHCP (dhcpcd). For example:

   a. `rm -rf /etc/dhcpcd`

   b. `rm -rf /etc/dhcpd`

2. Disable cron use for anyone but root and wheel. This limits the possibility of someone running an unauthorized program periodically

3. Disable Set User ID (SUID) status from dump/restore, cardctl, dosemu, news server programs, rsh, rlogin, mount, umount, ping, ping6, at, user-netctl, traceroute, traceroute6, if possible. The SUID bit is set when a particular program needs to access resources at a higher privilege level than it is normally allowed. For example, traceroute sets the TTL field directly rather than through the sockets interface on the packets it sends. Normally, only a program with root permissions is able to use this low-level interface; thus, traceroute normally is installed with the SUID bit enabled. Unless a pressing need exists in your environment for normal users to access the aforementioned utility programs, disable SUID on all these programs. Failure to remove this bit opens your systems to a number of exploits that result in privilege escalation to root level.

   To find suid programs, issue the following command:

```
find / -type f -perm -2000 -o -perm -4000 -print
```

   Then remove the SUID bit as follows:

```
chmod -s /bin/ping
chmod -s /sbin/ping6
chmod -s /bin/mount
chmod -s /bin/umount
chmod -s /usr/sbin/traceroute
chmod -s /usr/sbin/traceroute6
chmod -s /usr/sbin/usernetctl
chmod -s /usr/bin/at
chmod -s /usr/bin/newgrp
```

Are You 0wned?

Protect Yourself from Root Kits

Install chkrootkit for monitoring of root kits. Chkrootkit is a tool to check a local machine for signs of a root kit. It does this in a number of ways: it checks critical system binaries for signs of root kit modification; it checks to see if a network interface is in promiscuous mode; it checks for wtmp, wtmpx, lastlog, and utmp deletions; and it checks for LKM Trojan modifications. Make sure to add chkrootkit to daily crontab and monitor its results regularly.

4. Clean up mail:

```
cd /var/mail
cat /dev/null > *
chmod 000 *
```

5. Clean up /usr:

```
cd /usr
rm -rf rpms
rm -rf games
rm -rf dict
rm -rf X11R6
cd /usr/local
rm -rf games
```

6. Clean up /etc:

```
rm -rf /etc/X11
rm -rf /etc/yp.conf
```

A number of OS- and version-specific security tweaks exist. The following list is not exhaustive since many of these are environment-specific; however, these will give you some areas to focus on.

1. Enforce password aging.

2. Enforce limits on resources to prevent a DoS attack.

3. Password-protect boot loader.

4. Password-protect single user mode.

5. Add additional logging.

6. Disable apmd, NFS, Samba, PCMCIA, DHCP server, NNTP server, routing daemons, NIS, SNMPD, and GPM.

7. Disable printing and files related to lpd.

8. Activate TMPDIR protection.

9. Set umask to 077.

10. Restrict "." from the PATH variable.

11. Activate Internal security controls.

12. Apply security patches (see last section of this chapter).

Activation of Internal Security Controls

1. Configure TCP Wrappers by editing /etc/hosts.allow and /etc/hosts.deny. Put this first in /etc/hosts.allow. Then edit /etc/hosts.deny so that it reads ALL : ALL : DENY. Don't enter this until all the daemons are activated in /etc/hosts.allow.

   ```
   sshd  : ALL \
   : spawn /bin/echo SSH Connection on `/bin/date` from
       %h>>/var/log/messages \
               : allow
   in.ftpd : ALL : spawn /bin/echo FTP access from %h on
       `/bin/date`>>/var/log/messages : allow
   sshd : ALL : spawn /bin/echo SSH access from %h on
       `/bin/date`>>/var/log/messages : allow
   in.telnetd : ALL : spawn /bin/echo TELNET access from %h on
       `/bin/date`>>/var/log/messages : allow
   in.tftpd : ALL : spawn /bin/echo TFTP access from %h on
       `/bin/date`>>/var/log/messages : allow
   ```

2. Install Tripwire, a file system integrity-checking program for Windows and UNIX operating systems. The core of any computer system is the disk drive, whether the underlying objects are UNIX file systems, Windows NTFS, or the Registry. In general, making harmful changes to a computer system requires some type of modification to the data on disk, such as planting Trojan horse programs, back doors, root kits (a compressed group of files that allows a user to obtain system level privileges by exploiting a

security hole in the operating system), or by modifying critical system files such as /etc/passwd.

From a security perspective, one of the most important responsibilities of modern operating systems is to authenticate users and preserve privilege levels. In computer security, root (superuser or admin) privilege level is all powerful: Root kits allow attackers to steal these privileges and to cover their tracks. Trojan horses masquerade as common harmless programs but may carry programs that facilitate remote superuser access. Backdoors allow unrestricted, unauthorized hacker access to network assets.

Tripwire is one form of intrusion detection. Much like the secret agent trick of putting a hair on the doorknob to validate that no one has entered a room, Tripwire validates that critical system files have not been altered. Tripwire creates a secure database of file and directory attributes (including, if desired, complex cryptographic file hashes), which are then used to compare against to monitor if a file or directory has been altered. For example, if an attacker has broken in and added a bogus entry to the /etc/passwd file, Tripwire will alert.

Tripwire software is used for host-based intrusion detection (HIDS), file integrity assessment, damage discovery, change/configuration management, system auditing, forensics, and policy compliance. Host-based IDS software is able to monitor a system or application log file for unauthorized changes. Tripwire's integrity assessment detects external and internal attacks and misuse. Ultimately, the role of Tripwire is to notify system administrators of changed, added, and deleted files in some meaningful and useful manner. These reports can then be used for the purposes of intrusion detection, recovery, and forensic analysis.

To use Tripwire, you first must specify a configuration file that designates the directories and files that you want to protect. You then run Tripwire (with the initialize option) to create a database of cryptographic checksums that correspond with the files and directories specified in the configuration file. Tripwire then is run periodically via cron, and the current checksums are compared with the originals. If a file is altered, then the checksums will not match. To protect the Tripwire program, configuration file, and initialized database against corruption, be sure to transfer them to a medium that can be designated as physically write-protected, such as a CD-ROM.

a.   Edit /etc/tripwire/twcfg.txt. Here is a sample configuration.

```
ROOT                          =/usr/sbin
POLFILE                       =/etc/tripwire/tw.pol
DBFILE                        =/var/lib/tripwire/$(HOSTNAME).twd
REPORTFILE                    =/var/lib/tripwire/report/$(HOSTNAME)-
$(DATE).twr
SITEKEYFILE                   =/etc/tripwire/site.key
LOCALKEYFILE                  =/etc/tripwire/$(HOSTNAME)-local.key
EDITOR                        =/bin/vi
LATEPROMPTING                 =false
LOOSEDIRECTORYCHECKING        =false
MAILNOVIOLATIONS              =true   <- Change to false
EMAILREPORTLEVEL              =3
REPORTLEVEL                   =3
MAILMETHOD                    =SENDMAIL
SYSLOGREPORTING               =false        <- Change to true
MAILPROGRAM                   =/usr/sbin/sendmail -oi -t
```

b. As the root user, type /etc/tripwire/twinstall.sh at the shell prompt to run the configuration script. The twinstall.sh script will ask you for site and local passwords. These passwords are used to generate cryptographic keys for protecting Tripwire files. The script then creates and signs these files. When selecting the site and local passwords, you should consider the following guidelines:

c. Make the Tripwire passwords completely different from the root or any other password for the system.

d. Use unique passwords for both the site key and the local key.

e. The site key password protects the Tripwire configuration and policy files. The local key password protects the Tripwire database and report files. Warning: There is no way to decrypt a signed file if you forget your password. If you forget the passwords, the files are unusable and you will have to run the configuration script again.

f. Run /usr/sbin/tripwire --init in order to initialize the tripwire database. This may take a while. Once you finish these steps successfully, Tripwire has the baseline snapshot of your file system necessary to check for changes in critical files. After initializing the Tripwire database, you should run an initial integrity check.

```
/usr/sbin/tripwire --check
```

This check should be done prior to connecting the computer to the network and putting it into production. Figure 10.3 outlines the Tripwire processes.

Figure 10.3 A Diagram of Tripwire Processes

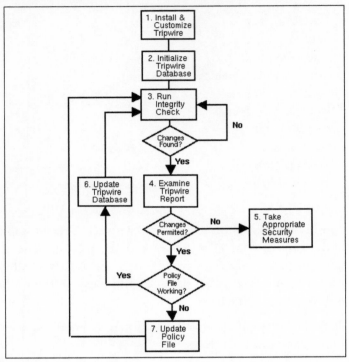

g. By default, the Tripwire RPM adds a shell script called tripwire-check to the /etc/cron.daily/ directory. This script automatically runs an integrity check once per day. You can, however, run a Tripwire integrity check at any time by typing the following command: /usr/sbin/trip-wire --check

h. To view a Tripwire report, type:

```
/usr/sbin/twprint -m r --twrfile \
/var/lib/tripwire/report/<report_name>. twr
```

i. Remove Tripwire install files: twcfg.txt, twinstall.sh, twpol.txt. and ftp the remaining files in tripwire directory to a secure server or burn them to disk.

j. Be sure to check the Tripwire reports regularly. Much like other types of forensic logging, if the reports are not viewed by humans at regular intervals, then they serve little purpose.

Activate iptables firewall

ftp rc.firewall.sh script to /etc/init.d

Start script by running: *sh rc.firewall.sh*

Firewall services can be checked by: *service iptables status*

Security Patching and Service Packs

In this section we'll put down some of our thoughts on Best Practices for the application and determination of appropriate service packs and security patches for VoIP-related client and server computers.

Service packs correct known problems and provide tools, drivers, and updates that extend product functionality, including updates, system administration tools, drivers, security updates, and additional components developed after the product was released. Service packs often contain many files, and are normally cumulative, but not always. Check this before you apply the service pack. Normally, service packs are packaged for easy downloading and installation. Patches, on the other hand, are usually specific to a particular file. Security patches eliminate (hopefully) security vulnerabilities. Oftentimes, security patches are released in response to the public circulation of exploit code. Service packs and patches often are interrelated, and it is important to check that the patch is workable for a particular service pack.

Before applying any service pack or patch, read all relevant documentation. Schedule server outages and be sure to have a complete set of backups available, in case a restoration is required. If possible, test the update(s) on noncritical infrastructure first. Develop and follow change control procedures. A good change control procedure has an identified owner, an audit trail for any changes, a defined announcement and review period, testing procedures, and a well-understood back-out plan. A good rule of thumb is: If you don't have a back-out plan, don't patch.

Only patch or update when you have to. It is likely that you have been part of a situation where a router or server function failed mysteriously. Typically, the vendor response is that you upgrade to a new operating system revision. The consequent upgrade then results in a number of new, unrelated problems. Murphy's Law dictates that this occurs only on the most critical infrastructure components at the most sensitive times. Alternatively, there are examples of a patch for one file that damages the functionality of another unrelated file.

Test before patching. Test after patching. Then, test again. If possible, monitor the updated production servers carefully for the first few days after the update.

Supporting Services

VoIP relies upon a number of ancillary services as part of the configuration process, as a means to locate users, for management, and to ensure favorable transport, among others. These include DNS, DHCP, LDAP, RADIUS, HTTP, HTTPS, SNMP, SSH, TELNET, NTP, and TFTP. Other services that modify QoS are also required. We recommend that those services that support the VoIP infrastructure be dedicated to that infrastructure. The following sections assume that the support infrastructure is protected from direct Internet traffic by a firewall, firewalls, IDS, IPS, or a combination of these.

DNS and DHCP Servers

DHCP is used in VoIP environments to provide an IP address and other relevant information such as the default gateway location, the subnet mask, the IP address of local DNS servers, the name and location of firmware and configuration servers, and other options. DHCP relies upon a broadcast mechanism to query for an IP address, so be sure to locate DHCP servers in separate broadcast domains in order to eliminate confusing addressing results.

DHCP services may be susceptible to a Rogue DHCP server attack. During boot-up, the IP phone sends a DHCP request for its own IP address and the address of a RAS server. Because DHCP replies are not authenticated, a rogue DHCP server can reply with erroneous information resulting in, at best, a Denial of Service, and at worst, routing to a server under the control of the attacker. One solution to this is to install an IDS on the VoIP-related subnets that could detect repeated DHCP requests (these are broadcast packets) and determine that an IP phone is having trouble booting. Alternatively, methods have been suggested (RFC3118) for authentication of DHCP messages. Unfortunately, few devices support these methods.

Tech Terms...

Acronym Soup

An Analog Telephony Adapter (ATA) is a device used to connect one or more analog telephones to a VoIP-based network. The ATA usually takes the form of a small box with a power adapter, one or more Ethernet ports, and one or more FXS telephone ports. Another way to think about an ATA is that it functions as an FXS to Ethernet gateway.

A Foreign eXchange Subscriber (FXS) port is a legacy term for an interface that connects to subscriber equipment (telephone, modem, or fax). An FXS interface points to the terminal endpoint equipment, and additionally, provides the following primary services to the subscriber device: Dial Tone, Battery Current, and Ring Voltage. You plug your phone into an FXS port.

The complementary member to an FXS is the Foreign eXchange Office (FXO) port. This interface receives POTS service, typically from a Central Office (CO). In other words an FXO interface points to the Telco office. If your ATA contains an FXO interface, then you connect this interface to the jack in the wall.

In May, 2005, a DoS exploit was announced that relied upon sending specially crafted DNS packets to Cisco IP phones, ACNS, Unity Express, and ATAs. The only fix for this was to upgrade to a fixed software revision. This illustrates the requirement to stay informed of current software vulnerabilities, and to maintain some type of regular patching/update cycle.

DNS services have a number of uses within a VoIP environment, the most important being IP address name resolution. In a simple configuration, DNS services may be used simply to map a URI (Uniform Resource Locator) to one or more IP addresses. As VoIP technology and infrastructure arrangements mature, DNS will play a more central role in converting E164 defined telephone numbers to IP addresses via the ENUM framework. One caveat in this arrangement is that synchronization and delegation of DNS servers must be planned and managed carefully in order for the system to function properly.

DHCP and DNS servers should be secured by hardening their respective operating systems, and in the case of DNS, by ensuring that the BIND daemon is patched and up-to-date. Running a recent version of BIND generally means that you are running the most secure version of BIND. Additionally, you should disallow queries from unauthorized nameservers, ensure that only your slave nameservers are allowed to update by requesting zone transfers, and BIND should be run with least privilege—jailing or chrooting the BIND daemon is always good practice. In high security environments it is worthwhile to run TSIG (transaction signatures) between nameservers in order to authenticate DNS messages (see DNS & BIND, Albitz & Liu, O'Reilly, 2001 for more detailed information).

DNS traffic also can be difficult to correctly firewall. DNS traffic runs over port 53 via TCP or UDP depending upon the transaction. The problem is that in recent major versions of BIND (8 and 9), nameservers, by default, send queries from random high-numbered ports to port udp/53 of the resolver (client). Resolvers also send their queries from random high-numbered ports to port udp/53 of the nameserver. One way to resolve (sorry for the pun) this issue is to *allow from any to port udp/53* in both directions on the firewall. However, this is not a particularly elegant solution in that the control is not very granular. A better solution is to use the *query-source* option to force BIND to send queries from port 53. This enables more stringent control of DNS traffic on the firewall.

LDAP and RADIUS Servers

LDAP (Lightweight Directory Access Protocol) is a protocol for accessing X.500 directory services. LDAP is the de facto standard for directory-based application, authentication. authorization, and search requests. An LDAP server is essentially a database optimized for read rather than read/write operations. LDAP services provide call routing and subscriber information within a VoIP environment. RADIUS (Remote Authentication Dial In User Service) is an AAA (authentication, authorization, and accounting) protocol for many different types of applications ranging from router and switch access to subscriber AAA in a VoIP environment.

The LDAP directory stores information about objects on a network and makes this information available to applications, users, and network administrators. Using LDAP, authorized network users can access resources anywhere on the network using a single login process. Within the enterprise, LDAP directories often comprise the corporate directory. Much of the data in these types of directories is considered security-critical data because it includes personal information including usernames, passwords, contact information, and, of course, telephone numbers and SIP URIs.

This leads to a conundrum: The location services provided by the LDAP directory server (or more typically, a cluster of these servers) must be quickly and easily accessible by anyone or any machine with the appropriate login credentials. On the other hand, these services must be completely inaccessible by any nonauthorized user. Complicating this scenario is that properly authenticated users must be given enough, and only enough, authorization so that they can access their cognate data and no other.

LDAP and RADIUS security tasks include hardening the operating system that the services reside upon and restricting access to port tcp/389 (LDAP) and ports tcp/1812 and tcp/1813 (RADIUS) to only those agents that require access. Additionally, most LDAP implementations provide for native (though complex) access control in the form of Access Control Lists (ACLs). Proper configuration of these ACLs is critical to securing your LDAP directory server; however, this task must be designed and implemented carefully.

Lastly, LDAP natively provides no protection against sniffing or active attackers, whereas RADIUS provides some protection based upon shared secrets. SSL v3 or TLS are recommended for securing LDAP data while in transmission. Normally these data are received on port tcp/636.

NTP

Time synchronization often is overlooked during the design of network infrastructure. On a stand-alone computer or network device such as a router or a switch, the time, which usually is based on inexpensive oscillator circuits, can drift by seconds each day. Over time, this drift leads to significant variation in the times of different network clocks. Why is this important for VoIP infrastructure and security?

To begin with, any servers or other networked devices that participate in clusters for load balancing or high availability will act inconsistently if their clocks are not synchronized. Network monitoring services (see the next section) rely upon an accurate clock for determining the root-cause of network outages or delays. In forensic analysis, DHCP leases can be tied to specific workstations if the clocks on all machines are accurately synchronized. Directory services require accurate clocks. Windows 2000 and Windows 2003 are significant examples of this since the default authentication protocol (Kerberos v5) for many domain functions uses the workstation time as part of the ticketing process. Most importantly, from a security point of view, any type of logging, particularly if logs from different hosts are stored on a remote server, relies upon accurate timestamps to correlate specific data with specific events.

For these reasons, it is recommended to create a time synchronization hierarchy as part of the foundation VoIP architecture.

SNMP

SNMP is vital in VoIP networks, particularly for monitoring discrete systems and for traffic supervision. In addition, many vendors use SNMP as part of the IP telephone configuration process. SNMP traffic, at least for versions 1 and 2, is encoded using ASN.1 syntax and BER encoding; however, it is not encrypted. SNMP v3 traffic can be encrypted.

Unfortunately, the default community strings associated with the most common versions of SNMP (v1 and v2) are well-known and easily guessed. These community strings act as passwords that allow access to the SNMP-managed device. The default read-only community string (public) allows a user to browse configuration information regarding the device or server. Information gathered in this manner can potentially be used to gain further access to the device.

SNMP messages, like syslog messages, can be stolen by eavesdroppers, and these data can be used to determine the state and configuration of networked devices. Routers and switches can be reconfigured as well by the appropriate SNMP commands. Thus, it is recommended to use SNMP v3 for monitoring and configuration of VoIP networks. If the use of SNMP v3 is not a valid option, due to network constraints or a lack of support by networked devices, then it is essential to restrict SNMP to subnets that are segregated from the Internet and from the balance of the network.

This can be accomplished in a number of ways including VLANs, firewalls, and access control lists. These methods are described in more detail in Chapter 13. Note that a number of different vendors' (UTstarcom, Cisco, and Hitachi, for example) IP phones have shipped in the past 18 months with default SNMP read/write strings. This allows any remote user to read, write, and erase the configuration of an affected device. Before you deploy your IP phones, check that the default community strings have been replaced by complex passwords. This highlights a key concept in securing SNMP on any type of network. Always check for the presence of default community strings and if they exist, change them to complex strings.

SSH and Telnet

SSH and Telnet are real-time protocols that often are used by VoIP system administrators for normal maintenance and troubleshooting. Telnet is a protocol commonly used for remote administration of servers and network devices. A major failing of Telnet is that it passes data in the clear; it uses no encryption. Usernames and passwords used to log into remote devices traverse the IP network unencrypted and are susceptible to interception. Although many network administrators believe that this risk is mitigated by the use of a switched network, techniques and tools exist that allow interception of switched traffic.

In the mid 1990s, as sniffer software became more readily available (i.e., free), system administrators began to search for a secure encrypting replacement for Telnet, rsh, rcp, and so on. SSLTelnet and SNP (Secure Network protocol) are two examples that have faded into history. SSH (Secure Shell) became the de facto choice for secure communication between networked devices. SSH allows an individual to log into another computer over a network, to execute commands on the remote machine, and to move files from one machine to another (SCP). It provides strong authentication and secure communications over insecure channels. A number of free SSH clients exist for both Windows and LINUX operating systems, and almost all servers support the SSH protocol.

Recently, several versions have been vulnerable to the CRC32 Compensation Attack exploit. If you plan to use a version of SSH based upon OpenSSH, be sure to install the most up-to-date version available, run SSH protocol 2, and be sure to disable the option to drop back to SSH protocol 1.

The message in this section is clear: There is no longer a place in any contemporary VoIP network for nonsecure, nonencrypted administrative maintenance or troubleshooting traffic.

Unified Network Management

Network management tools that are used on the data network can be used to monitor the entire converged infrastructure. This is one of the major advantages of a converged network. Existing network management tools may need to be updated to reflect the enhanced requirements of a VoIP network. If possible, management traffic should be segregated to an out-of-band, dedicated management network.

Proactive management of this complex environment ensures that the quality of voice calls will fall within acceptable limits. Voice quality is made up of both objective and subjective factors. The objective factors in assessing VoIP quality are delay, jitter, and packet loss. Delay is defined as the time it takes a packet to traverse the network from the sending node to the receiving node. It usually is estimated as the round-trip-time (RTT) divided by 2. Jitter is defined as the variance or change in delay times. If RTT are greater than 250 to 300 msec, then voice quality will suffer. All three measurements are interrelated. Studies have shown that the greater the jitter in a VoIP environment, the greater the packet loss. VoIP does not tolerate packet loss (dropped media packets are not resent), thus the greater the packet loss, the lower the voice quality. Active monitoring and management of voice quality in a VoIP environment is a must to help identify and reduce such undesirable occurrences.

If you are responsible for network monitoring in your own VoIP environment, then a number of tools—in a range from freeware to expensive commercial—are available to you. At the low end (price-wise, but not feature-wise) are tools like MRTG, NTOP, Nagios, and a host of other SNMP-based agent-managers. At the high end, tools like HP OpenView, Tivoli, and SMARTS not only discover and manage network objects, but in some cases, attempt to determine the root cause of network problems. The key security issue in rolling your own security monitoring infrastructure is that you segregate management traffic to a dedicated, secure, management network. The other key point is that managing your own network monitoring professionally requires that you dedicate human beings to the task of reading, analyzing, and acting upon the resultant data.

Many clients rely upon third-party remote management of VoIP infrastructure components. How do you choose between differing vendor offerings? What are the criteria you should use when making this decision? Hopefully, the next several paragraphs will give you some insight into this process.

First, you will require a secure and auditable path between your managed sites and the vendor sites that support remote delivery of services. One of the most challenging problems in remote management of large networks is the complexity of security administration. This can be a difficult issue to solve technically as mutual trust, at some point, becomes an issue. Technical workarounds for this include multiple layers of firewalls—some of which are managed by each party; coincident visualization of all encrypted traffic that spans the two networks; and strongly typed, enforced, and audited role-based access controls (RBAC).

You should specify that the remote management services incorporate a standards-based approach that enables secure maintenance access and monitoring for multivendor services support. Standards will enable visibility into the processes that are used to monitor your network. Check that all regulatory requirements that are relevant for your particular industry are met, including a strong audit trail for all transactions. Ensure that the remote management vendor provides a single point of alarm consolidation, ticketing, and inbound/outbound access to the corporate network; and that a customer self-service maintenance portal with unrestricted access to audit trail information and reports is available. Last, be certain that you retain access and control of the devices within your own infrastructure.

Sample VoIP Security Policy

In this section we'll discuss the components of a sample VoIP security policy.

Purpose

VoIP is a highly critical data application and as such, is subject to all the policies detailed in other data security policy sections (this assumes that the VoIP Security Policy module is part of a larger set of security policy modules). The purpose of this section is to provide an additional checklist to ensure that VoIP systems sharing the data network as a converged technology are implemented in a secure fashion.

Policy

Security in an IP telephony environment includes all the security features of traditional telephony and adds all the security concerns of the data network. IP telephony converts voice to data and places these data into IP packets. As such, these packets can be "sniffed" just like any other data packet on the network, thereby raising serious issues of confidentiality. The operating systems underlying IP-PBXs and other gateway devices are susceptible to the same attacks that regularly disrupt other types of servers.

Physical Security

IP-PBX equipment must be located in a locked room with limited access. This type of access must be provided as a user authentication system with either a key-card or biometric device. The use of a keypad alone to gain access is not permitted. All methods of gaining entry into the room must provide for a list of users that have accessed the room along with a date/time-stamp.

VLANs

Logical separation of voice and data traffic via VLANs is required to prevent the VoIP streams from broadcast collisions, and to protect data network problems from affecting voice traffic.

Softphones

Softphones that contain any type of advertising software must be banned in a highly secure environment. Softphone installation targets should be tested before deployment and those that do not encrypt user credentials should be prohibited.

Because a softphone is an application running on an operating system, its security depends principally upon the status of the underlying OS, and is subject to the same security concerns as any other communications program including e-mail, browsing, and IM.

Encryption

All VoIP systems should use a form of Media (RTP channel) Encryption in order to avoid the sniffing of VoIP data. All communications between network elements should be encrypted. Complete end-to-end IP voice encryption is recommended to mitigate the threat of eavesdropping attempts. Additionally, all administrative access to critical server and network components must use encrypted protocols such as SSL and/or SSH. All access to remote administrative functions should be restricted to connections to the switch itself or to a designated management PC.

Layer 2 Access Controls

The most comprehensive solution is to require all devices to authenticate on layer two using 802.1X before receiving layer three (IP) configuration settings.

Additionally, consider enabling port security as well as MAC address filtering on distribution switches. The port security feature of these devices provides the ability to restrict the use of a port to a specific MAC address or set of MAC addresses. It is generally considered that this is difficult to implement and maintain, but with proper planning, port security does not have to be difficult. Several third-party tools are available to help manage and maintain port security in enterprise environments.

Summary

In this chapter, we have discussed many of the ways that you can reuse portions of your existing security infrastructure as you prepare to add voice traffic to the mix. After you or your management has made the decision to move to a converged network, and before the new architecture is completed, it is important that one or more representatives of the security group participate in the architectural discussions. "Bolting on" security components and processes after the network and application architecture is finalized just doesn't work. Security as an afterthought usually results in a network that is insecure, as well as users that are frustrated because they now have to "do things differently."

Adding VoIP to your network may introduce additional risks, so your first step is to review your existing security policies. Do they exist at all? If so, are they current? Do most associates know where to find them? Do people understand their responsibilities?

In the section on Security Policies, we discussed the steps involved in formulation of policy. We talked about implementation and communication of the policy guidelines, as well as who should be involved in the process. A sample VoIP Security Policy module is located near the end of the chapter. Feel free to use this as a template for your own policies.

In the section on Physical Security, we discussed some of the measures and physical controls that are needed in a VoIP environment. A truly dedicated attacker, finding little means of accessing an organization's internal IP network over a public network such as the Internet, often will turn to physical penetration to bypass the organization's logical perimeter security controls. This is not just a theoretical vulnerability; numerous incidences of attackers using physical penetration to bypass logical perimeter security controls have been reported in the mainstream media. A comprehensive security strategy must consider the efficacy of physical perimeter security as well as its logical or technical perimeter security.

The section on Server Hardening went into some detail regarding hardening of specific platforms and the rationale for doing so. All hosts attached to the VoIP network should follow a standard build procedure and be subjected to hardening before they are connected to the network. One group within the organization should bear the responsibility for maintaining standard build and hardening guidelines for Windows, Linux, AIX, and other UNIX and UNIX-like operating systems. This group should define these guidelines, ensure that these hosts are hardened and patched before deployment, and ensure that patches are updated periodically as appropriate. This group should also maintain a central registry of individuals and groups running these operating systems so that periodic audits can be conducted to guarantee that the systems do not deviate from the established security baselines.

The section on Supporting Services described the functions and security characteristics of VoIP supplementary services. The servers that host these services should be hardened and patched per security policy guidelines. Hardening of these servers, as mentioned earlier, should follow the principle of "Least Privilege." This means that anything not required should be disabled. Turn off all unneeded services. Disable any features that are not in use. Remove unnecessary applications.

Last, the section on Unified Management detailed some of your responsibilities when designing the monitoring network for your VoIP infrastructure. Many open source network-monitoring tools exist that work as well as more expensive commercial packages. The trade-off is that the open source tools are usually more difficult to set up and maintain than their commercial counterparts. If you decide to outsource your network management tasks, make certain that you have defined in detail the SLAs, network topology, trust relationships, and reporting requirements.

This design period is an excellent time to inventory, unravel, and review your existing security infrastructure. It makes good business sense to reuse and recycle devices and processes that have worked in the past, and to eliminate those that don't work or those that do not provide a reasonable ROI.

At this point, you have updated your security policies to reflect the addition of voice to your data networks. You have physically secured the VoIP and data infrastructure components so that it is impossible (or at least unlikely) that unauthorized individuals have direct access to these components. You have hardened and patched servers, routers, switches, and other supporting devices so that they are resistant to common exploits. And you have determined how you will monitor your infrastructure.

In the following chapter, we'll look at methods for confirming that only authorized users have access to this infrastructure.

Solutions Fast Track

Security Policies and Processes

☑ A Security Policy provides the framework, justification, and metrics for all other security related development.

☑ A policy that is not consistently enforced is worse than having no policy at all.

☑ The most important step in security policy practices is communicating the policy contents to everyday users—these "human firewalls" are the best security investment an organization can make.

☑ Upgrading a data network to a Data + VoIP network is an ideal time to reexamine and revamp the security state of your support infrastructure.

Physical Security

☑ CCTV cameras that record to disk are inexpensive and useful security tools.

☑ Require more than one type of authentication for access into critical areas.

☑ Remember to lock doors and windows.

Server Hardening

☑ Turn off all unnecessary services and listening daemons.

☑ The risk of implementing the service pack or security patch should *always be less* than the risk of not implementing it.

☑ If you make the effort to generate log files, then review them regularly. Logged data are a great resource for understanding the day-to-day operation of your infrastructure.

Supporting Services

☑ If possible, dedicate your support infrastructure components to either data or VoIP networks but not both.

☑ Ensure that multiple DHCP servers do not coexist in the same broadcast domain.

☑ Ensure that SNMP community strings are not set to default values.

☑ Replace Telnet with SSH at every opportunity.

Unified Network Management

☑ Delay, jitter, and packet loss are the major network variables that impact VoIP quality.

☑ Always segregate management traffic on a dedicated, secure management network.

Frequently Asked Questions

The following Frequently Asked Questions, answered by the authors of this book, are designed to both measure your understanding of the concepts presented in this chapter and to assist you with real-life implementation of these concepts. To have your questions about this chapter answered by the author, browse to **www.syngress.com/solutions** and click on the **"Ask the Author"** form.

Q: Our security policy document is 300+ pages long. Is it comprehensive enough?

A: No one can read or understand a security policy that is that long. Try to keep it to a maximum of 40 to 50 pages.

Q: What's the best way to communicate the contents of our security policy?

A: There is no best way, but there are many ways. Post it on the company intranet or in the company paper. Put up security-related signs or magnets in computing areas. Publicly reward individuals who exemplify some example of security awareness.

Q: What's a root kit?

A: A root kit is a set of tools—usually contained in a single compressed file—used by an attacker during and after breaking into a computer system. These tools allow the attacker to maintain and mask his or her access to the system and use it for malicious purposes.

Q: Does Tripwire run on Windows?

A: Yes, Tripwire runs on Windows, Linux, BSD, and many network appliances.

Q: Is SNMP data natively secure?

A: SNMP versions 1 and 2 are not secure because they traverse the network unencrypted. SNMP v3 allows for encryption.

Q: What are stratum 1 and stratum 2 clocks?

A: The NTP primary (stratum 1) host designates an NTP time server available for public access with certain restrictions. Normally, only stratum 2 clocks should use these time sources.

Q: How is an LDAP database different from a normal database?

A: Typically, an LDAP database is designed for fast read operations, and the data normally is described in ASN.1 syntax.

Q: What is ENUM?

A: ENUM is a framework for converting E164 formatted telephone numbers into IPv4 addresses.

Chapter 11

Confirm User Identity

Solutions in this chapter:

- 802.1x and 802.11i
- Public Key Infrastructure
- Minor Authentication Methods

☑ Summary

☑ Solutions Fast Track

☑ Frequently Asked Questions

Introduction

Authentication is a measure of trust. The point of this chapter is to illustrate trust complexities and to cover authentication of both user identity and device identity. These two identities are not equal. Authentication in the networking world, in general, is based either on using a shared secret (you are authenticated if you know the secret) or on public key-based methods with certificates (you prove your identity by possessing the correct private key). Authentication establishes the identities of devices and users to a degree that is in accord with your security policies. Authorization, on the other hand, establishes the amount and type of network and application resources authorized individuals and devices are able to access.

Device authentication can be automated and made transparent to the user based upon assigning and verifying a unique profile for the device. This profile may include attributes such as model, serial number, MAC address, IP address, physical location, time-of-day, and so on, and may include a shared secret or a certificate. Device authentication literally blocks rogue endpoints from accessing any network resources. In a VoIP environment, this prevents malicious endpoints from placing unauthorized calls or causing other mischief. Some of the 802.1x and 802.11i standards described later in this chapter can be used as part of an automated device authentication process.

NOTE

Bluetooth security is based upon device authentication, not user authentication. Each device is either trusted or untrusted. Bluetooth devices are identified by unique 48-bit identifiers, much like Ethernet MAC addresses.

Everyone who has logged on to a computer is familiar with user authentication. Users identify themselves to an authenticator by presenting credentials. The most common of these is a username/password combination, although user authentication can also be accomplished using other means including biometric or token-based methods. Common network-based authentication methods include Windows domain authentication, NIS+, and Kerberos. Windows 2000 and later platforms offer two default authentication mechanisms: MS Kerberos and NTLM. Most users believe that logging on to an account in a Windows domain gives them access to the network. That is not true. When the Kerberos protocol (the default) is used for network authentication, the user's first access is to the domain's authentication service, which ultimately provides access to network resources.

In order to secure VoIP networks, the identity of both the user and the device must be verified. This can be accomplished in a number of ways. Network-based authentication methods such as those mentioned earlier in this chapter often are used, and in many environments, this user authentication is considered sufficient for virtually unrestricted access to network resources. However, as we argue in Chapter 1, network boundaries are disappearing, network users are increasingly mobile, more types and quantities of devices are registering with the network, and devices no longer even require a physical link to access network resources. The addition of VoIP resources to the existing infrastructure only adds to this complexity. The aforementioned mechanisms are not sufficient to cope with these new sophisticated technologies.

Some simple fixes are available. User identity can be confirmed using a method as simple as HTTP Digest authentication, and devices can simply be filtered by MAC address lists. These point solutions have their drawbacks. Both can be circumvented by attackers with minimal skills, and neither scale well. In order to confirm user and device identity on enterprise VoIP networks, system administrators will ultimately turn to 802.1x/EAP, a certificate infrastructure, or a combination of these. The remainder of this chapter discusses these two technologies.

Figure 11.1 shows the generic components involved in a model authentication scheme. The static beginning and end states are the device and user identities, and internal network access, respectively. The processes are access control and authorization. Much of this chapter is devoted to exploring these mechanisms.

Figure 11.1 General Authentication—Authorization Framework

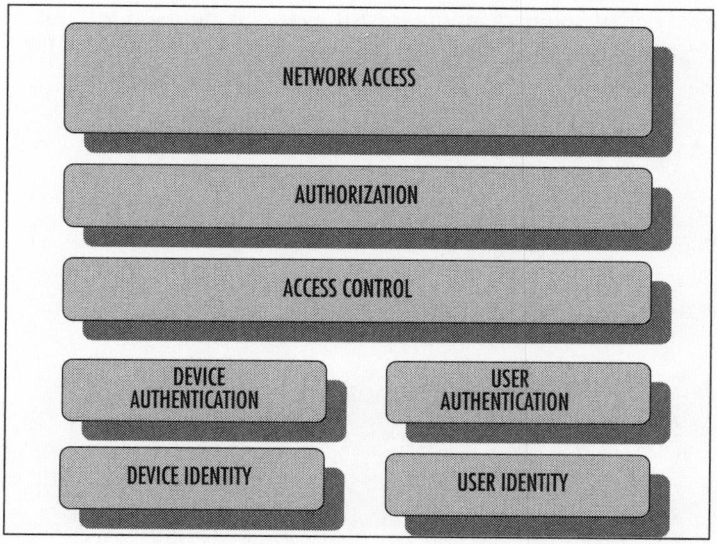

In H.323 environments the basis for authentication (trust) is defined by the endpoints of the communications channel. For a connection establishment channel, this may be between the caller (such as a gateway or IP telephone endpoint) and a hosting network component (a gateway or gatekeeper). For example, a telephone "trusts" that the gatekeeper will connect it with the telephone whose number has been dialed. The result of trusting an element is the confidence to reveal the privacy mechanism (algorithm and key) to that element. Given the aforementioned information, all participants in the communications path should authenticate any and all trusted elements. This is described in more detail in Chapter 5.

The SIP draft does not explicitly define authentication mechanisms. In contrast, SIP developers chose a modular approach—reusing the same headers, error codes, and encoding rules as HTTP. From RFC 3261:

> The fundamental security services required for the SIP protocol are: preserving the confidentiality and integrity of messaging, preventing replay attacks or message spoofing, providing for the authentication and privacy of the participants in a session, and preventing denial-of-service attacks. Bodies within SIP messages separately require the security services of confidentiality, integrity, and authentication. Rather than defining new security mechanisms specific to SIP, SIP reuses wherever possible existing security models derived from the HTTP and SMTP space.

SIP defines a set of security mechanisms that can be used by any SIP client or server to share authentication data (see Table 11.1).

Table 11.1 SIP Security Mechanisms

AUTHENTICATION METHOD	AUTHENTICATION TYPE	CONFIDENTIALITY	INTEGRITY
S/MIME	PUBLIC KEY INFRASTRUCTURE	YES	YES
TLS	PUBLIC KEY INFRASTRUCTURE	YES	YES
IPSEC	PUBLIC KEY INFRASTRUCTURE & PSK	YES	YES
HTTP 1.1 DIGEST	PRE-SHARED KEY	NO	NO

Since SIP's syntax is based on HTTP, it reuses HTTP Digest Authentication to authenticate endpoints. S/MIME, TLS, and IPSec can also be used to protect components of the SIP infrastructure. SIP can use TLS for signaling security between routing elements (hop by hop), as well as S/MIME for security of signaling end to end. TLS security is visible to users and other elements by using the "sips:" URI scheme, similar to "https:".

The threats in this category rely on the absence of cryptographic assurance of a request's originator. Attacks in this category seek to compromise the message integrity of a conversation and interfere with nonrepudiation. Oftentimes the goal of these attacks is economic or data theft. These threats demonstrate the need for security services that enable entities to authenticate the originators of requests and to verify that the contents of the message and control streams have not been altered in transit.

802.1x and 802.11i (WPA2)

The 802.1x protocol defines port-based, network access control that is used to provide authenticated network access (see Figure 11.2). Although this standard is designed for wired Ethernet networks, it has been adapted for use on 802.11 WLANs. It is simply a standard for passing EAP over a wired or wireless LAN.

Figure 11.2 EAPOL

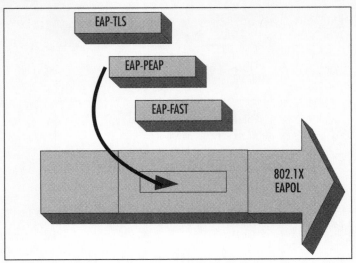

802.1x restricts unauthorized clients from connecting to a LAN. The client must first authenticate with an Authentication server, typically a RADIUS server, before the switch port is made available and the network can be accessed. EAP (Extensible Authentication Protocol) is a general authentication protocol that provides a framework for multiple authentication methods, including traditional passwords, token cards, Kerberos, Digital Certificates, and public-key authentication.

WEP (Wireless Equivalent Privacy) has famously been shown to be insecure (Anton Rager's wepcrack was the first publicly available tool for this— http://wepcrack.sourceforge.net/); however WEP protection of wireless connections is still better than no encryption at all. The Wi-Fi Alliance (a consortium of major vendors—http://wi-fi.org/) is responsible for drafting both the WPA (Wi-Fi Protected Access) and WPA2 standards. The Wi-Fi alliance also formed a VoWLAN (Voice over Wireless LAN) working group tasked with developing WMM (Wi-Fi Multimedia) QoS standards for VoIP and other multimedia over wireless networks.

WPA implements a subset of IEEE802.11i, and differs from WEP mainly in that it utilizes TKIP (Temporal Key Integrity protocol) and the EAP framework for authentication. 802.11i is a draft IEEE standard for 802.11 wireless network security. 802.11i, also known as WPA2, uses 802.1x as the authentication mechanism and the Advanced Encryption Standard (AES) block cipher for encryption. WEP and WPA use the RC4 stream cipher. Table 11.2 shows some of the key features of these three security standards.

Table 11.2 Security Standard Features

Protocol	Authentication	Cipher	Key Length	Key Management
WEP	None	RC-4	40/104	None
WPA	802.1x/EAP	RC-4	128	802.1x/EAP
WPA2	802.1x/EAP	AES	128	802.1x/EAP

It is helpful to think of 802.1x not as a single protocol but rather as a security framework using existing, and proven security standards that serves two critical security functions—authentication (PSK or PKI, for example) and encryption (TLS or AES, for example). Note that 802.1x does not define either authentication or encryption methods (in fact 802.1x can be used without encryption); rather these are defined largely through this choice of an EAP type.

Until the client is authenticated via 802.1x/EAP access control, the only protocol allowed through the port to which the client is connected is Extensible Authentication Protocol traffic. After authentication is successful, traffic can pass through the port.

802.1x/EAP Authentication

Now we'll define the terms associated with 802.1x/EAP authentication.

Supplicant (Peer)

This is the other end of the point-to-point link; the end that is being authenticated by the authenticator. Generally this term refers to the client in an EAP exchange.

Authenticator

Authenticator is a wireless access point (AP) or switch (NAS—Network Access Server). The authenticator maintains the network (WLAN or LAN) in closed state to all unauthenticated traffic. It does not do authentication directly, but instead tunnels the extensible authentication protocol (EAP) to an authentication server.

Authentication Server

The authentication server performs the actual client authentication and instructs the authenticator to allow or reject the supplicant's traffic. The authentication server is typically a RADIUS server.

Figure 11.3 illustrates the basic message flow in an 802.1x/EAP authentication scenario. This is an example of the most common 802.1x/EAP model —a Full/Pass-

Through state machine, which allows an NAS (network access server) or edge device to pass EAP Response messages to an Authentication Server where the authentication method resides. The NAS does not have to understand the request type and must be able to simply act as a passthrough agent for a back-end server. The NAS need look only for the success/failure code from the Authentication Server to terminate the authentication phase.

Figure 11.3 Generic EAP Authentication

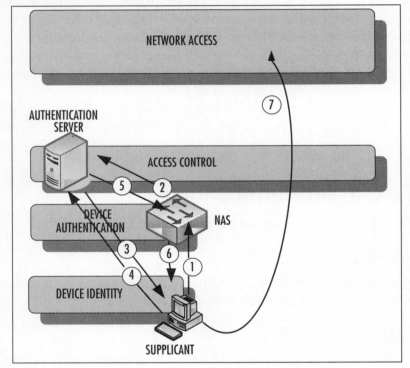

Tools & Traps …

AAA, RADIUS, and DIAMETER

RADIUS (Remote Authentication Dial In User Service) is an AAA (authentication, authorization, and accounting) protocol for applications such as network access or IP mobility. AAA is a term for a framework that allows methods to intelligently control access to computer resources, enforce policies, audit usage, and provide information necessary to bill for services. Because AAA services often are used to authenticate remote system administrators, availability is critical, and should always be provided by at least a pair of physically separated, dedicated AAA servers that serve as master and backup.

DIAMETER is a new extended AAA protocol that is designed to replace RADIUS. DIAMETER (a play on words, since diameter is twice the radius of a circle) is designed to enhance RADIUS functions and to fix several security problems (such as unencrypted CHAP response) that have plagued RADIUS in recent years.

In step 1, the supplicant (a workstation, wireless access point, IP phone, etc.) sends one or more requests to the NAS petitioning for access to the network. The NAS (step 2) passes the EAP message to the Authentication Server, which is almost always a RADIUS server. In step 3, the Authentication Server requests the credentials of the supplicant and specifies the type of credentials required to confirm the supplicant's identity. (Note here that the arrows between the RADIUS server and the client indicate logical, not physical, connectivity. All traffic between the two passes through the NAS.) The Authentication Server makes its decision to grant or deny access based upon Native RADIUS credentials. In step 4, the supplicant sends its credentials to the RADIUS server. Upon validating the supplicant's credentials, the Authentication Server transmits a success/failure message to the NAS (step 5). In step 6, if access is granted, the NAS opens the port to all traffic (as opposed to just EAPOL traffic) and data exchange between the authenticated LAN device and the LAN is allowed. If access is granted, then (step 7) the supplicant is able to access network resources.

You will notice that after access is approved, the supplicant has unrestricted access to network resources. Only the device identity has been authenticated. No authorization has been performed, nor has the user of the device been authenticated.

Figure 11.4 illustrates a more typical generic 802.1x transaction. The first several steps in this scenario are similar to the scenario we just described. In step 1, the supplicant (a workstation, wireless access point, IP phone, etc) sends one or more

requests to the NAS petitioning for access to the network. The NAS (Step 2) passes
the EAP message to the Authentication Server, which is almost always a RADIUS
server. In step 3, The Authentication Server requests the credentials of the supplicant
and specifies the type of credentials required to confirm the supplicant's identity.
(Note here that the arrows between the RADIUS server and the client indicate logical, not physical, connectivity. All traffic between the two passes through the NAS)

Figure 11.4 EAP Authentication with Authorization

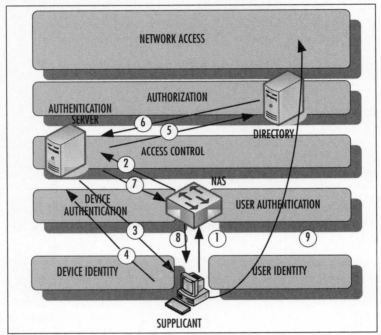

In step 5 the Authentication Server (RADIUS) forwards the access request to
the AD server. The AD server responds with a success or failure message, and if successful, also forwards the client's AD domain credentials in step 6. Upon validating
the supplicant's credentials, the Authentication Server transmits a success/failure message to the NAS (step 7). In step 8, if access is granted, the NAS opens the port to
all traffic. If access is granted, then (step 9) the supplicant is able to access authorized
network resources.

In this scenario, administrators can limit user access to specific VLANs, and via
Windows permissions, to most network resources. The specifics of authentication
and authorization depend upon the type of EAP policy chosen. There are a variety
of them, and we'll look at those most widely deployed.

EAP Authentication Types

Most of the more recent EAP types are made up of two components: an outer and an inner authentication type, separated by a forward slash—such as PEAPv0/EAP-MSCHAPv2. The outer type defines the method used to establish an encrypted channel between the client (peer) and the Authentication Server.

NOTE

The primary goal of the Transport Level Security (TLS) Protocol is to provide privacy and data integrity between two communicating applications. TLS is based on the Netscape SSL 3.0 Protocol Specification, although they are not interoperable. The protocol is composed of two layers: the TLS Record Protocol and the TLS Handshake Protocol, and is situated between ISO layers 3 and 4. Symmetric cryptography is used for data encryption (e.g., DES, RC4, AES, etc.). The keys for this symmetric encryption are generated uniquely for each connection. Message transport includes a message integrity check using a keyed MAC (SHA, MD5). These two elements ensure data confidentiality and integrity for each connection.

In Figure 11.5 an outer authentication method, PEAP, is negotiated between a client such as an IP phone or a workstation and a RADIUS authentication server. The intermediate NAS proxies the first several exchanges and then serves to passively mediate traffic in both directions. The NAS does not have knowledge of the keys used to instantiate the TLS tunnel, and thus, cannot be used to snoop on the encrypted traffic passing through it.

Figure 11.5 EAP Part I Outer Tunnel

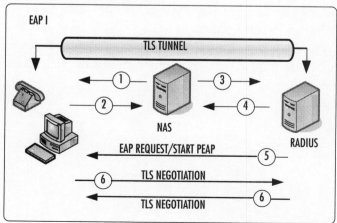

This outer tunnel verifies the server to the client using digital certificates.

Once the outer channel is established, the inner authentication type passes the user's credentials to the Authentication Server over this TLS encrypted tunnel for additional authentication of, typically, user credentials. Passing user credentials through the TLS encrypted tunnel protects them from exposure (see Figure 11.6).

Figure 11.6 EAP Part II Inner Tunnel

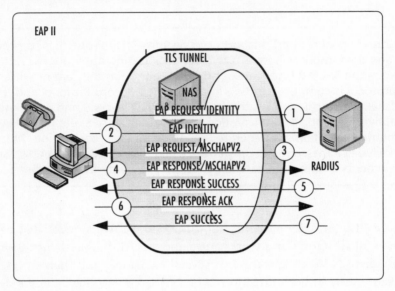

One of EAP's potential security vulnerabilities is that data exchanged as part of some of the outer authentication types, such as identity data, and the results of parameter negotiations are sent in the clear. This can result in a Denial-of-Service (DoS) condition since an attacker, for example, can flood the connection with different types of EAP notification messages.

In Table 11.3 some of the characteristics for the different types are summarized. In the last two fields more plus signs (+) equals greater difficulty and more strength, respectively.

Table 11.3 EAP Types Summary

EAP Type	Server Authentication	Client Authentication	Native Windows 2003 Support	Confidentiality	Integrity	Deployment Difficulty	Security Strength
EAP-TLS	Certificate	Certificate	Yes	TLS	+	+++++	+++++
EAP-PEAP	Certificate	Certificate, Smartcard, MS-CHAP-V2	Yes	TLS	+	++	++++
PEAPv0/ EAP-MS CHAPv2	Certificate	Certificate, Smartcard, MS-CHAP-V2	Yes	TLS	+	++	++++
EAP-TTLS	Certificate	PAP, CHAP, EAP, MS-CHAP-V2, Certificate	No	TLS	+	+++	++++
PEAPv1/ EAP-GTC	Password hash	Password hash (Token)	No	No	+	???	+++
EAP-SIM	128-bit secret	SIM secret	No	+/-	+/-	+++	++
EAP-FAST	Optional (PAC) password	Password (PAC)	No	+	+	+++	+++
LEAP	Password	Password	No	+	+	+++	+
MD5	None	None	Yes	-	-	+	+

Most of the newer EAP types defined by the Wi-Fi Alliance (those with the forward slash and EAP-SIM) are derived from this EAP type. EAP-PEAP and PEAPv0/EAP-MSCHAPv2 are the same thing. PEAPv1/EAP-GTC is a Cisco invention.

EAP-TLS

EAP-TLS (Extensible Authentication Protocol–Transport Layer Security) provides for certificate-based and mutual authentication of the client and the network. EAP-TLS is the most secure of the common EAP types, but requires a PKI (public key infrastructure) to manage and distribute client certificates. The TLS protocol has its roots in the Netscape SSL protocol, which was originally intended to secure HTTP. It provides either one-way or mutual authentication of client and server based on certificates. In its most typical use in HTTP, the client authenticates the server based on the server's certificate and establishes a tunnel through which HTTP traffic is passed. Username and password management in this scheme is irrelevant as identity is based upon possession of the appropriate private key. The obligatory overhead of a certificate management infrastructure normally precludes use of this EAP type.

EAP-PEAP

EAP-PEAP (Extensible Authentication Protocol–Protected Extensible Authentication Protocol) provides a method to transport secure authentication data, including legacy password-based protocols. PEAP accomplishes this by tunneling user credentials over a TLS tunnel between PEAP clients and an authentication server. EAP-PEAP is the best combination of security and ease of deployment in Windows environments today. EAP-PEAP requires only a server certificate (which is simple enough to create for testing using the native MS Certification Authority) and client side username/password combinations. EAP-PEAP is natively supported on Windows XP and Windows 2000 SP4 and above client platforms and IAS (Internet Authentication server). PEAPv0/EAP-MSCHAPv2 is the same thing as EAP-PEAP.

EAP-TTLS

EAP-TTLS (Extensible Authentication Protocol–Tunneled Transport Layer Security) is supported primarily by the Funk RADIUS people. EAP-TTLS, like PEAP, is also relatively easy to deploy (it requires only a server-side certificate) and quite secure since it tunnels user credentials inside of a TLS tunnel; however, this Funk Software invention has not been supported by Microsoft on clients or IAS server. Thus, EAP-TTLS requires the use of an additional software. TTLS and PEAP are similar in other ways, but there are differences: TTLS supports other EAP authentication methods and also supports inner authentication methods, PAP, CHAP, MS-CHAP, and MS-CHAPv2; whereas PEAP can tunnel only EAP-type protocols such as EAP-TLS, EAP-MS-CHAPv2, and EAP-SIM.

PEAPv1/EAP-GTC

PEAPv1/EAP-GTC (Extensible Authentication Protocol–Generic Token Card) was defined in RFC2284 along with one-time passwords, and MD5 was one of the initial set of EAP Types used in Request/Response exchanges. Cisco supports this type of PEAP (v1 vs. v0) and Microsoft supports only PEAPv0.

EAP-FAST

EAP-FAST (Extensible Authentication Protocol–Flexible Authentication via Secure Tunneling) was developed by Cisco. EAP-FAST authenticates both the client and the authentication server using a preshared secret known as the Protected Access Credential (PAC). EAP-FAST is a certificate-free replacement for LEAP. EAP-FAST is easy to implement in Windows/Cisco mixed environments, but this method is vulnerable to MITM (man in the middle) attacks in which an attacker can acquire the MS-CHAPv2 hash of the user's passwords, which can then be subjected to off-line dictionary attacks.

LEAP

LEAP (Lightweight Extensible Authentication Protocol) is an EAP authentication type used primarily in Cisco Aironet WLANs. LEAP supports strong mutual authentication, based upon a modified MS-CHAPv2 challenge/response, between the client and a RADIUS server using a logon password as the shared secret. It provides dynamic per-user, per-session WEP encryption keys. LEAP has been superseded by EAP-FAST due to the public availability of LEAP hash cracking tools such as ASLEAP. There is some disagreement regarding the value of complex password enforcement when using LEAP. When in doubt, use the longest, most complicated passwords that your userbase will agree to.

EAP-MD-5

EAP-MD-5 (Extensible Authentication Protocol–Message Digest) is an EAP authentication type that provides base-level EAP support. EAP-MD5-Tunneled is an EAP protocol designed for use as an inner authentication protocol within a tunneling protocol such as EAP- TTLS or EAP-PEAP. This has additional security features, but has not been widely deployed.

Notes from the Underground ...

RainbowCrack

Passwords are the most common form of computer authentication today. Password encryption is done using a one-way hashing algorithm such as MD5 or SHA-1. A one-way hash function, also known as a message digest, is a mathematical function that takes a variable-length input string and converts it into a fixed-length binary sequence that is computationally difficult to invert—that is, generate the original string from the hash. Conventional password crackers grab a word or string of wordlike tokens and run it though the hash algorithm. It then compares its generated hash with the target password hash. If they match, then the password has been discovered. The computationally expensive part of this process is the hash generation preceding the hash comparison, not the actual comparison process itself.

RainbowCrack is a general-purpose implementation of Philippe Oechslin's faster time-memory trade-off technique. In short, the RainbowCrack tool is an extremely fast and effective hash cracker. The simple but brilliant idea of time-memory trade-off is to do all the hash generation computation in advance and store the result in chains of files called "rainbow tables." It does take a long time to precompute the tables (it takes 2–3 days to generate the rainbow tables necessary to crack a lowercase-letters-only Windows (LM hash) password that's between 1 and 7 characters in length.), but after this one-time computation is finished, a time-memory trade-off cracker can crack passwords hundreds or thousands of times faster than a brute force cracker.

Inner Authentication Types

A number of inner authentication methods exist. The most commonly used is MS-CHAP-V2 because it is relatively secure and it is supported natively on all recent Microsoft clients. Additionally, PAP, CHAP, MD5, GTC, and other inner authentication methods exist but are not nearly as commonly used. Interestingly, even EAP itself can be tunneled within EAP.

MS-CHAP v2

MS-CHAP v2 is a one-way encrypted password, two-way authentication process that provides mutual authentication between peers (see Figure 11.7). It differs from MS-CHAP-V1 because it piggybacks an additional peer challenge (PCS) on the

Response packet and an additional authenticator response on the Success packet. Both the authenticating server and the client challenge and authenticate each other. The message flow is as follows:

Figure 11.7 MS-CHAP-V2

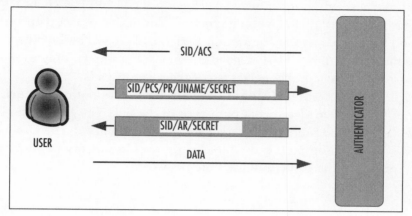

1. Authenticator sends a challenge consisting of a Session ID and random authenticator challenge string (ACS).

2. Client (peer) sends a response containing an encrypted one-way hash of the session ID, username, a peer challenge string (PCS), the peer response (PR), and the user password (secret).

3. Authenticator responds with another one-way hash (based on the client response) of a success/failure code, the authenticator response (AR), and the user's password (secret).

4. The peer verifies the authenticator response and begins communications if the response is successful. It disconnects on failure.

This authentication method depends upon a secret (password) known only to the authenticator and the peer. The secret is not sent over the link. A one-way hash function, also known as a message digest, is a mathematical function that takes a variable-length input string and converts it into a fixed-length binary sequence that is computationally difficult to invert—that is, generate the original string from the hash.

CHAP and MS-CHAP

CHAP was defined in RFC1994: PPP Challenge Handshake Authentication Protocol. CHAP (Challenge-Handshake Authentication Protocol) was initially used to verify client identity on PPP links using a three-way handshake. The handshake begins with the authenticator issuing a challenge to the client. The client responds with a digest calculated using a hashing function. The authenticator then verifies the response and acknowledges the connection if the match is successful, otherwise it terminates the connection. CHAP depends upon a secret known only to the authenticator and the client. The secret is not sent over the link.

MS-CHAP differs from CHAP in that MS-CHAP does not require that the shared secret be stored in cleartext at both ends of the link. The Microsoft client knows the hash method used by the server so it can reproduce it, effectively creating a "matching" password on both ends. The client proves its identity based on the fact that it can reproduce the hashed value of the password.

PAP

PAP (Password Authentication Protocol) is described in RFC1334. PAP provides a simple method for the peer to establish its identity using a two-way handshake. PAP is not a strong authentication method. Passwords are sent over the connection in cleartext and there is no protection from playback or repeated trial and error attacks.

MD5

MD5 (Message-Digest algorithm 5) is a widely used cryptographic hash function that results in a 128-bit hash value. The 128-bit (16-byte) MD5 hashes (also termed message digests) typically are represented as 32-digit hexadecimal numbers (for example, ec55d3e698d289f2afd663725127bace). EAP-MD-5 typically is not recommended for wireless LAN implementations because it may expose the user's password, and because several collision-based weaknesses have been demonstrated. It provides for only one way authentication – there is no mutual authentication of wireless client and the network. And very importantly it does not provide a means to derive dynamic, per-session wired equivalent privacy (WEP) keys.

GTC

Typically, password (PIN) information is read by a user from a token card device and entered as ASCII text into the client. GTC is similar to PAP in that passwords are sent in the clear.

Notes from the Underground …

Dictionary Attacks

Passwords can be broken in real-time (active) and offline (passive) modes. The premise of a dictionary attack is that by trying every possible combination or words (or tokens), an attacker ultimately will succeed in discovering user secret passwords. A dictionary attack relies on the fact that a password is often a common word, name, or concatenation of words or names with a minor modification such as a trailing digit or two. Longer passwords with a variety of characters (such as ^Y2o4uEA16r3-2e64A12EFing!) offer the greatest protection against dictionary attacks.

During an online dictionary attack, an attacker tries to actively gain network access by trying many possible combinations of passwords for a specific user. Online dictionary attacks can be prevented using password lockout mechanisms that lock out the user account after a certain number of invalid login attempts. Online attacks also generally show up in logs, which can indicate that this type of "loud" hacking activity occurred or is occurring. Offline attacks rely on the attacker's ability to capture and record data from the datastream usually by using a sniffer such as tcpdump or ethereal. These captured data can then be compared at leisure against tables of hashes until a password is discovered or the attacker gives up. The offline attacks can be thwarted by changing passwords regularly and limiting attackers' access to the datastream.

Public Key Infrastructure

The very starting point of Internet or VoIP security is to correctly identify the user or servicing nodes, called subjects, without leaving any room for impersonation or spoofing. Subjects include all the entities that hold or issue certificates such as an end entity or CA. IETF adopted Public-Key Infrastructure (PKI) as its basis for subject identification. PKI is known to satisfactorily meet the needs of deterministic, automated identification, authentication, access control, and authorization functions.

The IETF RFC 3280 specification profiles the format and semantics of certificates and Certificate Revocation Lists (CRL) for the Internet PKI. The goal of this specification is to develop a profile to facilitate the use of X.509 certificates within Internet applications. Such applications could include WWW, electronic mail, user authentication, and VoIP.

Public Key Cryptography Concepts

Within the PKI framework, who you are is defined by the private keys you possess. From the point-of-view of PKI authentication authorities, you are your private key. In order to understand PKI, you will first have to understand some basic cryptological concepts. In Figure 11.8 the concept of a secret key is presented. Alice and Bob often are used as examples of the two parties engaged in a secure communications channel, and we will use them here. In this case, Alice and Bob both possess the same secret key. This can be a password, a token, or some other form of secret. Alice encrypts the plaintext that she wishes to send to Bob using her secret key. After Bob receives the ciphertext, he decrypts it using the same secret. The fact that *the same key* is used for both encryption and decryption determines that this is a symmetric exchange.

Figure 11.8 Symmetric Key Cryptography

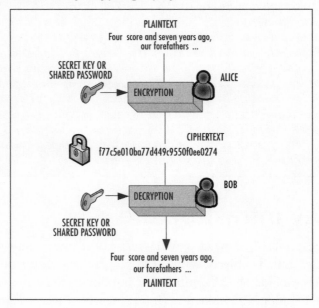

PKI relies on a public/private key combination. The public and private keys are mathematical entities that are related. One key is used to encrypt information and only the related key can decrypt that same information; however, if you know one of the keys, it is computationally unfeasible to calculate the other. Your public key is something that you make public. It is freely distributed and can be accessed by everyone. A corresponding (and unique) private key is something that you keep secret. It is not shared with anyone. Your private key enables you to prove, unequivocally, that you are who you claim to be.

In Figure 11.9, Alice uses public key cryptography to send a ciphertext to Bob. She first locates Bob's public key (normally from some type of directory service or from a previous secured document that Bob has sent to her) and encrypts the plaintext with Bob's public key. She sends the encrypted text to Bob. Only Bob has the corresponding private key that can be used to decode the ciphertext.

Note that in normal practice, for performance reasons, the actual ciphertext is encrypted using a secret key algorithm as shown in Figure 11.8. Symmetric algorithms are much faster than public/private key algorithms (asymmetric cryptography). A random key (the session key) is generated, and it is used with the symmetric algorithm to encrypt the information. The public key is then used to encrypt that key and both are sent to the recipient. The private key is then used to decrypt the session key, and the resulting session key is used to decrypt the actual data.

Figure 11.9 Public Key Cryptography

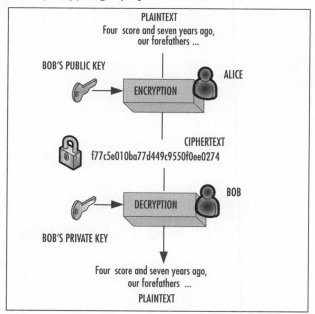

The developers of public key cryptography were economical with keys. Both the public and private key are used for more than just encrypting and decrypting data or session keys. The private key also is used to digitally sign the sent message so that the sender's identity is guaranteed. If the sender wishes to prove to a recipient that they are the source of the information (perhaps they accept legal responsibility for it), the sender uses his or her (or its) private key to digitally sign a message (a digital signature). Unlike a handwritten signature, a digital signature is different every time it is created. To create the digital signature, a hash of the message is signed (encrypted) with the sender's private key. The encrypted value either is attached to the end of the message or is sent as a separate file together with the message. The sender's public key that corresponds to this private key may also be sent with the message, either on its own or as part of a certificate.

The receiver uses the sender's public key to verify that the message hash calculated by the receiver (when certificates are used, the type of hashing algorithm will be included in the public key certificate sent with the message) is the same as the original hash. If the values match, the receiver is reasonably assured that the sender (the individual or device that owns the private key that corresponds with the public key) sent the information. The receiver also is reasonably assured that the information has not been altered since it was signed. This exchange forms the basis for two key security principles: nonrepudiation (the identity of the sender is verified) and message integrity (the contents of the message have not been altered in transit). Table 11.4 summarizes the intended use and owner of both public and private keys in public key cryptography.

Table 11.4 Key Usage in Pubic Key Cryptography

Function	Key Type	Key Owner
Encrypt Data	Public Key	Bob (Receiver)
Sign Data	Private Key	Alice (Sender)
Decrypt Data	Private Key	Bob (Receiver)
Verify Data Integrity	Public Key	Alice (Sender)

Architectural Model and PKI Entities

Figure 11.10 shows a simplified view of the architectural model assumed by the PKI specification. This model is analogous to the credit card infrastructure. Even though the data is encrypted differently, the ways in which the entities in the two structures interact with each other are conceptually similar. Each PKI entity is like an entity in the credit card infrastructure.

Figure 11.10 PKI Entities and Their Relationships

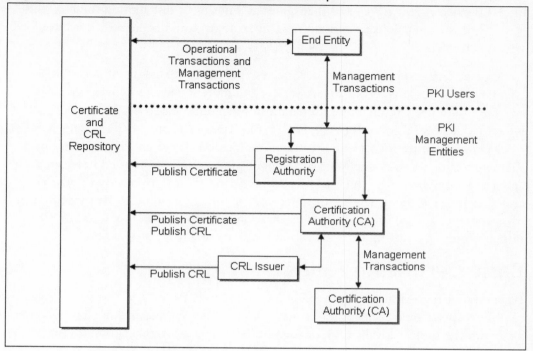

We'll now define the following PKI entities:

- **End Entity** User of PKI certificates and/or end-user system that is the subject of a certificate. Like a credit card reader in a retail store or restaurant, it reads a user certificate (credit card number) and queries the credit card company for the card holder's legitimacy and credit limits.

- **Certification Authority (CA)** A system that issues PKI certificates. Think of credit card application processing, which checks an applicant's credit history and issues a credit card.

- **Registration Authority (RA)** An optional system to which a CA delegates certain management functions.

- **CRL issuer** An optional system to which a CA delegates the publication of certificate revocation lists. This entity manages the equivalent of a stolen or lost credit card report and distributes certificate revocation information.

- **Repository** A system or collection of distributed systems that stores certificates and CRLs and that serves as a means of distributing these certificates and CRLs to end entities. An analogy would be a credit card holder database.

Operational protocols deliver certificates and CRLs (or status information) to client systems that use certificates. A variety of different ways to deliver certificates and CRLs are needed, including distribution procedures based on Lightweight Directory Access Protocol (LDAP), HTTP, File Transfer Protocol (FTP), and X.500.

Management protocols support online interactions between PKI user and management entities. For example, a management protocol might be used between a CA and a client system with which a key pair is associated, or between two CAs that cross-certify each other. The set of functions potentially needing to be supported by management protocols include user registration, client initialization, user certification, periodic key pair update, revocation request, and cross-certification.

Basic Certificate Fields

Basic certificate fields for X.509 version 3 are shown in Table 11.5. The To Be Signed (TBS) certificate field contains the names of the subject and issuer, a public key associated with the subject, a validity period, and other associated information. It usually includes extensions which hold additional optional information. The subject field identifies the entity associated with the public key stored in the subject public key field. It also distinguishes if a certificate is for an end entity, a CA, or a CRL. The Subject Public Key Info (SPKI) field is used to carry the public key and to identify the algorithm by which the key is used (e.g., RSA, DSA, or Diffie-Hellman).

The signature algorithm field contains the identifier for the cryptographic algorithm used by the CA to sign the certificate.

The signature value field contains a signature digitally added to the encoded TBS certificate. By generating this signature, a CA certifies the validity of the information in the TBS certificate. To be more specific, the CA certifies the binding between the public key material and the subject of the certificate.

Table 11.5 Basic Certificate Fields for X.509

Certificate Fields	Attribute	Type
TBS Certificate	Version	V1, v2, v3
	Certificate Serial Number	Integer
	Algorithm Id	Algorithm Object Id.
	Issuer	Name
	Validity	Not before time
		Not after time
	Subject	Name
	Subject Public Key Info	Algorithm Id
		Bit string
	Issuer Unique Id	Bit string
	Subject Unique Id	Bit string
	Extensions	
Signature Algorithm		Algorithm Id
Signature Value		Bit string

Certificate Revocation List

When a certificate is issued, it is expected to be in use for its entire validity period. However, various circumstances may cause a certificate to become invalid prior to the expiration of the validity period. Such circumstances include change of name, change of association between subject and CA (e.g., an employee terminates employment with an organization), and compromise or suspected compromise of the corresponding private key. Under such circumstances, the CA needs to revoke the certificate.

CRL is similar to notices of stolen or lost credit cards reported to other credit companies. The CA periodically issues a signed data structure called a CRL. A CRL is a time-stamped list identifying revoked certificates. The list is signed by a CA or CRL issuer and made freely available in a public certificate and CRL repository. Each revoked certificate is identified in a CRL by its certificate serial number. When a system employing certificates uses a certificate for verifying a remote user's digital signature, that system not only checks the certificate signature and validity, but also acquires a recent CRL and checks that the certificate serial number is not on that CRL.

Certification Path

If a public key user does not already hold a copy of the CA that signed the certificate including the CA's name, then it might need an additional certificate to obtain that public key. A sample scenario appears in Figure 11.11. Let's assume that Bob requested authentication from Alice with his certificate signed by CA1. But Alice, whose certificate was signed by CA2, does not have the public key for CA1, which is required to validate Bob's certificate. Then, Alice forms a certificate chain that contains both CA2's and her certificate and requests that CA1 provide a public key for CA1.

Figure 11.11 A Sample Certification Path

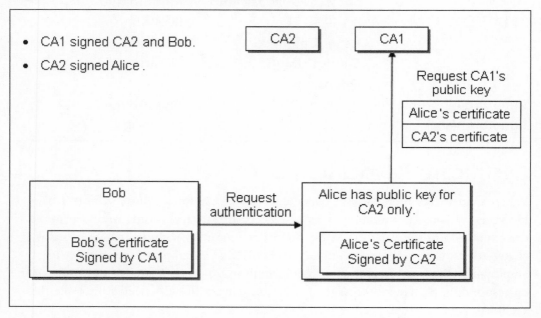

In general, a chain of multiple certificates might be needed that would make up a certificate containing the public key owner (the end entity) signed by one CA, and zero or more additional certificates originating from CAs signed by other CAs. Such chains, called certification paths, are required because a public key user is initialized with only a limited number of assured CA public keys. Certification path processing verifies the binding between the subject name and subject public key. This requires obtaining a sequence of certificates that support that binding.

Many organizations elect to create self-signed certificates for their public key infrastructure rather than purchase one or more from a Certificate Authority. In most cases, this is fine. However there are two differences between self-signed certificates and CA-signed certificates. SSL-enabled Web browsers normally recognize a CA-generated certificate and automatically allow a secure connection to be made, without prompting the user. Self-signed certificates usually generate an annoying (and sometimes to nontechnical users, frightening) pop-up. CAs also guarantee the identity of the organization that is providing services to the browser or other certificate-enabled device.

Before signing a certificate, a CA verifies the identity of the requesting organization. Thus, if your PKI is accessed by the public at large, you should provide a certificate signed by a CA so that people who visit or call know that your infrastructure is owned by the organization who claims to own it.

Minor Authentication Methods

Information security often is defined as a number of layers. The basis for this is the idea that every time and place a logical or physical impediment can be created that might reasonably stop an attacker (without hindering normal users' access to network resources) it should be done. 802.1x/EAP and PKI are large, complex layers, that when implemented and maintained correctly, result in highly secured access. There are a number of less expensive, less labor-intensive measures that administrators can take that also result in restricting network access to authorized devices.

MAC Tools

A basic security rule is that endpoints cannot be trusted until the identity of the endpoint is confirmed, or authenticated. In the case of VoIP, a method for authentication of IP phones is the hardware or MAC address. The MAC (Media Access Control) address is a six-byte address that usually is represented as hex numbers in the form AA-BB-CC-DD-EE-FF or AA:BB:CC:DD:EE:FF. The first three bytes represent the vendor ID and the remaining three bytes form a unique address for any network connected device. There are potentially 2^{48} or 281,474,976,710,656 possible MAC addresses. The Web site http://coffer.com/mac_find/ is useful for doing MAC/Vendor lookups.

MAC Authentication

If an IP phone with an unknown MAC address attempts to download a configuration from a registration server, then that device should not receive a configuration assuming automatic registration has been disabled. This setup prevents someone from placing a rogue phone or sniffer into the network, unless of course the person spoofs the MAC address in hopes of intercepting calls.

ARP Spoofing

ARP spoofing is an essential part of call interception. If an attacker cannot success-fully meddle with the switch's ARP table then eavesdropping is virtually eliminated. Of course, unrestrained console access to a switch also offers the chance for call interception; however, appropriate physical security controls and good passwords will minimize this threat. This topic and countermeasures are discussed in detail in Chapter 13.

Port Security

Since 802.1x is still an emerging technology, not all devices support it. Devices that do not support 802.1x can be controlled by Media Access Control (MAC) address authentication. Devices with static IP addresses that do not support 802.1x (such as printers and some IP phones) can be accommodated by utilizing various port secu-rity commands without the use of 802.1x (different switch vendors have different names for these commands). These devices should also be placed into their own VLAN.

Summary

As VoIP evolves, the requirements for user and device authentication and authorization will evolve as well. VoIP and other contemporary network services necessitate increased requirements for identity management both within and between organizational domains. Users often maintain multiple identities. IP endpoints proliferate. Individuals employ different usernames, passwords, and other identifying attributes in various online contexts, and then they have trouble remembering all these multiple usernames and passwords. The foundation of identity management is authentication services.

Authorized access begins with authentication. We are all familiar with different forms of authentication—from the password used to login to your computer to the key that unlocks your front door. The conceptual framework for authentication is made up of three factors: "something you have" (a key or certificate), "something you know" (a password or secret handshake), or "something you are" (a fingerprint or iris pattern). Authentication mechanisms validate users by one or a combination of these.

User and device identities are not the same and need to be verified independently. This can be accomplished in a number of ways. Microsoft Kerberos and NTLM authentication are the most widely used authentication schemes due to the large installed Windows 2000 and XP user base. These authentication schemes—particularly Kerberos—provide reasonable security, but Windows authentication is primarily a user authentication scheme, and many VoIP infrastructure components do not run on Windows. In addition, Windows authentication cannot be used to restrict access to the layer 2 network

The two most commonly used, general-purpose, user and device authentication methods are 802.1x/EAP and PKI. Though they are functionally unrelated, both define umbrella-like suites that provide frameworks for positively identifying users and devices based upon a spectrum of credentials. In addition, both of these approaches are extensible.

802.1x and 802.11i/WPA2 rely on an Authentication Server (usually a RADIUS server) and an Authenticator (usually a switch or wireless access point) to authenticate users and to proxy user credentials, respectively. 802.1x relies on EAP to carry out the authentication process. In the spirit of protocol isolation that has been successfully pulled off in the TCP/IP suite, 802.1x provides support for EAP, which provides a framework for multiple authentication methods, including traditional passwords, token cards, Kerberos, digital certificates and public-key authentication.

These EAP types normally are composed of an inner and outer type, and in many situations, inner and outer types can be mixed to correspond with an organization's specific security requirements.

PKI techniques, methods, and infrastructure components were developed principally to support secure information exchange over insecure networks such as the Internet where such features cannot otherwise be readily provided. PKI, however, can be used just as easily for information exchanged over private networks, including corporate internal networks. PKI can also be used to deliver cryptographic keys between users and devices (including IP phones and servers) securely.

Other point solutions can be used to limit network access to only authorized devices. These are normally vendor-dependent, and typically involve some type of MAC address filtering or access lists.

Solutions Fast Track

802.1x and 802.11i

- ☑ The 802.1x protocol defines port-based, network access control that is used to provide authenticated network access.

- ☑ EAP (Extensible Authentication Protocol) is a general authentication protocol that provides a framework for multiple authentication methods.

- ☑ Most of the more recent EAP types are made up of two components: an outer and an inner authentication type.

- ☑ The three components of an 802.1x infrastructure are the supplicant (client), the authenticator (NAS), and the authentication server (normally a RADIUS server).

- ☑ 802.11i also is known as WPA2.

Public Key Infrastructure

- ☑ Within the PKI framework, who you are is defined by the private keys you possess.

- ☑ The fact that the same key is used for both encryption and decryption determines a symmetric exchange.

- ☑ PKI relies on a public/private key combination.

☑ Public and private keys are mathematical entities that are related. One key is used to encrypt information and only the related key can decrypt that same information; however, if you know one of the keys, it is computationally unfeasible to calculate the other.

☑ The private key also is used to digitally sign the sent message so that the sender's identity is reasonably assured.

Minor Authentication Methods

☑ Information security is often defined as a number of layers. The basis for this is the idea that every time and place a logical or physical impediment can be created that might reasonably stop an attacker (without hindering normal users' access to network resources) it should be done.

☑ A basic security rule is that endpoints cannot be trusted until the identity of the endpoint is confirmed or authenticated.

☑ In the case of VoIP, a method for authentication of IP phones is the hardware or MAC address.

Frequently Asked Questions

The following Frequently Asked Questions, answered by the authors of this book, are designed to both measure your understanding of the concepts presented in this chapter and to assist you with real-life implementation of these concepts. To have your questions about this chapter answered by the author, browse to **www.syngress.com/solutions** and click on the **"Ask the Author"** form.

Q: What is TKIP?

A: TKIP (Temporal Key Integrity Protocol) changes encryption keys in every packet. TKIP also adds a rekeying mechanism to provide fresh encryption and integrity keys. This makes TKIP protected networks more resistant to cryptanalytic attacks involving key reuse.

Q: What is the difference between authentication and authrorization?

A: Authentication establishes the identities of devices and users. Authorization, on the other hand, establishes the amount and type of network and application resources authorized individuals and devices are able to access.

Q: Does my wireless card (supplicant) have to have any sort of special 802.1x compatibility to initiate a session with the access point, (i.e., tell it, "hello, I am here" and then be prompted for a password)? Or will just any old card work, as long as the access point is 802.1x compatible?

A: Yes, and no. You need 801.x supplicant running on the client. There are EAPOL messages exhanged between the supplicant (client) and the authenticator (access point). Both the client and the AP need to be 802.1x capable and compatible.

Q: Is EAPOL (EAP over LAN) equal to PEAP or they are compatible?

A: EAPOL can use PEAP as an inner or outer authentication type. They are different things.

Q: What is a digital certificate and what is it used for?

A: As part of the X.509 protocol, certificates are assigned by a trusted Certificate Authority and provide a strong binding between a party's identity and its public key.

Q: What is a one-way hash?

A: A one-way hash function converts an arbitrary amount of data into a fixed-length string (the hash). It is computationally expensive to reverse the transformation or to find collisions (hopefully). MD5 and SHA are examples of one-way hash functions.

Q: I am planning on using 802.1x/EAP to authenticate users and IP phones. What is the most secure way to do this without putting a certificate on each IP phone?

A: EAP-PEAP and EAP-TTLS requires only that a certificate be installed on the authentication server. EAP-PEAP is natively supported on recent Microsoft Windows platforms. EAP-TTLS is not. In addition, Microsoft IAS server includes RADIUS functionality. Funk Software (the major supporter of EAP-TTLS) also makes an industry standard RADIUS server. In a Windows environment, EAP-PEAP is probably the best in terms of security and ease of deployment.

Q: Can I place users, in particular VLANs, automatically using 802.1x?

A: Yes, in most cases. Most vendors support a number of types of RADIUS-based user identification, and support extensions that allow the RADIUS server to return information about which 802.1q VLAN number corresponds to a particular SSID.

Q: If my VoIP phone contains a multiport switch in the back of it and I plug my workstation into the phone, what authenticates the port on the wiring closet switch, my phone or my workstation?

A: This depends to some extent on your environment and VLAN structure. But in most cases, the phone will authenticate using 802.1x, thus allowing the workstation to piggyback on the authenticated connection.

Chapter 12

Active Security Monitoring

Solutions in this chapter:

- Network Intrusion Detection Systems
- Host-Based Intrusion Detection Systems
- Logging
- Penetration and Vulnerability Testing

☑ Summary

☑ Solutions Fast Track

☑ Frequently Asked Questions

Introduction

At this point, we have examined and hardened the working components of the existing security infrastructure, established procedures to confirm user and device identities, and logically separated voice and data traffic, thus allowing the network to now carry them. The next step in maintaining the security of this infrastructure is to monitor traffic and the state of key devices. This is accomplished by active monitoring.

Plenty of commercial and open-source tools exist to help with this, and in this chapter we will look at several categories of them. We won't, however, discuss in any detail the large commercial network monitoring suites like NetIQ, SMARTS, BMC Patrol, HP OpenView Operations, HP Network Node Manager NNM, IBM Tivoli, Nortel Optivity NMS, Cisco Ciscoworks, Sun Solstice SunNet Enterprise Manager, Micromuse, Computer Associates CA Unicenter, and Microsoft Operations Manager 2000 (MOM). While we recommend that organizations employ one or more of these enterprise tool suites (particularly to monitor network jitter, packet loss, and latency), the configuration, use, or integration of any one of these tool suites with VoIP network monitoring components is complex, dependent upon both the suite chosen for monitoring, and the peculiarities of each particular network. For these reason we will have to leave this discussion to another time.

A related class of tools for both monitoring and performance testing of VoIP networks include tools like Empirix Hammer, Brix Network Verifier, and Shunra's Virtual Enterprise. These tools use different techniques and metrics to monitor the functionality, performance, scalability, and robustness of VoIP networks to provide signaling and media quality data on every call. Administrators can monitor high-level network metrics via integration with their existing Network Management Systems or can drill into the details of any call down to individual protocol and network messages.

We will start off by discussing in more detail two intrusion detection (ID) technologies: NIDS (network-based) and HIDS (host-based). NIDS inspects all inbound and outbound network activity and identifies patterns of packet data that may indicate a network or system attack. NIDSs are normally arranged in a multiple-sensor-to-one-console configuration, where the sensors reside on dedicated appliances distributed at key network junctions, and report back to a central management console. HIDSs, on the other hand, normally reside on the server that they monitor. HIDS can also report back to a central management console. A third class of intrusion detection is exemplified by DShield or Symantec—distributed intrusion detection—where global system attacks are reported to, and consolidated by, a central management server. Intrusion detection is a requirement in contemporary networks since it is not possible to stay abreast of existing and potential threats to modern computing systems.

Next, we will take a look at logging, primarily focusing on syslog and SNMP. Syslog (system logger) provides a means to allow a machine to send event notification messages across IP networks to event message collectors (also known as syslog servers). The decision regarding how much and what types of data should be logged is a critical responsibility of the system administrator. However, in most modern systems the sheer amount of logging data generated by system loggers can easily overwhelm most system administrators. We have witnessed organizations that react to log events, not based upon the data contained in the logs, but rather according to the number of logs generated per some unit of time. In order to deal with this mass of data, many system administrators develop scripts or tools to examine the log files and extract the important information. These tools are important because, without them, log data is often ignored. SNMP (Simple Network Management Protocol) is the primary transport for most of the aforementioned large tool suites. There are, however, simple point solution SNMP tools available, and we'll offer suggestions regarding general SNMP usage.

TIP

"If you know the enemy and know yourself, you need not fear the result of a hundred battles. If you know yourself but not the enemy, for every victory gained you will also suffer a defeat."
—Sun Tzu

Finally, in this chapter, we will close with a section on penetration testing. Penetration testing is a means of monitoring the state of security controls on your VoIP network. The primary reason for testing systems or networks is to identify potential vulnerabilities and subsequently repair them. Penetration Testing (Pen Testing) is an intelligent combination of automated and manual examinations that are launched from either inside or outside the perimeter of a private network. This testing emulates the threat from hackers and other parties, and their attempts to enumerate and compromise visible services.

Although we are not aware of production ready VoIP-specific NIDS, several are rumored to be in development. As a note: Based upon data gathered from historical analysis of call flows, anomaly detection, particularly in a call center setting where traffic is more defined than in an entire converged network, may prove to be an effective NIDS strategy.

Network Intrusion Detection Systems

Network Intrusion Detection Systems (NIDSs) are designed to alert administrators when malicious or illegitimate traffic is detected. Malicious traffic can consist of worm or exploit-based code, while illegitimate traffic (often termed "misuse") consists of traffic that deviates from established security policy such as surfing porn sites or peer-to-peer connections. Network-based IDSs can monitor an entire, large network with only a few well-situated nodes or devices and impose little overhead on a network. NIDSs are found in most networked computing environments today because, no matter how well security controls are implemented, it is impractical to maintain defenses against all known and potential threats to networked systems and applications. In VoIP environments, NIDSs provide an additional layer of defense.

NIDS Defined

NIDSs detect suspicious activity in three ways. First, the security community maintains an extremely large database of specific attack signatures. These signatures are programmed into the NIDS sensor, and are updated on a regular basis. Examples of attack signatures include Code Red, NIMDA, DoS attacks, buffer overflows, ASP, and CGI vulnerabilities. Second, the NIDS sensors contain preprocessors that continuously monitor the network for anomalous behavior. Though not as specific as attack signatures, these anomalies are still highly effective for the detection of port scans, distributed network probes, new forms of buffer overflows, and Denial-of-Service attacks. Third, all NIDS appliances can apply and detect security policy deviations. These policy deviations include the detection of unauthorized network services, applications running on unusual ports, and backdoor/Trojan activity.

Signature-based NIDSs are essentially network sniffers combined with a database of attack signatures. One of the most difficult (and necessary) tasks when initially configuring the NIDS is the job of de-tuning it. It is important that the number of false positives be reduced; otherwise, they will make meaningful analysis of the data impossible.

Components

Most NIDSs are configured in a client- (sensor) to-server (management console) configuration. Many sensors normally report to one or several management consoles. Sensors can be dedicated appliances, can run as an application on a host running other applications, or can run independently in a virtual subsystem such as VMware or Xen. Note that if the sensor does not reside on a dedicated appliance, then the OS of the host computer should be hardened.

Because NIDSs do not reside in the datapath (normally one NIC is used as a sensor and a second NIC is used for management traffic), the sensor Ethernet interface can be configured in a number of ways as receive only. Sensor hardware requirements are not particularly strict since the sensor application normally inspects packets, and upon finding a signature or pattern match, sends the subsequent data upstream to the management console for processing and visualization.

The term "signature" refers to a set of conditions that, when met, indicate some type of intrusion event. Typical modern sensors contain a signature database consisting of 1000 to 2000 entries. Often, sensors inspect traffic based upon a mixture of signature matching as well as pattern matching. Pattern matching is based on looking for a fixed sequence of bytes in a single packet. A more sophisticated method is stateful pattern matching. Stateful pattern matching is useful when the intrusion signature spans more than a single packet. Similar to antivirus software, a signature-based IDS requires regular access to an up-to-date database of attack signatures so recent exploits are not missed.

Figure 12.1 is a simple illustration of the basic logic used by NIDS management stations when resolving an event reported by a remote sensor. The "Match IDS Rule" logic normally resides on the sensor. When a rule is matched (for example: `packet from outside to inside contains illegal SIP rerouting headers`"), the data is forwarded to the management console where it is prioritized, logged, and visualized.

Figure 12.1 NIDS Logic

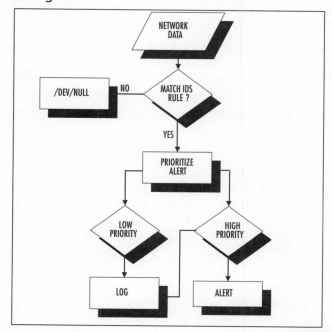

The management console (MC) hardware requirement is normally stricter than that of the sensor since the MC is responsible for data correlation from multiple sensors, as well as storage, alerting, and visualization. Often, the MC also includes an integrated sensor.

Types

NIDSs are normally classified according to the methods they use for attack detection; either as signature-based, or anomaly detection. Note, though, that almost all current NIDSs use a mixture of these approaches. Signature-based approaches, as mentioned earlier in this chapter, rely on some type of pattern matching. NIDS sensors parse the entire IP packet, and make decisions by means of a simple rule-based logic that is based upon signatures or regular expression matching. In other words, they compare the data within a packet payload to a database of predefined attack signatures (a string of bytes). Additionally, statistical or historical algorithms may supplement static pattern matching. Attack signatures usually consist of one or more of the following fields:

- Source and destination IP addresses, or an address or range
- TCP/UDP source and destination ports and ICMP type/code
- IP header flags and options
- TCP header flags and options
- A definition of the payload data to search (hex or ASCII)
- A starting point for the payload search (offset) and the search depth

Analysis of packet headers can be done economically since the locations of packet header fields are restricted by protocol standards. However, the payload contents are, for the most part, unconstrained. Therefore, searching through the payload for multiple string patterns within the datastream can be a computationally expensive task. The requirement that these searches be performed at wirespeed only adds to the cost.

Anomaly detection NIDSs are based on the assumption that normal traffic can be defined, and that attack or misuse patterns will differ from "normal" traffic. Heuristic-based signatures, on the other hand, use some type of algorithmic logic on which to determine their alarm decisions.

NOTE

Heuristic is the art and science of discovery and invention. The word comes from the same Greek root as "eureka," which means "I find." Heuristics defines a problem-solving technique in which the most appropriate solution is selected at successive stages of a program for use in the next step of the program. Heuristic approaches utilize simplification or an educated guess to reduce or limit the search for solutions. A heuristic can be a single algorithmic solution to a problem, but unlike an algorithm, heuristics does not guarantee optimal, or even feasible, solutions.

These algorithms are often statistical evaluations of the type of traffic being inspected. An example of a heuristic signature is a signature used to detect a port scan. This signature defines a particular threshold number of external probes against unique ports or a specific combination of ports. The signature may be further restricted by specification of the types of packets (for instance, SYN only) it reacts to. Interesting trends can be learned from these data, and it is possible to detect ongoing attacks based on these algorithms; however, the information that these systems provide is generally very nonspecific and requires extensive human investigation before actionable intelligence is gathered.

By creating baselines of normal behavior, anomaly-based NIDSs are able to detect when current network behavior deviates statistically from the norm. This capability theoretically gives an anomaly-based NIDS the capacity to detect new attacks that are either unknown or to detect attacks for which no signatures exist.

The major problem with this type of approach is that normal network traffic is difficult or impossible to define. Since normal network behavior can change easily and readily, anomaly-based NIDSs are prone to false positives. Additionally, inconsistency of detector performance, training issues (for example, how often an anomaly-based detection system should be retrained to ensure acceptable performance), and inadvertent incorporation of intrusive behavior into an NIDS concept of normal behavior during training negatively affect performance.

Placement

NIDSs should be located where they can most effectively monitor critical traffic. This doesn't necessarily mean that NIDSs should be placed where they can monitor the *most* traffic. In Figure 12.2, an example network is diagrammed. This network consists of a single Internet connection, a DMZ (demilitarized zone), and three internal VLANs, configured for voice users, workstations, and servers. The circular

network symbols signify routers or layer 3 switches, while the square network symbols signify layer 2 switches. The five NIDSs are shown as arrowed rectangular boxes.

Figure 12.2 NIDS Locations

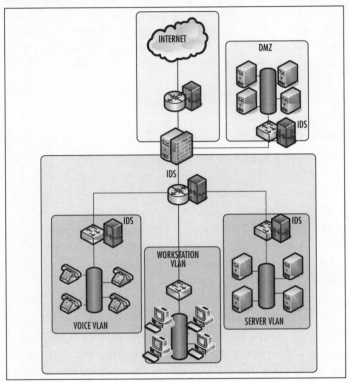

In this figure, an NIDS is located on the external side of the firewall to monitor
all inbound and outbound Internet traffic. NIDSs are located on internal layer 2
switches in the voice and server VLANs, and on the layer 3 switch that is used to
truck these connections. An additional NIDS is situated in the DMZ. In this architecture, the NIDSs will have access to all the network traffic, but are they all really
necessary?

Frankly, no. Several of the NIDSs are either redundant or will report so many
events as to be meaningless. The external NIDS is unnecessary since it is exposed to
the Internet. Even those of you with broadband connections realize that your single
IP address is constantly bombarded with exploit probes and port scans. The following is a sample from 30 minutes of scans against a typical home system.

```
~ # tail -f /var/log/messages | egrep -v "repeated"
Oct  3 00:27:33 ns1 /kernel: Connection attempt to TCP 192.168.20.20:135
from 24.193.208.77:2258 flags:0x02

Oct  3 00:30:26 ns1 /kernel: Connection attempt to TCP 192.168.20.20:901
from 211.172.40.72:4896 flags:0x02   swat

Oct  3 00:30:27 ns1 /kernel: Connection attempt to TCP 192.168.20.20:901
from 211.172.40.72:4896 flags:0x02   swat

Oct  3 00:30:58 ns1 /kernel: Connection attempt to TCP 192.168.20.20:445
from 83.37.160.160:3400 flags:0x02

Oct  3 00:31:00 ns1 /kernel: Connection attempt to TCP 192.168.20.20:135
from 24.199.122.40:3829 flags:0x02

Oct  3 00:31:01 ns1 /kernel: Connection attempt to TCP 192.168.20.20:135
from 24.199.122.40:3829 flags:0x02

Oct  3 00:31:01 ns1 /kernel: Connection attempt to TCP 192.168.20.20:445
from 83.37.160.160:3400 flags:0x02

Oct  3 00:31:01 ns1 /kernel: Connection attempt to TCP 192.168.20.20:135
from 24.199.122.40:3829 flags:0x02

Oct  3 00:31:43 ns1 /kernel: Connection attempt to UDP 192.168.20.20:137
from 66.63.173.19:1316            netbios-ns

Oct  3 00:31:47 ns1 /kernel: Connection attempt to UDP 192.168.20.20:137
from 66.63.173.19:1316

Oct  3 00:31:54 ns1 /kernel: Connection attempt to TCP 192.168.20.20:1433
from 212.33.102.36:2784 flags:0x02   mssql/slammer

Oct  3 00:32:03 ns1 /kernel: Connection attempt to UDP 192.168.20.20:137
from 66.63.173.19:1316

Oct  3 00:32:27 ns1 /kernel: Connection attempt to UDP 192.168.20.20:137
from 66.63.173.19:1316

Oct  3 00:33:01 ns1 /kernel: Connection attempt to UDP 192.168.20.20:137
from 66.63.173.19:1316

Oct  3 00:43:18 ns1 /kernel: Connection attempt to TCP 192.168.20.20:445
from 24.199.80.94:1831 flags:0x02

Oct  3 00:47:55 ns1 /kernel: Connection attempt to TCP 192.168.20.20:5000
from 24.84.67.76:4593 flags:0x02   UPnP backdoor

Oct  3 00:47:58 ns1 /kernel: Connection attempt to TCP 192.168.20.20:135
from 24.84.67.76:3254 flags:0x02

Oct  3 00:48:50 ns1 /kernel: Connection attempt to TCP 192.168.20.20:4899
from 69.60.111.98:1361 flags:0x02   Radmin exploit

Oct  3 00:49:26 ns1 /kernel: Connection attempt to TCP 192.168.20.20:135
from 24.199.105.227:3192 flags:0x02

Oct  3 00:52:19 ns1 /kernel: Connection attempt to TCP 192.168.20.20:5000
from 24.199.230.130:4456 flags:0x02

Oct  3 00:52:22 ns1 /kernel: Connection attempt to TCP 192.168.20.20:135
from 24.199.230.130:4276 flags:0x02
```

```
Oct  3 00:52:22 ns1 /kernel: Connection attempt to TCP 192.168.20.20:135
from 24.199.230.130:4276 flags:0x02

Oct  3 00:55:37 ns1 /kernel: Connection attempt to UDP 192.168.20.20:1029
from 203.21.20.30:30065            ICQNuke98

Oct  3 00:55:42 ns1 /kernel: Connection attempt to TCP 192.168.20.20:135
from 24.199.105.227:4103 flags:0x02

Oct  3 00:56:17 ns1 /kernel: Connection attempt to TCP 192.168.20.20:135
from 24.167.27.37:2995 flags:0x02
```

As you can see, most of this traffic is the result of automated scanning by worms and viruses, or by simple automated scanning tools. In an enterprise environment, where IDS and log data accumulates in copious amounts, these external data can be ignored. It is more important to focus on the events that occur within the firewall perimeter.

The NIDS situated on the layer 2 switches can also be eliminated since this traffic can be monitored at the central layer 3 switch. In addition, the management connection passes through the firewall and may allow an attacker to piggyback into the network if the sensor is compromised. Although there are no hard and fast rules for deploying NIDS, most system administrators deploy them on uplinks and at devices where many VLANs are trunked so that the fewest number of NIDSs can monitor the most traffic. In our sample network, two NIDSs are suitable to monitor most of the network traffic—one NIDS in the DMZ, and one on the central layer 3 switch.

Note that on the layer 3 switch, there are two interesting and separate traffic flows—one on the uplink between the switch and the firewall, and one port that trunks inter VLAN traffic. The choice of how to monitor both traffic flows depends on how the switch-NIDS connection is configured. Two common methods for allowing NIDS access to network traffic are port mirroring (spanning) and the insertion of a tap (we recommend NetOptics taps because they have two power connections and a wide choice of physical interfaces; check them out at www.netoptics.com). Port mirroring, depending upon its configuration, can enable the NIDS to inspect all of the traffic traversing the switch, and is an inexpensive option. However, some vendor's switches or OS revisions break when port mirroring is enabled. Be sure to check this with your vendor before connecting an NIDS. The second option, a network tap, is more expensive but offloads the mirroring to a separate device. In this simple example network setting, two network taps would have to be used to visualize all of the traffic—one on the uplink, and one on an inter VLAN port.

Important NIDS Features

Let's now discuss the important features of an NIDS.

Maintenance

Most NIDS systems support centralized installation, configuration, and updating since in an enterprise network a security administrator cannot physically access each sensor. In addition, most vendors support the automated download of signatures and software updates. Distribution and customization of the signature libraries and policies should be possible on a per-sensor basis and on a per-group basis (these groups should be defined by the security administrator) so the group signatures and policies do not have to be pushed to each sensor individually.

Communication between the IDS components (sensors and management console) should be encrypted using strong authentication (via key exchange or challenge). And as mentioned earlier, NIDS Ethernet interfaces should be stealthy. Transmission of data via the sensing interface is prohibited, unless it is configured intentionally (TCP resets, which we discuss later in this chapter, may be an exception).

Alerting

The management console should be configurable to support alerting via a variety of mechanisms, including SNMP traps, e-mail alerts, pager messages, syslog messages, SMS (short message service), IM, and console alerts.

Logging

All alerts and header and payload data should be automatically stored in a central event database that is backed up regularly via SCP or other secure means.

Extensibility

The NIDS should support simple integration of additional vulnerability assessment tools such as Nmap or Nessus, and should provide support the correlation of data from other IDSs (for example, NIDS and HIDS).

Response

Some NIDS are able to actively respond to attacks or misuse by interfering with the particular message stream that generated the alert. This is normally accomplished via targeted TCP resets that eventually tear down the connection, or by dynamically altering firewall rules or Access Control Lists to block the connection. These active-response NIDSs are often referred to as intrusion prevention systems (IPSs).

Most administrators do not activate these features because of the risk of blocking normal traffic. Imagine that this functionality was enabled on a system directly connected to the Internet. A clever attacker could send traffic to an IPS with the source address spoofed to that of an upstream router, and designed to trigger the IDS. The resultant blocking of the upstream router could effectively remove the organization from the Internet. In a VoIP environment where availability is a key metric, IPSs are not recommended because of this potential to obstruct voice traffic.

Limitations

NIDSs that rely upon signatures must constantly update the signature database. Obviously, pure signature matching NIDSs will not alert on attacks for which they have no signature. If signature definitions are too specific, signature-based IDSs may miss variations on known attacks. (A common technique for creating new attacks is to modify existing attacks.) Signature-based NIDSs can also impose noticeable performance problems on systems when numerous attack signatures are matched concurrently. Additionally, signature-based NIDS inspection can be evaded. Secure Networks showed in 1998 that attacks which exploit fundamental TCP/IP problems—insertion, evasion, and Denial-of-Service attacks—are able to elude NIDS detection. Dan Kaminsky recently showed he could send a series of fragmented packets to a NIDS that, based on the time and the operating system platform that they arrive at, reassemble into an attack for that platform that is not recognized by the NIDS.

Honeypots and Honeynets

A honeypot is a computer system that is shielded from the Internet by a router or firewall that is transparent to an attacker. The honeypot masquerades as a normal undefended system, yet it logs every action taken against it and every operation that is performed on it. The goal of a honeypot operator is to lure an attacker into hacking the system in hopes of learning all of the details of the attack. A honeypot is a system designed to illustrate the methods used by black-hats to probe for, and exploit, a system. Honeynets are networks that contain at least one honeypot. Typically, honeynets present a virtual network complete with virtual services and applications that look to an attacker like a real network.

Honeypots and honeynets are learning tools, and can also be useful as canaries (canaries were used in mines to provide an early warning to miners if air conditions turned sour). Unlike NIDSs and HIDSs, where false positives are a common nuisance, honeypots and honeynets, if configured correctly, do not have a measurable false positive rate. Honeynets are often configured so that their IP space resides within unoccupied IP space in an organization's internal network. In this configuration, anything that hits the honeynet is either an attack or a precursor to an attack since this IP space is supposedly unused. In its canary role, a honeynet can provide an early warning of a virus or worm attack.

Host-Based Intrusion Detection Systems

Host-based intrusion detection systems (HIDSs) are applications that operate on information collected from individual computer systems. This vantage point allows an HIDS to analyze activities on the host it monitors at a high level of detail; it can often determine which processes and/or users are involved in malicious activities. Furthermore, unlike NIDSs, HIDSs are privy to the outcome of an attempted attack since they can directly access and monitor the data files and system processes targeted by these attacks.

Tripwire (the reference model for many of the follow-on HIDSs) is described in more detail in the "Server Hardening" section of Chapter 10. Tripwire operates on MD5 hashes of critical system files, as defined by the system administrator. It is one model for host-based intrusion detection—like the secret agent trick of putting a hair on the doorknob, it lets you know if somebody's been changing things inside your system—but only *after* this occurs.

Alternatively, HIDSs can utilize information sources of two types, operating system audit trails, and system logs. Operating system audit trails are usually generated at the innermost (kernel) level of the operating system, and are therefore more detailed and better protected than system logs. System logs are much less obtuse and much smaller than audit trails, and are normally far easier to comprehend.

Most HIDS software, like Tripwire, establishes a "digital inventory" of files and their attributes in a known state, and uses that inventory as a baseline for monitoring any system changes. The "inventory" is usually a file containing MD5 checksums for individual files and directories. This must be stored offline on a secured, read-only medium that is not available to an attacker. On a server with no read-only media (a blade server, for example), one method to accomplish this is to store the statically compiled intrusion detection application and its data files on a remote computer. When you wish to run an HIDS report, SCP (secure copy) the remote files to /tmp (or its equivalent) on the target server and run them from there. When you modify any files on the server, re-run the application, and make a new data set, which should be stored on the remote computer.

HIDS surveillance is especially important on VoIP media, proxy, and registration servers and should be considered as part of the initial install package. Indeed, vendors such as Cisco are even making this part of the default installation. For instance, the

Cisco Security Agent (CSA) comes with every Call Manager license, and Avaya Media Servers ship with a web-enabled version of Tripwire installed and preconfigured.

The downside to HIDS use is that clever attackers who compromise a host can attack and subvert host-based HIDSs as well. HIDS can not prevent DoS attacks. Most significantly, a host-based IDS consumes processing time, storage, memory, and other resources on the hosts where such systems operate. HIDSs that operate in a client-server mode (most of them) can also add to network traffic congestion.

Logging

Interestingly, when discussing system logging, tired metaphors seem most apt. System log information "is a goldmine" of useful information, but searching through these data is "like trying to find a needle in a haystack." Tired metaphor or not, the preceding statement is true. Time-stamped logs generated by servers, gateways, firewalls, proxies, routers, and switches often contain invaluable security-related information, but system administrators are normally so overwhelmed with other maintenance and configuration chores that analyses of these logs is disregarded. The key to successful log analysis is to adopt the proper tools for your environment to automatically parse, visualize, and report summarized log data. For example, many organizations utilize MRTG (Multi Router Traffic Grapher—http://people.ee.ethz.ch/~oetiker/ webtools/mrtg/) to visualize router and switch SNMP network data.

Syslog

In its most simplistic terms, the syslog protocol provides a transport to allow a machine to send event notification messages across IP networks to event message collectors—also known as syslog servers. Syslog is an odd protocol in that it was implemented on many platforms before the protocol was ratified by the IEEE in RFC3164. Rather than begin by defining the protocol, RFC3164 starts with "*This document describes the observed behavior of the syslog protocol.*"

Syslog messages use UDP/514 for transport, increasing the possibility of losing packets and never noticing, and also making it easy for anybody to forge fake packets, either to insert log events, or to flood the server. Syslog, at this time, does not provide for encryption, so the messages are sent in the clear and can be sniffed by anyone on the wire. Recently, a proposed draft has been submitted that describes a mechanism to add origin authentication, message integrity, replay-resistance, message sequencing, and detection of missing syslog messages, but this is not commonly implemented. Several of the popular syslogd replacements (including syslog-ng) can use TCP for reliable delivery, and some add a checksum and/or cryptographic signature to each log event.

Syslog is native on most UNIX platforms, but is not available natively on Microsoft Windows. The most common Windows syslog daemon is Kiwi Syslog (www.kiwisyslog.com).

Syslog messages (ASCII-based) may be sent to local logs, a local console, a remote syslog server, or a remote syslog relay. The syslog facility collects messages and records them normally in log files in /var/log. A facility is defined as a subsystem which generates messages. What is recorded and where it is placed depends on the facility configuration file (syslog.conf). Syslog also uses severity (or priority to some) to classify log messages by importance. The severity levels, from least to most important, are

0 Emergency: system is unusable

1 Alert: action must be taken immediately

2 Critical: critical conditions

3 Error: error conditions

4 Warning: warning conditions

5 Notice: normal but significant condition

6 Informational: informational messages

7 Debug: debug-level messages

There is also a severity of none. A severity of none indicates that all messages should be discarded. Entries in syslog.conf indicate how messages from each facility at the various severity levels should be handled.

Here is a small section of a BSD syslog file:

```
Jan  9 14:46:50 ns1 /kernel: usb1: <VIA 83C572 USB controller>
on uhci1

Jan  9 14:46:50 ns1 /kernel: usb1: USB revision 1.0

Jan  9 14:46:50 ns1 /kernel: uhub1: VIA UHCI root hub, class
9/0, rev 1.00/1.00, addr 1

Jan  9 14:46:50 ns1 /kernel: uhub1: 2 ports with 2 removable,
self powered

Jan  9 14:47:00 ns1 login: ROOT LOGIN (root) ON ttyv0

Jan  9 14:47:18 ns1 /kernel: Connection attempt to UDP
192.168.20.20:162 from 192.168.20.1:24343

Jan  9 14:47:19 ns1 /kernel: Connection attempt to TCP
127.0.0.1:16001 from 127.0.0.1:1024
```

Note that the messages are ASCII based and are composed of three major space-delimited fields: the time and date stamp, the hostname and facility, and a text based message.

Configuration of syslog and syslog remote logging is trivial. Much more difficult than generating appropriate syslog messages is defining processes that determine how the logs are parsed, who is responsible for parsing, and what type of log entries result in actionable alerts.

In a VoIP environment, IP phones may generate syslog messages and servers almost certainly will. These messages should be sent to a centralized server where they are automatically parsed, and where reports are generated at least on a daily basis. These logs are a valuable and often ignored source of both intrusion detection events and system performance messages. For example, syslog can be configured to report failed logon attempts, sudo (a command that attempts to change a restricted user's permissions to system level or root privilege) attempts, or any action that interacts with the PAM subsystem (Pluggable Authentication Module—an authentication framework). Any message that refers to one of these events may indicate that an intrusion has occurred.

SNMP

The Simple Network Management Protocol (SNMP) is an application layer protocol that facilitates the exchange of management information between network devices. SNMP messages are encoded as ASN.1 binary using BER encoding, and run over UDP/161 and UDP/162. SNMP enables network administrators to manage network performance and to find and solve network problems. Three versions of SNMP exist: SNMP version 1 (SNMPv1), SNMP version 2 (SNMPv2), and SNMP version 3 (SNMPv3). SNMPv1 and SNMPv2 have a number of features in common, but SNMPv2 offers enhancements, such as additional protocol operations. Neither version provides for any authentication or encryption. SNMPv3 includes, among other things, a model for access control and security as well as for a new architecture. SNMPv3 has yet to attain wide acceptance; thus, SNMPv1 and SNMPv2 still predominate.

An SNMP network normally consists of three key components: managed devices, agents, and network-management systems (NMSs). A managed device is a network node that contains an SNMP agent. Almost every networked device functions as a managed device. An agent is a network-management software module that resides in a managed device. An agent has local knowledge of management information and translates that information into a form compatible with SNMP. An NMS executes applications that monitor and control managed devices. NMSs provide the bulk of the processing and memory resources required for network management. Applications such as HP Openview or Tivoli are examples of NMSs.

Managed devices are monitored and controlled using three basic SNMP commands: read, write, and trap. These commands are defined as follows:

- The **read** command is used by an NMS to monitor managed devices.

- The **write** command is used by an NMS to control managed devices.

- The **trap** command is used by managed devices to asynchronously report events to the NMS.

Additionally, NMS and other applications (such as GetIF; see www.wtcs.org/snmp4tpc/getif.htm) can read and display the Management Information Base (MIB). A MIB is a (sometimes vendor-supplied) collection of information about the managed device that is organized hierarchically. The MIB contains fields that list all of the data the managed device can make available to the NMS.

SNMP community strings and some device configuration data are often among the first findings in penetration tests or vulnerability assessments. Most administrators forget about this threat or simply ignore it.

The best method for securing SNMP today is to turn it off. In VoIP networks, most IP-enabled telephones use SNMPV1 and SNMPv2 for configuration and performance monitoring. Thus, it is often impossible to disable this service. If you must run SNMP over your internal networks, then adopt the following practices:

- Immediately change the default read/write community strings

1. Do not use the default "public" or "private" string.

2. Do not use a string that would be easy to guess, such as the company's name or phone number.

3. Do not use a text-only string; use an alphanumeric string (both text and numerals).

4. Use both uppercase and lowercase letters (community strings are case-sensitive).

5. Use a community string that is at least eight characters long.

- Employ ingress and egress filtering at the nearest network border, or limit SNMP to specific management and configuration VLANs.

- Allow SNMP traffic to only a few authorized internal hosts. Only a few network management systems need to initiate SNMP request messages. Thus, administrators can configure SNMP agents to prohibit request messages from unauthorized hosts.

Penetration and Vulnerability Testing

Penetration/vulnerability tests are useful tools for determining the current security posture of an organization. These tests are also ideal for testing detection and response capabilities. Given that many computer emergency response teams are unprepared and inexperienced, these tests provide a great opportunity to gain experience in a consequence-free exercise.

TIP

"Not everything that can be counted counts, and not everything that counts can be counted."
    —A. Einstein

Penetration/vulnerability testing deals only with the "how" dimension of threats. It is a requirement for high-rated secure systems, ratings above B1 of the Secure Computer System Trusted Evaluation Criteria (TCSEC). In most industries, these penetration tests or "pen-tests" have become a required audit component. They can also be used as "shock therapy" to convince skeptical managers of their vulnerability to attack threats.

Penetration/vulnerability testing can not prove or even demonstrate that a system is flawless. It is an empirical method and unable to say much about undiscovered flaws. It is as thorough and comprehensive as the talent, knowledge, skill, and diligence of the team members—the goal being to demonstrate that the given network security architecture effectively balances risks and costs—to verify security controls so that the hacker "goes away before he gets in."

NOTE

"Desirable characteristics for the penetration testing team include experience, people knowledgeable of the target system, creative folks with bizarre ideas on associations of software modules, software development methods and tools, operating systems' control structure, resource allocation, input/output, human interfaces, and memory management. Successful testers are individuals who are detail oriented, careful thinkers, and persistent."
Handbook for the Computer Security Certification of Trusted Systems
Naval Research Laboratory
NRL Technical Memorandum 5540:082A.

A report in a SANS Security Alert, dated May 2000, provided an interesting perspective on this issue: A small number of flaws in software programs are responsible for the vast majority of successful Internet-based attacks. A few software vulnerabilities account for the majority of successful attacks because most attackers don't like to do extra work. They exploit the best known flaws—the "low-hanging fruit"—with the most effective and widely available attack tools.

And they count on organizations not fixing the problems.

What Is a Penetration/Vulnerability Test?

These tests or pseudo-attacks are conducted by an objective evaluation team and emulate an attack on one or more computer systems to discover ways to breach the system's security controls, to obtain sensitive information, to obtain unauthorized services, or to simulate damage to the system by denying service to legitimate users. Security testing comprises a detailed inventory of network assets and a set of controlled attacks intended to find vulnerabilities in those network assets. The words attack and test are used to mean the same in the context of a security assessment.

Penetration tests (pen-tests) usually refer to tests against perimeter defenses, while vulnerability testing refers to tests against specific systems (host, applications, or networks). External assessments can be loosely defined as testing that is launched from outside the perimeter of the private network. This kind of testing emulates the threat from hackers and other external parties and is often concerned with breaching firewalls and other forms of perimeter security. On the other hand, for vulnerability testing the analyst is located somewhere within the perimeter of the private network and emulates the threat experienced from internal staff, consultants, disgruntled employees, or, in the event of unauthorized physical access or a compromise of the perimeter security, a hacker. The general rule of thumb is that internal threats comprise more than 60 percent of the total threat portfolio.

Testing can consist of something as simple as an Nmap or Nessus scan, or it can be as detailed as tests against a multitiered business application architecture requiring months of code review and application testing. The ground rules for testing define successful completion. Testing is successfully concluded when:

- A defined number of flaws are found.

- A set level of penetration time has transpired.

- A dummy target object is accessed by unauthorized means.

- The security policy is violated sufficiently.

- Money and resources are exhausted.

- Internal resources are accessed.

- Transaction data is captured.

- A particular program or transaction is executed.

- Access is gained to any user account.

- Access is gained to a root/administrative account.

- Network management systems are subverted.

- The ability to remotely control resources is demonstrated.

Methodology

The team should thoroughly investigate target systems and networks in a structured manner, documenting their findings as they proceed. The goal is to attempt to identify all the *significant* vulnerabilities on the network—including their location and implications—and provide recommendations for securing the affected systems. Testing results in a comprehensive, operational review or "snapshot" of the state of the network. Testing should include an analysis of the external network from the perspective of an outside hacker, and/or a review of the internal network from the perspective of a disgruntled employee or contractor.

Discovery

The discovery process takes advantage of publicly available information that relates to your organization. Internet search engines, Whois databases, network registrars, DNS servers, and company Web sites are all sources of information. This phase can yield data that your organization might wish to protect. Table 12.1 lists a number of recommended tools used during the discovery phase. All of these are either native UNIX tools or are freeware, with the exception of WSPingPro.

Table 12.1 Common Security Testing Tools

Discovery	Scanning	Vulnerability Assessment
Whois	Hping	tcpdump
SamSpade	Nmap	Voipong
WSPingPro	LDAPMiner	Wepcrack
SuperScan	scanrand	GetIf
dig	NetStumbler	Nessus
nslookup	Kismet	Retina
ping	Nikto	Brute
traceroute	PSTools	WinFingerprint
TCPTraceroute	WSPingPro	Lophtcrack5
	SQLPing 2	ISS Internet Scanner
	ToneLoc	SnagIT
	Dsniff	@stake Proxy
	SuperScan	Ethereal
		Ettercap
		Amap
		John the Ripper
		Netcat

Scanning

Scanning or fingerprinting utilizes a variety of automated, non-intrusive scans. Nmap is a recommended tool for this step. Foundstone's SuperScan is another useful tool at this stage. Results of these scans should be constantly monitored in order to minimize bandwidth issues and to ensure that the scanning process does not result in loss of network connectivity for any networked devices. If any device fails under this type of scanning, that is a finding in itself.

It may be useful to emulate specific IP phones when testing VoIP gateways. For testing H.323 gateways or gatekeepers, the OpenH323 project offers OpenPhone, which has a GUI for Windows clients and command-line options for Linux distributions.

For testing SIP proxies, registrars, and gateways, many sites (such as sipXphone and YATE) have open-source SIP clients that are quite configurable. SJ Labs' SJphone softphone (www.softjoys.com) is also useful for testing in a VoIP environment, and is free for 30 days. SIPsak and SIPbomber are also useful SIP proxy testing tools. Callflow (http://callflow.sourceforge.net/) can be very useful for examining and understanding the alterations in calling message sequences that can result when performing SIP testing.

As an indication of the maturity of this field, SiVuS (www.vopsecurity.org) has been released. SiVuS is the first publicly available vulnerability scanner for VoIP networks that use the SIP protocol.

Vulnerability Assessment

Vulnerability assessment, one of the most important phases of penetration testing, occurs when your team maps the profile of the environment to publicly known or, in some cases, unknown vulnerabilities. Tools such as Nessus, Retina, and ISS Internet Scanner are all good choices at this stage. An excellent listing of the top 75 security tools can be found at www.insecure.org/tools.html.

When vulnerability testing VoIP networks, it is not necessary to test every IP phone. Because of the oftentimes, sheer number of IP phones, vulnerability testing has the potential to generate enough network traffic that voice quality is negatively affected. Testing one particular IP phone per vendor is often adequate since configurations should be functionally identical.

In most VoIP environments, it is possible to identify IP phones by their SNMP signature. Calling the IP phone directly—thus, bypassing any gateways or gatekeepers—can sometimes yield interesting information.

Exploitation

The exploitation phase begins once the target system's vulnerabilities are mapped. The testers will attempt to gain privileged access to a target system by exploiting the identified vulnerabilities. This may take the form of running an exploit tool such as scalp.c or iis5hack.c, or launching a password guessing attack using THC-Hydra, a network authentication cracker. (An excellent resource of known/default accounts and associated passwords is located at www.phenoelit.de/dpl/dpl.html.)

Reporting

Throughout the testing, the team should maintain a detailed journal of activities to account for effects and results of the testing procedures. This record will serve to distinguish the test team's activities from any other anomalies that occur during the course of the penetration test. Some techniques for capturing these data include the use of echo and logging. When appropriate, the use of screen captures may be an option.

- Detailed results of the testing performed
- What the results indicate
- Recommendations on types of corrective actions

One internal measure that can be used to quantify a particular vulnerability is a "Threat Index." This index is based upon two independent metrics: perceived risk (Table 12.2) and an estimated frequency (Table 12.3). The subsequent two-part identifier is formed by combining these two results, and is placed in the 3X3 matrix. The Threat Index (TI) has several purposes: First, it is used to rapidly prioritize a discovered vulnerability. Severe or high TIs (see Table 12.4) require immediate attention, and may also require more in-depth analysis by testers. Second, the TI can be used to rapidly code particular vulnerabilities. For example, if a newly discovered vulnerability is ranked with a TI of H1, all members of the team immediately understand that this is a severe problem that requires immediate action, while a TI of L3 indicates an insignificant issue.

Table 12.2 Risk Categories

High Risk (H)	Loss of critical proprietary information, system disruption, or severe environmental damage
Medium Risk (M)	Loss of proprietary information, severe occupational illness, or major system or environmental damage
Low Risk (L)	Minor system or environmental damage

Table 12.3 Modified Department of Defense Frequency Categories

Frequent (1)	Likely repeated occurrences
Occasional (2)	Possibility of repeated occurrences
Improbable (3)	Practically impossible

Table 12.4 Threat Index

	High Risk (H)	Medium Risk (M)	Low Risk (L)
Frequent (1)	H1	M1	L1
Occasional (2)	H2	M2	L2
Improbable (3)	H3	M3	L3

Your organization can apply these criteria in any way you see fit. The point is to determine as objectively as possible a method to prioritize threats against your infrastructure. You may even use different rankings based upon different portions of the network infrastructure—for example, when testing data services, threats to data integrity may be particularly important, compared to voice services, where threats that negatively impact availability may be critical.

In Table 12.4, any vulnerability with a threat index of H1, H2, M1, M2, and L1 requires immediate attention.

Summary

An appropriate firewall policy can minimize the exposure of your internal networks. However, attackers are evolving their attacks and network subversion methods. These techniques include e-mail-based Trojan horses, stealth scanning techniques, and attacks which bypass firewall policies by tunneling access over allowed protocols such as ICMP, HTTP, or DNS. Attackers are also getting better at using the ever-growing list of application vulnerabilities to compromise the few services that are allowed through a firewall.

Firewalls and Access Control Lists are requisite security controls in any enterprise, but they are not sufficient in contemporary networks. Active monitoring of the network and attached devices provides not only one or more additional layers of defense, but also supplies data that may have a forensic utility. Active monitoring consists of the following types of activities: network monitoring, network intrusion detection, host-based intrusion detection, syslog, and SNMP logging. Penetration and vulnerability testing monitors and validates existing security controls.

On enterprise networks, network monitoring is typically managed by a comprehensive tool suite such as OpenView. Traffic patterns and quantities, and device state are common measurements. These tools supply data that can be useful to security administrators, particularly when combined with the results of recent penetration/vulnerability tests or with NIDS/HIDS data. Unfortunately, the correlation of these data is difficult even when using tools such as SMARTS (a root-cause correlation engine), because of the overwhelming amount of data that must be organized.

NIDS and HIDS are complementary intrusion detection technologies. NIDS monitors the network for malicious or unauthorized traffic and HIDS monitors critical servers for changes to significant files and directories. Both relay event data to a central management console for logging and visualization. Most current NIDSs use a combination of signature (pattern or regex) and anomaly-based detection. Both of these methods have benefits and drawbacks. Signature-based detection is quick, effective, and popular, but it won't catch attacks that don't have signatures. Anomaly detection is theoretically a better method for detecting attacks, but suffers from the basic problem that it is difficult to define "normal" traffic on a network.

Although functionally dissimilar, SNMP and syslog both provide transport for event messages over the network from agents or endpoints to a centralized information repository. SNMP is a highly structured, binary-formatted message type, while syslog messages are ASCII-based and relatively arbitrary within the confines of three defined fields. Neither protocol is encrypted. Thus, SNMP and syslog messages should always be limited to a constrained management network.

Penetration and vulnerability testing is both art and science. These assessments are only as good as the people and tools used to perform them. In today's environment most types of penetration/vulnerability assessment have been commoditized due to the ready availability of scanning and vulnerability assessment tools.

Some tools, such as Nessus (which until recently was open source), make it possible for naïve administrators to perform at least baseline vulnerability scans on their networks. In this case, we recommend that an experienced security analyst be brought in to analyze the data since all of the vulnerability scanners report various false alarms. One important note is that the results of a test only reflect the security status during the testing period. Even minor administrative and architectural changes to the environment performed only moments after a penetration test can alter the system's security profile.

Solutions Fast Track

Network Intrusion Detection Systems

☑ Network Intrusion Detection Systems (NIDSs) are designed to alert administrators when malicious or illegitimate traffic is detected.

☑ Network-based IDSs can monitor an entire, large network with only a few well-situated nodes or devices and impose little overhead on a network.

☑ NIDSs are normally classified according to the methods they use for attack detection—either as signature-based or as anomaly detection.

☑ NIDSs should be located where they can most effectively monitor critical traffic.

☑ Communication between the IDS components (sensors and management console) should be encrypted using strong authentication.

Host-Based Intrusion Detection Systems

☑ HIDSs are applications that operate on information collected from individual computer systems.

☑ Tripwire is the reference model for many of the follow-on HIDSs.

☑ Most HIDS software establishes a "digital inventory" of files and their attributes in a known state, and uses that inventory as a baseline for monitoring any system changes.

Logging

☑ The key to successful log analysis is to adopt the proper tools for your environment to automatically parse, visualize, and report summarized log data.

☑ Syslog messages use UDP/514 for transport.

☑ The syslog protocol provides a transport to allow a machine to send event notification messages across IP networks to event message collectors (also known as syslog servers).

☑ Syslog messages (ASCII-based) may be sent to local logs, a local console, a remote syslog server, or a remote syslog relay.

☑ The Simple Network Management Protocol (SNMP) is an application layer protocol that facilitates the exchange of management information between network devices.

☑ An SNMP network normally consists of three key components: managed devices, agents, and network-management systems (NMSs).

☑ If you must use SNMP, immediately change the values of the default read/write community strings

Penetration and Vulnerability Testing

☑ Penetration/vulnerability tests are useful tools for determining the current security posture of an organization.

☑ Penetration tests (pen-tests) usually refer to tests against perimeter defenses, while vulnerability testing refers to tests against specific systems (host, applications, or networks).

☑ The results of a penetration/vulnerability test only reflect the security status during the testing period. Even minor administrative and architectural changes to the environment performed only moments after a penetration test can alter the system's security profile.

Frequently Asked Questions

The following Frequently Asked Questions, answered by the authors of this book, are designed to both measure your understanding of the concepts presented in this chapter and to assist you with real-life implementation of these concepts. To have your questions about this chapter answered by the author, browse to **www.syngress.com/solutions** and click on the **"Ask the Author"** form.

Q: What's the difference between a network intrusion detection system (NIDS) and a host-based intrusion detection system (HIDS)?

A: An NIDS inspects all inbound and outbound network activity and identifies patterns of packet data that may indicate a network or system attack. An HIDS, on the other hand, normally resides as an application on the server that it monitors.

Q: What is the Windows equivalent of syslog?

A: Windows doesn't really have a native equivalent. The eventlog service enables event log messages issued by Windows-based programs and components to be viewed in Event Viewer.

Q: I've set up *<myfile>* to log to syslog, but it's not working. What should I do?

A: Make sure you have an entry in your syslog.conf file to save the apropriate messages. Don't forget to send a SIGHUP to your syslogd so that it re-reads its conf file. Also, remember that syslogd does not create log files. You need to create the file before syslogd will log to it (for example, touch /var/log/myfile).

Q: If you have multiple security devices reporting to a remote syslog server, what is the best way to parse or separate the logs?

A: Log parsing is difficult to do in an efficient, scalable manner. A number of commercial products claim to parse various formats and store the information in a backend database. Numerous open-source log parsing projects exist at Freshmeat or SourceForge. Also, simple shell, awk, or perl scripts can be used.

Q: Should my company be running our own honeypot or honeynet?

A: Probably not. Most organizations still have problems completing and maintaining basic security controls. Honeypots and honeynets are primarily learning tools. Most honeynets are run in academia, the military, and government.

Q: I'm looking for a utility that enables me to change community names on multiple devices from a single management console. Where can I find one?

A: Because the methodology for setting community strings is not standardized, every type of device/agent version may have a different mechanism for handling this chore. Therefore, there are no "single console" products for setting community strings. For this to be feasible, you would have to be able to differentiate every agent type, and know how that particular vendor/system/agent handles it.

Q: What is RMON?

A: The Remote Network Monitoring MIB is an SNMP MIB for the remote management of networks. While other MIBs usually are created to support a network device whose primary function is other than management, RMON was created to provide management of a network. RMON is one of the many SNMP-based MIBs that are on the IETF Standards track.

Q: What are red-teams and blue-teams?

A: In penetration testing, a red-team approach means that the testers adopt a stealthy posture—that is, they take on the role of an untrusted attacker attempting to sneak into the network. Blue-team signifies an approach where the tester is an insider and test tool collateral "noise" is not an issue.

Chapter 13

Logically Segregate Network Traffic

Solutions in this chapter:

- **VLANs**
- **QoS and Traffic Shaping**
- **NAT and IP Addressing**
- **Firewalls**
- **Access Control Lists**

☑ **Summary**

☑ **Solutions Fast Track**

☑ **Frequently Asked Questions**

Introduction

One of the principal advantages of converging voice and data is to save money and to simplify administration and management by running both types of traffic over the same physical infrastructure. With this in mind, it is ironic that most of the engineering effort expended during the VoIP architecture design phase focuses on logically separating this same voice and data traffic.

Packetized voice is indistinguishable from any other packet data at Layers 2 and 3, and thus is subject to the same networking and security risks that plague data-only networks. The general idea that motivates the logical separation of data from voice is the expectation that network events such as broadcast storms and congestion, and security-related phenomena such as worms and DoS attacks, that affect one network will not impact the other. This is the principal consequence of compartmentalization.

In practice, system and security administrators have a number of options to realize this logical division. Packet headers can be manipulated in order to separate datagrams and datastreams at Layer 2, to provide certain classes of packets with preferential treatment or more bandwidth; and to alter source and destination IP addresses. Firewalls (particularly VoIP-aware firewalls), application layer gateways (ALGs), routers, and switches are inserted in the datapath to monitor and control traffic streams. Many devices now support robust access control lists (ACLs) that are used to fine-tune network and application access. Encryption is used often to ensure data and signal channel authentication, integrity, and privacy, but the encryption process results in subtle and not-so-subtle interactions with the methods that manipulate packet headers.

Maintaining and securing contemporary data and voice networks is complex stuff—something not recommended for naïve system administrators. Gone are the days when networks could be pieced together in an ad hoc fashion in order to support gopher, e-mail, and ftp. Modern VoIP/data networks must be designed to support a sometimes bewildering array of applications—all with their own unique service requirements and SLAs—in an open, yet secure environment.

To this end, in this chapter we look at the methods used to segregate voice and data into logically isolated networks that run over the same physical infrastructure. Figure 13.1 shows the components of this architecture. The primary elements of the security architecture are VLANs, QoS scheduling, firewalls, NAT and intelligent IP address space management, and ACLs. Encryption also plays a role in this. We will look at each of these technologies in more detail in the following sections.

Figure 13.1 is a diagram of a VoIP/data reference network that illustrates the major security components involved in logical segregation of network traffic types. At the border between the Internet and the internal network, firewalls, ALGs, and router-based ACLs provide the first line of defense or security layer against illicit traffic and attackers. Within the internal domains, VLANs, QoS, private IP addresses, and NAT segregate VoIP traffic from other data network traffic, and VoIP-aware firewalls and router-based ACLs manage traffic between the two domains. Softphones may or may not span both domains depending upon an organization's sensitivity to risk.

Figure 13.1 Converged Reference Network

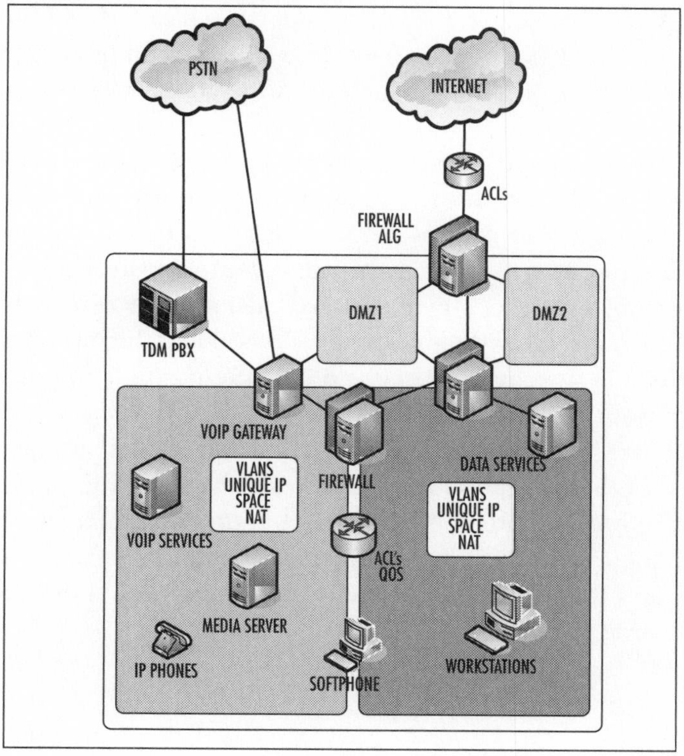

VLANs

Logical separation of voice and data traffic via VLANs is recommended in order to prevent data network problems from affecting voice traffic and vice versa. In a switched network environment, VLANs create a logical segmentation of broadcast or collision domains that can span multiple physical network segments. VLANs remove the need to organize and manage PCs or softphones based upon physical location, and can be used to arrange endpoints based upon function, class of service, class of user, connection speed, or other criteria. The separation of broadcast domains reduces traffic to the balance of the network. Effective bandwidth is increased due to the elimination of latency from router links. Additional security is realized if access to VLAN hosts is limited to only hosts on specific VLANs and not those that originate from other subnets beyond the router.

VLANs, or virtual LANs, can be thought of as logically segmented networks mapped onto physical hardware. One or more VLANs can coexist on a single physical switch. The predominant VLAN flavor is IEEE 802.1Q, as defined by the IEEE. Prior to the introduction of 802.1q, Cisco's ISL (Inter-Switch Link) was one of several proprietary VLAN protocols. ISL is now deprecated in favor of 802.1q. VLANs operate at layer 2 of the OSI model. However, a VLAN often is configured to map directly to an IP network or subnet, which gives the appearance that it is involved at layer 3.

VLANs can be configured in various ways—by protocol (IP or IPX, for example) or based on MAC address, subnet, or physical port. They can be static, dynamic, or port-centric. Mechanistically, VLANs are formed by either frame-tagging or frame-filtering. Frame-tagging, the more common mechanism, requires adding and removing a unique, 2-byte L2 frame identifier so that switches may appropriately send and receive their cognate VLAN traffic. Frame-filtering relies upon the participating switches building and communicating a filtering database in order to forward traffic to its correct VLAN.

In Figure 13.2, dotted lines represent VLAN 2 and solid lines represent VLAN 10. The presence of the two lines that form a trunk between the top level switches should not be taken to indicate that there are two physical connections. Servers and workstations are logically isolated based upon their physical location. If a New York workstation requires the services of a Los Angeles server, then those data are routed between the top level switches.

Figure 13.2 Location-Based VLANs

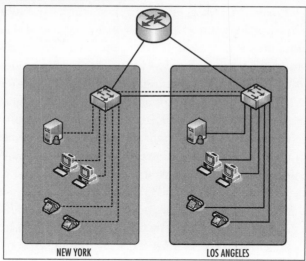

In Figure 13.3, dotted lines represent VLAN 2, solid lines represent VLAN 10, and dash–dot lines represent VLAN 100. The presence of the three lines that form a trunk between the top level switches should not be taken to indicate that there are three physical connections. In the network shown in Figure 13.3, broadcast traffic in the telephone subnet will not be seen by hosts in the workstation subnet.

Figure 13.3 Function-Based VLANs

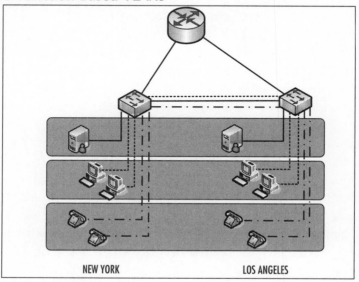

VLANs provide some security and create smaller broadcast domains by creating logically separated subnets. Broadcasts are a common, sometimes noisy phenomenon in data networks. Creating a separate VLAN for voice reduces the amount of broadcast traffic (and unicast traffic on a shared LAN) the telephone will receive. Separate VLANs can result in more effective bandwidth utilization, and reduce the processor burden on IP telephones and PCs by freeing them from having to analyze irrelevant broadcast packets. Management traffic can be segregated on a management VLAN so that SNMP and syslog traffic do not interfere with data traffic. This also has the benefit of adding a layer of security to the management network. Additionally, VLANs can be used in conjunction with various quality of service mechanisms (see next section) to further isolate and prioritize voice traffic.

The consequences of DoS attacks can be mitigated by logically separating voice and data segments into discrete VLANs. Segregation of network traffic requires that IP traffic pass through a Layer 3 device, thereby enabling the traffic to be inspected at the ACL level. VLAN segregation forces any DoS packets through the ACLs on the layer 3 device. The use of packet filtering or stateful firewall inspection at these junctions also is recommended. As a side note, user authentication prior to the user's accessing the telephony device also will reduce the possibility of internal DoS attacks.

VLAN Security

VLAN and layer 2 security is a complex topic, partially because of the uneven support by switch vendors for appropriate datalink safeguards and because many of the exploitable vulnerabilities arise due to misconfiguration of available safeguards. The single most important rule with regard to this topic is to absolutely ensure that unauthorized individuals do not have access to the switch console. Additionally, terminal access to the console should either require strong authentication (RADIUS or AAA) and be restricted to a small set of management PCs, or should be eliminated altogether.

VLAN function depends upon the presence or absence of tag information. If the integrity of the tag information is assured, then the logical security afforded by VLANs is as legitimate as physical security. The key is to certify that tag information originates from the appropriate hosts and is unchanged in transit. A number of controls exist to verify this information such as ARP inspection, DHCP spoofing, VACLs (VLAN ACLs), private and dynamic VLANs, port security, and 802.1X admission controls, but implementation of these is vendor specific and beyond the scope of this section. Additionally, the IEEE 802.1 Working Group has established drafts, particularly, 802.1aj, that decompose security when two related MACs are in a relay configuration.

VLANs and Softphones

Softphones present a security challenge in a VoIP environment, particularly if VLANs are employed as a major security control. Several popular softphones (such as X-Lite) store credentials unencrypted in the Window's registry even after uninstallation of the program. Many softphones contain advertising software that attempts to "phone home" with private user information. Host-based IDS or firewall applications have limited use in this situation because softphones require that PC-based firewalls open a number of high UDP ports as part of the media stream transaction. Additionally, any special permissions that the VoIP application has within the host-based firewall rule set will apply to all applications on that desktop (e.g., peer-to-peer software may use SIP for bypassing security policy prohibitions).

Tools & Traps…

Watch What You Plug into That Phone

We recently observed a situation where plugging in a single phone brought down a substantial piece of the network. The IP phone had two RJ45 plugs in the back and a technician mistakenly plugged both of these into a nearby access switch running STP. No one realized (until later) that the IP phone failed to bridge spanning tree BPDUs. The resulting broadcast storm took out several core switches. This problem was solved temporarily with a bit of glue and some RJ45 plugs.

The most important rule for securing softphones is to harden the underlying operating system. Malware that affects any other application software on the PC can also interfere with voice communications. The flip-side is also true—malware that affects the VoIP software will affect all other applications on the PC and the data services available to that PC (a separate VoIP phone would not require access to file services, databases, etc.). Softphones that contain any type of advertising software must be banned in a secure environment. Softphone installation targets should be tested before deployment and those that do not encrypt user credentials should be prohibited.

Because PC workstations are necessarily on the data network, using a softphone system conflicts with the requirement to separate voice and data networks since the principle of logically separating voice and data networks is defeated because the PC must reside in both domains. One solution to this is dual home workstations—

dedicate one NIC to the data domain and one NIC to the voice domain. This arrangement still allows for possible routing of information between domains via a workstation. Cisco recently has introduced a Certificate Trust List (CTL) that contains among other information, the IP addresses of trusted VoIP peers. However, this feature is available only in selected IP phones and requires, for the most part, setup and maintenance of a complex certificate infrastructure. Additionally, unless complex host firewall rules are implemented, non-VoIP related data can enter the voice domain from workstations. Frankly, there is no single good security solution to the issue of softphones on workstations in split voice/data environments. In a highly secure environment, your best choice is to ban them via policy and monitor for illicit usage via IDS or IPS.

QoS and Traffic Shaping

VoIP has strict performance requirements. The factors that affect the quality of data transmission are different from those affecting the quality of voice transmission. For example, data generally is not affected by small delays. The quality of voice transmissions, on the other hand, is lowered by relatively small amounts of delay. VoIP call quality depends on three network factors, as mentioned earlier:

- **Latency** The time it takes for a voice transmission (or any transmission) to travel from source to destination is increased as packets traverse each security node. Primary latency-producing processes are firewall/NAT traversal, negotiation of long ACLs, and traffic encryption/decryption.

- **Jitter (erratic packet delays)** Jitter may be increased, because in many circumstances, jitter is a function of hop count.

- **Packet loss** The number of non-QoS-aware routers and firewalls that ignore or fail to properly process Type of Service (ToS) fields in the IP header can influence packet loss.

In the absence of QoS or Traffic shaping, data networks operate on a best-effort delivery basis, which means that all data traffic has equal priority and an equal chance of being delivered in a prompt manner. However, when network congestion occurs, all data traffic has an equal chance of being dropped and/or delayed. When voice data is introduced into a network, it becomes critical that priority is given to the voice packets to insure the expected quality of voice calls. The mechanisms used to accomplish this are generically referred to as traffic shaping.

Traffic shaping is an attempt to organize network traffic in order to optimize or guarantee performance and/or bandwidth. Traffic shaping relies upon concepts such as classification, queue disciplines, scheduling, congestion management, quality of service (QoS), class of service (CoS), and fairness.

Common CoS models include the Differentiated Services Code Point (DiffServ or DSCP, defined in RFC 2474 and others) and IEEE 802.1Q/p. DSCP specifies that each packet is classified upon entry into the network. The classification is carried in the IP packet header, using 6 bits from the deprecated IP type-of-service (ToS) field to carry the classification (code point) information, which ranges from 0 through 63. Generally, the higher number equates to higher priority.

802.1Q defines the open standards for VLAN tagging. Twelve of the 16 bits within the two Tag Control Information bytes are used to tag each frame with a VLAN identification number. 802.1p uses three of the remaining bits (the User Priority bits) in the 802.1Q header to assign one of eight different classes of service (0 = low priority; 8 = high priority).

Quality of Service involves giving preferential treatment of particular classes or flows of traffic primarily by manipulating queues and scheduling. A service quality is then negotiated.

Examples of QoS are CBWFQ (Class Based Weighted Fair Queuing), RSVP (RESERVATION Protocol–RFC 2205), MPLS, (Multi Protocol Label Switching–RFC 1117 and others). CoS, or tagging, is ineffective in the absence of QoS because it can only mark data. QoS relies on those tags or filters to give priority to data streams.

Networks with periods of congestion can still provide excellent voice quality when using an appropriate QoS/CoS policy. The recommendation for switched networks is to use IEEE 802.1p/Q. The recommendation for routed networks is to use DiffServ Code Points (DSCP). The recommendation for mixed networks is to use both.

The main purpose of these technologies is to ensure that application performance remains satisfactory regardless of network conditions. In general, they all work by categorizing traffic into discrete subsets that are processed with different priorities. For this reason, QoS techniques may be useful in protecting VoIP networks from a significant security threat—Denial of Service. A number of authors have shown that some VoIP architecture components including IP telephones, SIP proxies, and H.323 gateways may freeze and crash when attempting to process a high rate of packet traffic. QoS can provide some security for these devices during DoS attack either by prioritizing unauthorized data low and/or by prioritizing VoIP high. This measure (security layer) will mitigate the consequences of a DoS attack on applications that share the same physical bandwidth.

The downside of all this is that traffic shaping is, at times, a stew of poorly interoperable technologies and techniques. This ad hoc nature makes a true end-to-end

QoS strategy sometimes difficult to implement. If possible, provide enough bandwidth resources to meet the expected peak demands with a substantial safety margin. Note also that the implementation of some security measures can degrade quality of service.

These security-related complications are bulleted at the beginning of this section, and range from interruption or prevention of call setup by misconfigured firewall rules to encryption-produced latency and delay variation (jitter). There is no single best method at present to optimize traffic shaping on VoIP networks without taking into account the relationship of these technologies with the security measures implemented within your environment.

NAT and IP Addressing

Network Address Translation (NAT) is a method for rewriting the source and/or destination addresses of IP packets as they pass through a NAT device, which is often a router or firewall that separates two realms or domains on the Internet. NAT was first officially proposed (RFC1631) in 1994 as a temporary solution to the problems of IP address space depletion and the rapidly increasing size of route tables. Addresses, at that time, were divided into two classes: local and global addresses. Today we normally refer to these addresses as either private or public, and the private IP space often is referred to as RFC1918 addresses. Per RFC1918, the Internet Assigned Numbers Authority (IANA) reserved three blocks of the IP address space for private internets:

- 10.0.0.0–10.255.255.255 (10/8 prefix)
- 172.16.0.0–172.31.255.255 (172.16/12 prefix)
- 192.168.0.0–192.168.255.255 (192.168/16 prefix)

NAT commonly is used to enable multiple hosts on private networks to access the Internet using a single public (Internet routable) IP address. Note that although NAT most commonly is used to map IP addresses from internal private IP space to the public IP space, NAT can be used to map between any two IP address domains. Additionally, NAT provides a security function by segregating (hiding) private hosts from the publicly routed Internet. This short-term kludge has had an enormous impact on the day-to-day functioning of the Internet, and has special relevance to system administrators who are charged with securely transporting VoIP packet data across network boundaries.

How Does NAT Work?

To a system on the Internet, a NAT device appears to be the source/destination for all traffic originating from behind the NAT device. Hosts behind a NAT device do not have true end-to-end Internet connectivity and cannot directly participate in Internet protocols that require initiation of TCP connections from outside the NAT device, or protocols that split signaling and media into separate channels.

A NAT device examines and records certain IP header information from each packet within an active IP connection. It uses these connection data to multiplex or demultiplex traffic depending upon the direction of the traffic flows. Multiplexing, in this case, means that two or more traffic streams are combined into a single outbound channel; demultiplexing refers to the process of separating a complex inbound traffic stream into single traffic streams (see Figure 13.4).

Figure 13.4 Multiplexing and Demultiplexing

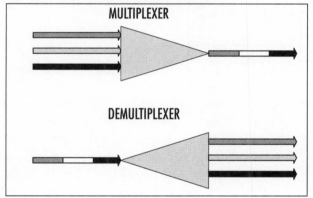

NAT devices manipulate a subset of the IP header information. In order to comprehend the sometimes complex interaction of NAT, encryption, and VoIP protocols, you will have to understand the IP header fields and how they are altered during the NAT and encryption processes. It is not necessary for you to understand these concepts if you are concerned only with a NAT device's ability to hide internal network topology from the Internet, but as part of the process of securing VoIP communications, this information is critical. Get to know the header diagrams shown in Figure 13.5. You'll be seeing them frequently.

Figure 13.5 IP, TCP, and UDP Headers

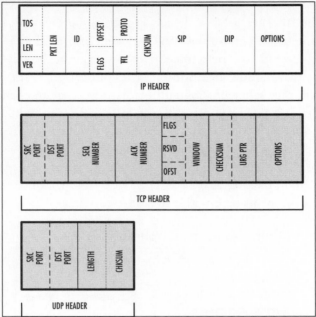

Note that the rest of this section applies only to IPv4 packets. IPv6 resolves most of the following issues, but it just hasn't caught on yet. The IP header normally consists of 20 bytes of data. The TCP header also normally consists of 20 bytes of data. An options field exists within each header that allows further bytes to be added, but normally this is not used. The UDP header is 8 bytes in length. Both the TCP and UDP headers reside in the data field of an IP packet. In Figure 13.5, the data field is to the right of the options field for IP and TCP headers and to the right of the CHKSUM field in the case of the UDP header.

NAT devices monitor, record, and alter the source IP address (SIP), destination IP address (DIP), and checksum (CHKSUM) fields within IP headers. NAT also modifies the checksum fields of both TCP and UDP packets since these checksums are computed over a pseudo-header that conceptually consists of the source and destination IP addresses, and the protocol and length fields for TCP. The UDP checksum is calculated over a pseudo-header that consists of the source and destination IP addresses, the UDP header and data. As for ICMP Query packets, no further changes in the ICMP header are required as the checksum in the ICMP header does not include the IP addresses. These checksum fields will prove particularly troubling as we modify VoIP packets by encryption over NAT.

In response to the pseudo-header complexities, RFC1631 suggests that:

NAT must also look out for ICMP and FTP and modify the places where the IP address appears. There are undoubtedly other places, where modifications must be done. Hopefully, most such applications will be discovered during experimentation with NAT.

Though these were bright individuals it seems to me unlikely that they would have imagined that their complex solution would prove to be a major complication to end-to-end application availability on today's contemporary internetworks. Figure 13.6 shows how NAT alters four header fields.

Figure 13.6 NAT Alters Four Header Fields

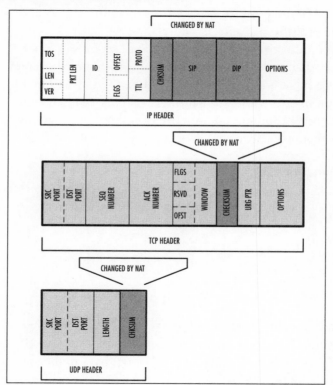

NAT Has Three Common Modes of Operation

Depending upon networking requirement and topology requirements, NAT is manifested in one of three related modes. Static NAT refers to a one-to-one mapping or correspondence between internal and external IP addresses. In this case, the number of internal IP addresses equals the number of external addresses (see Figure 13.7).

Figure 13.7 Static NAT

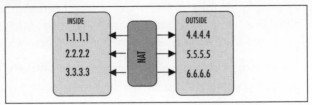

The NAT device maintains a lookup table of internal and external addresses in order to manage translations in a stateless manner. Static NAT has utility in mapping the private internal IP addresses of critical infrastructure servers and network appliances to a unique globally available IP address.

Dynamic NAT in its original form consisted of an outside pool or collection of public IP addresses that were used on a first-come, first-served strategy (see Figure 13.8). Each unique single internal address could be used by any member of the outside pool to communicate with external Internet hosts. Consequently, the size of the outside pool member set limited the number of inside users that could connect externally. A built-in timeout mechanism allowed external pool members to be reused.

Figure 13.8 Dynamic NAT

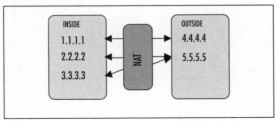

The third and probably most common style of NAT is derived functionally from Dynamic NAT since it reuses a smaller pool or a single external IP address to proxy for all the internal IP addresses. This NAT is known by a number of names, including Network Address Port Translation (NAPT), Port Address Translation (PAT), Full Cone NAT (From the STUN RFC3489), hiding NAT, and masquerading NAT. This type of NAT (we'll call it NAPT to keep things organized) works to preserve state by maintaining a lookup table of source IP, destination IP, source port, and destination port. This 4-tuple is almost always guaranteed to be unique within a given conversation stream. You'll find NAPT operating in almost all home broadband and in most large enterprise networking scenarios. Figure 13.9 shows an example of NAPT.

Figure 13.9 Network Address Port Translation

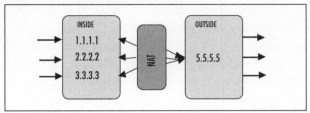

So a normal scenario that occurs when moving TCP traffic between two domains running NAT at each edge is shown in Figure 13.10.

In addition to these three NAT modes, STUN (we'll see this later) has defined a three types of NAT that map more or less to these three modes. These are cone NAT, restricted NAT, and symmetric NAT. We'll talk more about these in the section on STUN and TURN.

Figure 13.10 Normal NAT Process with TCP

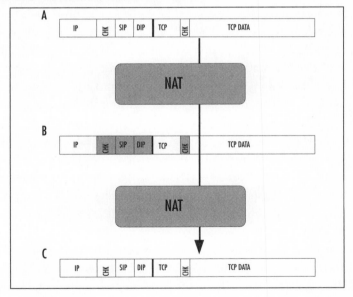

Section A of Figure 13.10 shows the TCP/IP packet header prior to NAT. After passing through the first NAT edge device (section B), the four header fields are modified: the three IP header fields—source address, destination address, and checksum—and the TCP header checksum. After passing through the second NAT edge device, the original header fields are regenerated (section C). The same is true for UDP in this situation, except that if the UDP checksum is zero, it will not be altered.

You may naturally ask by now, why is NAT such an issue for VoIP? Well, when we begin to combine NAT and protocols such as H.323 and SIP that partition the signaling and media channels; and, to make things even more interesting, embed IP addresses in the signaling channel, it will be important to understand how, when, and where NAT manipulates these fields. When we add encryption into the mix, NAT adds further complexity to these systems. Additionally, note that NAT stores its address mapping information in binding tables, and that these bindings are only initiated by outbound traffic. NAT breaks the choreography of SIP session flow. Encryption adds further complexity to these systems.

NAT and Encryption

As IPsec VPNs became popular, NAT became an impediment to their initial widespread implementation. I'll use the IPsec model to develop a description of the interactions between NAT and encryption since it is one of the more popular Internet encryption systems and has potential value in VoIP networks. The IP security (IPsec) protocol was defined by the Internet Engineering Task Force (IETF) to provide security for IP networks. IPsec is a large protocol suite designed to provide the following security services for IP networks: Data Integrity, Authentication, Confidentiality, and Application-transparent Security. IPSec secures packet flows and key transmission. Since we are interested in NAT and encryption, we'll ignore most of the protocol suite including key exchange (IKE), and the various hash and encryption algorithms, and focus instead on the protocols that are used to secure packet flows.

The AH and ESP protocols can operate in two modes: Transport Mode can be visualized simply as a secure connection between two concurring hosts. In Tunnel Mode—more of a "VPN-like" mode—IPsec completely encapsulates the original IP datagram, including the original IP header, within a second IP datagram. ESP and AH normally are implemented independently, though it's possible (but uncommon) to use them both together.

The Authentication Header (AH) and the Encapsulating Security Payload (ESP) are the two main network protocols used by IPsec. The AH provides data origin authentication, message integrity, and protection against replay attacks, but has no provision for privacy—data is not encrypted. The key to the AH authentication process is the inclusion in the AH header of an Integrity Check Value (ICV) —a hash based upon a secret key that is calculated over a subset of the original IP header fields, *including the source and destination IP addresses.* AH guarantees (if implemented correctly) that the data received is identical to the data sent, and asserts the identity of the true sender. AH provides authentication for as much of the IP header as possible, as well as for upper level protocol data. However, some IP header fields (SIP, DIP, TTL, CHKSUM, and optionally, TOS, FLAGS, and OPTIONS) change in transit. The values of such fields usually are not protected by AH. In transport mode, AH is inserted after the IP header and before the upper layer protocol (TCP, UDP, ICMP, etc.) header. In tunnel mode, the AH header precedes the encapsulated IP header. Figure 13.11 shows the AH transport and tunnel modes.

Figure 13.11 Authentication Header: Transport and Tunnel Modes

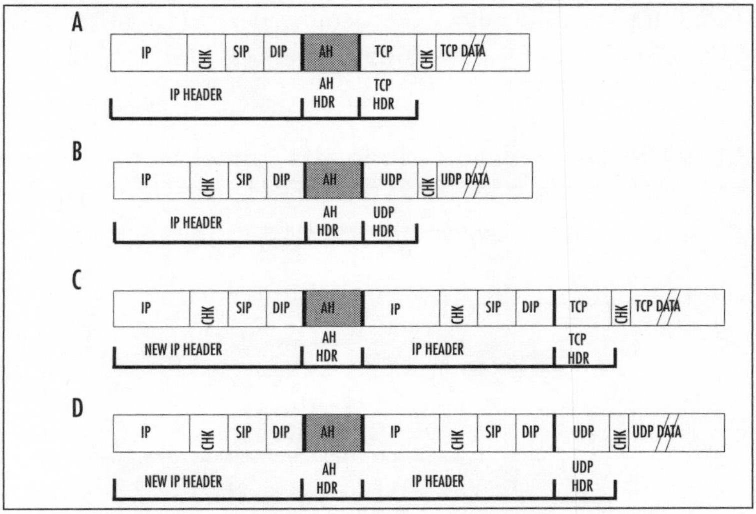

In Figure 13.11, sections A and B show the location of the AH header in transport mode. Sections C and D show the location of the AH header in tunnel mode. The data field in all packets is not to scale (indicated by the double slanted lines). You can see from this figure that tunnel mode AH adds an additional 20 bytes to the length of each packet. None of the fields in this figure are encrypted.

NOTE

The key to the incompatibility of NAT and IPsec AH is the presence of the ICV, whose value depends partially on the values of the source and destination IP addresses, the IP header checksum, and either the TCP or UDP header checksum. The AH ICV calculation takes into account the mutable and predictable header fields that change as the packet moves from hop to hop through the network, but because intermediate devices do not share the secret key, they cannot recalculate the correct ICV after NAT has altered the aforementioned original header fields.

ESP, on the other hand, was used initially only for encryption; authentication functionality was subsequently added. The ESP header is inserted after the IP header and before the upper layer protocol header (transport mode) or before an encapsulated IP header (tunnel mode).

Figure 13.12 shows the location of the ESP header in both transport mode (sections A and B) and tunnel mode (sections C and D) for TCP (sections A and C) and UDP (sections B and D). In transport mode, the original IP header is followed by the ESP header. The rightmost field contains the ESP trailer and optionally, the ESP authorization field. Only the upper-layer protocol header, data, and the ESP trailer (also, optionally, the ESP authorization field) is encrypted. The IP header is not encrypted.

Figure 13.12 ESP Header: Transport Mode and Tunnel Mode

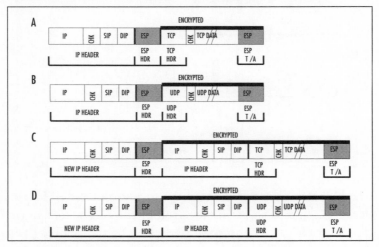

In transport mode, ESP encrypts the entire packet. This means that the entire original IP datagram, including the original IP and protocol header, is encrypted. In this mode, when IP traffic moves between gateways, the outer, unencrypted IP header contains the IP addresses of the penultimate source and destination gateways, and the inner, encrypted IP header contains the IP source and destination addresses of the true endpoints. However, even though ESP encrypts most of the IP datagram in either transport or tunnel mode, ESP is relatively compatible with NAT, since ESP does not incorporate the IP source and destination addresses in its keyed message integrity check. Still, ESP has a dependency on TCP and UDP checksum integrity through inclusion of the pseudo-header in the calculation. As a result, when checksums are calculated, they will be invalidated by passage through a NAT device (except in some cases where the UDP checksum is set to zero).

NAT traversal using ESP leads to a catch-22. NAT must recalculate the TCP header checksums used to verify packet integrity, because as was showed earlier, NAT modifies those headers. If NAT updates the header checksum, ESP authentication will fail. If NAT does not update the checksum, TCP verification will fail. One way around this, if the transport endpoint is under your control, is to turn off checksum verification, but I'm not aware of anyone who has done this in production environments. A second, more common means to do this is to NAT before IPSec; don't perform IPSec before NAT. This can be accomplished by locating the NAT device logically behind the IPsec device. The most common form of NAT traversal used today relies on encapsulating IPsec packets in UDP in order to bypass NAT devices. The IPsec packet is encapsulated in a meta-UDP packet and the meta-UDP packet is stripped off after it passes through the NAT device. This enables NAT and IPsec to function together but none of these are hardly elegant solutions.

NAT as a Topology Shield

NAT provides a security function by segregating private hosts from the publicly routed Internet. Depending upon your addressing requirements, NAT can isolate, to some extent, your VoIP network IP space from the balance of your internal network IP space. The large number of private RFC1918 IP addresses allows system architects to intelligently address hosts and other network elements based upon location, function, or other criteria during the design phase of the VoIP network.

External hosts cannot directly access a particular internal host if a NAT intervenes since the external host has no way of targeting its payload to a chosen IP address. Of course, when addresses are assigned dynamically, it becomes even more problematic for an attacker to point to a specific host within the NAT domain. This may help protect internal hosts from external malicious content. At worst, NAT is an additional layer of security controls that you implement as part of your overall security architecture.

The IPsec model is instructive in that it illustrates a complex interaction between encryption and NAT. However, IPsec is not the only functional or proposed security mechanism for VoIP environments. SSL/TLS, S/MIME, HTTP 1.1 digest, and ZRTP have also been proposed as security instruments. Nor are all environments as simple as the symmetric examples we have seen where one or more devices reside on opposite sides of a NAT device. Asymmetric or hairpin call routing (a call from one phone behind a NAT to another phone behind the same NAT), in an environment where basic NAT and encryption issues have been resolved, can cause communications to fail. The point here is to introduce some of the concepts that you will come across as you design and troubleshoot in this area. We'll see in the next section how encryption, NAT, and VoIP protocols work (or don't work) together.

Firewalls

Firewalls are a key component of virtually any network security architecture. Firewalls demarcate inside from outside, trusted from nontrusted networks, and they are used to separate VoIP from data on internal networks. Two significant issues affect firewall performance with regard to VoIP: The first is that the boundary between inside and outside or trusted and nontrusted networks gradually is becoming less clear; the second is that most firewalls fail to adequately process VoIP packets and sessions, particularly (as you were forewarned) if those session and packets are encrypted.

A Bit of Firewall History

Traditionally, firewalls have provided a physical and logical demarcation between the inside and the outside of a network. The first firewalls were basically just gateways between two networks with IP forwarding disabled. Most contemporary firewalls share a common set of characteristics:

1. They are single points between two or more networks where all traffic must pass (choke point).
2. They can be configured to allow or deny IP (and other protocol) traffic.
3. They provide a logging function for audit purposes.
4. They provide a NAT function.
5. Their operating systems are hardened.
6. They often serve as a VPN endpoint.
7. They fail closed—that is, if the firewall crashes in some way, no traffic is forwarded between interfaces.

Shallow Packet Inspection

Steven Bellovin classically stated, "Firewalls are barriers between 'us' and 'them' for arbitrary values of 'them.'"

Shallow packet inspection, in contrast to deep packet inspection, inspects only a few header fields in order to make processing decisions. IP packet filtering firewalls all share this same basic mechanism: As an IP packet traverses the firewall, the headers are parsed, and the results are compared to a rule set defined by a system administrator. The rule set, commonly based upon source and/or destination IP address, source and/or destination port, or a combination of the two, defines what type of traffic is subsequently allowed or denied. Packet filtering (and the code that performs these tasks) based upon parsing of IP headers has been common for many years.

Tools & Traps…

Thank Goodness for GUIs

Interestingly, some early (and not particularly popular) packet-filtering implementations required that the system administrator define specific byte fields with the packet headers, and the specific byte patterns to match against. Imagine setting up and troubleshooting a 100-field rule set on one of these systems!

Stateful Inspection

Stateful Inspection Firewall Technology, a term coined by Check Point Software Technologies, described a method for the analysis and tracking of sessions based upon source/destination IP address and source/destination ports. A stateful inspection firewall registers connection data and compiles this information in a kernel-based state table. A stateful firewall examines packet headers and, essentially, remembers something about them (generally source/destination IP address/ports). The firewall then uses this information when processing later packets. Interestingly, Lance Spitzner (www.spitzner.net/) showed that, contrary to what we would expect, sequence numbers and other header information is not utilized by Check Point in order to maintain connection state tracking. Stateful packet inspection firewalls, like packet filtering firewalls, have very little impact on network performance, can be implemented transparently, and are application independent.

Medium-Depth Packet Inspection

Application layer proxies or gateways (ALG) are a second common type of firewall mechanism. ALGs peer more deeply into the packet than packet filtering firewalls but normally do not scan the entire payload. Unlike packet filtering or stateful inspection firewalls, ALGs do not route packets; rather the ALG accepts a connection on one network interface and establishes the cognate connection on another network interface. An ALG provides intermediary services for hosts that reside on different networks, while maintaining complete details of the TCP connection state and sequencing. In practice, a client host (running, for example, a Web browser application) negotiates a service request with the AP, which acts as a surrogate for the host that provides services (Web server). Two connections are required for a session to be completed—one between the client and the ALG, and one between the AP and the server. No direct connection exists between hosts.

Additionally, ALGs typically possess the ability to do a limited amount of packet filtering based upon rudimentary application-level data parsing. ALGs are considered by most people to be more secure than packet filtering firewalls, but performance and scalability factors have limited their distribution. An adaptive (coined by Gauntlet), dynamic, or filtering proxy is a hybrid of packet filtering firewall and application layer gateway. Typically, the adaptive proxy monitors traffic streams and checks for the start of a TCP connection (ACK, SYN-ACK, ACK). The packet information from these first few packets is passed up the OSI stack and if the connection is approved by the proxy security intelligence, then a packet filtering rule is created on the fly to allow this session. Although this is a clever solution, UDP packets, which are stateless, cannot be controlled using this approach.

Although current stateful firewall technologies and ALGs provide for tracking the state of a connection, most provide only limited analysis of the application data. Several firewall vendors, including Check Point, Cisco, Symantec, Netscreen, and NAI have integrated additional application-level data analysis into the firewall. Check Point, for example, initially added application proxies for Telnet, FTP, and HTTP to the FW-1 product, but have since replaced the Telnet proxy with an SMTP proxy. Cisco's PIX fix-up protocol initially provided for limited application parsing of FTP, HTTP, H.323, RSH, SMTP, and SQLNET. Both vendors since have added support for additional applications. To sum up, the advantages of ALGs is that they do not allow any direct connections between internal and external hosts; they often support user and group-level authentication; and they are able to analyze specific application commands inside the payload portion of data packets. Their drawbacks are that ALGs tend to be slower than packet filtering firewalls, they are not transparent to users, and each application requires its own dedicated ALG policy/processing module.

Deep Packet Inspection

To address the limitations of Packet Filtering, Application Proxies, and Stateful Inspection, a technology known as Deep Packet Inspection (DPI) was developed (or marketed). DPI analyzes the entire packet, and may buffer, assemble, and inspect several related packets as part of a session. DPI operates at L3–L7 of the OSI stack.

DPI engines parse the entire IP packet, and make forwarding decisions by means of a rule-based logic that is based upon signature or regular expression matching. That is, they compare the data within a packet payload to a database of predefined attack signatures (a string of bytes). Additionally, statistical or historical algorithms may supplement static pattern matching.

The issue with DPI is that packet data contents are virtually unstructured compared with the highly structured packet headers (review the previous section on NAT for more details). Analysis of packet headers can be done economically since the locations of packet header fields are restricted by protocol standards. However, the payload contents are, for the most part, unconstrained. Searching through the payload for multiple string patterns within the datastream is a computationally expensive task. And as wire speeds increase, the requirement that these searches be performed at wire speed adds to the cost. Additionally, because the threat signature database is dynamic, it must be easily updateable—this rules out the use of normal ASICs. Promising approaches to these problems include a software-based approach (Snort implementing the Boyer-Moore algorithm) and a hardware-based approach (FPGAs running a Bloom filter algorithm).

Tools & Traps…

FPGAs

FPGAs (Field Programmable Gate Arrays) are a class of general-purpose digital logic chips. Some of the larger FPGA vendors are Xilinx and Altera. FPGAs are dynamically programmable, support a wide range of signal processing, and offer true parallel processing. They may provide the hardware solution for processing entire packet streams at multigigabit wire speeds.

Deep Packet Inspection is a promising technology in that it may help to solve these problems. DPI engines are situated at network boundaries where bandwidth and security controls are logically implemented. New, programmable ASICs coupled with efficient algorithms can realistically parse the entire contents of each packet at gigabit speeds. Also, combining Firewall and IDS within a single device should simplify device configuration and management. But there are concerns as well.

One of the primary benefits of the traditional firewall/IDS deployment is that the failure of one component does not leave the network completely unprotected.

Deploying devices with separate functionality also prevents being locked into a single solution and vendor.

Particular attention must be paid to firewall and deep packet inspection configurations to make sure they don't introduce unacceptable latency. Implementation of some security measures can degrade QoS. These complications range from interruption or prevention of call setup by firewalls to encryption-produced latency and delay variation (jitter).

VoIP-Aware Firewalls

With a basic understanding of NAT, encryption, and firewall technologies under our belts, it is now possible to appreciate the challenges of securing VoIP traffic without either throwing away your firewalls or obstructing call flow. The basic problem is twofold: firewall administrators are loath to open up a range of high ports (> 1024) that will allow uncontrolled connections between external and internal hosts, and firewalls often rewrite information that is necessary for VoIP signaling traffic to succeed. In the first case, call parameter traffic, media traffic, and media control traffic travel on arbitrary high ports. In the second case, the general rule in this fraction of the H.323 protocol suite is that IP address information and port numbers are exchanged within the data stream of the preceding connection. Obviously, since SIP and H.323 are separate protocols, they have different firewall requirements. First, we'll look at H.323.

H.323 Firewall Issues

For basic voice call setup H.323 requires at least the ports shown in Table 13.1 to be opened.

Table 13.1 Basic VoIP Call Setup

FUNCTION	PORT	PROTOCOL
Gatekeeper discovery	1718	UDP
Gatekeeper RAS	1719	UDP
Q.931 Call Signaling (Setup)	1720	TCP
H.245 Signaling (Call parameters)	1024–65535	TCP
RTP/RTCP (Media)	1024–65535	UDP
H.235 Secure Signaling	1300	TCP

The sequence of H.323 call setup and control depends upon the presence or absence of a gatekeeper (see Chapter 5 for more details). In the example shown in Figure 13.13, we will assume that the network consists of a single gatekeeper and two H.323 endpoints (endpoints can be telephones, gateways, MCUs, etc.) using direct signaling. A generic H.323 call sequence begins with one endpoint (EP1) initiating a gatekeeper discovery process that opens ports UDP/1718. If successful, RAS messages are sent over port UDP/1719 as part of the registration and admission process. EP1 then sends a call signaling setup message to EP2 over TCP/1720. After EP2 registers with the gatekeeper, it sends several H.225 messages to EP1 over port TCP/1720 and the call is established. At this point in the exchange, three static bidirectional ports have been opened—two between EP1 and the gatekeeper and one between EP1 and EP2 (we can ignore the ports opened between EP2 and the gatekeeper for this discussion).

Figure 13.13 H.323 Communications Ports

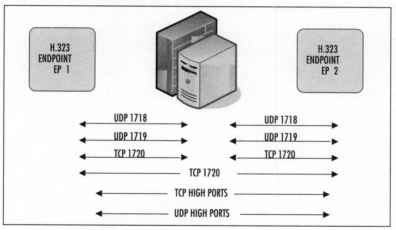

After call establishment, an H.245 call control channel is established over TCP. A subset of RAS messages include IP addressing information in the payload, typically meant to register an endpoint with a gatekeeper or learn about another registered endpoint. The ephemeral port numbers for this connection are established by the preceding H.225/Q.931 signaling traffic (are contained within the data portion of the Q.931 message). After capabilities exchange over the H.245 control channel, media (RTP and RTCP) port and real (rather than private) IP addresses are exchanged. This information again is transported within the data portion of the H.245 message. Q.931 tunneling of H.245 messages or Q.931 multiplexing can reduce the number of ports opened, but the problem with H.323 and firewalls that do NAT should now be apparent—in order to properly route messages to the real, rather than public, address, a NAT firewall or proxy must inspect each signaling and control channel for the correct ports and IP addresses, and rewrite them appropriately.

Since H.323 relies greatly on dynamic ports, packet filtering firewalls are not a particularly favorable solution, as every port greater than 1024 has to be opened bidirectionally for a call to take place. Thus, firewall solutions supporting H.323 must at least dismantle and inspect signaling packets (H.245, H.225.0) and statefully open the firewall ports for both H.245 control packets and bidirectional UDP media packets as well. As if this is not enough complexity, the signaling and control messages are binary encoded according to ASN.1 rules. ASN.1 parsers have been exploited in a variety of implementations, and parsing takers time, adding latency to an already latency-sensitive application.

Notes from the Underground...

Problems with Parsers

In 2004, the University of Oulu Secure Programming Group (OUSPG) tested the effects of sending modified Setup-PDUs to a number of differing vendor H.323 implementations. Modified Setup-PDUs are TCP/IP packets that carry the H.225/Q.931 initial signaling information (protocol identifier, source address, called number, etc.) encoded according to ASN.1 PER (Packed Encoding Rules). The H.225 Setup-PDU is an excellent test candidate for several reasons: the Setup-PDU contains many information elements, whose length and type are variable; the Setup PDU is normally the first packet exchanged during H.323 communication; and affected systems can be rebooted quickly for additional testing. OUSPG prepared a test suite containing approximately 4,500 modified Setup-PDUs, and fed these to each tested H.323 device. They found that many systems that implement H.323 are vulnerable to one or more of these malformed PDUs—affected devices typically crashed or experienced 100% CPU utilization.

These failures result from insufficient bounds checking of H.225 messages as they were parsed and processed by affected systems. These errors are primarily due to problems in low-level byte operations with vendor ASN.1 PER/BER PDU decoders, as mentioned earlier. Depending upon the affected system and implementation, these attacks result in system crash and reload (DoS), or in the case of systems that parse these data (such as Microsoft ISA server), execution of code within the context of the security service.

Continued

> Additionally, we have found privately that flooding multiple, malformed GRQ (Gatekeeper Request) packets to the gatekeeper results in the disconnection of a number of vendor's IP phones.

SIP Firewall Issues

Unlike H.323, SIP's syntax is based on HTTP. ASCII is more economically parsed than PER encoded PDUs. Like H.323 though, the topology of SIP sessions differs from that of an HTTP, SMTP session in that connections can and will be initiated from parties outside of the firewall. This would be akin to a Web server requesting that you browse its site. The SIP connection topology is similar to IM (Instant Messaging) topologies where callers (session initiators) can exist on either side of the firewall.

Typically, SIP infrastructure consists of User Agents (UAs—normally IP phones or softphones), SIP Proxies (SP), and SIP Registrars (SR). For a careful and thorough analysis of the attacks that can be promulgated against SIP infrastructure see Ofir Arkin's excellent treatment at www.sys-security.com/index.php?page=voip.

SIP sessions can be broken down into three constituents: locating the called person, session setup, and media transport. In the context of traversing firewalls and NAT, SIP's primary problem relates to determination of the "real" IP addresses of end users or UAs, which are often located in private IP address space. Unlike H.323, SIP does not cascade IP address and port numbers within control packets. However, as is the case with H.323, SIP, when used as a VoIP application, opens bidirectional UDP media channels over random high ports.

WARNING

Recent issues that affect Cisco SIP Proxy Server (SPS) [Bug ID CSCec31901] demonstrate the problems SIP implementers may experience due to the highly modular architecture of this protocol. The SSL implementation in SPS (used to secure SIP sessions) is vulnerable to an ASN.1 BER decoding error similar to the one described for H.323. This example illustrates a general concern with SIP: As the protocol links existing protocols and services together, all the classic vulnerabilities in services such as SSL, HTTP, SMTP, and IM may resurface in the VoIP environment.

SIP-aware firewalls will need to address these two issues. A helper proxy and registrar, closely associated with the firewall, can allow SIP location services to function in the presence of NAT. The Ingate firewall is one example of this approach. The high ports for RTP media channels are negotiated during the session setup phase, remain open for the duration of the call, and should be closed immediately after the call's termination. A SIP-aware firewall will have to manage these channels by opening a "pinhole" in the firewall rule set that temporarily allows these channels.

Bypassing Firewalls and NAT

H.323 and SIP have proven so difficult to manage with modern firewalls that some system administrators have given up, and instead, have implemented VoIP controls at other points: on the network perimeter, outside the perimeter, or in specially designated VoIP-DMZs. To secure calls from remote systems, NIST, in its excellent document, *SP 800-58: Security Considerations for Voice Over IP Systems*, suggests the use of VPNs to eliminate all the processing issues associated with NAT, firewalls, and encryption; however, as NIST points out, VPNs don't scale well.

There are literally dozens of proposals and hundreds of acronyms for managing VoIP sessions. My personal favorite is AYIYA (anything in anything). One of the examples mentioned in this proposal is tunneling IPv6-in-UDP-in-IPv4! My sense is that if the protocol requires this much convolution, perhaps we need to revisit the protocol itself. Unsurprisingly, no one of these approaches that follow has become dominant to date.

One successful solution to these issues is the development of Session Border Controllers (SBCs). SBCs are a class of dedicated network devices, generally located at the network perimeter, that offload VoIP security, NAT traversal, and media and signaling processing. SBCs are high-powered, complicated network devices. The primary function of most SBCs is to serve as a VoIP-aware NATing firewall. As long as packet latencies remain low and scale uniformly on both media and signaling channels, there is no need to split these functionalities.

However, for more complex operations on the media stream, such as transcoding and silence detection and/or suppression, one or more additional DSP (digital signal processing) farms, controlled by the SBC, can be added. Offloading DSP resources to a separate device will help lower SBC prices by providing additional transcoding capability only when the enterprise requires additional capabilities.

SBCs are often purpose-built to enable a spectrum of services, including real-time IP, support for H.323, SIP, and MGCP, deep-packet processing, traffic management, classification, reporting, and billing. SBCs also provide for lawful intercept. For more information about SBCs, you can check out the following vendors: Acme Packet, Ditech (Jasomi), Juniper (Kagoor), Netrake, Newport Networks, and Tekelec.

Tools & Traps...

CALEA

In 1994, the Communications Assistance for Law Enforcement Act (CALEA) was signed. In August 2005, in response to a request from the DEA and FBI, the FCC ruled that VoIP must comply with CALEA—that is, that VoIP must be capable of lawful intercept. This seems to mean that common carriers, facilities-based broadband Internet access providers, and providers of interconnected VoIP services must accommodate law enforcement wiretaps at any time.

A number of experts have commented that that it's one thing to demand that VoIP applications comply with CALEA, and it is quite another to require that the Internet be reengineered at the protocol level to provide wiretapping services. This area of law affects you if you are involved in design or maintenance of a VoIP network. We discuss CALEA in Chapter 15.

Because of their complexity, SBCs are expensive and management intensive; thus, in the near future, SBCs will be available to only carriers and large organizations.

Midcom (Middlebox protocol) is an interesting concept that may yet organize all the additional components proposed as adjuncts to firewalls. Essentially, midcom promises to allow applications, using a common language, to signal their requirements to trusted third parties such as firewalls, SBCs, IPSes (intrusion prevention systems), and NATs. Additionally, midcom supports abstraction of various VoIP processing components (for example, ASN.1 parsing or stateful inspection). Asterisk reportedly uses midcom to enable an IP PBX to indicate to a firewall which ports the PBX requires open. Although promising, the midcom protocol has yet to be finalized by the IETF.

STUN, TURN, and ICE

The following protocols and frameworks are methods for enabling SIP, but not H.323, to work in the presence of NATs. STUN (Simple Traversal of UDP through NATs) is a client-server protocol designed to enable an endpoint to discover its public IP address and the type of NATs between the endpoint and its peer. The

STUN protocol describes a STUN-enabled client in private IP space and its means of communication with a public STUN server. The public STUN server informs the private client of the client's public IP presence (IP address and port) within a SIP session. The following list of public STUN servers was active at the time of this writing:

- stun.fwdnet.netn   69.90.168.14
- stun.fwd.orgn   64.186.56.73
- stun01.sipphone.comn   69.0.208.27
- stun.softjoys.comn   69.3.254.11
- stun.voxgratia.orgn   83.103.82.85
- stun1.vovida.orn   128.107.250.38
- xtunnels1.xten.nen   64.69.76.23

STUN is relatively successful in residential VoIP deployments, but it is not an enterprise solution for a number of reasons. Key among these are STUN does not support TCP (TCP conformance is mandated by the SIP draft), and STUN does not work in the presence of symmetric NATs (the binding table entry for a symmetric NAT is based on source IP and port, and destination IP and port), which are the most common type of NATs in the enterprise.

STUN has been enhanced by the addition of the TURN protocol (Traversal Using Relay NAT). TURN is identical in syntax and general operation to STUN, but differs in behavior. In a simplified STUN exchange, the private STUN client sends a UDP packet to a public STUN server. The STUN server copies the last (closest to the STUN server) public IP address and mirrors this information to the private STUN client. No resources or bandwidth are allocated, but the private STUN client is now aware of its public IP presence. The first TURN message, on the other hand, is part of an authentication exchange. Authentication is required because a TURN server allocates its own resources (processing time, NIC, etc.) as part of its role as a proxy/relay for the private TURN client. TURN complements STUN in that TURN works with symmetric NATs and relays both TCP and UDP. This performance comes at a price, however: TURN requires multiple relays, which adds to latency. Because both of these protocols (as well as other related NAT traversal strategies such as UPNP, RSIP, and UDP hole punching) have strengths and weaknesses, a framework called Interactive Connectivity Establishment (ICE) has been proposed to coordinate these protocols. ICE explains how to use the other protocols for NAT traversal.

Skype has been fabulously successful as a peer-to-peer voice application. Many feel that Skype's success has pushed leading vendors such as Microsoft to support ICE. ICE (see IETF draft-rosenberg-sipping-ice-00 for more information, 2003) is not a protocol. It is best understood as a method, determined by additional SDP attributes, for enabling SIP traffic through multiple independent NATs by utilizing STUN, TURN, or other servers and protocols. ICE basically allows a privately addressed IP device to interrogate trusted external partners about public IP and NAT environment. In the author's own words:

> ICE always works, independent of the types or number of NATs. It always represents the cheapest solution for a carrier. It always results in the minimum voice latency. It can be done with no increase in call setup delays. It is far less brittle than STUN. ICE also facilitates the transition of the Internet from IPv4 to IPv6 ...

Quite a list, but it is not clear, for all of its promises, that ICE will catch on. Interestingly, like the ICE framework, Skype attempts to connect peers directly. Failing that, it apparently uses a modified STUN/TURN-like mechanism to bypass NAT firewalls. In the event, that this fails, Skype circumvents firewalls by emulating HTTP traffic on TCP ports 80 and 443.

The general issue with most of these approaches is that admission/egress control between the external and internal networks becomes more decentralized and less manageable as additional security and security adjunct components are added. Multiple chokepoints require more resources to defend them. Management and change control will become more difficult since firewall administrators will have to learn to configure and maintain additional devices that are likely from different vendors.

Access Control Lists

Network access control lists (ACLs) are table-like data structures that normally consist of a single line divided into three parts: a reference number that defines the ACL; a rule (usually permit or deny); and a data pattern, which may consist of source and/or destination IP addresses, source and/or destination port numbers, masks, and Boolean operators. Other patterns are used, but the ones listed are most common. ACLs generally are applied to the ingress or egress side of an interface.

As a packet traverses the interface, the ACL is scanned from top to bottom—in the exact order that it was entered—for a pattern that matches the incoming packet. Figure 13.14 shows the process flow for an access control list. In this case, a packet enters at the top and as it negotiates the ACL structure, some portion or portions of the packet are tested for a match at each rule-node. If the match succeeds, then related processing takes place; if there is no match, then the packet data is tested by the next lower node. A default rule should always be added to process any packets that traverse the entire ACL structure. Note that in this figure, an ACL rule has called an additional ACL. This type of ACL organization leads to exceptionally fine filtering granularity, but these complex rule sets, unless carefully designed, can be computationally expensive, slowing traffic unacceptably.

Figure 13.14 ACL Flow Diagram—Decision Based upon Match/No Match

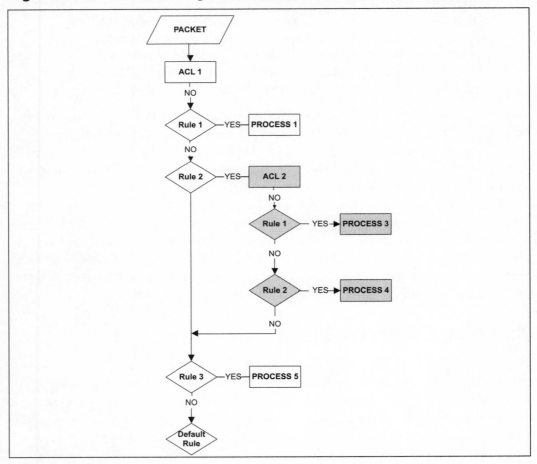

A general rule-of-thumb is that outbound ACLs are more efficient than inbound ACLs since the inbound logic must be applied to every packet, but the outbound logic is applied only to those packets exiting a particular interface. ACLs normally are applied at layers 3 and 4 of the OSI model, but some vendors (Cisco and

Extreme, for example) offer layer 2 ACLs, and others (Alteon/Nortel, for example) offer ACLs at layers 5 and above.

ACLs, in coordination with VLANS, QoS, and firewalls, are powerful tools for segregating VoIP traffic from other traffic. Appendix A, which is available on the Solutions site at www.syngress.com, contains information that can be used to construct detailed ACLs in a multivendor VoIP environment. Additional services may be permitted or denied based upon the client's infrastructure requirements. Example ACLs in Appendix A provide a foundation on which to customize your policy.

Summary

Logically separate data from voice traffic. Plan on establishing at least two VLANs and put your VoIP system components on a separate dedicated VLAN with 802.1p/q QoS (Quality of Service) and priority VLAN tagging. Limit physical and terminal access to your switch consoles to only authorized personnel.

Traffic shaping normally is associated with ensuring performance, but it also plays a role in security. Voice and data on separate logical VLANs share the same physical bandwidth. If hosts on the data VLAN become infected with viruses or worms that flood the network with traffic, VoIP traffic may remain unaffected if traffic shaping has been configured correctly to ensure that VoIP traffic has priority. The reverse is also true.

Access control lists find new utility at layer 3 of the internal networks, acting to fine-tune and control traffic. Keep ACLs simple and apply them only to egress ports in order to minimize their processing requirements.

Network Address Translation (NAT) will continue to be a major obstacle in VoIP migrations until Ipv6 becomes commonly adopted. Encryption across a NAT device is particularly problematic as both H.323 and SIP embed layer-3 routing and signaling information inside the IP datagram payload.

There is still no simple solution for securely handling calls that originate externally. Packet filtering and stateful inspection firewalls can open a "pinhole" through which outbound replies can pass. However, particularly in the case of SIP-based solutions, private translated internal IP addresses prevent incoming calls from reaching the correct recipient.

One promising approach is to combine an application layer gateway with a stateful packet filtering firewall. In this approach, an ALG software module running in close logical proximity to a NAT firewall device updates payload and header data made invalid by address translation. Complicating this solution is that the ALG software must be configured to be aware of the internal network architecture; and it requires that the ALG software understand the higher-layer protocol that it needs to "patch," thus each protocol requires a separate ALG module.

One particular technology that looks promising with regard to making firewalls intelligent and VoIP-aware is Deep Packet Inspection (DPI). Deep Packet Inspection may enhance firewall capabilities by adding the ability to dynamically open and close ports for VoIP application traffic—essentially collapsing Intrusion Detection (IDS) functionality into the firewall appliance so that both a firewall and an in-line IDS are implemented on the same device.

Unfortunately, some of these products have been shown to be vulnerable to exploitation of software defects in their DPI inspection engines. These data suggest that the addition of these enhanced functions to firewalls may weaken, rather that strengthen network perimeter security.

The bottom line is that organizations must be able to differentiate and control traffic types based upon the contents of the application payload as networked application traffic and threats to that traffic evolve.

Solutions Fast Track

VLANs

- ☑ Separate voice and data traffic via VLANs.

- ☑ VLANs provide security and make smaller broadcast domains by creating logically separated subnets.

- ☑ Disable unused ports and put them in a unique unused VLAN. This is a simple but effective means to prevent unauthorized access.

- ☑ For a good discussion of L2 access controls see www.cisco.com/en/US/products/hw/switches/ps708/products_white_pap er09186a008013159f.shtml.

QoS and Traffic Shaping

- ☑ QoS and traffic-shaping VoIP has strict performance requirements.

- ☑ VoIP quality is negatively affected by increased latency, jitter, and packet loss.

- ☑ QoS can provide some security against DoS attacks.

NAT and IP Addressing

- ☑ Network Address Translation (NAT) is a method for rewriting the source and/or destination addresses of IP packets.

- ☑ NAT also rewrites TCP and UDP checksums based upon a pseudo-header.

- ☑ Hosts behind a NAT device do not have true end-to-end Internet connectivity and cannot directly participate in Internet protocols that require initiation of TCP connections from outside the NAT device, or protocols that split signaling and media into separate channels.

☑ The key to the incompatibility of NAT and the IPsec AH mode is the presence of the Integrity Check Value (ICV).

☑ NAT provides a security function by segregating private hosts from the publicly routed Internet.

Firewalls

☑ Firewall mechanisms include packet filtering, stateful inspection, application layer gateways, and deep packet inspection.

☑ Packet Filtering firewalls inspect only a few header fields in order to make processing decisions.

☑ Application layer gateways provide intermediary services for hosts that reside on different networks, while maintaining complete details of the TCP connection state and sequencing.

☑ Deep Packet Inspection analyzes the entire packet, and may buffer, assemble, and inspect several related packets as part of a session.

☑ H.323 calls are difficult to firewall because IP addresses and ports are embedded in each previous packet stream, because packets are ASN.1 PER encoded, and because media and signaling take place on different channels, some of which are dynamically created.

☑ SIP, when used as a VoIP application, is difficult to firewall because NAT often hides the "real" IP address of endpoints, and because media and signaling take place on different channels, some of which are dynamically created.

Access Control Lists

☑ Access control lists (ACLs) are table-like data structures.

☑ A general rule-of-thumb is that outbound ACLs are more efficient than inbound ACLs.

☑ ACLs provide extremely granular control of traffic streams if configured correctly.

Frequently Asked Questions

The following Frequently Asked Questions, answered by the authors of this book, are designed to both measure your understanding of the concepts presented in this chapter and to assist you with real-life implementation of these concepts. To have your questions about this chapter answered by the author, browse to **www.syngress.com/solutions** and click on the **"Ask the Author"** form.

Q: How much security do VLANs provide?

A: It depends. For example, if you allow unauthorized access to the switch console, then VLANs offer no security at all. If however, you can guarantee the integrity of VLAN tags (not an easy task), then the resulting security controls are equal to physical security controls.

Q: I thought IPsec worked with NAT. I VPN into the office this way.

A: IPsec AH mode does not work with NAT. IPsec in ESP mode sometimes works with NAT. Your packets probably are encapsulated in UDP packets that are stripped at the VPN endpoint.

Q: Why haven't you discussed the protocols such as SCCP (skinny)?

A: I've tried to limit this to the main protocols. There are hundreds of related and proposed protocols, and it's not clear which will prevail. And I've tried to keep this vendor-neutral.

Q: What other steps can I take to secure my SIP infrastructure?

A: Block SIP requests directed to broadcast addresses at your router in order to protect your site from being used as an intermediary in a UDP-based DoS attack. Also block inbound ports 5060/UDP, 5060/TCP, and 5061/TCP (SIP over TLS) to any devices that do not participate directly in the SIP infrastructure.

Q: What type of firewall should I use?

A: It depends upon your environment and the applications that you need to protect. I think that in the near future the following statement will be axiomatic: In order to securely control all types of traffic, organizations must be able to differentiate traffic types based upon the contents of the application payload.

Q: Which is better, SIP or H.323?

A: What a question… Again, it depends on your requirements. H.323-based VoIP systems outnumbered SIP systems early in the deployment stage, but SIP-based systems have gained ground. If IMS (IP Multimedia Subsystem) takes off, then I expect almost all future systems to be SIP-based.

Chapter 14

IETF Encryption Solutions for VoIP

Solutions in this chapter:

- **Suites from the IETF**

- **S/MIME: Message Authentication**

- **TLS: Key Exchange and Signaling Packet Security**

- **SRTP: Voice/Video Packet Security**

☑ **Summary**

☑ **Solutions Fast Track**

☑ **Frequently Asked Questions**

Introduction

There are two competing breeds of VoIP signaling protocols, H.323 from the ITU and SIP from the IETF. Accordingly, there are also two groups of VoIP security protocols accompanying each of them. One for H.323 is a group of protocols named H.235.x and the other for SIP is TLS, S/MIME, and SRTP. They are not completely exclusive to each other. Some components are overlapped, such as X.509 digital certificate, TLS secured transport, and SRTP encryption. In this chapter, we will put our main focus on protocol suites for SIP from the IETF, and then a brief introduction to ITU suites (H.235 group); pointers to individual components are presented for the investigative reader.

NOTE

In addition to the IETF standards discussed in this chapter, there are ITU standards for implementation of these and other encryption and authentication standards within the H.323 family of protocols. The suite of H.323-related security standards is known as the H.235 hierarchy and is discussed in more detail within Chapter 5.

Suites from the IETF

Realizing the security issues present in VoIP, the IETF picked up three landmark security protocols in the SIP standard—Transport Layer Security (TLS), Secure/Multipurpose Internet Mail Extensions (S/MIME), and Secure Real-Time Transfer Protocol (SRTP)—to be used for securing SIP service. The basic approach consisted of adding a security layer below the existing VoIP protocol rather than crafting a new security protocol. The layered architecture is shown in Figure 14.1. The advantage of this approach is that existing protocol implementation can be reused for secured communication by adding security layers.

Figure 14.1 Layered Architecture of VoIP Security Protocol

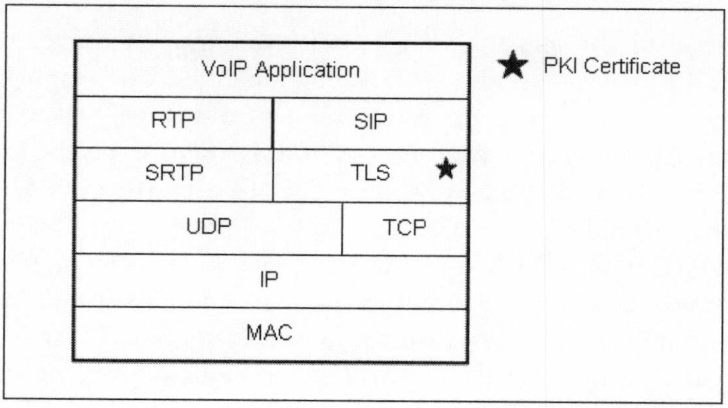

In general, TLS, which was chosen to protect SIP signaling messages, provides an upper layer secured tunnel to its peer entity. It is basically a successor of Secure Sockets Layer (SSL) version 3. The Service Data Unit (SDU) from the upper layer is encrypted before transmission. At the other end, the received Protocol Data Unit (PDU) is decrypted and passed to the upper layer. Each entity at both ends must have a legitimate certificate issued from a Certificate Authority (CA), which is mandatory for the TLS handshake operation. SIP signaling is passed through the secured tunnel.

SRTP is used to secure voice/video media from possible eavesdropping and tampering. It secures the confidentiality of RTP payloads and the integrity of all RTP packets by adopting the Advanced Encryption Standard (AES) as a default encryption/decryption algorithm using a symmetric cryptographic key. It also protects against replayed packet attack. The most sensitive issue in SRTP use is how the secret key can be shared between two communicating nodes. Embedding the key manually in all the phones is too cumbersome and error prone. For efficiency, RTP and SRTP can be implemented as one layer, rather than two separate layers. TLS and SRTP are the key components that play a major role in securing VoIP service.

However, there must be supporting protocols or an infrastructure that can authenticate users, validate node/user certificates, and exchange cryptographic keys. Each of these elements should work together in harmony to provide secured VoIP service.

S/MIME: Message Authentication

To secure Internet mail, the message must be protected from tapping or tampering, and the sender and receiver must also be correctly identified. The reason why Spam e-mail is thriving these days is that the e-mail sender can be easily faked or spoofed.

Secure/Multipurpose Internet Mail Extensions (S/MIME), specified in the Certificate Handling (RFC 3850) and Message Specification (RFC 3851) RFCs, provide a standard for public key encryption and for signing e-mail encapsulated in the popular MIME format. S/MIME provides the following cryptographic security services for electronic messaging applications: authentication, message integrity, non-repudiation of origin (using digital signatures), and data confidentiality (using encryption). S/MIME is not restricted to mail. It can be used with any transport mechanism that transports MIME data, such as HTTP or SIP message bodies (and certain SIP headers).

S/MIME applies to the message body overall, but the SIP standard also provides a mechanism to apply S/MIME to protect sensitive headers. Message bodies like SDP are encrypted with S/MIME to keep integrity and remain confidential. However, the header information such as To, From, Call-ID, CSeq, and Contact cannot remain confidential end to end. They are indispensable information for intermediaries, such as SIP proxy servers, firewalls, or UAS, to establish the requested call. To overcome this issue, the information is provided in both plaintext and an S/MIME encrypted format in a SIP message. So the intermediaries may have access to the information without being bothered to decrypt them. And the final recipient with a proper key to decrypt the information can compare the decrypted ones with plaintext to check message integrity and the sender's identity.

To understand how an S/MIME-based system delivers messages secured to its destination, an understanding of the fundamentals of PKI-based messaging system is necessary. Figure 14.2 shows the overall operation and flow of keys and messages within and between the systems.

1. The raw message is digested using a digestion algorithm. Without digestion, it takes a much longer time to process raw messages with digital signatures. The digestion, or hashing, reduces the message size to one adequate for signing.

2. Alice signs the digested message using a digital signature algorithm and appends the signature to the original message and to her certificate.

3. A session key is randomly generated and used to encrypt the message, certificate, and signature using an encryption algorithm.

4. The random session key is encrypted by Bob's public key using a public key encryption algorithm and wrapped into the encrypted message. The resulting message, which is shown as a shaded box, is transmitted to the receiver.

5. On the receiver side, a random session key is retrieved first by decrypting it with Bob's private key using the same algorithm that appears in step 4.

6. With the recovered session key, the encrypted messages, certificate, and signature are all decrypted using the same algorithm as that in step 3. In this way, data confidentiality is achieved. Now, Bob needs to check to see if the message is really signed by Alice and has to make sure that it has not been tampered with while being transmitted.

7. Using the same algorithm that appears in step 1, the message is digested.

8. Bob verifies that Alice's certificate is legitimate. If it is, Alice's public key is retrieved from the certificate.

9. Using the same algorithm that appears in step 2, the digested value is signed with Alice's public key.

10. The computed signature is compared with the received one. If it does not match, the message has been tampered with. The tampering occurred from outside of the network. Authentication, message integrity, and nonrepudiation therefore are achieved.

During the previous operation, four PKI security primitives were used: digestion, encryption, public key encryption, and digital signature. S/MIME basically specifies which algorithm to use to carry out the four primitives, to format the message, and how to handle the message after the security primitives are applied.

Figure 14.2 S/MIME Message Sending Process

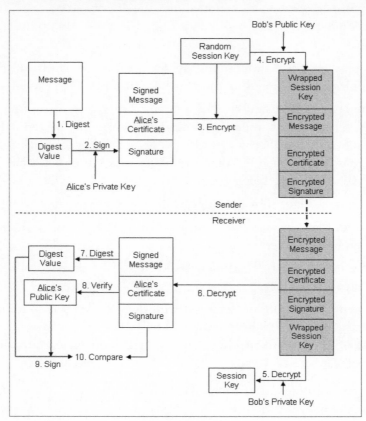

S/MIME Messages

To certify the sender or receiver, X.509 PKIX (RFC 3280) is adopted. S/MIME messages are a combination of MIME bodies and Cryptographic Message Syntax (CMS) content types.

Sender Agent

Before using a public key to provide security services, the S/MIME agent verifies that the public key is valid. Sending agents should include any certificates for the user's public key(s) and associated issuer certificates. This increases the likelihood that the intended recipient can establish trust in the originator's public key(s).

It should include at least one chain of certificates up to, but not including, a CA that it believes the recipient can trust as authoritative.

Receiver Agent

Receiving agents handle an arbitrary number of certificates of arbitrary relationship to the message sender and to each other in an arbitrary order. These agents do not simply trust any self-signed certificates as valid CAs, but use another mechanism, not discussed here, to determine if this is a CA that should be trusted.

E-mail Address

Sending agents force the e-mail address in the From or Sender header in a mail message to match an Internet mail address in the signer's certificate. Receiving agents check to see that the address in the From or Sender header of a mail message matches an Internet mail address, if present, in the signer's certificate.

TLS: Key Exchange and Signaling Packet Security

TLS is based on SSL protocol version 3. The IETF standardized TLS published as RFC 2246 in January of 1999. SSLv3 is incompatible with TLS by design. TLS is a protocol that provides a secure channel between two machines. It has facilities for protecting data in transit and for identifying its peer by checking the peer's X.509 certificate.

The secure channel is transparent, meaning that the data passed through the channel is unchanged. The data is encrypted between client and server, but the data that one end writes is exactly what the other end reads. Transparency allows nearly any protocol that can be run over TCP to be run over SSL/TLS with only minimal modification, which is very convenient. As depicted in Figure 14.1, TLS sits right above the TCP layer and below the SIP layer meaning that a message at the SIP layer is encrypted by TLS and transmitted through a TCP connection.

Each entity at both ends must have a legitimate certificate issued from a CA. Think of TLS as a transport layer like TCP on which you send SIP messages. There are open source *OpenSSL* APIs that can be used to set up TLS connections programmatically. Once the SSL connection is established, you basically write to the SSL socket, just as you would write to a TCP socket. The SIP message is transferred through the secured channel to its peer.

> **WARNING**
>
> Many enterprises, rather than buying certificates from assured CAs, create their own CAs and issue certificates to their internal users. It may work well between the internal users. But when they want to establish secured communication with another enterprise, their certificates cannot be certified by a common root because the two enterprises do not have a publicly verifiable CA in common.

Certificate and Key Exchange

Figure 14.3 shows the handshake between client and server. The purpose of the handshake is first so that the server and client can agree on a set of algorithms that will be used to protect the data. Second, they need to establish a set of cryptographic keys that will be used by those algorithms.

Figure 14.3 SSL Handshakes for Certificate and Key Exchange

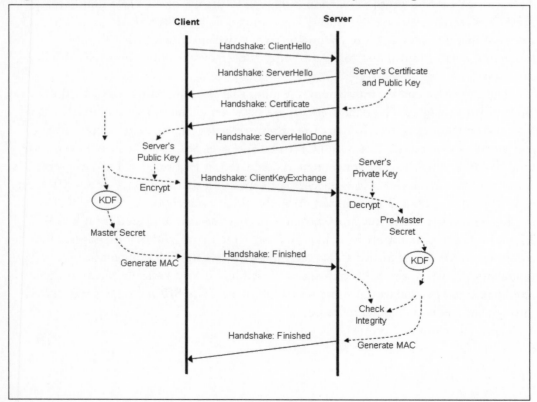

Figure 14.3 depicts the case where the client challenges the server's authentication. A detailed explanation of Figure 14.3 follows:

1. With the ClientHello and ServerHello message, the client and server agree on a list of algorithms they will use.

2. The server's certificate and public key are contained in the Certificate Message.

3. The client generates a random number, called a Pre-Master Secret key. Upon receiving a Certificate message, it checks authentication of the server's certificate and extracts its public key. The Pre-Master Secret key is encrypted by the server's public key and sent via the ClientKeyExchange message to the server. Meanwhile, the Key Derivation Function (KDF) generates a master key derived from the Pre-Secret Master key.

4. On the server side, the ClientKeyExchange message is decrypted by the server's private key, resulting in the Pre-Master Secret key. Using the same KDF as the client, the master key is derived from the Pre-Master Secret key.

5. With the master key, the client generates the Message Authentication Code (MAC) of the entire previous message it received from the server and sends it via a Finished message to the server.

6. With the master key, the server generates a MAC of the entire previous message it received from the client and sends it via a Finished message to the client.

7. Both the server and the client check the integrity of the received MAC with all the messages they have sent so far.

8. If the check is successful, both server and client share the same Master Secret key.

Figure 14.4 shows how data from the upper layer is encapsulated by the TLS/SSL layer. After data is fragmented, MAC is appended before being encrypted. Then the SSL/TLS record header, containing content type, length, and SSL version, is attached to the encrypted text. There are four types of content: application, alert, handshake, and change cipher specification. The packets described in Figure 14.4 fall into application type and the messages for certification and key exchange in Figure 14.3 are grouped into handshake type.

Figure 14.4 SSL/TLS Record Protocol

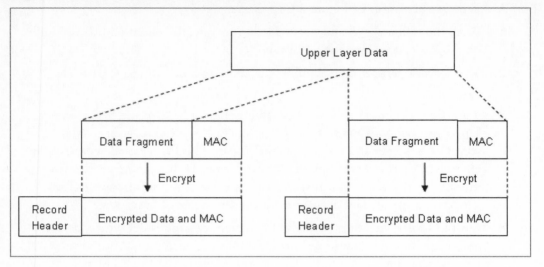

SRTP: Voice/Video Packet Security

SRTP, specified in RFC 3711, describes how to protect telephony media for encryption of the RTP packet payload, for authentication of the entire RTP packet, and for packet replay protection:

1. Confidentiality of RTP packets protects packet payloads from being read by entities without the secret encryption key.

2. Message authentication of RTP packets protects the integrity of a packet against forgery, alteration, or replacement.

3. Replay protection ensures that the session address (IP address, User Datagram Protocol (UDP) port, and Synchronization Source RC (SSRC)) do not experience a DoS attack.

The protocol is located between the RTP application and RTP transport layers, sitting like a "bump in a stack." It secures the confidentiality of RTP payloads and the integrity of all RTP packets by adopting the AES using a symmetric crypto-graphic key. The payloads from the RTP application are encrypted and encapsulated into an SRTP packet.

The most sensitive issue in using SRTP is how the secret key is shared between two nodes communicating in secret. The keys for these services are associated with the stream triple <IP address, UDP port, SSRC> and are called *SRTP cryptographic context*.

Unfortunately, key management for SRTP is a huge issue with the associated IETF standards since there have been multiple proposals, MIKEY and SDP Security Description (sdescription), on the table for years. Many implementation options exist within those schemes and a lot of unresolved implementation details caused early SRTP solutions in the market to use improper negation vehicles like the SIP INFO message or proprietary headers. As of the writing of this book (February 2006), all the interoperable SRTP implementations on the market are using proprietary negotiation or key management techniques that are nonstandard, although several vendors indicate that their sdescriptions-based solutions will be released shortly.

Multimedia Internet Keying

Multimedia Internet Keying (MIKEY) is a simple key management solution intended to be used for one-to-one, simple one-to-many, and small size groups. It provides three different ways to transport or establish traffic encryption key (TEK): with the use of a preshared key, public-key encryption, and Diffie-Hellman (DH) key exchange.

The preshared key method and the public-key method are both based on key transport mechanisms, where the actual TGK (TEK Generation Key) is pushed securely to the recipient(s). In the Diffie-Hellman method, the actual TGK is derived instead from the Diffie-Hellman values exchanged between the peers.

Session Description Protocol Security Descriptions

SDP Security Descriptions specify a new SDP attribute called *crypto*, which is used to signal and negotiate cryptographic parameters for SRTP media streams. The definition of the crypto attribute is limited to one-to-one unicast media streams. It assumes that the underlying service of secured data transport protocol, IPSec, TLS, or SIP S/MIME, protects the SDP message containing the crypto attribute. The attribute describes the cryptographic suite, key parameters, and session parameters for the preceding unicast media line.

```
a=crypto:<tag> <crypto-suite> <key-params> [<session-params>]
```

where tag is a decimal number used as an identifier for a particular crypto attribute; crypto-suite is an identifier that describes the encryption and authentication algorithms like AES_CM_128_HMAC_SHA1_80; key-params consist of method and actual keying information; and session-params is specific to a given transport, and use of them is OPTIONAL.

Providing Confidentiality

A confidentiality service is obtained by encrypting the payload so that only the sender and receiver in possession of the keys can read it. Figure 14.5 shows one key stream block, $\mathbf{B}_{i,j}$, which is the AES encryption of the initial value (IV) with key. The IV is computed from the 48-bit packet index, the 32-bit SSRC, and the 112-bit salting key. All these parameters are left-shifted and exclusive-or'ed.

Each IV is encrypted along with the key to produce a pseudorandom block of 128 bits, shown as $\mathbf{B}_{i,j}$. Each 128-bit block is exclusive-or'ed with an associated block of RTP payload plaintext to produce a block of cipher text, which covers either part of or the entire payload. Both the encryption and decryption processors run the key stream generator with the packet index, SSRC, and salting key; each processor synchronously produces the key stream $\mathbf{B}_i,*$—a stream of concatenated AES blocks.

Figure 14.5 SRTP Packet Encryption

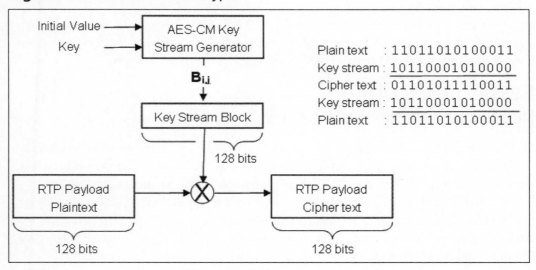

Message Authentications

An integrity service is obtained by running a one-way hash function on the message using a cryptographic key so that the receiver can ensure that the sender of the message possessed a secret key and that no party lacking that cryptographic key modified the message while in transit.

Figure 14.6 shows how the message authentication works overall. The one-way function, Hash-based Message Authentication Code with Secure Hashing Algorithm 1 (HMAC-SHA1), is run over the header and payload with a secret key. The sender writes the HMAC-SHA1 hash into the authentication tag, and the receiver runs the same computation and checks its result against the tag. If the two do not match, the message authentication is said to fail and the packet is discarded.

Figure 14.6 SRTP Packet Authentications

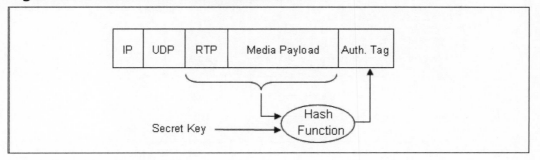

Replay Protection

SRTP packet-index determination deciphers the index of an invalid as well as a valid packet. There can be no integrity check until the authentication key is determined. SRTP replay protection is the first line of defense against packets sent by an attacker.

To counter replay attack, Rollover Counter (ROC) and sliding window are used. The 16-bit sequence number from the RTP header is added to the 32-bit SRTP ROC that is stored in the cryptographic context to get the 48-bit sequence number, which is the SRTP packet index for the particular packet. The packet index is encrypted with other parameters to generate key stream segments.

As Figure 14.7 depicts, a received packet index must fall within range of the sliding window, and its corresponding "Received ?" bit must not be checked in order for the packet to be passed to the next processing step. If the packet does not meet the criteria, it is discarded. If an attacker chooses a sequence number at random, and the window size is 64, there is a 99.9 percent likelihood $(1-64/2^{16})$ that the packet will be discarded before more computationally intense message authentication is applied.

Figure 14.7 Sliding Window for Packet Replay Protection

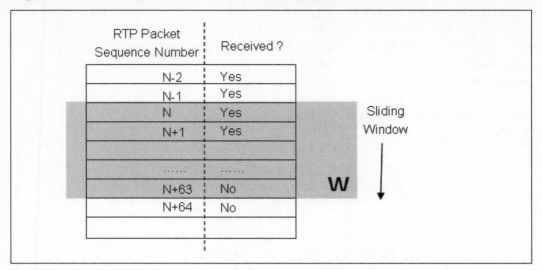

Summary

A brief tutorial on VoIP-related security standards was given, which focused on IETF standards. TLS and SRTP were presented as mainstream protocols to protect VoIP signaling and voice media, respectively. However, these protocols cannot operate alone. The supporting infrastructure, X.509 certificate profile, and S/MIME secured message format were introduced.

IETF RFCs

The following requests for comments were either referenced in this chapter or are recommended for further reading:

> *S/MIME Version 2 Message Specification (RFC 2311)*
> *S/MIME Version 2 Certificate Handling (RFC 2312)*
> *Cryptographic Message Syntax (RFC 2630) made obsolete by RFC 3369*
> *Diffie-Hellman Key Agreement Method (RFC 2631)*
> *S/MIME Version 3 Certificate Handling (RFC 2632) made obsolete by RFC 3850*
> *S/MIME Version 3 Message Specification (RFC 2633) made obsolete by RFC 3851*
> *Enhanced Security Services for S/MIME (RFC 2634)*
> *Methods for Avoiding the 'Small-Subgroup' Attacks on the Diffie-Hellman Key Agreement Method for S/MIME (RFC 2785)*
> *Use of the KEA and SKIPJACK Algorithms in CMS (RFC 2876)*
> *Use of the CAST-128 Encryption Algorithm in CMS (RFC 2984)*
> *Use of the IDEA Encryption Algorithm in CMS (RFC 3058)*
> *Electronic Signature Policies (RFC 3125)*
> *Domain Security Services Using S/MIME (RFC 3183)*
> *Electronic Signature Formats for Long Term Electronic Signatures (RFC 3126)*
> *Reuse of CMS Content Encryption Keys (RFC 3185)*
> *Triple-DES and RC2 Key Wrapping (RFC 3217)*
> *Password-based Encryption for SMS (RFC 3211) made obsolete by RFC 3369*
> *Preventing the Million Message Attack on CMS (RFC 3218)*
> *Use of ECC Algorithms in CMS (RFC 3278)*
> *Compressed Data Content Type for Cryptographic Message Syntax (CMS) (RFC 3274)*
> *Cryptographic Message Syntax (RFC 3369) made obsolete by RFC 3852*
> *Cryptographic Message Syntax (CMS) Algorithms (RFC 3370)*
> *Advanced Encryption Standard (AES) Key Wrap Algorithm (RFC 3394)*
> *Implementing Company Classification Policy with the S/MIME Security Label (RFC*

3114)

Wrapping a Hashed Message Authentication Code (HMAC) Key with a Triple-Data Encryption Standard (DES) Key or an Advanced Encryption Standard (AES) Key (RFC 3537)

Use of the RSAES-OAEP Key Transport Algorithm in Cryptographic Message Syntax (CMS) (RFC 3560)

Use of the Advanced Encryption Standard (AES) Encryption Algorithm in Cryptographic Message Syntax (CMS) (RFC 3565)

Use of the Camellia Encryption Algorithm in CMS (RFC 3657)

S/MIME Version 3.1 Certificate Handling (RFC 3850)

S/MIME Version 3.1 Message Specification (RFC 3851)

Cryptographic Message Syntax (CMS) (RFC 3852)

Securing X.400 Content with S/MIME (RFC 3854)

Transporting S/MIME Objects in X.400 (RFC 3855)

Use of the SEED Encryption Algorithm in Cryptographic Message Syntax (CMS) (RFC 4010)

Use of the RSASSA-PSS Signature Algorithm in Cryptographic Message Syntax (CMS) (RFC 4056)

Examples of S/MIME Messages (RFC 4134)

X.509 Certificate Extension for Secure/Multipurpose Internet Mail Extensions (S/MIME) Capabilities (RFC 4262)

Internet X.509 Public Key Infrastructure Certificate and Certificate Revocation List (CRL) Profile (RFC3280)

Suites from the IETF

☑ The IETF picked up three landmark security protocols in the SIP standard—Transport Layer Security (TLS), Secure/Multipurpose Internet Mail Extensions (S/MIME), and Secure Real-Time Transfer Protocol (SRTP)?to be used for securing SIP service.

☑ TLS, which was chosen to protect SIP signaling messages, provides an upper layer secured tunnel to its peer entity.

☑ SRTP is used to secure voice/video media from possible eavesdropping and tampering. It secures the confidentiality of RTP payloads and the integrity of all RTP packets by adopting the Advanced Encryption Standard (AES) as a default encryption/decryption algorithm using a symmetric cryptographic key.

S/MIME: Message Authentication

☑ To secure Internet mail, the message must be protected from tapping or tampering, and the sender and receiver must also be correctly identified.

☑ S/MIME provides the following cryptographic security services for electronic messaging applications: authentication, message integrity, nonrepudiation of origin (using digital signatures), and data confidentiality (using encryption).

☑ Message bodies in SIP like SDP are encrypted with S/MIME to keep integrity and remain confidential.

TLS: Key Exchange and Signaling Packet Security

☑ TLS, a successor of SSL, is a protocol that provides a secure channel between two machines. It has facilities for protecting data in transit and for identifying its peer by checking the peer's X.509 certificate.

☑ The secure channel is transparent, meaning that the data passed through the channel is unchanged.

☑ A SIP message is transferred through the secured channel to its peer.

SRTP: Voice/Video Packet Security

☑ SRTP describes how to protect telephony media for encryption of the RTP packet payload, for authentication of the entire RTP packet, and for packet replay protection.

☑ It secures the confidentiality of RTP payloads and the integrity of all RTP packets by adopting the AES encryption algorithm and a symmetric cryptographic key.

☑ The most sensitive issue in using SRTP is how the secret key is shared between two nodes communicating in secret. Currently, there are many options within proposed key exchange schemes and a lot of unresolved implementation details. A lot of early SRTP implementations use things like INFO for negotiation or other proprietary tricks.

☑ Two SRTP key exchange schemes, MIKEY and SDP security descriptions, are proposed so far. The first one establishes separate secured channel for key exchange, and second one uses channel established by TLS layer and sends keys in plaintext.

Frequently Asked Questions

The following Frequently Asked Questions, answered by the authors of this book, are designed to both measure your understanding of the concepts presented in this chapter and to assist you with real-life implementation of these concepts. To have your questions about this chapter answered by the author, browse to **www.syngress.com/solutions** and click on the **"Ask the Author"** form.

Q: How vulnerable is current VoIP service if it is not protected at all?

A: It is highly susceptible to security attack. If the RTP media stream is promiscuously monitored by an intruder, the voice conversation can be tapped easily because the media stream runs unencrypted. As signaling protocol is exchanged in plaintext, the contents can be easily peeked, analyzed, and altered. After a simple analysis, the attacker can easily generate a BYE message in SIP protocol to terminate an existing VoIP connection. The attacker can effortlessly launch a Denial of Service attack by dumping hundreds of SIP INVITE message to call a server or to a particular phone.

Q: Are those protocol suites mentioned in this chapter sufficient enough to protect VoIP service?

A: Not necessarily. The suites protect only VoIP service-related resources like voice media stream and signaling messages. The call servers and phones are basically Internet data devices with the same IP stack as any regular computers and networking devices. So, they also are prone to the same kind of attacks as to the data devices such as well-known DoS, virus, buffer overrun, password hacking, man-in-the-middle, and so forth. To build a successfully secured VoIP network, one must take the two aspects into account, not just one of them.

Q: Who is entitled to issue an X.509 certificate and sign it digitally?

A: Theoretically, everybody can issue the X.509 certificate and sign it as long as the right certificate generation software (self-signed scheme) is used. This is analogous to a case where a person issues his or her own driver's license and signs it him- or herself, which will be trusted by no one. So, the certificate must be issued by a trustworthy entity that everybody puts faith in and relies on.

Q: Is there a vendor that manufactures VoIP call servers and phones adopting the protocol suites mentioned in this chapter?

A: Big VoIP players have a whole line of secured VoIP products, from phones to call servers. Small ones are specialized in one or more secured phones, gateways, voice-mail servers, and call servers. However, the issue is compatibility between products from different vendors. As implementation of the security protocol is in a rudimentary stage, it is not easy to configure the phones/servers, and industrywide compatibility is stilll questionable.

Chapter 15

Regulatory Compliance

Solutions in this chapter:

- SOX: Sarbanes-Oxley Act

- GLBA: Gramm-Leach-Bliley Act

- HIPAA: Health Insurance Portability and Accountability Act

- CALEA: Communications Assistance for Law Enforcement Act

- E911: Enhanced 911 and Related Regulations

- EU and EU Member States' eCommunications Regulations

☑ Summary

☑ Solutions Fast Track

☑ Frequently Asked Questions

Introduction

The past decade has seen an explosion of government regulation that will directly or indirectly affect VoIP implementation security. Some of these regulations can be addressed by selecting and implementing compliant equipment, but the vast majority of these are *operational* in nature, meaning that to ensure compliance you'll need to pay more attention to (1) how your IP communications systems are designed and (2) how your organization's business and IT operations groups are using the equipment once it's live.

For this chapter, each applicable set of regulations will be discussed separately. What you'll want to ask yourself in each section is:

- Does this regulation apply to me and my organization (or my client's organization)?

- Who in my organization has responsibility for overall compliance with this regulation? In some cases, the answer may be you if there isn't already someone designated, but for many of these regulations your organization is likely to have a person or group specifically designated as the lead for addressing compliance, particularly with regulations for which security is only an ancillary component of the overall regulation.

- Is it likely that my systems and/or operations are not compliant with this regulation today? If you suspect that remediation is necessary, it's important to raise the concern to the appropriate level of management in a way that allows the issue to be corrected and reduce the risk of fines, negative publicity, or worse.

WARNING

Always consult experienced legal counsel (or your organization's audit or compliance department) for legal advice with regulatory issues that could materially affect your organization. Although this chapter highlights the most common regulatory concerns surrounding VoIP, it cannot provide complete guidance for every situation or jurisdiction. For instance, VoIP itself is considered illegal in certain countries when it bypasses national carriers (sometimes known as PTTs) who may have a telecommunications monopoly. And new data privacy laws around the world seem to appear monthly.

NOTE

Despite the aforementioned caveat, you may find that the compliance experts available to you are not familiar with VoIP and how to apply broad regulations like GLBA or HIPAA to voice and other real-time communications systems. To help with these situations, pay special attention to the "Tools & Traps" sidebars in this chapter. They will provide specific guidance for you to share with a specialized compliance expert in that area of regulation.

Don't be surprised, however if your expert chooses to ignore the additional information. Many of the experts I've met with over the years prefer to apply these regulations narrowly and don't want to open the door to unanticipated compliance costs (common concern for internal experts) or expand the scope of compliance work without having the billable expertise to address it (typical for external experts). If that happens to you, just make sure to complete your due diligence by advising your organization's responsible executive (corporate counsel or chief compliance office) of your concerns in writing and leaving the matter in their hands.

In the next six sections, we'll review regulations that may affect you or your organization. You may safely skip some of them, so here's a quick way to tell which sections won't apply to you and your organization:

- If your organization is not public (listed on any U.S. stock exchange), then you can skip SOX.

- If your organization isn't involved with banking, consumer finance, securities, or insurance, then you can skip GLBA.

- If your organization doesn't handle any medical records (don't forget your HR department and any health insurance-related records when considering this question), you can skip HIPAA.

- If you're not a telecommunications carrier (or effectively replace one, like a university does for on-campus students, for example), then you can skip CALEA.

- If you don't have any physical locations in the United States or provide phone service there, you can skip E911.

- If you don't have any customers, suppliers, or operations in an EU country, then you can skip the EU section, though if you operate in a state or country with data privacy regulations then this section might still be relevant.

SOX: Sarbanes-Oxley Act

Enacted in response to corporate scandals at Enron, Tyco, and Worldcom during 2001, the Sarbanes-Oxley Act of 2002 was designed to bolster confidence in the financial reporting of publicly traded corporations in the United States. When he signed the Act into law, President Bush hailed it as "the most far reaching reforms of American business practices since the time of Franklin Delano Roosevelt." Since that time, an estimated $5 billion has been spent by U.S.-listed corporations to comply with the act.

SOX Regulatory Basics

Let's take a few minutes to go through the Sarbanes-Oxley Act and what it requires, starting with what the regulations themselves explicitly require. Then we'll look at related recommendations that SOX consultants and auditors are likely to recommend above and beyond the explicit legal requirements.

Direct from the Regulations

When it comes to VoIP or any other IP application, Section 404 is the only part of SOX that even remotely applies. Section 404 isn't long but since it's been the basis for hundreds (perhaps thousands) of costly IT reporting and process changes ultimately attributed to Sarbanes-Oxley over the past few years, I'm going to reproduce it in its entirety—but first here's the simple version:

- 404(a) requires an annual report from management regarding the effectiveness of internal controls.

- 404(b) requires an independent auditor to report on (and attest to) management's annual report.

So we're really just talking about two reports here: one that's signed by the officers of a company, and another that's signed by their independent auditor (typically from a large accounting and consulting firm). However, since a negative report could have huge consequences in the stock market, being able to produce an acceptable report supported by your auditor is a big deal

Here's the actual text of Section 404 of the Sarbanes-Oxley Act of 2002:

Section 404 Management Assessment Of Internal Controls

(a) RULES REQUIRED- The Commission shall prescribe rules requiring each annual report required by section 13 of the Securities Exchange Act of 1934 (15 U.S.C. 78m) to contain an internal control report, which shall—

(1) state the responsibility of management for establishing and maintaining an adequate internal control structure and procedures for financial reporting; and

(2) contain an assessment, as of the end of the most recent fiscal year of the issuer, of the effectiveness of the internal control structure and procedures of the issuer for financial reporting.

(b) INTERNAL CONTROL EVALUATION AND REPORTING- With respect to the internal control assessment required by subsection (a), each registered public accounting firm that prepares or issues the audit report for the issuer shall attest to, and report on, the assessment made by the management of the issuer. An attestation made under this subsection shall be made in accordance with standards for attestation engagements issued or adopted by the Board. Any such attestation shall not be the subject of a separate engagement.

Now, if you've been part of an internal "SOX audit" you may be saying to yourself, "So where does it say I need to have complex passwords and encrypted links and quarterly user reviews and vulnerability testing and so forth?" And that's an excellent question because, of course, it doesn't say that at all. In fact, even the new internal controls audit standard ("Auditing Standard No. 2" or AS2) created by the Public Company Accounting Oversight Board (an organization created by the Act) addresses information technology only in terms of internal controls.

However, since Section 404 clearly states that the independent auditor must validate management's internal controls report, this gives management a strong incentive to defer to the auditor. As many large public companies found out in 2004 and 2005, a "disclaimer opinion" from an auditor suggesting that a company's internal controls are inadequate tends to push down its stock price. Thus, the security best-practices advice given by an auditor or SOX consultant is very likely to be driven down through an organization as if the law itself required it when that's not strictly true.

Nevertheless, since Section 404 speaks in terms of "internal controls," it only makes sense to ask what an internal control really is. The commonly accepted definition comes from the Committee of Sponsoring Organizations of the Treadway Commission (COSO):

> Internal control is broadly defined as a process, effected by an entity's board of directors, management and other personnel, designed to provide reasonable assurance regarding the achievement of objectives in the following categories:
>
> ■   Effectiveness and efficiency of operations.
>
> ■   Reliability of financial reporting.
>
> ■   Compliance with applicable laws and regulations.

What's most important to note about this definition is that it's *not* made in terms of technology (although organizations routinely use information technology as a *part* of the implementation of many internal controls). It's not just a report, or a policy, or a line of code by itself; rather it's an entire operational process. Given that definition, it's easy to see that SOX really doesn't care if you're using VoIP or telepathy for your business communications so long as any associated internal controls (such as those for billing) are adequate. The critical standard to be met in designing a control is "reasonable assurance"—not absolute assurance. According to COSO, adequate controls should provide visibility and focus but cannot be expected to take the place of effective management:

> The likelihood of achievement is affected by limitations inherent in all internal control systems. These include the realities that judgments in decision-making can be faulty, and that breakdowns can occur because of simple error or mistake. Additionally, controls can be circumvented by the collusion of two or more people, and management has the ability to override the system. Another limiting factor is that the design of an internal control system must reflect the fact that there are resource constraints, and the benefits of controls must be considered relative to their costs.

In other words, design with the assumption that management can make appropriate executive decisions given the necessary background and context. If your control provides that level of input to decision-makers, it is adequate.

What a SOX Consultant Will Tell You

External auditors and other SOX consultants hired by your company have many incentives to provide broad, conservative guidance regarding SOX best practices. Why? First, given Arthur Andersen's collapse in the wake of the Enron debacle, one lesson learned by the large audit firms was the importance of giving conservative guidance even if management might take issue with the cost/benefit ratio. Keep in mind, however, that your company's independent auditor is prevented by SOX from offering nonaudit (consulting) services, so these recommendations may force another consulting firm to join the process.

For these additional consultants, comprehensive recommendations on their part tend to increase the length and scope of their billable engagements. And they don't have to worry about jeopardizing a long-term audit relationship through a failed project. So with your management more concerned about passing the next SOX audit than the business value being derived from SOX-related work, a SOX consultant is much more likely to recommend embarking on a comprehensive security strategy in the name of SOX compliance. And the independent auditor has no good reason to suggest to management that the extra work is unnecessary, as that could only increase their liability in the post-Enron world.

If you're involved with security, that dynamic is a double-edged sword. On the plus side, some security best practices that you may have unsuccessfully lobbied for in the past are suddenly now the new law of the land in your company, with the full support of your CIO and CFO arriving in the name of SOX compliance. On the other hand, all sense of perspective when it comes to risk management seems to have been lost in the process. Millions of dollars are spent to implement solutions like enterprise role definition (ERD), single sign-on (SSO), and identity and access management (IAM). At the same time, labor-intensive tasks like a quarterly user review that cannot be outsourced to consultants are taking large chunks of time from the operational resources that you need in order to address risks not tied to SOX at all. And good security practices not tied to SOX may fall off the management's radar screen entirely.

So what specific recommendations are you likely to get from a SOX consultant for a VOIP system? Primarily, these are security best practices you may already be familiar with. Here's what you might expect in a thorough SOX examination of a VoIP system that is deemed to have internal financial controls (because of external billing or internal chargebacks, for example):

- **Logging and audit trails** Does your VoIP system log administrative changes and provide basic usage logs (in this case, Call Detail Records (CDRs) or something equivalent)? If a billing process requires those logs then what is protecting them? More broadly, are the associated internal controls around that billing system adequate? Are lists of authorized administrators and users reviewed for accuracy on a periodic basis (at least annually)?

- **Password complexity** Does your organization enforce consistent requirements for password complexity across applications, including the VoIP system? For example, a password must be at least eight characters with at least one uppercase letter and one non-alpha character. Also, are default administrative passwords changed to comply (or default users removed)?

- **Password expiration** Does your organization enforce consistent expiration timeframes (example: 90 day expiration, 10 day warning) for passwords across all applications, including the VoIP system? Also, are accounts with expired passwords removed after a set timeframe?

- **Database user management** Do associated databases enforce password complexity and expiration rules? Are default database users removed or assigned new passwords that comply?

- **Server (and database) vulnerability management** Do associated servers/databases receive regular vulnerability scans, virus scans with regular updates, and security patches as part of a vulnerability and patch management system?

- **Server hardening** Are unnecessary services, packages, and tools removed from the VoIP system? Are all VoIP processes running as a nonprivileged user?

- **Encrypted IP communications** Do all administrative and operational links prevent user data, passwords, and any other sensitive information from being seen in the clear? This means that Telnet and ftp have been replace with their TLS-based equivalents (like ssh, sftp), external database connectivity runs over TLS, and (on a VoIP system) that signaling and media encryption are used.

- **Role–Based Access Control (RBAC)** Do you have a fine-grained authorization scheme that allows you to grant access to each administrative and functional capability independently? For VoIP systems, that means that there are separately granted administrative permissions for each major area of configuration (such as networking, PSTN integration, user administration, etc.) and user-level permissions for different classes of features, calling restrictions, and so on.

- **Segregation of Duties (SoD)** Have you separated administrative, operational, and audit roles within your VoIP system so that, for instance, an auditor can gain access to system logs without having the ability to change settings? To properly implement SoD, you will need to support RBAC.

- **Identity and Access Management (IAM) with Provisioning** Have you tied the VoIP system's user and administrative identities back to enterprisewide directories and authentication schemes? In other words, do users and administrators accessing the VoIP system use the same IDs and passwords on the VoIP system as they would on other enterprise applications? Do directory attributes like groups enable automatic assignment of roles in the VoIP system's RBAC scheme? Does VoIP system deprovisioning (or disablement) happen automatically for a user that has been removed from the enterprisewide directory upon termination? Optional: Are new employees able to be provisioned automatically to the VoIP system as part of the on–boarding process?

- **Enterprise Role Definition (ERD)** Has your organization identified across its business applications the employee roles and access required by those roles to be able to map the VoIP system's roles into that enterprise scheme? Have those roles been screened for Segregation of Duties conflicts with the VoIP system included? Note that RBAC and IAM with Provisioning typically are required for an ERD system to work smoothly in practice.

Tools & Traps…

Core SOX Compliance Issues
for IP Communications Systems

The only direct SOX impacts to VoIP and other communications systems are likely to be billing related if your VoIP system is part of a service billed to others or if your SOX controls team considers it to be part of an internal control around PSTN usage costs being billed back to your company. Of course, indirect impacts through IT security policies around user, password, logging, systems, and database management are all likely since the VoIP system is a part of the overall IT infrastructure of your organization.

The SOX issue most likely to be ignored by your SOX team: internal controls for controlling VoIP calls that route through the PSTN create financial obligations (i.e., long-distance charges) so long as your long distance isn't fixed-cost (or free), since abuse of IP communications systems could have a material financial impact on your organization. In SOX terms, that means that the same controls used with critical financial systems should be evaluated for applicability to IP communications systems as well.

SOX Compliance and Enforcement

It may surprise you to know that most of the Act itself is focused on new practices and penalties for independent auditors, not public companies. The Sarbanes–Oxley Act created the Public Company Accounting Oversight Board (PCAOB) to address the audit processes used for public companies. The Act gives the PCAOB the authority to register, investigate, and discipline public accounting firms and auditors. Oversight of the PCAOB falls to the Securities and Exchange Commission (SEC). Penalties for certain white-collar crime were increased and the SEC has some additional civil enforcement tools as part of the Act, but in general all nonaudit compliance and enforcement for SOX remains within the enforcement frameworks previously established at the SEC.

Certification

Compliance is evaluated on an annual basis by two groups: the management of the public company itself (typically through your internal audit or compliance group) for the management report asserting that internal controls are adequate (i.e., compliant with Sarbanes-Oxley requirements); and the company's independent auditor for their attestation—either unqualified support of management's report or a "disclaimer opinion" that raises concerns about the adequacy of internal controls. Just to complete the attestation process each year, large companies can be charged up to $1 million or more by their independent auditor—over and above the fees paid for basic corporate audit work. These costs (and potential conflicts the process can create with EU Data Protection directives) have prompted a number of European firms to de-list from American stock exchanges.

SOX has no notion of "product certification" like some of the other regulations in this chapter.

Enforcement Process and Penalties

Auditors and auditing organizations are investigated and sanctioned by the Public Company Accounting Oversight Board (PCAOB), and corporate officers and corporations are investigated and sanctioned by the SEC. For the PCAOB, the maximum penalty for "violations committed in the preparation and issuance of audit reports," was $110,000 in 2005 for an individual and $2.1 million for an entity. And the SEC maximum penalty in 2005 for "intentional or knowing conduct, including reckless conduct, or repeated instances of negligent conduct" was $800,000 for an individual and $15.825 million for an entity.

The Act itself increased the maximum penalty for mail, securities, and wire fraud to up to 25 years imprisonment, and established maximum penalties for CEOs and CFOs that made willful and knowing violations of financial statement and disclosure rules punishable by a fine of not more than $500,000 and/or imprisonment of up to five years. The latter garnered a lot of press at the time and resulted in increased attention to SOX by corporate chiefs.

Both the SEC and PCAOB have processes in place to accept both anonymous tips and formal complaints. For the SEC, tips can be sent to enforcement@sec.gov and online forms can be found at www.sec.gov. The PCAOB can accept tips at tips@pcaobus.org or online at www.pcaobus.org.

GLBA: Gramm-Leach-Bliley Act

The US Gramm-Leach-Bliley Act of 1999—commonly referred to as GLBA—is landmark legislation that completely reorganized the statutory and legislative framework in place since the 1930s for the banking and financial services market. Of particular note is Title V, Subtitle A, Section 501, which requires that banking, consumer finance, securities, and insurance companies develop and meet new standards for protection of consumer privacy and safeguarding of financial institution infrastructure. Although VoIP systems were not specifically called out in the Act itself, the Federal Deposit Insurance Corporation (FDIC) and other financial regulatory agencies subsequently have issued VoIP-specific guidance to be used by regulated entities.

GLBA Regulatory Basics

Because the regulatory scope of GLBA is extensive and we really are interested only in the privacy and security effects of the legislation (and specifically, how they interact with VoIP systems), we will limit our discussion to Title V–PRIVACY. For those in the security community, every security reference to GLBA that you've seen is tied back to Title V, and we will review its contents later in this chapter. In addition, we will discuss supplementary guidance from consultants and regulators (including the FDIC VoIP recommendation) to help you understand what your organization will need for your VoIP system to operate in compliance with GLBA.

Direct from the Regulations

Title V is broken out into two subtitles. Subtitle A, "Disclosure of Nonpublic Personal Information," is where we will center most of our attention, particularly in Section 501. Subtitle B, "Fraudulent Access to Financial Information" criminalizes the act of using false pretenses to obtain financial information from an institution except under certain law-enforcement and investigative exclusions. We won't spend any more time with Subtitle B, but if you ever find yourself investigating someone's financial information you would be wise to familiarize yourself with its contents.

Of the 10 sections in subtitle A, I am only going to reproduce section 501 in its entirety, since it is the basis for all of the GLBA security recommendations I encounter. The other nine talk through privacy definitions, enforcement, and the creation of detailed regulations from the GLBA. In any case, Section 501 is what we want to be most familiar with, and it is fairly straightforward:

SEC. 501. PROTECTION OF NONPUBLIC PERSONAL INFORMATION.

(a) PRIVACY OBLIGATION POLICY- It is the policy of the Congress that each financial institution has an affirmative and continuing obligation to respect the privacy of its customers and to protect the security and confidentiality of those customers' nonpublic personal information.

(b) FINANCIAL INSTITUTIONS SAFEGUARDS- In furtherance of the policy in subsection (a), each agency or authority described in section 505(a) shall establish appropriate standards for the financial institutions subject to their jurisdiction relating to administrative, technical, and physical safeguards—

(1) to insure the security and confidentiality of customer records and information;

(2) to protect against any anticipated threats or hazards to the security or integrity of such records; and

(3) to protect against unauthorized access to or use of such records or information which could result in substantial harm or inconvenience to any customer.

From this point onward, I'll use the commonly accepted terminology for the rules created by this section. 501(a) and subsequent joint regulations are collectively known as the *privacy rule* and 501(b) with its joint regulations is called the *safeguarding rule*. Later in this chapter, you'll notice that HIPAA regulations follow a similar model, except the latter is called "security" instead of "safeguarding."(That's the way I think about GLBA as well: privacy + security.)

After the GLBA was signed, the Secretary of the Treasury, the National Credit Union Administration (NCUA), the Federal Trade Commission (FTC), and the Securities and Exchange Commission (SEC) were required to create appropriate regulations as part of Title V. The resulting documents can be found at the FTC at www.ftc.gov/os/2000/05/glb000512.pdf and the Office of the Comptroller of the Currency (OCC) at www.occ.treas.gov/ftp/release/0509fin.pdf. Detailed requirements for the privacy disclosures and opt-out procedures are spelled out in detail within these two documents (and if you're like me, you receive the annual privacy disclosures they require in droves from financial institutions). In general, there are no VoIP considerations within the privacy rule that aren't more directly addressed by the safeguarding rule, so we're going to spend the rest of this section on the safeguarding rule.

Detailed regulations for the safeguarding were finalized in 2001 as the "Interagency Guidelines Establishing Information Security Standards" (see www.fdic.gov/regulations/laws/rules/2000-8660.html or www.ots.treas.gov/docs/2/25231.pdf for a typical copy), and it is these rules that you will want to become most familiar with, in particular, part III:

III. Development and Implementation of Information Security Program

A.   Involve the Board of Directors.   The board of directors or an appropriate committee of the board of each bank holding company shall:
1. Approve the bank holding company's written information security program; and
2. Oversee the development, implementation, and maintenance of the bank holding company's information security program, including assigning specific responsibility for its implementation and reviewing reports from management.

B.   Assess Risk.   Each bank holding company shall:
1. Identify reasonably foreseeable internal and external threats that could result in unauthorized disclosure, misuse, alteration, or destruction of customer information or customer information systems.
2. Assess the likelihood and potential damage of these threats, taking into consideration the sensitivity of customer information.
3. Assess the sufficiency of policies, procedures, customer information systems, and other arrangements in place to control risks.

C.   Manage and Control Risk.   Each bank holding company shall:
1. Design its information security program to control the identified risks, commensurate with the sensitivity of the information as well as the complexity and scope of the bank holding company's activities. Each bank holding company must consider whether the following security measures are appropriate for the bank holding company and, if so, adopt those measures the bank holding company concludes are appropriate:
a. Access controls on customer information systems, including controls to authenticate and permit access only to authorized individuals and controls to prevent employees from providing customer information to unauthorized individuals who may seek to obtain this information through fraudulent means.
b. Access restrictions at physical locations containing customer information, such as buildings, computer facilities, and records storage facilities to permit access only to authorized individuals;
c. Encryption of electronic customer information, including while

in transit or in storage on networks or systems to which unauthorized individuals may have access;

d. Procedures designed to ensure that customer information
system modifications are consistent with the bank holding company's information security program;

e. Dual control procedures, segregation of duties, and employee
background checks for employees with responsibilities for or access
or customer information;
{{4-29-05 p.6120.37}}

f. Monitoring systems and procedures to detect actual and
attempted attacks on or intrusions into customer information systems;

g. Response programs that specify actions to be taken when the
bank holding company suspects or detects that unauthorized individuals have gained access to customer information systems,
including appropriate reports to regulatory and law enforcement
agencies; and

h. Measures to protect against destruction, loss, or damage of
customer information due to potential environmental hazards, such
as fire and water damage or technological failures.

2. Train staff to implement the bank holding company's information security program.

3. Regularly test the key controls, systems and procedures of the
information security program. The frequency and nature of such
tests should be determined by the bank holding company's risk
assessment. Tests should be conducted or reviewed by independent
third parties or staff independent of those that develop or maintain
the security programs.

D.   Oversee Service Provider Arrangements.   Each bank
holding company shall:

1. Exercise appropriate due diligence in selecting its service
providers;

2. Require its service providers by contract to implement appropriate measures designed to meet the objectives of these
Guidelines; and

3. Where indicated by the bank holding company's risk assessment, monitor its service providers to confirm that they have satisfied their obligations as required by paragraph D.2. As part of this
monitoring, a bank holding company should review audits, sum-

maries of test results, or other equivalent evaluations of its service providers.

E.   Adjust the Program.   Each bank holding company shall monitor, evaluate, and adjust, as appropriate, the information security program in light of any relevant changes in technology, the sensitivity of its customer information, internal or external threats to information, and the bank holding company's own changing business arrangements, such as mergers and acquisitions, alliances and joint ventures, outsourcing arrangements, and changes to customer information systems.

F.   Report to the Board.   Each bank holding company shall report to its board or an appropriate committee of the board at least annually. This report should describe the overall status of the information security program and the bank holding company's compliance with these Guidelines. The reports should discuss material matters related to its program, addressing issues such as: risk assessment; risk management and control decisions; service provider arrangements; results of testing; security breaches or violations and management's responses; and recommendations for changes in the information security program.

G.   Implement the Standards.
    1. Effective date. Each bank holding company must implement an information security program pursuant to these Guidelines by July 1, 2001.
    2. Two-year grandfathering of agreements with service providers. Until July 1, 2003, a contract that a bank holding company has entered into with a service provider to perform services for it or functions on its behalf satisfies the provisions of section III.D., even if the contract does not include a requirement that the servicer maintain the security and confidentiality of customer information, as long as the bank holding company entered into the contract on or before March 5, 2001.

These are the standards against which financial regulators will evaluate your organization if it falls under the GLBA. For VoIP systems, the primary concern will be to ensure that risk management and security processes for compliance include the VoIP infrastructure and that your organization's security standards developed for GLBA compliance will be applied to your IP communications systems as well.

What a Financial Regulator or GLBA Consultant Will Tell You

Until July 2005, when the FDIC provided very specific and detailed VoIP guidance, it was not uncommon for GLBA experts to consider voice communications systems to be outside the scope of GLBA's safeguarding rule. In what's known as a Financial Institution Letter or FIL (in this case FIL–69–2005—see www.fdic.gov/news/news/financial/2005/fil6905.html for a complete copy); the FDIC made it clear that VoIP systems must be included in GLBA risk assessment reports and processes. In their highlights, the FDIC noted:

- VoIP is susceptible to the same security risks as data networks if security policies and configurations are inadequate.

- The risks associated with VoIP should be evaluated as part of a financial institution's periodic risk assessment, with status reports submitted to the board of directors as mandated by section 501(b) of the Gramm-Leach—Bliley Act (GLBA). Any identified weaknesses should be corrected during the normal course of business.

This effectively told regulators and institutions that they will be expected to include IP communications systems in their GLBA compliance planning and reporting going forward. The FDIC VoIP security recommendation follows:

> Financial institutions can access various publicly available sources to develop VoIP security policies and practices. Widely accepted best practices are published by the National Institute of Standards and Technology (NIST), the agency responsible for developing information security standards for federal agencies (Special NIST Publication 800-58, Security Considerations for Voice over IP Systems, can be found at http://csrc.nist.gov/publications/nist-pubs/800-58/SP800-58-final.pdf.)

> Financial institutions contemplating the use of VoIP technology should consider the following best practices. Details of these best practices are further discussed in the attached "Voice over Internet Protocol Informational Supplement."

- Ensure that the institution has examined and can acceptably manage and mitigate the risks to information, systems operations and continuity of essential operations when implementing VoIP systems.

- Assess the level of concern about security and privacy. If warranted and practical, do not use "softphone" systems, which implement VoIP using an ordinary PC with a headset and special software.

- Carefully review statutory requirements for privacy and record retention with competent legal advisors.

- Develop appropriate network architecture.

- Use VoIP-ready firewalls and other appropriate protection mechanisms. Financial institutions should enable, use and routinely test security features included in VoIP systems.

- Properly implement physical controls in a VoIP environment.

- Evaluate costs for additional backup systems that may be required to ensure continued operation during power outages.

- Consider the need to integrate mobile telephone units with the VoIP system. If the need exists, consider using products implementing WiFi Protected Access (WPA), rather than Wired Equivalent Privacy (WEP).

- Give special consideration to emergency service communications. Automatic location services are not always as available with VoIP as they are with phone calls made through the PSTN.

When a financial institution decides to invest in VoIP technology, the associated risks should be evaluated as part of a financial institution's periodic risk assessment and discussed in status reports submitted to the board of directors as mandated by section 501(b) of the Gramm-Leach-Bliley Act. Any identified weaknesses should be corrected during the normal course of business.

The aforementioned FDIC VoIP Informational Supplement can be downloaded at www.fdic.gov/news/news/financial/2005/fil6905a.html if you'd like to get more detail on the points covered in the previous section of this chapter. Since it rehashes points covered in detail elsewhere in this book, I will leave this as an exercise for you, dear reader.

Tools & Traps…

Core GLBA-Compliance Issues for IP Communications Systems

Although GLBA does not have specific rules for VoIP, its integration with the rest of your organization's data network clearly puts it in scope of GLBA safeguarding provisions. This was reinforced by FDIC FIL-69-2005, which suggests nine specific GLBA risk management activities for VoIP systems:

- Include VoIP systems into general risk management and continuity planning
- Avoid softphone systems (where warranted and practical)
- Review privacy and records retention approach within VoIP system
- Review VoIP network architecture as part of overall network architecture
- Enable and test VoIP security features; use VoIP-ready firewalls
- Implement appropriate physical controls on VoIP systems
- Consider costs of additional backup systems required during power outages
- Avoid WEP on wireless VoIP; use WPA instead
- Consider E911 location service implications

In addition to the items highlighted by the FDIC, the same user, password, log, and database management policies used for data applications should also be applied to IP communications systems.

GLBA Compliance and Enforcement

Enforcement of Title V of the GLBA falls to 57 different regulators in three classes: federal functional regulators, state insurance authorities, and the Federal Trade Commission as follows:

- **State insurance authorities in each state** Insurance providers
- **Securities and Exchange Commission (SEC)** Brokers, dealers, investment advisors and investment companies
- **Office of the Comptroller of the Currency (OCC)** National banks
- **National Credit Union Administration (NCUA)** Federally insured credit unions
- **Board of Governors of the Federal Reserve System (FRB)** Member banks of the Federal Reserve System (other than national banks), branches and agencies of foreign banks (except federal branches, federal agencies, and insured state branches of foreign banks), commercial lending companies owned or controlled by foreign banks, organizations operating under section 25 or 25A of the Federal Reserve Act, and bank holding companies and their nonbank subsidiaries or affiliates not subject to the SEC or state authorities
- **Board of Directors of the Federal Deposit Insurance Corporation (FDIC)** Banks insured by the FDIC (except Federal Reserve System members), insured state branches of foreign banks, and their nonbank subsidiaries or affiliates not subject to the SEC or state authorities
- **Director of the Office of Thrift Supervision (OTC)** Savings associations insured by the FDIC and their nonbank subsidiaries or affiliates not subject to the SEC or state authorities
- **Federal Trade Commission (FTC)** All others

No Certification

GLBA has no concept of certification, either for institutions, individuals, or products.

Enforcement Process and Penalties

The FDIC, NCUA, OTS, OCC, and FRB use uniform principles, standards, and report forms created by the Federal Financial Institutions Examination Council (FFIEC). The FFEIC has gathered together a broad set of IT-related presentations, examination booklets, and other resources (www.ffiec.gov/ffiecinfobase/index.html) that provide an excellent guide to what their examiners will be looking for in an information security examination. For the banks and other financial institutions that fall under these agencies, GLBA enforcement is part of the overall enforcement regime that is standardized by the FFIEC.

Each of the 57 possible regulators has discretion over sanctions and penalties for privacy or safeguarding rule violations (for Subtitle B there are criminal penalties but these don't apply to the privacy or safeguarding rules, only to criminal access to financial data under fraudulent pretenses), so penalties may vary. Also, civil suits can be brought against financial institutions that violate the GLBA privacy rule.

HIPAA: Health Insurance Portability and Accountability Act

Within the U.S. Health Insurance Portability and Accountability Act of 1996, Congress adopted a broad range of reforms and standards designed to improve healthcare and health insurance and move toward electronic transaction processing and recordkeeping.. As part of the 1996 Act, Congress acknowledged the need for privacy standards, but it failed to produce them in time to meet its own deadline; that job fell to the Department of Health and Human Services (HHS), which issued the final rule for privacy in December 2000. The final security rule was issued by HHS in February 2003.

HIPAA Regulatory Basics

The privacy and security mandates that can affect VoIP systems are found in Title II, Subtitle F, Part C – Administrative Simplification. There are three aspects to Title II: Privacy, Code Sets, and Security. HHS has issued detailed regulations for all three, but the only two that can apply to VoIP systems are Privacy and Security.

Critical to understanding HIPAA is the concept of Protected Health Information (PHI) or Individually Identifiable Health Information (IIHI). Think of IIHI or PHI as any set of information that contains health-related data for an individual that can be traced back to that person. In order to share health-related information with other individuals or groups that participate in a patient's care, a Covered Entity (organization subject to HIPAA) must first receive the patient's consent to share that PHI with those participants (insurance, billing, physicians, hospitals, pharmacies, and so forth). Protection of PHI by a Covered Entity is the objective of the HIPAA Privacy Rule and Security Rule.

Direct from the Regulations

Privacy in HIPAA is addressed in Section 264 (of Title II, Subtitle F, Part C). The HHS Privacy Rule is based on this text in the Act:

> The recommendations under subsection (a) shall address at least the following: (1) The rights that an individual who is a subject of individually identifiable health information should have. (2) The procedures that should be established for the exercise of such rights. (3) The uses and disclosures of such information that should be authorized or required.

Three years and over 52,000 comments later, the first HHS Final Rule for Privacy was published, and after four more amendments (the last of which was in April 2003) the "Standards for Privacy of Individually Identifiable Health Information" had reached its present form (for a copy of the combined Privacy and Security regulations along with enforcement and penalty information, go to www.hhs.gov/ocr/combinedreg-text.pdf). In general, the Policy Rule applies more to an organization's procedures independent of technology, so it makes more sense to dig into HHS Security Rule, "Security Standards for the Protection of Electronic Protected Health Information," which is based on this text in Section 1173 of the Act:

> (1) SECURITY STANDARDS.—The Secretary shall adopt security standards that—
>
> (A) take into account—(i) the technical capabilities of record systems used to maintain health information; (ii) the costs of security measures; (iii) the need for training persons who have access to health information;(iv) the value of audit trails in computerized record systems; and (v) the needs and capabilities of small health care providers and rural health care providers (as such providers are defined by the Secretary); and
>
> (B) ensure that a health care clearinghouse, if it is part of a larger organization, has policies and security procedures which isolate the activities of the health care clearinghouse with respect to processing information in a manner that prevents unauthorized access to such information by such larger organization.
>
> (2) SAFEGUARDS.—Each person described in section 1172(a) who maintains or transmits health information shall maintain reasonable

and appropriate administrative, technical, and physical safeguards—

(A) to ensure the integrity and confidentiality of the information;

(B) to protect against any reasonably anticipated—(i) threats or
hazards to the security or integrity of the information; and (ii)
unauthorized uses or disclosures of the information; and

(C) otherwise to ensure compliance with this part by the officers
and employees of such person.

Notice the way that security is broken out in the Act—this structure is carried
forward into the HHS Security Rule (and believe me, without that knowledge it's
hard to make sense of the Rule).

The Security Rule

Within the Security Rule, there are general requirements that outline what a covered entity is required to document for compliance overall. Specific requirements
then follow in four main categories: Administrative, Physical, and Technical
Safeguards, plus Organizational Requirements. Understanding the difference
between the first three is crucial to following the Security Rule:

Administrative safeguards are administrative actions, and policies
and procedures, to manage the selection, development, implementation, and maintenance of security measures to protect electronic
protected health information and to manage the conduct of the
covered entity's workforce in relation to the protection of that
information.

Physical safeguards are physical measures, policies, and procedures to protect a covered entity's electronic information systems
and related buildings and equipment, from natural and environmental hazards, and unauthorized intrusion

Technical safeguards means the technology and the policy and
procedures for its use that protect electronic protected health
information and control access to it.

With this in mind, let's start with the general requirements and objectives for the security rule, and the flexibility allowed in implementing and documenting standards in each of the four categories:

(a) General requirements. Covered entities must do the following:

(1) Ensure the confidentiality, integrity, and availability of all electronic protected health information the covered entity creates, receives, maintains, or transmits.

(2) Protect against any reasonably anticipated threats or hazards to the security or integrity of such information.

(3) Protect against any reasonably anticipated uses or disclosures of such information that are not permitted or required under subpart E of this part.

(4) Ensure compliance with this subpart by its workforce.

(b) Flexibility of approach.

(1) Covered entities may use any security measures that allow the covered entity to reasonably and appropriately implement the standards and implementation specifications as specified in this subpart.

(2) In deciding which security measures to use, a covered entity must take into account the following factors:

(i) The size, complexity, and capabilities of the covered entity.

(ii) The covered entity's technical infrastructure, hardware, and software security capabilities.

(iii) The costs of security measures.

(iv) The probability and criticality of potential risks to electronic protected health information.

This flexibility is key to making your compliance document less painful to write. When you find that a vendor's equipment or solution does not provide a technical solution to a given standard, you can usually assemble an administrative solution that provides an acceptable workaround. And for those items that are not required (marked as Addressable in the Security Rule), you can still be compliant if you document why implementation of that item isn't reasonable or appropriate. Specifically,

(d) Implementation specifications. In this subpart:

(1) Implementation specifications are required or addressable. If an implementation specification is required, the word "Required" appears in parentheses after the title of the implementation specification. If an implementation specification is addressable, the word "Addressable" appears in parentheses after the title of the implementation specification.

(2) When a standard adopted in § 164.308, § 164.310, § 164.312, § 164.314, or § 164.316 includes required implementation specifications, a covered entity must implement the implementation specifications.

(3) When a standard adopted in § 164.308, § 164.310, § 164.312, § 164.314, or § 164.316 includes addressable implementation specifications, a covered entity must—

(i) Assess whether each implementation specification is a reasonable and appropriate safeguard in its environment, when analyzed with reference to the likely contribution to protecting the entity's electronic protected health information; and

(ii) As applicable to the entity—

(A) Implement the implementation specification if reasonable and appropriate; or

(B) If implementing the implementation specification is not reasonable and appropriate—

(1) Document why it would not be reasonable and appropriate to implement the implementation specification; and

(2) Implement an equivalent alternative measure if reasonable and appropriate.

With this in mind, I want to skip ahead to the documentation standard so that you understand why documentation is so critical for HIPAA compliance:

(b)(1) Standard: Documentation.

(i) Maintain the policies and procedures implemented to comply with this subpart in written (which may be electronic) form; and

(ii) If an action, activity or assessment is required by this subpart to be documented, maintain a written (which may be electronic) record of the action, activity, or assessment.

(2) Implementation specifications:

(i) Time limit (Required). Retain the documentation required by paragraph (b)(1) of this section for 6 years from the date of its creation or the date when it last was in effect, whichever is later.

(ii) Availability (Required). Make documentation available to those persons responsible for implementing the procedures to which the documentation pertains.

(iii) Updates (Required). Review documentation periodically, and update as needed, in response to environmental or operational changes affecting the security of the electronic protected health information.

You may never need to produce that documentation, but if your organization is subject to an investigation or a compliance review and you don't have it ready, you and your organization could face significant penalties.

WARNING

It's tempting to think of HIPAA documentation as something you can ask the VoIP (or other product) vendor to take care of for you, but there are two reasons why I don't recommend it. First, the vendor is not on the hook for your HIPPA processes; suppose they agreed to document a process for you, but it's one that you can't reasonably implement—it's your organization that will be held responsible by regulators, not the vendor. Second, remember that HIPAA is about your organization's operational *processes*, not any specific software or hardware. Unless you're hiring a consultant specifically for that purpose, asking an equipment vendor to document that process for you makes about as much sense as asking your local car dealer to pass a driving test for you . Maybe you get a salesman who takes you up on it just to close the sale, but that doesn't really make it appropriate or legal (and it won't make you a safe driver).

So what needs to be documented? Each of the items within the four main categories of the security rule: Administrative, Physical, and Technical Safeguards, plus Organizational Requirements. Since these are lengthy sections, I'm going to summarize and highlight specific parts from each that are likely to come into play with VoIP systems. You'll want to consult the Security Rule for specific details if you believe a listed standard will apply to the VoIP system.

Administrative Safeguards with VoIP Applicability

- Documented security management process to prevent, detect, contain, and correct security violations. Required elements: risk analysis, risk management, sanction policy, and logging/activity review.

- Authorization policies and procedures must be established to grant access to PHI only to those who require it. Addressable elements: Authorization and/or supervision, workforce clearance procedure, termination procedure.

- Security awareness and training program. Addressable elements: security reminders, malicious software protection, log-in monitoring, password management.

- Security incident procedures. Required elements: response and reporting.

- Contingency plan. Required elements: data backup plan, disaster recovery plan, emergency mode operation plan. Addressable elements: testing and revision procedures, applications and data criticality analysis.

Physical Safeguards with VoIP Applicability

- Physical access controls implementation. Addressable elements: contingency operations, facility security plan, physical access control and validation procedures, maintenance records.

- Device and media controls. Required elements: disposal, media reuse. Addressable elements: accountability, data backup and storage.

Technical Safeguards with VoIP Applicability

- Access control. Required elements: unique user identification, emergency access procedure. Addressable elements: automatic logoff, encryption and decryption.

- Audit controls (record of activity within systems containing PHI).

- Integrity. Addressable element: authentication mechanism (for PHI).

- Authentication (individual and entity seeking access to PHI).

- Transmission security. Addressable elements: integrity controls, encryption.

Organizational Requirements

These will generally not have any VoIP applicability except in the unusual case where there is a business relationship established with a service provider with access to recorded information containing PHI.

Other Considerations

Don't assume that because VoIP runs over IP it is considered to be "transmission via electronic media" by HIPAA. Within HHS General Administrative Requirements there is an official definition stating that:

> Certain transmissions, including of paper, via facsimile, and of voice, via telephone, are not considered to be transmissions via electronic media, because the information being exchanged did not exist in electronic form before the transmission

In general this excludes VoIP from HIPAA so long as the transmission is not recorded. Recording is the critical distinction. Within that same section HHS notes:

> Health information means any information, whether oral or
> recorded in any form or medium, that: (1) Is created or received by
> a health care provider, health plan, public health authority,
> employer, life insurer, school or university, or health care clearing-
> house; and (2) Relates to the past, present, or future physical or
> mental health or condition of an individual; the provision of health
> care to an individual; or the past, present, or future payment for
> the provision of health care to an individual.

From this, we see that a *recorded* VoIP call or voicemail clearly will fall within the scope of the HIPAA Privacy and Security Rules even though a nonrecorded call would not.

What a HIPAA Consultant Will Tell You

My experience with HIPAA consultants is that few of them have thought much about what happens when you record a VoIP conversation and what documentation is required for the system overall when you do. Nearly all agree that VoIP by itself does not create any HIPAA requirements. The question is how much documentation is required for voicemail and other call recording technologies.

Given the flexibility that the Security Rule allows, my suggestion is to document just that part of the system involved in recording, but even with that limited scope there will be plenty to document. If the VoIP system includes or interfaces with an Interactive Voice Response (IVR) system, that may need to be documented as well if it can be used as a gateway to PHI contained on a database system behind it.

Tools & Traps…

Core HIPAA-Compliance Issues for IP Communications Systems

Although HIPAA regulations only briefly touch on voice communication systems at all, several general principles still apply. First, the use of VoIP by itself does not create any electronic records unless some related system is recording a session containing Protected Health Information (PHI). In that case, the system doing the recording will fall under HIPAA requirements. This means that voice messaging and call recording equipment may require fully documented HIPAA-compliant operational processes. Second, if a VoIP-related system (such as a VoiceXML

Continued

server) is a gatekeeper to databases or other record-keeping systems that contain PHI, then HIPAA also will apply. Another example of this is an IVR system that front-ends patient records or billing systems.

HIPAA Compliance and Enforcement

The Department of Health and Human Services (HHS) delegated compliance and enforcement of the HIPAA Privacy Rule to the Office for Civil Rights (OCR) along with authority for allowing exceptions where certain state laws may conflict with HIPAA . The Centers for Medicare and Medicaid services (CMS) received delegated responsibility from HHS for enforcing the security rule, transactions, and code set standards (and identifiers standards when those are published). Through its Office of HIPAA Standards (OHS), CMS will enforce these rules and continue to enforce the insurance portability requirements under Title I of HIPAA.

No Certification

No official certification process exists for covered entities under HIPAA, although HHS did receive authority to perform compliance reviews as part of the Act. Products are not certified as part of HIPAA (although it's not uncommon to see them promoted as if they were). Regardless, documentation as specified in the Security Rule and Privacy Rule must exist and might be reviewed by a business partner, for example, as part of a due-diligence process. Other than that, the only time you would have to produce it is if you are investigated by HHS or OCR in response to a complaint or as part of a compliance review.

Enforcement Process and Penalties

In general, OCR acts on Privacy Rule violations in response to complaints that are registered with it. OCR requires written notification but does accept e-mail at OCRComplaint@hhs.gov (see "How to File a Health Information Privacy Complaint" at www.hhs.gov/ocr/privacyhowtofile.htm for more details). CMS has stated that the enforcement process for its portion of HIPAA will be primarily complaint-driven, although their primary strategy is to achieve "voluntary compliance through technical assistance." Penalties would be imposed as a last resort. When a complaint is received (typically through their Web site at www.cms.hhs.gov/Enforcement or via mail), CMS first allows the provider the opportunity to demonstrate compliance (or submit a plan for corrective action). Only if the provider fails to respond would penalties be considered.

The Administrative Simplification Compliance Act (ASCA) permits the Secretary of HHS to exclude noncompliant covered entities from the Medicare program. In addition, the original HIPAA legislation permits civil monetary penalties of not more than $100 for each violation, with a cap of $25,000 per calendar year. In addition, criminal penalties can be imposed for certain wrongful disclosures up to a $250,000 fine and 10 years imprisonment for willful conduct.

CALEA: Communications Assistance for Law Enforcement Act

The Communications Assistance for Law Enforcement Act first arrived from the U.S. Congress in 1994 with a simple goal: improving wiretapping effectiveness for law-enforcement in an increasingly digital PSTN. Advances in telecommunications made prior wiretapping methods less effective and CALEA was intended to force all carriers and carrier-grade equipment vendors to provide consistent and accessible electronic monitoring capabilities. For private equipment, including PBX and similar business-class voice equipment, CALEA doesn't apply except when that equipment was deemed a "substantial replacement" for the public telephone service.

Between 1994 and 2004, CALEA eventually progressed to a rough set of technically feasible standards backed by FCC regulations (and deep involvement by the Federal Bureau of Investigation (FBI) and Department of Justice (DOJ), though packet communications was still a CALEA minefield. These VoIP and broadband issues came to a head in August 2004 when the FCC issued a Notice of Proposed Rulemaking and Declaratory Ruling (NPRM) for public comment, stirring up anew the privacy and civil-liberties debate (see the sidebar, "CALEA and the Xbox?"). Lost to many observers was the fact the new NPRM might now be broad enough to force enterprises, universities, and other previously excluded organizations that deploy VoIP to become subject to the revised regulations. Although several requests for clarification on that topic still are pending at the FCC, it's clear these rules could substantially affect the design and deployment of enterprise VoIP.

If you're a carrier (of Voice, VoIP, or even just broadband IP), CALEA regulation is already a certainty (although in the case of broadband, there is a lot of work remaining even to agree on the technical standards, and the FBI has yet to specify capacity requirements as required by the Act). And in spite of the fact that in November 1994, the FCC had ruled that VoIP was a "data service" for other regulatory purposes, the FCC and DOJ agreed that data services were still within the scope of CALEA. Although predictable, this nevertheless came as a shock to many carriers who had in recent years become comfortable with the FCC hands-off approach to data networks and VoIP despite pressure from the FBI and Department of Justice (DOJ).

Notes from the Underground...

CALEA and the Xbox?

With the latest CALEA guidance for broadband, it's applicability to VoIP and data networks that has become a new privacy battleground. Groups Like the Electronic Frontier Foundation have been heavily involved in the debate, and from their perspective, the consequences of the revised CALEA rules could have long-ranging—and possibly dire—consequences:

> "If the FBI gets its way, the NPRM's tentative regulations will only be the tip of the iceberg. Soon, software companies, under threat of an expansive definition of CALEA's requirements, will face economic incentives to create email and IM programs that are surveillance-ready. Many computer game consoles that people can use to play over the Internet, such as the Xbox, allow gamers to chat with each other while they play. If any communication program running on the Internet has to be CALEA-compliant before being bought and sold, what would stop law enforcement from pushing for a tappable Xbox?"

Although it remains to be seen just how far the FCC and DOJ take enforcement of CALEA, it seems unlikely that serious enforcement will happen outside of the carrier space (with the possible exception of organizations like universities that provide phone service over a large campus).

Figure 15.1 shows a timeline for the development of the CALEA.

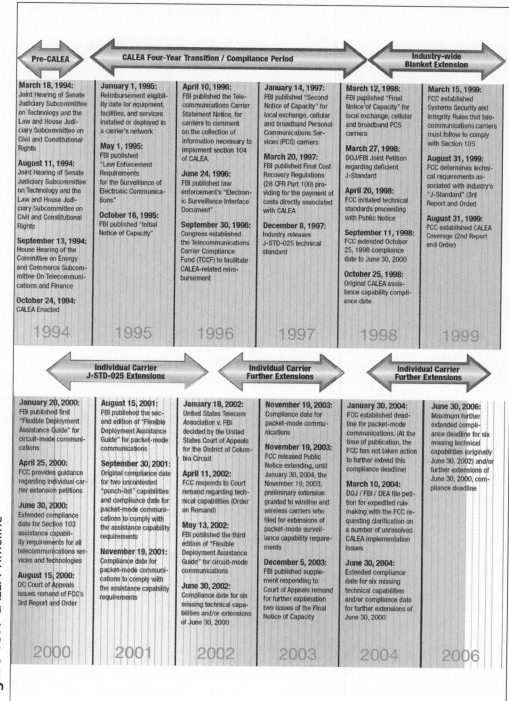

Figure 15.1 CALEA Timeline*

* Published in the Communications Assistance for Law Enforcement Act (CALEA) Flexible Deployment Assistance Guide, Fourth Edition

Since the publication of this guide, the following developments have taken place:

- September 23, 2004: FCC rules that all "push-to-talk" services are subject to CALEA

- September 23, 2005: FCC responds to DOJ / FBI / DEA petition and issues Notice of Proposed Rulemaking (NPRM) that will require broadband and VoIP providers to comply with CALEA; compliance deadline will be 18 months after final order.

CALEA Regulatory Basics

Several critical documents are required reading for those wanting to understand the intent of the original Act, and subsequent VoIP policy from the FCC, FBI, DOJ, and other agencies, particularly in the context of VoIP and its place in the latest CALEA rules. Here's the short list; we'll cover each of these in more detail later in the section:

- The 1994 Act itself as passed by Congress (see www.askcalea.net/calea.html for a full copy) broadened wiretap applicability to new telecommunications technologies and added a new requirement to gather "call-identifying information" as part of a legal communications intercept.

- J-STD-025, "Lawfully Authorized Electronic Surveillance" published by the Telecommunications Industry Association (TIA) as a result of work started in 1995 to address CALEA; known initially as TIA/EIA SP 3580. J-STD-025 was first published by TIA in December, 1997. (The current version required for FCC compliance is J-STD-025-A, published by the TIA in December, 2000—available for purchase at www.tiaonline.org/standards/catalog/ for nonmembers.)

- FCC "CALEA Third Report and Order,? August 31, 1999 (for a full copy, see www.fcc.gov/Bureaus/Engineering_Technology/Orders/1999/fcc99230.pdf or .txt), defined capability requirements in terms of J-STD-025 for wireline, cellular, and broadband PCS carriers, and specified that six of the nine additional capabilities in the FBI "CALEA punch list" for J-STD-025 would be required for CALEA compliance (subsequently incorporated into J-STD-025-A).

- DOJ, FBI and Drug Enforcement Agency (DEA), "Joint Petition for Expedited Rulemaking" (www.askcalea.net/docs/20040310.calea.jper.pdf)

filed before the FCC March 10, 2004 requested clear rules for how CALEA will be implemented on a wide variety of services, including packet technologies generally and VoIP specifically. Although not itself a regulation, this document serves as a roadmap for FCC rulemaking that will take place in 2006 and beyond, directly affecting VoIP service providers.

- FCC "First Report and Order and Further Notice of Proposed Rulemaking," FCC 05-153 (get a copy at www.askcalea.net/docs/20050923-fcc-05-153.pdf or at www.fcc.gov), September 23, 2005, issued in response to the March 2004 Joint Petition.

Direct from the Regulations

The basic technical requirements of the Act can be found in the first part of Section 103. In a nutshell, when a court order is present, the law enforcement requires access to all communications and their surrounding context without letting the target discover the "wiretap" (known in CALEA as a "lawful intercept"):

SEC. 103. ASSISTANCE CAPABILITY REQUIREMENTS.

(a) CAPABILITY REQUIREMENTS- Except as provided in subsections (b), (c), and (d) of this section and sections 108(a) and 109(b) and (d), a telecommunications carrier shall ensure that its equipment, facilities, or services that provide a customer or subscriber with the ability to originate, terminate, or direct communications are capable of—

(1) expeditiously isolating and enabling the government, pursuant to a court order or other lawful authorization, to intercept, to the exclusion of any other communications, all wire and electronic communications carried by the carrier within a service area to or from equipment, facilities, or services of a subscriber of such carrier concurrently with their transmission to or from the subscriber's equipment, facility, or service, or at such later time as may be acceptable to the government;

(2) expeditiously isolating and enabling the government, pursuant to a court order or other lawful authorization, to access call-identifying information that is reasonably available to the carrier—

(A) before, during, or immediately after the transmission of a wire or electronic communication (or at such later time as may be acceptable to the government); and

(B) in a manner that allows it to be associated with the communication to which it pertains, except that, with regard to information acquired solely pursuant to the authority for pen registers and trap and trace devices (as defined in section 3127 of title 18, United States Code), such call-identifying information shall not include any information that may disclose the physical location of the subscriber (except to the extent that the location may be determined from the telephone number);

(3) delivering intercepted communications and call-identifying information to the government, pursuant to a court order or other lawful authorization, in a format such that they may be transmitted by means of equipment, facilities, or services procured by the government to a location other than the premises of the carrier; and

(4) facilitating authorized communications interceptions and access to call-identifying information unobtrusively and with a minimum of interference with any subscriber's telecommunications service and in a manner that protects—

(A) the privacy and security of communications and call-identifying information not authorized to be intercepted; and

(B) information regarding the government's interception of communications and access to call-identifying information.

Bottom line: CALEA even at this level not only requires the media itself for a VoIP call, but a good deal of signaling information as well (labeled "call-identifying information" in the Act). In addition, you must facilitate the process and provide appropriate equipment to enable the surveillance to take place, although some cost recovery is permitted (this is an open issue, however, as you'll see in the 2004 Joint Petition). If you're a carrier (or substantial replacement for one) and fall under CALEA, every communications service that you provide to your customers must be capable of meeting these requirements.

NOTE

Although these terms are by no means unique to CALEA, it's useful to review the different types of legal interception available to Law Enforcement Agencies (LEAs) today:

1. Pen Register—what numbers were called by the target?
2. Trap and Trace—what numbers called the target?
3. Interception (Title III)—recorded conversation of the target (plus the other two items in this list). Most of the time, CALEA talks about this type of legal intercept.

The rest of the act lays out specific regulatory mandates and responsibilities, mainly targeted at the FCC. Sections 102, 104, 107, and 109 mandate that the FCC establish regulations for systems security and integrity, associated technical requirements, and determinations for specific equipment, facility, or services. An important compliance concept is also part of Section 107 and are known as "Safe harbor standards." Section 107(a)(2) of CALEA allows a carrier to be deemed in compliance with CALEA's capability requirements in Sections 103 and 106 if it complies with an appropriate publicly available technical standard. Also in Section 107 is a provision that allows a carrier to petition for an extension of the CALEA deadline when appropriate standards or technology isn't available. Here's the complete text of Sections 106 and 107:

SEC. 106. COOPERATION OF EQUIPMENT MANUFACTURERS AND PROVIDERS OF TELECOMMUNICATIONS SUPPORT SERVICES.

(a) CONSULTATION- A telecommunications carrier shall consult, as necessary, in a timely fashion with manufacturers of its telecommunications transmission and switching equipment and its providers of telecommunications support services for the purpose of ensuring that current and planned equipment, facilities, and services comply with the capability requirements of section 103 and the capacity requirements identified by the Attorney General under section 104.

(b) COOPERATION- Subject to sections 104(e), 108(a), and 109 (b) and (d), a manufacturer of telecommunications transmission or switching equipment and a provider of telecommunications support services shall, on a reasonably timely basis and at a reasonable charge, make available to the telecommunications carriers using its equipment, facilities, or services such features or modifications as are necessary to permit such carriers to comply with the capability requirements of section 103 and the capacity requirements identified by the Attorney General under section 104.

SEC. 107. TECHNICAL REQUIREMENTS AND STANDARDS; EXTENSION OF COMPLIANCE DATE.

(a) SAFE HARBOR-

(1) CONSULTATION- To ensure the efficient and industry-wide implementation of the assistance capability requirements under section 103, the Attorney General, in coordination with other Federal, State, and local law enforcement agencies, shall consult with appropriate associations and standard-setting organizations of the telecommunications industry, with representatives of users of telecommunications equipment, facilities, and services, and with State utility commissions.

(2) COMPLIANCE UNDER ACCEPTED STANDARDS- A telecommunications carrier shall be found to be in compliance with the assistance capability requirements under section 103, and a manufacturer of telecommunications transmission or switching equipment or a provider of telecommunications support services shall be found to be in compliance with section 106, if the carrier, manufacturer, or support service provider is in compliance with publicly available technical requirements or standards adopted by an industry association or standard-setting organization, or by the Commission under subsection (b), to meet the requirements of section 103.

(3) ABSENCE OF STANDARDS- The absence of technical requirements or standards for implementing the assistance capability requirements of section 103 shall not—

(A) preclude a telecommunications carrier, manufacturer, or telecommunications support services provider from deploying a technology or service; or
(B) relieve a carrier, manufacturer, or telecommunications support services provider of the obligations imposed by section 103 or 106, as applicable.

(b) COMMISSION AUTHORITY- If industry associations or standard-setting organizations fail to issue technical requirements or standards or if a Government agency or any other person believes that such requirements or standards are deficient, the agency or person may petition the Commission to establish, by rule, technical requirements or standards that—

(1) meet the assistance capability requirements of section 103 by cost-effective methods;

(2) protect the privacy and security of communications not authorized to be intercepted;

(3) minimize the cost of such compliance on residential ratepayers;

(4) serve the policy of the United States to encourage the provision of new technologies and services to the public; and

(5) provide a reasonable time and conditions for compliance with and the transition to any new standard, including defining the obligations of telecommunications carriers under section 103 during any transition period.

(c) EXTENSION OF COMPLIANCE DATE FOR EQUIPMENT, FACILITIES, AND SERVICES-

(1) PETITION- A telecommunications carrier proposing to install or deploy, or having installed or deployed, any equipment, facility, or service prior to the effective date of section 103 may petition the Commission for 1 or more extensions of the deadline for complying with the assistance capability requirements under section 103.

(2) GROUNDS FOR EXTENSION- The Commission may, after consultation with the Attorney General, grant an extension under this subsection, if the Commission determines that compliance with the assistance capability requirements under section 103 is not reasonably achievable through application of technology available within the compliance period.

(3) LENGTH OF EXTENSION- An extension under this subsection shall extend for no longer than the earlier of—

(A) the date determined by the Commission as necessary for the carrier to comply with the assistance capability requirements under section 103; or
(B) the date that is 2 years after the date on which the extension is granted.

(4) APPLICABILITY OF EXTENSION- An extension under this subsection shall apply to only that part of the carrier's business on which the new equipment, facility, or service is used.

These extensions, once routine, are now scrutinized much more closely by the FCC, FBI, and DOJ. Even for packet-based solutions like VoIP, the existence of adequate technical standards is forcing equipment manufacturers and carriers to show compliance with CALEA.

J-STD-025 and Other Technical Standards

Shortly after CALEA was enacted, work began in Subcommittee TR-45.2 of the Telecommunications Industry Association (TIA) to create an appropriate technical interface between Law Enforcement Agencies (LEAs) and carriers. Interim standard J-STD-025 was developed specifically to define services and features required by CALEA for "wireline, cellular, and broadband PCS carriers to support lawfully-authorized electronic surveillance, and specifies interfaces necessary to deliver intercepted communications and call-identifying information to a law enforcement agency."

NOTE

J-STD-025 and subsequent TIA technical standards referenced by FCC regulations—although available to the public—are not free. They can be purchased on the TIA Web site (see www.tiaonline.org/standards/CALEA_JEM for more information) or through the Alliance for Telecommunications Industry Solutions (ATIS—see www.atis.org/atis/docstore/ for more information). In general, most of the standards referenced in this section require membership or document fees to be paid in order to access the associated standard.

Originally published in December, 1997, J-STD-025, the standard was the subject of a March 27, 1998, Joint petition to the FCC from the DOJ and FBI, which argued that it was deficient in nine specific areas. This list commonly is referred to as the FBI "punch list" of additional capabilities, six of which were subsequently required by the FCC and incorporated into the revised J-STD-025-A specification, published by TR-45.2 in May, 2000.

Since that time, a number of standards have been developed by other industry groups and are recognized by the FBI and FCC as meeting the safe harbor provisions of CALEA. Many of these have been coordinated with ongoing TIA TR45 LAES work on J-STD-025. Among these standards are:

- TIA TR45 LAES J-STD-025B for CDMA2000 packet data intercepts

- T1P1 T1.724 for GPRS packet data intercepts

- T1S1 T1.678 for VoIP and other wire-line data intercepts

- PKT-SP-ESP-I03-40113 for PacketCable data intercepts

- AMTA Electronic Surveillance for ESMR Dispatch Version 1.0 for ESMR Push-To-Talk intercepts

- American Association of Paging Carriers (AAPC) Paging Technical Committee (PTC) CALEA Suite of Standards, Version 1.3 for Traditional Paging, Advanced Messaging, and Ancillary Services (see www.pagingcarriers.org/ptc.asp for this freely available standard)

FCC CALEA Third Report and Order (August 1999)

By 1999, the FCC was ready to require all carriers to implement the capabilities of the TIA J-standard and six FBI punch list capabilities by June 30, 2002. Packet-mode communications capability (including VoIP) was to be implemented by September 30, 2002 (though in practice CALEA extensions for packet continued routinely until late 2005). In addition, the FCC reached important conclusions regarding location information (not directly specified by the Act itself) and packet-mode communications capabilities. The FCC press release states:

Actions Regarding the Interim Standard (J-STD-025)

The FCC concluded the following regarding the location information and packet-mode communications capabilities of the interim standard:

Location information: The FCC required that location information be provided to law enforcement agencies (LEAs) under CALEA's assistance capability requirements for "call-identifying information," provided that a LEA has a court order or legal authorization beyond a pen register or trap and trace authorization. The FCC found that location information identifies the "origin" or "destination" of a communication and thus is covered by CALEA. The FCC, however, did not mandate that carriers be able to provide LEAs with the precise physical location of a caller. Rather, it permitted LEAs with the proper legal authorization to receive from wireline, cellular, and broadband PCS carriers only the location of a cell site at the beginning and termination of a mobile call.

Packet-mode communications: The FCC required that carriers provide LEAs access to packet-mode communications by September 30, 2001. However, the Commission acknowledged that significant privacy issues had been raised with regard to the J-STD-025 treatment of packet-mode communications. Under the J-STD-025, law enforcement could be provided with access to both call identifying information and call content, even where it may be authorized only to receive call identifying information. Accordingly, the FCC invited TIA to study CALEA solutions for packet-mode technology and report to the FCC by September 30, 2000 on steps that can be taken, including particular amendments to the interim standard, that will better address privacy concerns.

Actions Regarding the Capabilities Requested by DoJ/FBI

Of the nine items in the DoJ/FBI punch list, the following capabilities were required by the FCC:

Content of subject-initiated conference calls— A LEA will be able to access the content of conference calls initiated by the subject under surveillance (including the call content of parties on hold), pursuant to a court order or other legal authorization beyond a pen register order.

Party hold, join, drop on conference calls— Messages will be sent to a LEA that identify the active parties of a call. Specifically, on a conference call, these messages will indicate whether a party is on hold, has joined, or has been dropped from the conference call.

Subject-initiated dialing and signaling information— Access to dialing and signaling information available from the subject will inform a LEA of a subject's use of features (e.g., call forwarding, call waiting, call hold, and three-way calling).

In-band and out-of-band signaling (notification message)— A message will be sent to a LEA whenever a subject's service sends a tone or other network message to the subject or associate (e.g., notification that a line is ringing or busy, call waiting signal).

Timing information— Information will be sent to a LEA permitting it to correlate call-identifying information with the call content of a communications interception.

Dialed digit extraction—The originating carrier will provide to a LEA on the call data channel any digits dialed by the subject after connecting to another carrier's service., pursuant to a pen register authorization. The FCC found that some such digits fit within CALEA's definition of call-identifying information, and that they are generally reasonably available to carriers

In requiring the six punch list capabilities, the FCC noted that it determined that five of them constitute call-identifying information that is generally reasonably available to carriers and therefore is required under CALEA. The FCC found that although the cost to carriers of providing some of these five capabilities is significant, no automatic exemptions will be provided. Exclusions must be filed and approved on a case-by-case basis.

The following punch list items were not required by the FCC:

Surveillance status—Carriers would have been required to send a message to a LEA to verify that a wiretap had been established and was functioning correctly.

Continuity check tone (C-tone)— Electronic signal would have alerted a LEA if the facility used for delivery of call content interception failed or lost continuity.

Feature status— A LEA would have been notified when, for the facilities under surveillance, specific subscription-based calling services were added or deleted.

The FCC found that these three capabilities, although potentially useful to LEAs, were not required by the plain language of CALEA. However, carriers are free to provide these capabilities if they wish to do so.

DOJ-FBI-DEA Joint Petition for Expedited Rulemaking (March 2004)

Given CALEA's stated purpose, namely to "preserve law enforcement's ability to conduct lawful electronic surveillance despite changing telecommunications technologies," the DOJ, FBI, and DEA felt that key aspects of the law and its original intent were not being addressed by the FCC, carriers, and equipment manufacturers. The petition states:

> CALEA applies to all telecommunications carriers, and its application is technology neutral. Despite a clear statutory mandate, full CALEA implementation has not been achieved. Although the Commission has taken steps to implement CALEA, there remain several outstanding issues that are in need of immediate resolution.
>
> To resolve the outstanding issues, law enforcement asks the Commission to:
>
> (1) formally identify the types of services and entities that are subject to CALEA;
>
> (2) formally identify the services that are considered "packet-mode services";
>
> (3) initially issue a Declaratory Ruling or other formal Commission statement, and ultimately adopt final rules, finding that broadband access services and broadband telephony services are subject to CALEA;
>
> (4) reaffirm, consistent with the Commission's finding in the CALEA Second Report and Order, that push-to-talk "dispatch" service is subject to CALEA;
>
> (5) adopt rules that provide for the easy and rapid identification of future CALEA-covered services and entities;

(6) establish benchmarks and deadlines for CALEA packet-mode compliance;

(7) adopt rules that provide for the establishment of benchmarks and deadlines for CALEA compliance with future CALEA-covered technologies;

(8) outline the criteria for extensions of any benchmarks and deadlines for compliance with future CALEA-covered technologies established by the Commission;

(9) establish rules to permit it to request information regarding CALEA compliance generally;

(10) establish procedures for enforcement action against entities that do not comply with their CALEA obligations;

(11) confirm that carriers bear sole financial responsibility for CALEA implementation costs for post-January 1, 1995 communications equipment, facilities and services;

(12) permit carriers to recover their CALEA implementation costs from their customers; and

(13) clarify the cost methodology and financial responsibility associated with intercept provisioning.

In general, existing FCC rules are incomplete, inconsistent, or otherwise inadequate in these areas and you should expect to see new or clarified regulations from the FCC over the next few years that address the DOJ/FBI/DEA concerns. Many of these will directly impact VoIP systems design and operational practices within carriers.

FCC First Report and Order and Further Notice of Proposed Rulemaking, (September, 2005)

In response to the DOJ–FBI–DEA Joint Petition, the FCC ruled that CALEA does apply to providers of certain broadband and interconnected VoIP services. From the FCC press release:

> The Commission found that these services can essentially replace conventional telecommunications services currently subject to wiretap rules, including circuit-switched voice service and dial-up

Internet access. As replacements, the new services are covered by the Communications Assistance for Law Enforcement Act, or CALEA, which requires the Commission to preserve the ability of law enforcement agencies to conduct court-ordered wiretaps in the face of technological change.

The Order is limited to facilities-based broadband Internet access service providers and VoIP providers that offer services permitting users to receive calls from, and place calls to, the public switched telephone network. These VoIP providers are called interconnected VoIP providers.

The Commission found that the definition of "telecommunications carrier" in CALEA is broader than the definition of that term in the Communications Act and can encompass providers of services that are not classified as telecommunications services under the Communications Act. CALEA contains a provision that authorizes the Commission to deem an entity a telecommunications carrier if the Commission "finds that such service is a replacement for a substantial portion of the local telephone exchange."

Because broadband Internet and interconnected VoIP providers need a reasonable amount of time to come into compliance with all relevant CALEA requirements, the Commission established a deadline of 18 months from the effective date of this Order, by which time newly covered entities and providers of newly covered services must be in full compliance. The Commission also adopted a Further Notice of Proposed Rulemaking that will seek more information about whether certain classes or categories of facilities-based broadband Internet access providers – notably small and rural providers and providers of broadband networks for educational and research institutions – should be exempt from CALEA.

The Commission's action is the first critical step to apply CALEA obligations to new technologies and services that are increasingly used as a substitute for conventional services. The Order strikes an appropriate balance between fostering competitive broadband and advanced services deployment and technological innovation on one hand, and meeting the needs of the law enforcement community on the other.

The potential impact of this ruling is huge and will reverberate within the VoIP and broadband communities over the next few years. What is perhaps most surprising is the determination that broadband data services will need to support a lawful intercept function. Lawsuits have already been filed (partly over the unfunded mandate the FCC created for higher education: an estimated $7 billion in CALEA implementation costs are expected for colleges and universities alone, according to EDUCAUSE). Much of the story has yet to be written but the impact of this round of FCC rulemaking on the VoIP community will be hard to overstate. How this will affect Skype and other consumer services in the long run remains to be seen, but in the meantime this FNPR has served as a shot across the bow of the VoIP industry.

Telecommunications Carrier Systems Security and Integrity Plan

The FCC mandates that carriers file this plan as part of their CALEA compliance. From the FCC CALEA page:

> CALEA also requires telecommunications carriers to file with the Commission information regarding the policies and procedures used for employee supervision and control, and to maintain secure and accurate records of each communications interception or access to call-identifying information. In particular, all carriers that must comply with CALEA's capacity and capability requirements must also comply with 47 C.F.R. §§64.2100 - 64.2106 of the Commission's rules (available at www.access.gpo.gov/ nara/cfr/waisidx_03/47cfr64_03.html) by filing with the Commission a Telecommunications Carrier Systems Security and Integrity Plan. Resellers of local exchange services, both facilities-based and switchless, must also comply with these rules by filing a Systems Security and Integrity Plan.

What a CALEA Consultant Will Tell You

First and foremost, it's very important to know for sure if your organization is required to comply with CALEA. At this point, the FCC has issued extensive guidance but it still does not cover all cases. A CALEA expert can help guide you through existing precedent and determine which—if any—of the services offered by your organization must be compliant with CALEA. From there, identifying any safe harbor standards accepted by the FCC and FBI is the next step. If you can implement one or more safe harbor standards, then do it and consider yourself lucky.

If you can't, you'll need some help determining which section to file under (107 or 109) so that the FCC can grant you a little breathing room while you figure out what your long-term solution will be (presumably with the help of your VoIP system vendor(s). Unfortunately, today's VoIP systems are a little behind the curve on implementing CALEA standards, and if your software or hardware providers don't already have a plan to address CALEA, you may want to consider alternatives since the FCC has signaled that it will no longer routinely grant deferrals and other exceptions when adequate technical solutions exist and are available to the market.

Tools & Traps…

Core CALEA-Compliance Issues for IP Communications Systems

Unlike regulations like HIPAA, GLBA, or SOX, within CALEA there is more focus on equipment capabilities and standards as part of CALEA compliance. Know which standard to apply (start with J-STD-025B or T1.678 for VoIP). Retrofitting a compliant solution over a noncompliant system can be difficult and expensive for VoIP, so if you are required to comply with CALEA, make sure that your equipment (or software) supplier evaluation / procurement process adequately screens for CALEA support, and be sure to stay on top of FCC filings (and the latest FCC orders, since VoIP rules under CALEA are still being worked out). Consider filing a comment with the FCC if you're reading this early enough in the rulemaking process.

CALEA Compliance and Enforcement

In general, the FCC (with input from the DOJ and FBI) is responsible for compliance (although there are minor aspects of CALEA that the DOJ can enforce directly).

Certification

Individual LEAs can be CALEA-certified, but in general that term isn't applied to equipment or carriers. Equipment sold to carriers can (and should) be CALEA Section 106-compliant in the sense that if it meets a standard accepted by the FCC (and/or FBI in some cases where a technical standard hasn't been adopted by the FCC regulations directly). Use of CALEA-compliant equipment by a carrier will bring Section 107 Safe Harbor provisions into play to deem that service to be CALEA-compliant. In general, however, it is a carrier and associated service that can be certified as compliant, by meeting Section 103 requirements directly with the agreement of the FBI (these have been phased out as technical standards now fill the gap that once required this FBI consent) or by meeting FCC mandates and Filing directly with the FCC for certifaction.

Enforcement Process and Penalties

The FCC requires appropriate CALEA filings by each carrier and can impose fines when those filings are missing, incomplete, or otherwise not in line with CALEA regulations. At this point, there have been no major fines but the threat of fines has kept most carriers on top of all required filings. With the inclusion of VoIP it will be interesting to see if the FCC takes a "get tough" stance on CALEA enforcement once the current set of VoIP and packet-related CALEA lawsuits has been resolved.

Elliott Eichen at Verizon suggests a "Four-Step Process" to describe the regulatory experience surrounding CALEA (and E911) compliance; it rings particularly true for me:

1. Denial: "Not us!"

2. Depression: "We can't do it technically."

3. Anger: "This is going to cost a fortune!"

4. Acceptance: "CALEA and E911 are not going away; let's make it work."

E911: Enhanced 911 and Related Regulations

Within the United States and Canada, 911 is the official national emergency number; calls to 911 are directed to the most appropriate Public Safety Answering Point (PSAP) dispatcher for local emergency medical, fire, and law enforcement agencies via specialized infrastructure. Enhanced 911 (E911) systems automatically show the PSAP a calling number telephone number and location for wireline phones using the Automatic Location Identifier (ALI) database (maintained specifically for PSAP use, it translates a phone number from Automatic Number Identification (ANI) to a physical location). In 1996 the FCC established the wireless E911 program; which, when fully implemented, will provide a PSAP with a precise location for wireless 911 calls. Figure 15.2 is an example of an enhanced 911 system.

In this example, the ALI Location Database translates an ANI identifier into a physical location that can be used for emergency dispatch.

Given all the progress around E911 it may come as a surprise to you that 911 failures due to incomplete VoIP E911 design have led to several high-profile, preventable deaths (accompanied by lawsuits and demand for increased regulation). In fact, the rise of VoIP carriers that are interconnected with the PSTN has been accompanied by two massive breakdowns in E911 capability that eventually forced an urgent VoIP E911 order from the FCC in June, 2005. The first involves VoIP carriers not having adequate interconnection arrangements to pass E911 calls. But the second is the more interesting problem. What happens when you can register a VoIP phone over an IP network from any physical location in the world (so long as it can be connected to the Internet)?

Figure 15.2 An Enhanced 911 System

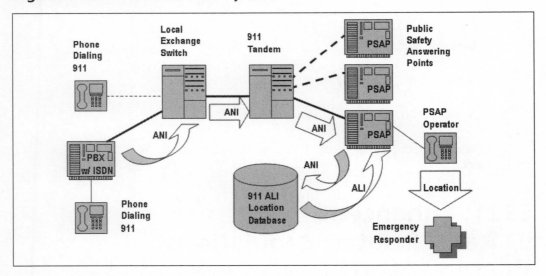

E911 Regulatory Basics

There are several dimensions to E911, the most important being the distinction between wireline and wireless regulations. But in this section we will focus exclusively on the FCC VoIP E911 rulings in 2005 that have added an important new dimension to FCC rules for E911.

Direct from the Regulations

On June 3, 2005 the FCC released the *VoIP 911 Order* requiring interconnected VoIP providers to provide their new and existing subscribers with 911 service no later than November 28, 2005. The FCC accompanying press release gives an excellent summary of the resulting regulations:

> Specifically, as a condition of providing interconnected VoIP service, each interconnected VoIP provider must, in addition to satisfying the subscriber notification, acknowledgment, and labeling requirements set forth in section 9.5(e) of the Commission's rules.

- Transmit all 911 calls to the public safety answering point (PSAP), designated statewide default answering point, or appropriate local emergency authority that serves the caller's "Registered Location." Such transmissions must include the caller's Automatic Numbering Information (ANI) [ANI is a system that identifies the billing account for a call and, for 911 systems, identifies the calling party and may be used as a call back number] and Registered Location to the extent that the PSAP, designated statewide default answering point, or appropriate local emergency authority is capable of receiving and processing such information;

- Route all 911 calls through the use of ANI and, if necessary, pseudo-ANI [Pseudo-ANI is "a number, consisting of the same number of digits as ANI, that is not a North American Numbering Plan telephone directory number and may be used in place of an ANI to convey special meaning. The special meaning assigned to the pseudo-ANI is determined by agreements, as necessary, between the system originating the call, intermediate systems handling and routing the call, and the destination system], via the Wireline E911 Network, [a "dedicated wireline network that: (1) is interconnected with but largely separate from the public switched telephone network; (2) includes a selective router; and (3) is utilized to route emergency calls and related information to PSAPs, designated statewide default answering points, appropriate local emergency authorities or other emergency answering points."] and make a caller's Registered Location available to the appropriate PSAP, designated statewide default answering point or appropriate local emergency authority from or through the appropriate Automatic Location Identification (ALI) database;

- Obtain from each of its existing and new customers, prior to the initiation of service, a Registered Location; and

■ Provide all of their end users one or more methods of updating their Registered Location at will and in a timely manner. At least one method must allow end users to use only the same equipment (such as the Internet telephone) that they use to access their interconnected VoIP service.

Compliance Letters

Additionally, given the vital public safety interests at stake, the VoIP 911 Order requires each interconnected VoIP provider to file with the Commission a Compliance Letter on or before November 28, 2005 detailing its compliance with the above 911 requirements. To ensure that interconnected VoIP providers have satisfied the requirements set forth above, we require interconnected VoIP providers to include the following information in their Compliance Letters:

■ **911 Solution**: This description should include a quantification, on a percentage basis, of the number of subscribers to whom the provider is able to provide 911 service in compliance with the rules established in the VoIP 911 Order. Further, the detailed description of the technical solution should include the following components:

1. **911 Routing Information/Connectivity to Wireline E911 Network**: A detailed statement as to whether the provider is transmitting, as specified in Paragraph 42 of the VoIP 911 Order, "all 911 calls to the appropriate PSAP, designated statewide default answering point, or appropriate local emergency authority utilizing the Selective Router, the trunk line(s) between the Selective Router and the PSAP, and such other elements of the Wireline E911 Network as are necessary in those areas where Selective Routers are utilized." If the provider is not transmitting all 911 calls to the correct answering point in areas where Selective Routers are utilized, this statement should include a detailed explanation why not. In addition, the provider should quantify the number of Selective Routers to which it has interconnected, directly or indirectly, as of November 28, 2005.

2. **Transmission of ANI and Registered Location Information:** A detailed statement as to whether the provider is transmitting via the Wireline E911 Network the 911 caller's ANI and Registered Location to all answering points that are capable of receiving and processing this information. This information should include: (i) a quantification, on a percentage basis, of how many answering points within the provider's service area are capable of receiving and processing ANI and Registered Location information that the provider transmits; (ii) a quantification of the number of subscribers, on a percentage basis, whose ANI and Registered Location are being transmitted to answering points that are capable of receiving and processing this information; and (iii) if the provider is not transmitting the 911 caller's ANI and Registered Location to all answering points that are capable of receiving and processing this information, a detailed explanation why not.

3. **911 Coverage:** To the extent a provider has not achieved full 911 compliance with the requirements of the VoIP 911 Order in all areas of the country by November 28, 2005, the provider should: 1) describe in detail, either in narrative form or by map, the areas of the country, on a MSA basis, where it is in full compliance and those in which it is not; and 2) describe in detail its plans for coming into full compliance with the requirements of the order, including its anticipated timeframe for such compliance.

- **Obtaining Initial Registered Location Information:** A detailed description of all actions the provider has taken to obtain each existing subscriber's current Registered Location and each new subscriber's initial Registered Location. This information should include, but is not limited to, relevant dates and methods of contact with subscribers and a quantification, on a percentage basis, of the number of subscribers from whom the provider has obtained the Registered Location.

- **Obtaining Updated Registered Location Information:** A detailed description of the method(s) the provider has offered its subscribers to update their Registered Locations. This information should include a statement as to whether the provider is offering its subscribers at least one option for updating their Registered Location that permits them to use the same equipment that they use to access their interconnected VoIP service.

■   **Technical Solution for Nomadic Subscribers**: A detailed description of any technical solutions the provider is implementing or has implemented to ensure that subscribers have access to 911 service whenever they use their service nomadically.

The Bureau notes that in an October 7, 2005 letter submitted in WC Docket Nos. 04-36 and 05-196, AT&T outlined an innovative compliance plan that it is implementing to address the Commission's 911 provisioning requirements that take effect on November 28, 2005. In letters filed on October 21, 2005 in these dockets, MCI and Verizon each outlined similar compliance plans. Each of these plans includes an automatic detection mechanism that enables the provider to identify when a customer may have moved his or her interconnected VoIP service to a new location and ensure that the customer continues to receive 911 service even when using the interconnected VoIP service nomadically. These plans also include a commitment to not accept new interconnected VoIP customers in areas where the provider cannot provide 911 service and to adopt a "grandfather" process for existing customers for whom the provider has not yet implemented either full 911 service or the automatic detection capability.

The Bureau applauds the steps undertaken by AT&T, MCI and Verizon and strongly encourages other providers to adopt similar measures. The Bureau will carefully review a provider's implementation of steps such as these in deciding whether and how to take enforcement action. Providers should include in their November 28, 2005, Compliance Letters a detailed statement as to whether and how they have implemented such measures. To the extent that providers have not implemented these or similar measures, they should describe what measures they have implemented in order to comply with the requirements of the VoIP 911 Order.

Although we do not require providers that have not achieved full 911 compliance by November 28, 2005, to discontinue the provision of interconnected VoIP service to any existing customers, we do expect that such providers will discontinue marketing VoIP service, and accepting new customers for their service, in all areas where they are not transmitting 911 calls to the appropriate PSAP in full compliance with the Commission's rules.

What an E911 Consultant Will Tell You

This is a very active and emerging space, particularly around VoIP E911, but the National Emergency Number Association (NENA) has some excellent recommendations in this area. They have published a 9-1-1 System Reference Guide (go to www.nena.org for more information) that is "a single-source reference for PSAP and Selective Router administrative data"—invaluable information for a VoIP carrier that needs to comply with the new FCC order. Also underway is a NG E9-1-1 Program, a public-private partnership to improve the nation's 9-1-1 system and provide necessary VoIP and PSAP standards to make deployable VoIP E911 more achievable.

Tools & Traps...

Core E911-Compliance Issues for IP Communications Systems

As with CALEA, there is a bit more focus on equipment capabilities and standards as part of compliance. However, retrofitting a compliant solution over a noncompliant system isn't necessarily difficult and expensive if it's well planned. Regardless, E911 should be a critical part of your vendor-facing solution evaluation / procurement process.

For enterprise VoIP systems, the critical considerations involve local regulations that require accurate information for ALI tables. Many enterprise system vendors have location databases, capabilities for end-user location self-reporting, and partnerships with third-party solutions for maintaining location information even when IP phones are moved.

E911 Compliance and Enforcement

The FCC and the National Association of Regulatory Utility Commissioners (NARUC) formed the Joint Federal/State VoIP Enhanced 911 Enforcement Task Force to facilitate compliance with FCC VoIP 911 rules as well as any necessary enforcement. The Task Force is made up of FCC staff and representatives from various State PUCs, and operates in conjunction with NENA, the Association of Public Safety Communications Officials, and various state and local emergency authorities. The Task Force's mission is to "develop educational materials to ensure that consumers understand their rights and the requirements of the FCC's VoIP 911 Order; develop appropriate compliance and enforcement strategies; compile data; and share best practices."

Self-Certification

At this point, the FCC process requires a self-certification by each VoIP carrier that must be filed with the FCC. As standards emerge, some form of product certification for VoIP E911 may eventually take place.

Enforcement Process and Penalties

Despite the number of extensions granted by the FCC in 2005, a number of fines and other penalties have been levied recently against noncompliant VoIP carriers. State and local agencies also are involved in enforcement and follow their own enforcement regimes.

EU and EU Member Sates' eCommunications Regulations

In April 2002, a European Union (EU) regulatory framework for electronic communications was adopted and went into effect in July 2003. In its introduction to the framework, the EU Information Society Directorate-General explains:

> The convergence of the telecommunications, media and information technology sectors demands a single regulatory framework that covers all transmission networks and services. The EU regulatory framework addresses all communications infrastructure in a coherent way, but does not cover the content of services delivered over and through those networks and services. There are five different directives: the Framework Directive[6] (2002/21/EC) and four specific directives, being the Authorisation Directive[7] (2002/20/EC),

the Access Directive[8] (2002/19/EC), the Universal Service Directive[9] (2002/22/EC) and the Privacy Directive[10] (2002/58/EC). In addition, the Competition Directive (2002/77/EC) applies.

The objectives set out in the EU regulatory framework are:

–To promote competition by fostering innovation, liberalising markets and simplifying market entry;

–To promote the single European market and;

–To promote the interest of citizens.

All Member States are required to implement the EU framework in their national law. The framework lays down the role of Member States and national regulatory authorities, the rights and obligations for market players, and the rights of users of electronic communications networks and services. In addition, Member States may take measures justified on the grounds of public health and public security as set out in the EC Treaty, for example by imposing requirements for legal interception or critical infrastructure protection, and such measures are not covered by the EU regulatory framework.

What many non-EU readers may not realize is the degree to which EU regulations (particularly privacy regulations) will force specific policy and practice outside of the EU. Its effects (particularly with respect to VoIP) will be briefly discussed in this final section. At the present, the EU IS Directorate-General is soliciting public comment on VoIP policy for input into a future regulatory regime for VoIP.

EU Regulatory Basics

Seven active EU Communications Directives with potential VoIP Implications that your organization may need to consider are listed here. Note that each of these directives is required to be expressed within the law for each EU nation, which may have additional regulatory measures of their own. In some cases (such as with the German Data Privacy Law) national laws are considerably more restrictive than the overall EU directive. Here is the list:

- **Directive 97/66/EC** Processing of personal data and protection of privacy (up to October 30, 2003)

- **Directive 2002/58/EC** Privacy and electronic communications (from October 31, 2003 onward)

- **Directive 2002/19/EC** Access and interconnection

- **Directive 2002/20/EC** Authorization of electronic communications networks and services (i.e., allocation of radio frequencies)

- **Directive 2002/21/EC** Common regulatory framework

- **Directive 2002/22/EC** Universal service and users' rights relating to electronic communications networks and services

- **Directive 2002/77/EC** On competition in the markets for electronic communications services

Although VoIP is directly or indirectly addressed in each of these, this section will focus on the only VoIP security concern addressed in the EU electronic communications regulations, namely the privacy and electronic communications directive.

Direct from the Regulations

Central to understanding EU privacy laws are the broad definitions used for personal data and its processing. We will focus on Directive 2002/58/EC since it establishes the minimum go-forward privacy framework for EU member states going forward with respect to electronic communications services. Note that despite specific references to ISDN and mobile networks in this directive, subsequent guidance from the EU IS Directorate-General has indicated that VoIP services will be expected to comply with this directive as well. Here is the relevant text within the directive:

Article 3 - Services concerned

1. This Directive shall apply to the processing of personal data in connection with the provision of publicly available telecommunications services in public telecommunications networks in the Community, in particular via the Integrated Services Digital Network (ISDN) and public digital mobile networks.

2. Articles 8 (www.bild.net/dataprEU1.htm#HD_NM_8), 9 (www.bild.net/dataprEU1.htm#HD_NM_9) and 10 (www.bild.net/dataprEU1.htm#HD_NM_10) shall apply to sub-

scriber lines connected to digital exchanges and, where technically possible and if it does not require a disproportionate economic effort, to subscriber lines connected to analogue exchanges.

3. Cases where it would be technically impossible or require a disproportionate investment to fulfill the requirements of Articles 8 (www.bild.net/dataprEU1.htm#HD_NM_8), 9 (www.bild.net/dataprEU1.htm#HD_NM_9) and 10 (www.bild.net/dataprEU1.htm#HD_NM_10) shall be notified to the Commission by the Member States.

Article 4 - Security

1. The provider of a publicly available telecommunications service must take appropriate technical and organizational measures to safeguard security of its services, if necessary in conjunction with the provider of the public telecommunications network with respect to network security. Having regard to the state of the art and the cost of their implementation, these measures shall ensure a level of security appropriate to the risk presented.

2. In case of a particular risk of a breach of the security of the network, the provider of a publicly available telecommunications service must inform the subscribers concerning such risk and any possible remedies, including the costs involved.

Article 5 - Confidentiality of the communications

Member States shall ensure via national regulations the confidentiality of communications by means of public telecommunications network and publicly available telecommunications services. In particular, they shall prohibit listening, tapping, storage or other kinds of interception or surveillance of communications, by others than users, without the consent of the users concerned, except when legally authorized.

Article 8 - Presentation and restriction of calling and connected line identification

1. Where presentation of calling-line identification is offered, the calling user must have the possibility via a simple means, free of

charge, to eliminate the presentation of the calling-line identification on a per-call basis. The calling subscriber must have this possibility on a per-line basis.

2. Where presentation of calling-line identification is offered, the called subscriber must have the possibility via a simple means, free of charge for reasonable use of this function, to prevent the presentation of the calling line identification of incoming calls.

3. Where presentation of calling line identification is offered and where the calling line identification is presented prior to the call being established, the called subscriber must have the possibility via a simple means to reject incoming calls where the presentation of the calling line identification has been eliminated by the calling user or subscriber.

4. Where presentation of connected line identification is offered, the called subscriber must have the possibility via a simple means, free of charge, to eliminate the presentation of the connected line identification to the calling user.

5. The provisions set out in paragraph 1 shall also apply with regard to calls to third countries originating in the Community; the provisions set out in paragraphs 2, 3 and 4 shall also apply to incoming calls originating in third countries.

6. Member States shall ensure that where presentation of calling and/or connected line identification is offered, the providers of publicly available telecommunications services inform the public thereof and of the possibilities set out in paragraphs 1, 2, 3 and 4.

Article 9 - Exceptions

Member States shall ensure that the provider of a public telecommunications network and/or publicly available telecommunications service may override the elimination of presentation of the calling line identification:

(a) on a temporary basis, upon application of a subscriber requesting the tracing of malicious or nuisance calls; in this case, in accordance with national law, the data containing the identification of the calling subscriber will be stored and be made available by the provider of a public telecommunications network and/or publicly available telecommunications service;

(b) on a per-line basis for organizations dealing with emergency calls and recognized as such by a Member State, including law enforcement agencies, ambulance services and fire brigades, for the purpose of answering such calls.

Article 10 - Automatic call forwarding

Member States shall ensure that any subscriber is provided, free of charge and via a simple means, with the possibility to stop automatic call forwarding by a third party to the subscriber's terminal.

Article 11 - Directories of subscribers

1. Personal data contained in printed or electronic directories of subscribers available to the public or obtainable through directory enquiry services should be limited to what is necessary to identify a particular subscriber, unless the subscriber has given his unambiguous consent to the publication of additional personal data. The subscriber shall be entitled, free of charge, to be omitted from a printed or electronic directory at his or her request, to indicate that his or her personal data may not be used for the purpose of direct marketing, to have his or her address omitted in part and not to have a reference revealing his or her sex, where this is applicable linguistically.

2. Member States may allow operators to require a payment from subscribers wishing to ensure that their particulars are not entered in a directory, provided that the sum involved is reasonable and does not act as a disincentive to the exercise of this right.

3. Member States may limit the application of this Article to subscribers who are natural persons.

Article 12 - Unsolicited calls

1. The use of automated calling systems without human intervention (automatic calling machine) or facsimile machines (fax) for the

purposes of direct marketing may only be allowed in respect of subscribers who have given their prior consent.

2. Member States shall take appropriate measures to ensure that, free of charge, unsolicited calls for purposes of direct marketing, by means other than those referred to in paragraph 1, are not allowed either without the consent of the subscribers concerned or in respect of subscribers who do not wish to receive these calls, the choice between these options to be determined by national legislation.

3. Member States may limit the application of paragraphs 1 and 2 to subscribers who are natural persons.

What an EU Data Privacy Consultant Will Tell You

In addition to the EU eCommunications framework, you may need to worry about data contained in corporate directories. Any collection, use, disclosure, or other processing about an individual that resides within the EU requires careful handling that goes far beyond that prescribed by the privacy provisions contained in U.S. law for GLBA or HIPAA with their associated regulations. This can create legal issues within the EU regardless of whether the individuals are employees, consumers, suppliers, or other legal entities. Cross-border data transfer restrictions may prohibit the transfer of such data to a jurisdiction without an equivalent data protection regime. For export to the United States, the FTC provides a Safe Harbor program that can meet this test, but there are significant tradeoffs to taking this route so you should consult with an EU data privacy expert before committing to this route. In many respects, addressing EU data privacy rules is more art than science.

Tools & Traps…

Core EU-Compliance Issues for IP Communications Systems

EU member countries do have important differences in data privacy rules, so be sure to consult appropriate experts for the countries in which you operate. Rules for VoIP as an eCommunication service may vary somewhat from the data-centric rules used for data applications. Unless your organization is a vendor or carrier, most other EU compliance issues will be addressed by purchasing equipment and services approved for sale within the EU.

EU Compliance and Enforcement

Within the EU and member states, compliance and enforcement happens at several levels. Some member states, such as Germany, have enforcement of privacy and electronic communication laws at a more local level as well as on a national basis. Decisions at the national level can be appealed at the EU level, and critical precedents are often set at this level.

No Certification

In general, the EU and member countries do not have certification processes for the privacy and eCommunications regulation.

Enforcement Process and Penalties

Data privacy fines can be stiff within the EU and its member states, though they do vary considerably by jurisdiction.

Summary

Unfortunately, the trend is clearly heading toward *more* regulation, not less. By the time you read this, another VoIP-affecting regulation will have been enacted in some part of the world. In the United States, regulations like California's SB 1386 (which forces security breach notifications or end-to-end encryption of Social Security and credit card numbers and could impact you if you operate a VoIP call center) are being considered at the U.S. federal level and by other countries around the world.

Solutions Fast Track

SOX: Sarbanes-Oxley Act

☑ Focus on any internal financial controls that may exist within your VoIP system.

☑ Consider applicability of cross-IT security standards to your VoIP system.

GLBA: Gramm-Leach-Bliley Act

☑ Make sure that your VoIP system is included in risk management processes for GLBA compliance plans.

☑ Consider FDIC VoIP recommendations when evaluating GLBA compliance.

☑ Document VoIP system compliance as you would any other part of the data infrastructure.

HIPAA: Health Insurance Portability and Accountability Act

☑ Pay special attention to VoIP components or adjuncts that record calls or conversations.

☑ Don't forget Interactive Voice Response (IVR) systems when evaluating HIPAA impact to VoIP systems.

☑ Ensure you have complete documentation per HIPAA requirements.

CALEA: Communications Assistance for Law Enforcement Act

☑ Don't assume you're not considered a carrier (or substantial replacement) for CALEA purposes—if you provide communication services to the public in any form the new rules may apply to you too.

☑ Find an appropriate technical standard and drive your software or equipment vendor toward compliance.

☑ Be sure to file all necessary paperwork with the FCC.

E911: Enhanced 911 and Related Regulations

☑ Be sure to investigate and comply with local regulations that mandate ALI support, even if you're not a carrier.

☑ If you are a VoIP carrier, you must provide E911 services or risk substantial penalties or fines.

EU and EU Member States' eCommunications Regulations

☑ Remember that VoIP services are treated equally with other communications services in the eCommunications regulatory framework.

☑ Pay close heed to data privacy regulations and any export of private data.

☑ Remember to investigate privacy and other regulatory policies at the national level as well.

Frequently Asked Questions

The following Frequently Asked Questions, answered by the authors of this book, are designed to both measure your understanding of the concepts presented in this chapter and to assist you with real-life implementation of these concepts. To have your questions about this chapter answered by the author, browse to **www.syngress.com/solutions** and click on the **"Ask the Author"** form.

Q: Where can I go for more information about SOX compliance and SOX-related resources?

A: The Sarbanes-Oxley Compliance Journal has a good summary of their articles at at www.s-ox.com/resources/.
The Securities and Exchange Commision has a SOX page at www.sec.gov/spotlight/sarbanes-oxley.htm.
The Public Company Accounting Oversight Board operates www.pcaobus.org with audit-related information.

Q: How do information security frameworks like ISO 17799, COSO, and CoBIT relate to SOX?

A: The Cyber Security Industy Alliance has published an excellent report on this topic, "IT Security and Sarbanes-Oxley Compliance: Conference Summary of Findings and Conclusions," which can be found online at www.csialliance.org/resources/pdfs/CSIA_PostSox_Summit_Report.pdf.

Q: Where can I go to learn more details about HIPAA?

A: The HHS/OCR Web site is excellent. Go to www.hhs.gov/ocr/hipaa/. Another excellent site with a large FAQ is the CMS site at http://cms.hhs.gov/HIPAAGenInfo/ (click on the "Questions" link on the top menu bar to get there).

Q: Where can I go to learn more details about CALEA?

A: 1. The FBI CALEA Implementation Unit runs a very well designed, comprehensive Web site—www.AskCALEA.com—aimed at telecommunications carriers and law enforcement personnel.
2. The FCC also runs an equally comprehensive CALEA site focusing on FCC regulations at www.fcc.gov/calea/ (and within the IATD sub-site at

www.fcc.gov/wcb/iatd/calea.html—note that while they look similar, there are differences between the two).

3. TIA standards and related CALEA information can be found at www.tiaonline.org/standards/CALEA_JEM.

4. For a privacy-advocate's point of view, try the Electronic Frontier Foundation's CALEA pages at www.eff.org/Privacy/Surveillance/CALEA/ or the Electronic Privacy Information Center (EPIC) at www.epic.org/privacy/wiretap/.

Q: If my organization successfully files a Section 109 (or 107) petition with the FCC to avoid implementing CALEA requirements within our current VoIP systems, will that make us exempt from CALEA?

A: The FCC has stated that "a carrier's obligation to comply with all CALEA requirements is only deferred by FCC grant of a section 109 (or section 107) petition. No qualifying carrier is exempt from CALEA." Any change in equipment or services could require full CALEA compliance in the future.

Q: What does CALEA require from the carrier if encryption is used?

A: If a carrier possesses the keying material, it must decrypt the communications when a lawful interception order is presented, but if the encryption is not provided by the carrier then it has no responsibility for decryption of the target communications.

Q: Where can I find more help on E911 and VoIP?

A: Start with www.fcc.gov/911/ for the basics. The National Emergency Number Association (NENA) is involved with E911 and VoIP at several levels, including the creation of advanced standards for PSAP and VoIP—see www.nena.org for details. Other helpful information about VoIP and E911 can be found at www.voip911.gov.

Q: Where can I go for more details about EU and EU member countries' electronic communications and data privacy regulations?

A: A good place to start is http://europa.eu.int/information_society/policy.

Chapter 16

The IP Multimedia Subsystem: True Converged Communications

Solutions in this chapter:

- IMS Architecture
- Communication Flow in IMS
- IMS Security Architecture
- IMS Security Issues

☑ Summary
☑ Solutions Fast Track
☑ Frequently Asked Questions

Introduction

The IP Multimedia Subsystem (IMS) is a next-generation multimedia communication framework that encompasses mobile, fixed, packet-switching, and traditional circuit-switching communication systems. It has been proposed by the Third Generation Partnership Project (3GPP) and uses the Voice over Internet Protocol (VoIP) framework, especially the Session Initiation Protocol (SIP) standard. The 3GPP is a standards organization driven by wireless carriers and equipment manufacturers and aims at producing globally applicable specification and reports for Third Generation (3G) Mobile Systems based upon GSM (Global System for Mobile Communication). The 3GPP also is working with the Internet Engineering Task Force (IETF) on SIP-related standards. The goal of the IMS is to provide a wide spectrum of services with ease and consistency. These services include videoconferencing, Push-to-Talk (PTT), Text-to-Speech (TTS), instant messaging (IM), content sharing, and multipart gaming. To achieve this goal, IMS uses an open standard IP protocol and extension of SIP.[1]

SIP is standardized by the IETF as multimedia signaling protocol. Its architecture is highlighted by a User Agent (UA), which is a terminal, and a set of servers, including proxy server, registration server, redirection server, and so on. From its inception, SIP has been gaining momentum due to its open architecture and extensibility to mobile device and multimedia communication. Because SIP signaling protocol is based on Hypertext Transfer Protocol (HTTP) and ASCII-based encoding, it is easy to understand. SIP also sits side by side with a standard media protocol named Real-time Transport Protocol (RTP), also standardized by the IETF. RTP is a vehicle with which any kind of multimedia can be transmitted as long as the media is digitized with a proper codec. For instance, one of the popular voice codecs in VoIP systems is G.711. This codec samples voice streams at 8,000 times/sec, also digitizing and transmitting them at 64K bit/sec. With a G.711 codec, each packet has a 160-byte payload (214 packet size with header information), and each VoIP phone sends 50 packets in one second. If there is a need for compression, a VoIP phone can transmit the digital voice with a compressed format (for instance 8K in G.729 format), thereby saving bandwidth. Video can be easily transmitted with SIP and RTP protocols if it is digitized with an appropriate format such as H264 or any of the MPEG series formats such as MPEG1, MPEG2, MPEG4, or H.264.

IMS architecture extends to the SIP and 3GPP architecture and adds several components suitable for mobile communication. It was driven originally by the 3GPP to boost the packet-switched services and attract more users to the packet-switched domain. To do so, it adds three important features in the GSM-based packet-switched network that already offers Internet services such as surfing the Web and accessing e-mail:

1. It requires QoS (Quality of Service) in a session, so that the quality of service can be met. Existing packet-switched network does not guarantee the quality of service and users may have a fluctuation of service depending on the situation.

2. It adds a flexible charging mechanism so that operators are able to charge appropriately for multimedia services. For example, operators can charge the video conferencing based upon the time used or any other reasonable measure rather than the bandwidth that the service consumes, which may end up being unacceptable to a customer.

3. It provides integrated services to users and offers ample room for third parties to provide services. Operators don't need to stick to the services that the large equipment vendors offer, but have flexibility to offer a variety of services developed by third parties.

The architecture of IMS extends the SIP and 3GPP architecture and adds several components that are suitable for mobile communication. The following sections discuss IMS architecture and how it can be used in the available forms of mobile communications.

IMS Architecture

IMS originally was designed for mobile carrier networks, but with the addition of Telecoms & Internet converged Services & Protocols for Advanced Networks (TISPAN) in release 7, fixed carrier networks are also included. The goal is to enable carrier-grade services that let people use only one phone with one number, address book, and voicemail bank, taking advantage of cheap, high-speed connectivity in their fixed-line home or office setting, while accommodating mobility in the wide-area mobile phone network. IMS goals also include a seamless handover of calls between fixed-line and mobile networks. Service providers can service users irrespective of their location, access technology, or type of phone. Internetworking with existing phone systems is also allowed.

Access Network

The user can connect to an IMS network using various methods, all of which use standard Internet Protocol (IP). IMS terminals can register directly into an IMS network when they roam in another network or country (the visited network). An IMS terminal can be a mobile phone or a fixed IP device attached to a Universal Integrated Circuit Card (UICC) with a user profile. The UICC is a removable smart card that contains a small data store for subscription information, authentication keys, a phonebook, and messages. These devices can use IPv6 (also IPv4 in Early IMS) and run SIP User Agents. Fixed access, mobile access, and wireless access are all supported.

Core Network

The core network provides call control and handles mobility. It also takes care of high-level security, such as location updating and authentication. Core network functions are described in the next section.

User Database

The Home Subscriber Service (HSS) is the central user database supporting IMS network entities that actually are handling the calls/sessions. It contains the user profiles, performs authentication and authorization of the user, and can provide information about the user's physical location. A network can have more than one HSS when there are too many subscribers to be handled by a single HSS. In this case, IMS can have a Subscriber Location Function, which is a simple database that maps user addresses to the appropriate HSS.

Call/Session Control

Several types of SIP servers (proxies) collectively known as the Call/Session Control Function (CSCF), are employed to process SIP signaling packets in the IMS. A Proxy-CSCF is the first point-of-contact SIP server (in the signaling plane) when the UA (User Agent) tries to get into the system. It can be placed either in the visited network (in full IMS networks) or in the home network (when the visited network is not yet IMS compliant). A Proxy-CSCF is assigned to an IMS terminal during registration, and does not change for the duration of the registration. It sits in the path of all signaling messages, and can inspect every message that it authenticates and establishes an Internet Protocol Security (IPSec) security association with the IMS terminal. This prevents spoofing and replay attacks and protects the privacy of the user. Other nodes trust the P-CSCF, and do not have to authenticate the user again. In SIP point of view, P-CSCF is taking the role of inbound/outbound proxy server.

An Interrogating-CSCF (I-CSCF) is a SIP proxy located at the edge of an administrative domain. Its IP address is published in the DNS of the domain, so that remote servers (e.g., a P-CSCF in a visited domain, or an S-CSCF in a foreign domain) can find it, and can use it as an entry point for all SIP packets to the domain. The I-CSCF queries the HSS using the DIAMETER Cx and Dx interfaces to retrieve the user location, and then routes the SIP request to its assigned Serving-CSCF (S-CSCF). An S-CSCF is a SIP server, but performs session control as well. It is located in the home network. The S-CSCF uses DIAMETER Cx and Dx interfaces to the HSS to download and upload user profiles. It processes SIP registrations, which allows it to bind the user location (e.g., the IP address of the terminal) and the SIP address. See Figure 16.1 for a diagram showing the relationships between these IMS call control functions.

Application Servers

An Application Server (AS) is a SIP component that offers value-added services like instant messaging and that resides either in the user's home network or in a third-party location. The third party could be a network or simply a stand-alone AS.

Application servers host and execute services, and interface with the S-CSCF using SIP. This allows third-party providers easy integration and deployment of their value-added services to the IMS infrastructure. Depending on the actual service, the AS can operate in SIP proxy mode, SIP UA mode, or SIP Back-to-Back User Agent (B2BUA) mode. An AS can be located in the home network or in an external third-party network. If it is in the home network, an AS can query the HSS with the DIAMETER Sh interface (for SIP-AS and Open Service Access–Service Capability Server (OSA-SCS) or the Match Protocol (MAP) interface (for IP Multimedia–Service Switching Function (IM-SSF)). DIAMETER is an extensible ASCII-based messaging protocol to enable Authorization, Authentication, and Accounting (AAA) function in IP and multimedia network. It improves the RADIUS protocol in the aspect of increased size of attributed data, more reliable transport, improved flow control, elimination of packet loss and enhanced session control. IMS uses DIAMETER protocol in several places for AAA using different interfaces.

Figure 16.1 Simplified Architecture

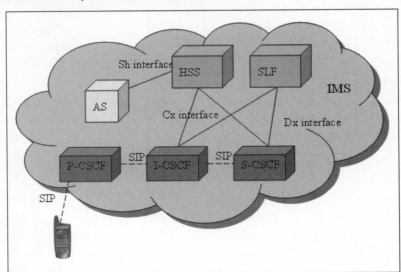

As shown in Figure 16.1, Cx interface connects an I-CSCF (or S-CSCF) and HSS. Likewise the Dx interface specifies an interaction between the I-CSCF (or S-CSCF) and SLF. The I-CSCF or S-CSCF may use the Cx or Dx interface for the following reasons:

1. To assign an S-CSCF to a user.

2. To download the authentication vector of the user, which is stored in the HSS.

3. To authorize the user to roam in a visited network.

On the other hand, Sh is defined between an AS and the HSS. It provides a data storage and retrieval type of functionality such as allowing an Application Server to download data from the HSS.

Media Servers

A Media Resource Function (MRF) provides a media source in the home network. It is used for playing announcements (audio/video), multimedia conferencing (e.g., mixing of audio streams), TTS conversion, speech recognition, and real-time transcoding of multimedia data (i.e., conversion between different codecs).

Breakout Gateway

A Breakout Gateway Control Function (BGCF) is a SIP server that includes routing functionality based on telephone numbers. It is used only when calling from the IMS to a phone in a circuit-switched network, such as the Public Switched Telephone Network (PSTN) or the Public Land Mobile Network (PLMN).

Application Level Gateway

An IMS Application Level Gateway (ALG) provides application-specific functions at the SIP/ Session Description Protocol (SDP) protocol layer to perform interconnection between two operator domains. It enables communication between IPv6 and IPv4 SIP applications.

Communication Flow in IMS

IMS supports the mobility of the UA, representing the user device or terminal. Hence, the UA can be either in the Home network or in the Visited network, as shown in Figure 16.2. Suppose that a UA tries to register his or her device from the visited network. Note that Serving General Packet Radio Service (GPRS) Support Node (SGSN) and Gateway GPRS Support Node (GGSN) are functional nodes for packet switching data services across the fixed and radio network. GPRS is defined by the 3GPP and is employed to connect mobile cellular users to the Public Data Network (PDN). Within the GSM network GPRS shares the network databases, radio access network, and employee functions known as the Packet Control Unit (PCU), SGSN, and GGSN.

First, the UA generates a SIP REGISTER message, which goes through the GGSN and SGSN. It reaches a P-CSCF near the UA. The P-CSCF plays the role of Proxy Server in SIP and relays the request to another I-CSCF in the Home Network. The I-CSCF looks up the HSS and decides if the user is authenticated or not based on the authentication information that the Register message carries.

When a UA makes a call to the destination user, the message goes through the same path except that I-CSCF figures out the location of the user, referring to the HSS, and sends the message to the S-CSCF that covers the destination user. Because the HSS has the up-to-date user profile and user location, the message can route to the correct user location no matter whether or not roaming takes place.

Figure 16.2 Typical Communication Flow

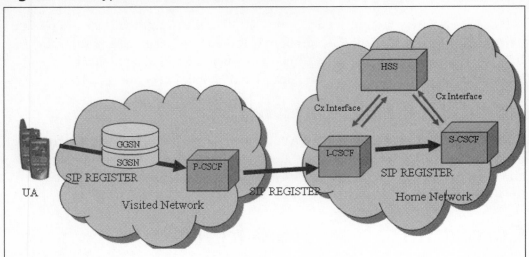

Once the user is registered, a system sends the reregister message periodically. Reregistration, however, is not mandatory. But, when a user moves to another location, an appropriate reregister SIP message has to be sent to the HSS, so that it always keeps the up-to-date location information.

When a UA makes a call, it sends an INVITE message to the P-CSCF and passes through the same initial path as the REGISTER message does. The only difference is that I-CSCF looks up the HSS, finding the destination location, and relays the message to the S-CSCF near the destination UA. Once the destination UA accepts the INVITE message and goes through the three-way handshaking (INVITE/OK/ACK), both UAs start sending the media packets (mostly using RTP) through the media gateway. Note that the media path is not necessarily the same as the signaling path. The communication ends when either of the UAs sends the BYE message to the other party and tears down the media communication.

IMS Security Architecture

IMS has its own security architecture in addition to the general 3GPP security architecture named Network Domain Security.[4,5] Network Domain Security addresses security issues at the IP layer and recommends IPSec as the basic security mechanism among Security Gateways (SEGs). SEG is a security component that sits in each network domain and communicates with SEGs of the destination domain. As shown in Figure 16.3, the IMS-specific security covers the security issues between the IP Multimedia Services Identity Module (ISIM) and HSS (path 1), UA and P-CSCF (path 2); the Network Domain Security covers the other paths that are implementing IP protocol (paths 3, 4, 5). ISIM and UA collectively are called UE (User Equipment). Suppose that P-CSCF and S-CSCF are located in different networks, each of which implements its own security policy. In this case, all the traffic between P-CSCF and S-CSCF traverse two SEGs in such a way that packets are encrypted in a SEG and decrypted in the other end of SEG. The two SEGs have their own security binding (Key exchange and encryption/decryption algorithm), implementing IPSec.

Figure 16.3 IMS-Specific Security

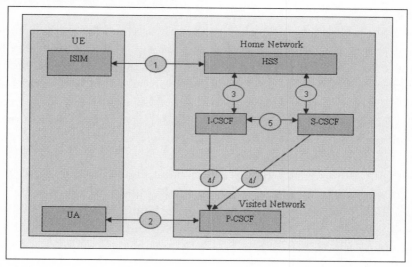

The Security mechanisms of paths 1 and 2 are specified in the security document as follows: [5]

1. Provides mutual authentication. The HSS delegates the performance of subscriber authentication to the S-CSCF. However the HSS is responsible for generating keys and challenges. The long-term key in the ISIM and the HSS is associated with the user private identity (IMPI). The subscriber will have one network internal IMPI and at least one external user public identity (IMPU).

2. Provides a secure link and a security association between the User Equipment (UE) and a P-CSCF for protection of the Gm reference point.

IMS security covers the initial secure authentication that occurs between the ISIM and the HSS in which user devices are authenticated through a secure link. Once the user device is authenticated and allowed to use IMS, the IMS security provides a secure communication mechanism through which all the information can be transmitted.

To summarize IMS security, all the UAs are authenticated before they are allowed to get into the system. The HSS is the central component for the security policy. The HSS gives commands for what kinds of security algorithm is used and provides correct authentication information for all the users. Each UA or ISIM, which is a term indicating the collection of IMS security data and functions on a Universal Integrated Circuit Card (UICC), has built-in authentication information in the UIUC.

IM-subscribers have their profile information stored in HSS in their home network. At registration, an S-CSCF is assigned to the subscriber by the I-CSCF. The subscriber profile will be downloaded to the S-CSCF over the Cx-reference point from the HSS (Cx-Pull). When a subscriber requests access to the Network, the assigned S-CSCF decides if the subscriber is allowed to continue with the request or not; that is, Home Control (Authorization of IM-services). These procedures are carried out with a security association, so that all the information can be transmitted encrypted, and therefore, not tampered with.

The authentication message flow is described in Figure 16.4.[5] If a user is permitted to get into the IMS service, at least an IMPU has to be registered in HSS in advance and the corresponding IMPI has to be authenticated. When a UE wants to be registered, it sends a SIP REGISTER message to the SIP registrar (in this case the corresponding S-CSCF).

Figure 16.4 Authentication Message Flow in IMS

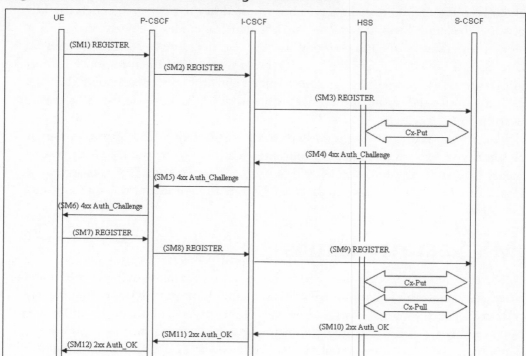

The SIP REGISTER is passed to I-CSCF and to the corresponding S-CSCF that refers to HSS, and retrieves all the authentication information of the user from HSS with the CS-Pull method. S-CSCF uses an Authentication Vector (AV) to conduct authentication and key agreement with the user, where the AV consists of five elements: a random number RAND, an expected response XRES, a Cipher Key (CK), an Integrity Key (IK), and an authentication token AUTN. If S-CSCF has no valid AV, S-SCSF sends an AV request to HSS together with the number of AVs (for instance, n) wanted.

Upon receipt of the AV request from S-CSCF, HSS sends an ordered array of n AVs. Once S-CSCF receives them, it uses them on a first-in/first-out basis and sends them for authentication challenge to users. The S-CSCF sends a SIP 4xx Auth_Challenge, that is, an authentication challenge to the UE including the challenge RAND, the authentication token AUTN in SM4. The challenge also includes the IK and the CK for the P-CSCF. The S-CSCF also stores the RAND sent to the UE for use in case a synchronization failure should occur.

When the P-CSCF receives SM5 it stores the key(s) and forwards the rest of the message to the UE, so that the key is not revealed in the clear text. When the UE gets the challenge, SM6, it takes the AUTN, which includes the MAC and a sequence number SQN and checks if the MAC is the same as XMAC and the SQN is correct. If both checks are successful, UE computes the authentication information, response RES using the random number, and authentication token. Then the UE puts it into the Authorization header and sends it back to the P-CSCF that forwards it to the S-CSCF.

When S-CSCF receives the SM9, it retrieves the active XRES for that user and checks the validity of the authentication information sent by the UE. If the user is successfully authenticated, the S-CSCF sends a SIP 2xxx Auth_OK message to I-CSCF that forwards the same message to the UE and completes the authentication procedure.

IMS Security Issues

IMS was from its inception designed to be secure to eliminate many of the vulnerability issues that plague existing packet-based communication systems. The security of IMS has been especially fortified with the built-in security functions of IPv6. For instance, the use of IPSec would eliminate the vulnerabilities such as eveasdropping, tampering, and IPSpoofing. However, it is expected to take a substantial amount of time to fully migrate from the existing IPv4-based network to IPv6. Hence 3GPP came up with a compromise solution called early IMS. Early IMS uses IPv4 and it is expected that this model will be a popular implementation in the early stages of IMS. Some early IMS may not be fully compliant with the security features defined in TS 33.203 because of the potential lack of support ISIM interface and inability to support the IPSec on some UE platforms. [5] Because IMS implementation is based on SIP, it also carries as many security vulnerabilities as SIP. With the full IMS implementation based on IPv6 and when the security is put in place, it is inevitable that IMS will have Denial of Service (DoS) attacks.

SIP Security Vulnerabilities

First let's review some of the security vulnerabilities of SIP, so that we can better understand the security issues faced by early IMS. SIP was designed to make the communication system standard and open to any other system compliant with SIP standards. SIP has many security vulnerabilities and is susceptible to being breached by hackers. The following list presents several well known SIP vulnerabilities.

Registration Hijacking

SIP has a registration hijacking vulnerability that is similar to man-in-the-middle attacks. An attacker sniffs a REGISTER message from a legitimate user and modifies it with its own address as the contact address. Getting this fake message, the SIP registrar updates the contact address belonging to the legitimate address with the fake address. When incoming calls are received for the legitimate users, the proxy server refers to the registrar and redirects all the incoming calls to the fake address, which makes the man-in-the-middle attack successful.

IP Spoofing/Call Fraud

An attacker impersonates another legitimate user with spoofed ID and sends an INVITE or REGISTER message. In IPv4, there is no way to block IP spoofing when SIP messages are sent in clear text and an attacker is able to use an arbitrary IP address easily. Hence, when an arbitrary IP address is sent to the registrar with the legitimate user account, the incoming calls that follow are transferred to the wrong address and are never sent to the correct user. When an INVITE message is sent to a user with an arbitrary destination IP address, the call is never sent through or connected to the hacker's terminal. If a hacker can use a legitimate IP address and make a call with that IP, he or she can execute call fraud and make free calls.

Weakness of Digest Authentication

SIP recommends the use of the HTTP digest authentication that is based on the MD5 digest algorithm. However, the MD5 digest algorithm is weak and cannot be used in an authentication system requiring high security. At the same time, SIP digest authentication algorithm does not include all header fields, which can be forged as well.

INVITE Flooding

A hacker keeps sending INVITE messages with a fake address and paralyzes the user terminal or SIP proxy server. This attack is quite similar to SYN Flood attacks in TCP connections.

BYE Denial of Service

A SIP signaling packet by default is sent in clear text and can be tampered with. If a hacker sniffs legitimate INVITE messages, he can counterfeit a legitimate BYE message and can send it to one of the communicating parties, resulting in tear-down of the ongoing conversation.

RTP Flooding

RTP Flooding is related to media transmission. Most media transmissions are based on RTP once the communication is set up with SIP signaling.[7] With RTP Flooding, a hacker makes fake RTP packets and bombards either of the ends with the fake RTP packets, resulting in quality degradation or terminal reboot.

Spam over Internet Telephony (SPIT)

A SPIT threat sends unsolicited calls to legitimate users that contain mostly prerecorded messages and that annoy people or congest a voicemail system to overflowing.[8]

Early IMS Security Issues

Early IMS refers to IMS systems that are not compliant with full IMS security. One of the key characteristics of early IMS is that it does not use the security binding between UE and P-CSCF, and thus it provides neither the integrity nor the message confidentiality that should be afforded to messages passed among UE, HSS, and P-CSCF. Therefore, IPSec is not used. Yet, the lower level Network Domain Security might provide security among lower level components such as SEGs.

Early IMS security addresses the threat of IP spoofing and presents a way to avoid this threat if full IMS security is not in place.[6] As exists in SIP vulnerability, IP spoofing enables hackers to use an IMS account or IP address freely. To prevent IP spoofing, early IMS security recommends the use of a RADIUS server in connection with HSS to check the IP address of the IMPU. Early IMS security features combined with the use of a RADIUS server and HSS restricts use to only one IMPU at a time and registers it with the legitimate IP address. Hence, multiple IMPUs cannot be used at the same time for individual users. Because of this restriction, users are not allowed the use of multiple devices such as mobile phones, VoIP phones, and Personal Digital Assistant (PDA)s. Once the IMPU is registered with the legitimate IP address, the hacker is not able to spoof his IP address with a legitimate user account, since it does not match in the RADIUS server.

However, there are still several security vulnerabilities left in early IMS security. Because early IMS does not use passwords or secure keys, it might be easy for the hacker to sniff the legitimate REGISTER message and counterfeit it. Once the legitimate user deregisters from the HSS, the hacker is able to reregister with his or her own IP address bound to the legitimate user account and get into the system. When the hacker gets into the system with his or her own IP address, the legitimate user is no longer able to get into the system. This vulnerability is just one aspect of early IMS security issues. There are still DoS attacks and SPIT issues that leave early IMS systems unprotected.

One thing to note is that early IMS security does not adopt HTTP digest authentication as in SIP, which requires a user account with its password and then encrypts them with a digest algorithm.[1] One of the main reasons for this is that HTTP digest can allow multiple users to get into the system at the same time if they share the same account and password. This makes appropriate billing difficult and thus, can have an impact on the service provider's revenue.

Full IMS Security Issues

Full IMS security includes the security architecture that implements IPv6 and IPSec among IMS components. All user terminals (collectively called UE) have security keys and can encrypt messages as well as include digital signatures for secure authentication. These characteristics protect from eavesdropping, tampering with messages, and IP spoofing. Full IMS security also is designed to block potential replay attacks since the encryption is based on the random numbers generated by HSS that are valid for a certain period of time.

Full IMS security tends to eliminate many of the vulnerabilities posed by SIP. Yet, full IMS contains a certain degree of DoS vulnerabilities and SPIT problems. An attacker can capture the encrypted packets and figure out the IP addresses of P-CSCF or S-CSCF if transport mode is used with IPSec. Attackers can also bombard servers with massive DoS attacks with SYN Flooding or other kinds of attacks. If the network has a firewall and implements appropriate security policies such as rate limiting, the hacker at least might be able to use up all the network bandwidth and disrupt IMS services. Full IMS security is also vulnerable to SPIT attacks. A legitimate UE is able to get into the system and send SPIT attacks to target users easily. It can also compromise many servers and mastermind distributed DoS SPIT attacks using the compromised servers. It may be quite difficult to detect DoS SPIT attacks since each compromised server acts like normal users, occasionally sending stealth calls. Therefore, a proper protection mechanism is still to be designed.

Summary

IMS promises a nice integration of IP and cellular networks. It allows both users and operators to take advantage of benefits of both sides. A mobile phone user gets comprehensive services available in both cellular network and Internet. At the same time, the embedment of QoS (Quality of Service) in the communication session improves the preservation of service quality. It prevents the users from suffering the quality degradation. Operators can also benefit from it since they have flexible control over charging mechanism. They can select the appropriate charging method based upon the bandwidth or duration of time, so that they have higher revenue. Also the operator can select third-party services on top of the given services freely, which allows the operator to provide a variety of service to users.

IMS enables many feature sets of convergence services but opens the IP network to security vulnerabilities. IMS addresses some security issues like unauthorized use, privacy, and denial of services. A built-in IPSec makes it hard to do packet forgery, eavesdropping, and IP spoofing and session hijacking. Nevertheless, there is still room for the hackers to disrupt the service by layer 2 and 3 DoS attacks and Voice Spam attacks. Additional security mechanisms like spam blockers and IPS are needed to prevent these attacks.

References

1. *SIP: Session Initiation Protocol*, IETF RFC 3261, www.ietf.org/rfc/rfc3261.txt, June 2002.
2. ETSI TS 123 002 V6.10.0, Digital cellular telecommunications system (Phase 2+); Universal Mobile Telecommunications System (UMTS); Network architecture, December 2005.
3. Peter Howard, *Sipping IETF51 3GPP Security and Authentication*, September 2001, www3.ietf.org/proceedings/01aug/slides/sipping-7/.
4. *ETSI TS 133 210 V7.0*, Digital cellular telecommunications system (Phase 2+); Universal Mobile Telecommunications System (UMTS); 3G security; Network Domain Security (NDS); IP network layer security (3GPP TS 33.210 version 7.0.0 Release 7), December 2005.
5. *ETSI, ETSI TS 133 203 V7.0.0*, Digital cellular telecommunications system (Phase 2+); Universal Mobile Telecommunications System (UMTS);3G security; Access security for IP-based services, 3GPP, December 2005.
6. *ETSI TR 133 978 V6.3.0*, Universal Mobile Telecommunications System (UMTS); Security aspects of early IP Multimedia Subsystem (IMS) (3GPP TR 33.978 version 6.3.0 Release 6), December 2005.

7. *RTP: A Transport Protocol for Real Time Application*, IETF RFC 3550, July 2003, www.ietf.org/rfc/rfc3550.txt.

8. Dongwook Shin and Choon Shim, *Voice Spam Control with Gray Leveling, 2nd VoIP security Workshop*, June 2006, Washington D.C.

Solutions Fast Track

IMS Architecture

☑ In IMS architecture, a network consists of an access network and a core network. An access network can be any network that connects user terminals to the core network such as WLAN (wireless LAN) or cable network.

☑ The core network is the main part of the IMS architecture, which consists of an HSS (Home Subscriber Server), one or more SIP servers as CSCF (Call/Session Control Functions), and several AS (Application Servers).

☑ The HSS is the main database that has user profiles including user authentication and location information. The CSCF has three categories: P-CSCF (Proxy –CSCF), I-CSCF (Interrogating-CSCF), and S-CSCF (Serving-CSCF).

☑ An Application Server (AS) is a SIP component that offers value-added services like instant messaging and that resides either in the user's home network or in a third-party location.

Communication Flow in IMS

☑ When a user terminal sends a SIP message (note that IMS uses SIP as its communication method), the message go through the access network and reaches the P-SCCF, the first point of contact in IMS network.

☑ P-CSCF relays the message to I-CSCF, a SIP proxy located at the edge of an administrative domain.

☑ If the message is SIP-REGISTER, the I-CSCF looks up the HSS and decides if the user is authenticated or not based on the authentication information that the REGISTER message carries.

☑ If the message is SIP-INVITE, I-CSCF retrieves an S-CSCF that nears the destination user from HSS and relays the message to the S-CSCF that finally sends the message to the user terminal.

IMS Security Architecture

☑ IMS security architecture covers the mutual authentication between a user terminal and the HSS and the secure link between a user terminal and its Proxy-CSCF.

☑ IMS security supports IPSec and assumes that the user terminal has its own security key.

☑ The HSS has user authentication information and authenticates the user based upon the information that the user sends through a secure link.

IMS Security Issues

☑ The communication of IMS is based upon SIP signaling that has several security vulnerabilities.

☑ The full IMS security supports IPSec and mutual authentication between the user terminal and HSS, which eliminates most security vulnerabilities including eavesdropping, tampering, session hijacking, and identity theft.

☑ Early IMS security does not support IPSec and has vulnerabilities, including eavesdropping and identity theft. Moreover, both full IMS and early IMS are vulnerable to DoS (Denial of Service) and SPIT (Spam over Internet Telephony) attack.

Frequently Asked Questions

The following Frequently Asked Questions, answered by the authors of this book, are designed to both measure your understanding of the concepts presented in this chapter and to assist you with real-life implementation of these concepts. To have your questions about this chapter answered by the author, browse to **www.syngress.com/solutions** and click on the **"Ask the Author"** form.

Q: What is the VoIP signaling protocol used in IMS?

A: Session Initiation Protocol (SIP). SIP is standarized by IETF and widely used in VoIP.

Q: Is IPv6 part of the IMS standard?

A: Yes, it recommends IPv6. However, it allows early IMS to use IPv4 as an alternative.

Q: What are typical SIP methods used for DoS attacks?

A: There are several SIP methods, but INVITE and REGISTER are used most commonly for DoS attack because these commands request the most resource allocation.

Q: Is the SPIT (Spam over Internet Telephony) issue addressed in IMS?

A: No, SPIT is inherted from VoIP.

Q: What information is kept in Home Subscriber Server?

A: User authentication and location information.

Chapter 17

Recommendations

Solutions in this chapter:

- **Reuse Existing Security Infrastructure Wisely**
- **Confirm User Identity**
- **Active Security Monitoring**
- **Logically Segregate VoIP from Data Traffic**

☑ **Summary**

☑ **Solutions Fast Track**

☑ **Frequently Asked Questions**

Introduction

As organizations have migrated most of their key information and business resources to the Internet, network administrators have been charged with the task of connecting mutually distrustful organizations and people without the benefits of centralized management. This is one factor that has led to exposure of sensitive corporate information. There are many examples of theft of credit card databases, customer lists, and other intellectual property in the media today. Remote workers typically access their entire corporate network from the comfort of their home offices. Unfortunately, however, attackers do, too.

The amount of traffic posted to vulnerability mailing lists such as Bugtraq has exploded over the past several years. The amount of information on network vulnerabilities is so pervasive that companies such as SecurityFocus (Symantec) and Ernst & Young commercially sell subscriptions to vulnerability digests, automatically tailored to a company's profile of operating systems and network hardware. Clearly, security is at the forefront of everyone's mind.

And yet, information theft continues to occur.

The Internet evolved in a world without predators. In the recent past denial-of-service attacks were viewed as illogical and undamaging. The Internet today is hostile, and it takes only a tiny percentage of miscreants to do a lot of damage. Causing damage doesn't even require particularly advanced skills anymore, as automated tools abound in the public domain. And organizations are becoming dependent on the Internet for reliability.

TIP

"In a world in which the total of human knowledge is doubling every 10 years, our security can rest only on our ability to learn."
—Nathaniel Brandon.

Security means different things to different people, and security aims can clash. To some, security means limiting data disclosure to the intended set of recipients or protecting the contents of data while in transit. To others, it means monitoring communications to catch terrorists or tracking down the bad guys. Some people just wish to be able to communicate in privacy. This is a good thing if you are engaged in an online eBay transaction, but a bad thing (for us) if you are Osama Bin Laden.

In this book, we have described the existing telecommunications infrastructure and the state of communications to come. We have discussed in detail various protocols and implementations because we believe that securing an infrastructure depends on the administrator's understanding of that particular infrastructure. We have pointed out the security challenges that face organizations and individuals as they move forward with adopting voice over IP (VoIP) technologies.

In this chapter, we will reiterate the tools and processes that we have found to work well for securing VoIP environments. Security administrators have at least five general tool sets to work with: the existing security infrastructure, authentication and authorization tools, the ability to logically segregate traffic, active security monitoring, and encryption. All these tool sets should be used to provide as many layers of defense as possible without encumbering the network with so many controls and control-related traffic that it becomes unusable.

Intelligent Defense in Depth is the cornerstone of contemporary security philosophy. Figure 17.1 illustrates many of the defensive layers that a typical security contemporary infrastructure comprises. We will talk more about this later in this chapter.

Figure 17.1 Defense in Depth

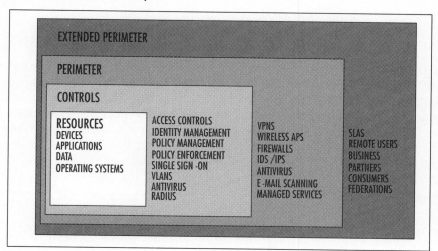

Reuse Existing Security Infrastructure Wisely

Your organization may already have many of the tools and infrastructure necessary to provide adequate VoIP security solutions, so don't reinvent the wheel. Augment existing policies and practices when you can and build on the voice and data practices that may already exist in your organization. Let's briefly review some of these areas of shared focus.

Security Policies and Processes

Securing a converged VoIP and data network begins with the formulation, implementation, and communication of *effective* security policies. This is true for pure data networks as well. Security policy provides metrics against which costs can be justified, drives security awareness, and provides the framework for technology and process. Once policy is in writing, less time will be spent debating security issues. Policy formulation is an important step toward standardization of security processes for everyone.

> **TIP**
>
> In information technology, gap analysis is the study of the differences between two different states of information systems or applications. Often one state describes the existing state, and the other state is a description of the desired end state. The metrics or variables that describe each end state are chosen to best represent a particular organization's characteristics. Often gap analysis is used for the purpose of determining how to get from an existing state to the desired new state.

We presented a gap analysis technique that can be used to establish "where you are" and "where you want to be" with regards to security policies. The point of the gap analysis is to engage affected individuals in defining, on paper (or in a spreadsheet), the existing security controls and the controls that will be required when adding VoIP to the existing infrastructure. Once finished, a road map exists that defines what processes and hardware need to be changed, reallocated, added, or removed.

Physical Security

Physical security is an essential part of any security environment. Physical security refers to the protection of building sites and equipment (and all other information and software contained therein) from theft, intrusion, vandalism, natural disaster, manmade catastrophes, and accidental damage (e.g., from electrical surges, extreme temperatures, and spilled coffee).

Unless VoIP traffic is encrypted, anyone with physical access to the organization's LAN can potentially connect network-monitoring tools and eavesdrop on telephone conversations. Although conventional telephone lines can also be monitored when physical access is obtained, most offices have many more points to connect to a LAN without arousing suspicion. Even if encryption is used, physical access to VoIP servers and gateways may allow an attacker to do traffic analysis (i.e., determine which parties are communicating, and how often they communicate). Adequate physical control should be in place to restrict access to VoIP network components. Physical security measures, including barriers, locks, access control systems, and guards, are the first line of defense.

When adding VoIP to existing data networks, one particular physical requirement stands out—electrical power or Power over Ethernet (PoE).

> **NOTE**
>
> **Power over Ethernet (POE):** The IEEE 802.3af standard (found here: http://standards.ieee.org/getieee802/802.3.html), defines delivery of up to 15.4 watts per port to Ethernet devices, typically using 48 volts. The standard specifies around 350 mA per connection, so at 48V, this results in 16W to a device.

The biggest consideration when using PoE is the overall power draw to the switch itself and dissipating the heat that results. Overall power consumption and cooling are very important factors to consider when deploying PoE. At a 15.4W default setting, total power can add up very quickly. Backup UPS power may also need to be upgraded to support the total draw to the switch. Additionally, the A/C system may need to be upgraded to keep equipment from overheating. Before installing a large number of PoE devices, you'll need to make sure that the overall power and cooling budgets are considered.

Server Hardening

All hosts attached to the VoIP network should follow a standard build procedure and be subjected to hardening before they are connected to the network. One group within the organization should bear the responsibility for maintaining standard build and hardening guidelines for Windows, Linux, AIX, and other UNIX and UNIX-like operating systems. This group should define these guidelines, ensuring that these hosts are hardened and patched before deployment and that patches are updated periodically as appropriate. This group should also maintain a central registry of individuals and groups running these operating systems so that periodic audits can be conducted to guarantee that the systems do not deviate from the established security baselines.

Supporting Services

VoIP relies on a number of ancillary services as part of the configuration process, as a means to locate users, for management, and to ensure favorable transport, among others. These include DNS, DHCP, LDAP, RADIUS, HTTP, HTTPS, SNMP, SSH, TELNET, NTP, and TFTP. Other services that modify QoS are also required. We recommend that those services that support the VoIP infrastructure be dedicated to that infrastructure.

The servers that host these services should be hardened and patched per security policy guidelines. Hardening of these servers, as mentioned earlier, should follow the principle of "Least Privilege." The Least Privilege principle includes the following guidelines:

- Anything not required should be disabled.

- Turn off all unneeded services.

- Disable any features that are not in use.

- Remove unnecessary applications.

Combine Network Management Tools and Operations

Network management tools that are used on the data network should be used to monitor the entire converged infrastructure. This is one of the major advantages of a converged network. Existing network management tools may need to be updated to reflect the enhanced requirements of a VoIP network. If possible, management traffic should be segregated to an out-of-band, dedicated management network. We recommend several free tools for network, device, and application monitoring. MRTG is an SNMP-based tool for visualizing network traffic patterns and trends. It can also monitor any SNMP-based device. Big Brother is another free tool that allows network managers to quickly visualize the state of remote applications and services.

Security Elements...

A Simple Security Deployment Test

A simple test to decide whether or not to deploy a specific VoIP security control is to ask the following questions:
What threats does this prevent?
Is it transparent to end-users?
Does it require extensive IT management and retraining?
Does it degrade network performance?
Does it include security functionality compatible with current and future standards?

Confirm User Identity

When we talk about VoIP security and attacks against that infrastructure, what are we really talking about? What types of attacks should we expect? Attackers will eavesdrop—that is, they will compromise connections or a device that provides a "hop" for the connection, and they will listen in to the conversation. In addition to listening in, they may steal the conversation, or they may modify elements of the conversation while it is in progress. The attacker may decide that it is more interesting to play or replay recorded messages, or they may attempt to deceive a listener at one end of the conversation into thinking that they are talking to someone else. If this succeeds, the attacker may trick the listener into sending the attacker personal information or into running a malicious program that turns the listener's computer into a spam–spewing zombie.

The most important way to prevent these attacks is to unambiguously determine the identities of the people or devices at both ends of the conversation. This is called *authentication*.

Authentication is a measure of trust. Authentication in the networking world is generally based either on using a shared secret (you are authenticated if you know the secret) or on public key-based methods with certificates (you prove your identity by possessing the correct private key).

Authenticators ask, "Who are you?"

Authorizers ask, "Should you be doing that?"

Authentication establishes the identities of devices and users to a degree that is in accord with your security policies. Authorization, on the other hand, establishes the amount and type of network and application resources authorized individuals and devices are able to access.

Figure 17.2 shows an authentication/authorization stack. This isn't a stack in the ISO sense, but it illustrates several key features: Both users and devices should be authenticated. These are often related but different processes. Authentication can be separated from authorization.

Figure 17.2 Security Framework

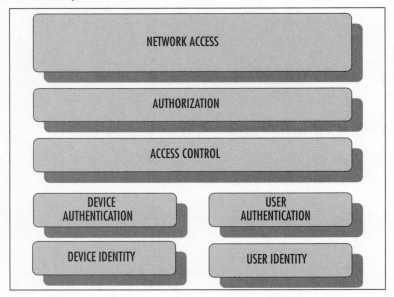

In H.323 environments the basis for authentication (trust) is defined by the endpoints of the communications channel. For a connection establishment channel, this may be between the caller (such as a gateway or IP telephone endpoint) and a hosting network component (a gateway or gatekeeper). SIP does not explicitly define authentication mechanisms. In contrast, SIP developers chose a modular approach—reusing the same headers, error codes, and encoding rules as HTTP.

802.1x and 802.11i

802.1x restricts unauthorized clients from connecting to a LAN. The client must first authenticate with an authentication server, typically a RADIUS server, before the switch port is made available and the network can be accessed. EAP (Extensible Authentication Protocol) is a general authentication protocol that provides a framework for multiple authentication methods.

Most of the more recent EAP types are made up of two components: an outer and an inner authentication type, separated by a forward slash, such as PEAPv0/EAP-MSCHAPv2. The outer type defines the method used to establish an encrypted channel between the client device (peer) and the authentication server. Once the outer channel is established, the inner authentication type passes the user's credentials to the authentication server over this TLS encrypted tunnel for additional authentication of, typically, user credentials.

We recommend that 802.1x be used for authentication for both devices and users on both wired and wireless VoIP networks. EAP-TLS should be used if a PKI exists; otherwise, we recommend EAP-PEAP for environments that are biased heavily toward Windows clients, and either EAP-PEAP or EAP-TTLS for those that are not. Additionally, depending on the RADIUS vendor, VLAN membership and other credentials should be designated by components of the 802.1x infrastructure.

Public Key Infrastructure

Within the PKI framework, who you are is defined by the private keys you possess. From the point of view of PKI authentication authorities, you are your private key. PKI relies on a public/private key combination. The public and private keys are mathematical entities that are related. One key is used to encrypt information, and only the related key can decrypt that same information; however, if you know one of the keys, it is computationally unfeasible to calculate the other.

Many organizations have tested PKI on a small to medium scale with different degrees of success. Most security consultants strongly recommend that these efforts be continued and expanded. Many organizations have discovered that the costs of deploying and maintaining a PKI are repaid in more widely applicable security and identity control mechanisms. On VoIP networks, a PKI provides a coherent security strategy because it can unambiguously guarantee the identities of users and devices, while preserving interoperability with authentication mechanisms such as 802.1x or 802.11i, federated identity management schemes, and many single sign-on formats.

Active Security Monitoring

Active monitoring of the network and attached devices not only provides one or more additional layers of defense but also supplies data that may have forensic utility. Active monitoring consists of the following types of activities: network monitoring, network intrusion detection, host-based intrusion detection, and syslog and SNMP logging. Penetration and vulnerability testing monitors and validates existing security controls.

NIDS and HIDS

Network intrusion detection systems (NIDSs) are designed to alert administrators when malicious or illegitimate traffic is detected. Malicious traffic can consist of worm or exploit-based code, while illegitimate traffic (often termed, "misuse"), such as surfing porn sites or per-to-peer connections, consists of traffic that deviates from established security policy. A host-based IDS (HIDS) consists of applications that operate on information collected from individual computer systems. This vantage point allows a HIDS to analyze activities on the host it monitors at a high level of detail; it can often determine which processes and/or users are involved in malicious activities. Furthermore, unlike a NIDS, a HIDS is privy to the outcome of an attempted attack, as it can directly access and monitor the data files and system processes targeted by these attacks.

Use of both a NIDS and a HIDS is recommended. NIDSs should be distributed so as to monitor traffic at key chokepoints—network junctions where different types of traffic merge. NIDSs are often located on uplinks where they have access to the most traffic. Ensure that NIDSs sensor-to-management-console traffic is encrypted, and that the sensors are de-tuned so that the mass of false positives does not obscure real events. Also be sure that operators have defined escalation processes to follow when a valid security event occurs.

HIDSs should be installed on every server classified as critical to the VoIP infrastructure. These include supporting servers (DNS, RADIUS, DHCP, NTP, etc.), gateways, proxies, directory servers, database servers, and firewalls. HIDS reports should be monitored regularly – in real time, if possible.

Logging

Syslog (system logger) provides a means to allow a machine to send event notification messages across IP networks to event message collectors, also known as syslog servers. Native syslog messages are not encrypted. Thus, syslogging should be utilized only on contained internal networks. Alternatively, some drop-in syslog replacements offer encryption as part of heir feature set. Their use is recommended.

IP phones can be reconfigured and rebooted via SNMP commands. Unfortunately, the default community strings associated with the most common versions of SNMP (v1 and v2) are well known and easily guessed. These community strings act as passwords that allow access to the SNMP-managed device. The default read-only community string (public) allows a user to browse configuration information regarding the device or server. Information gathered in this manner can potentially be used to gain further access to the device. SNMP messages, like syslog messages, can be stolen by eavesdroppers, and this information can be used to determine the state and configuration of networked devices.

Thus, it is recommended to use SNMP v3 for monitoring and configuration of VoIP networks. If the use of SNMP v3 is not a valid option, it is essential to restrict SNMP to subnets that are segregated from the Internet and from the balance of the network. Additionally, read/write community strings must be changed from their defaults.

TIP

"The search for security—in the law and elsewhere—is misguided. The fact is... security can only be achieved through constant change, adapting old ideas that have outlived their usefulness to current facts."
—William Osler.

Penetration and Vulnerability Testing

These tests or pseudo-attacks are conducted by an objective evaluation team and emulate an attack on one or more computer systems of interest to discover ways to breach the system's security controls, obtain sensitive information, obtain unauthorized services, or simulate damage to the system by denying service to legitimate users.

Security testing should be performed at least quarterly and after any major infrastructure changes. Some of these exercises can be done by internal testers. This serves multiple purposes: it saves money; it helps the testers learn about the network environment; it teaches them about recent security vulnerabilities and exploit tools; and it rewards them, since many network administrators are often curious about security practices. Most of the security scanning and vulnerability scanning tools are now automated, and while you may want to recruit security experts to analyze the data, these tools are particularly adept at pointing out the low-hanging fruit type of vulnerabilities—the kind most often exploited by attackers.

You may want to schedule additional external testing to validate the results obtained from internal test, as well as generate the appropriate data required for compliance with your particular regulatory or audit requirements.

Logically Segregate VoIP from Data Traffic

Packetized voice is indistinguishable from any other packet data at layers 2 and 3, and thus is subject to the same networking and security risks that plague data-only networks. The general idea that motivates the logical separation of data from voice is the expectation that network events (e.g., broadcast storms and congestion or security-related phenomena such as worms and DoS attacks that affect one network) will not impact the other.

Logically separate data from voice traffic. Plan on establishing at least 2 VLANs and put your VoIP system components on a separate dedicated VLAN with 802.1p/q QoS (Quality of Service) enable and priority VLAN tagging. Limit physical and terminal access to your switch consoles to only authorized personnel.

VLANs

Logical separation of voice and data traffic via VLANs is recommended to prevent data network problems from affecting voice traffic and vice-versa. VLANs, or virtual LANs, can be thought of as logically segmented networks mapped onto physical hardware. VLANs operate at layer 2 of the OSI model. However, a VLAN is often configured to map directly to an IP network or subnet, thereby appearing that it is involved at layer 3. Logical separation of voice and data traffic via VLANs is recommended to prevent data network problems from affecting voice traffic and vice-versa.

NOTE

Softphones security revisited: Malware that affects any other application software on the PC can also interfere with voice communications. The flip-side is also true: malware that affects the VoIP software will affect all other applications on the PC and the data services available to that PC (a separate VoIP phone would not require access to file services, databases, and so on). Because a softphone resides on a PC, the principle of logically separating voice and data networks is defeated because the PC must reside in both domains.

Security issues: Many softphones contain advertising software that "phones home" with private user information.

Several popular softphones (such as X-Lite) store credentials unencrypted in the Windows registry even after uninstallation of the program.

Softphones require that PC-based firewalls open a number of high UDP ports as part of the media stream transaction. Additionally, any special permissions that the VoIP application has within the host-based firewall ruleset will apply to all applications on that desktop (e.g., peer-to-peer software may use SIP for bypassing security policy prohibitions).

Steps to secure softphones: Softphones that contain any type of advertising software must be banned in a highly secure environment. Softphone installation targets should be tested before deployment, and those that do not encrypt user credentials should be prohibited.

Because a softphone is an application running on an operating system its security depends principally upon the status of the underlying OS, and is subject to the same security concerns as any other communications program including e-mail, browsing and IM.

Approval prior to the use of any IP softphone agent software must be authorized.

Personal installation and use of private softphones are prohibited.

All softphones must utilize a separate dedicated NIC for VoIP VLAN access.

Ensure that all IP Phones and softphones are both: VLAN aware and reside in the voice VLAN

In a switched network environment, VLANs create a logical segmentation of broadcast or collision domains that can span multiple physical network segments. VLANs remove the need to organize and manage PCs or softphones based on physical location. They also can be used to arrange endpoints based on function, class of service, class of user, connection speed, or other criteria. The separation of broadcast domains reduces traffic to the balance of the network. Effective bandwidth is increased due to the elimination of latency from router links. Additional security is realized if access to VLAN hosts is limited to only hosts on specific VLANs and not those that originate from other subnets beyond the router

In addition, the consequences of DoS attacks can sequestered from the balance of the network by logically separating voice and data segments into discrete VLANs.

QoS and Traffic Shaping

In the absence of QoS or traffic shaping, data networks operate on a best-effort delivery basis, which means that all data traffic has equal priority and an equal chance of being delivered promptly. However, when network congestion occurs, all data traffic has an equal chance of being dropped and/or delayed. When voice data is introduced into a network, it becomes critical that priority is given to the voice packets to ensure the expected quality of voice calls.

Some VoIP security measures can erode the performance of a network connection to the point where QoS is jeopardized. Most of the delays caused by security come from key generation and message exchanges during authentication and key exchange. Encryption can be accomplished relatively quickly.

NOTE

Encryption speeds: An AES encryption, without hardware acceleration, takes about 50 microseconds, for instance. But the key generation and exchange process can last up to 500ms, which is unacceptable for a real-time VoIP application. Overall, establishing a security association with IPSec requires anywhere from 2 to 10 seconds. TLS achieves better performance, but it still needs approximately 1.5 seconds to form a security association.

Firewalls

Firewalls have provided a physical and logical demarcation between the inside and the outside of a network. The first firewalls were basically just gateways between two networks with IP forwarding disabled. Most contemporary firewalls share a common set of characteristics: (1) it is a single point between two or more networks where all traffic must pass (choke point); (2) it can be configured to allow or deny IP (and other protocol) traffic; (3) it provides a logging function for audit purposes; (4) it provides a NAT function; (5) the operating system is hardened; (6) it often serves as a VPN endpoint; and (7) it fails closed—that is, if the firewall crashes in some way, no traffic is forwarded between interfaces.

Table 17.1 provides a noninclusive listing of common VoIP-related ports and services.

Table 17.1 Common VoIP Ports and Services

SERVICE	PORT
Skinny	TCP 2000-2002
TFTP	UDP 69
MGCP	UDP 2427
Backhaul (MGCP)	TCP 2428
Tapi/Jtapi	TCP 2748
HTTP	TCP 8080/80
SSL	TCP 443
SCCP	TCP 3224
Transport traffic	16384-32767
SNMP	UDP 161
SNMP trap	UDP 162
DNS	UDP 53
NTP	UDP 123
LDAP	TCP 389
H.323RAS	TCP 1719
H.323 H.225	TCP 1720
H.323 H.245	TCP 11000-11999
H.323 Gatekeeper Discovery	UDP 1718
SIP	TCP 5060
SIP/TLS	TCP 5061

There is still no simple solution for securely handling calls that originate externally. Packet filtering and stateful inspection firewalls can open a "pinhole" through which outbound replies can pass. However, particularly in the case of SIP-based solutions, private translated internal IP addresses prevent incoming calls from reaching the correct recipient.

In the near term, we recommend that organizations investigate the use of either VoIP-aware firewalls, application-layer gateways (ALGs), or session border controllers (SBCs) to manage and secure voice traffic that crosses the firewall. Alternatively, if the voice endpoints are located on the internal side of the firewall and all sessions can be virtually tunneled (via RAS users), we recommend that all voice traffic be encapsulated in a virtual private network (VPN).

NAT and IP Addressing

Network address translation (NAT) is a method for rewriting the source and/or destination addresses of IP packets as they pass through a NAT device. NAT devices manipulate a subset of the IP header information. NAT devices monitor, record, and alter the source IP address (SIP), destination IP address (DIP), and checksum (CHKSUM) fields within IP headers. NAT also modifies the checksum fields of both TCP and UDP packets since these checksums are computed over a pseudo-header that conceptually consists of the source and destination IP addresses, and the protocol and length fields for TCP. NAT provides a security function by segregating private hosts from the publicly routed Internet.

NAT will continue to be a major obstacle in VoIP migrations until Ipv6 becomes commonly adopted. Encryption across a NAT device is particularly problematic as both H.323 and SIP embed layer-3 routing and signaling information inside the IP datagram payload. The recommendation for NAT is the same as the aforementioned recommendation for firewalls—deployment of VoIP-aware perimeter devices should be investigated.

Access Control Lists

Network access control lists (ACLs) are tablelike data structures that normally consist of a single line divided into three parts: a reference number that defines the ACL, a rule (usually permit or deny), and a data pattern, which may consist of source and/or destination IP addresses, source and/or destination port numbers, masks, and Boolean operators. ACLs, in coordination with VLANs, QoS, and firewalls, are powerful tools for segregating VoIP traffic from other traffic.

ACLs should be implemented at layer 3 junctions between VoIP and data networks. In a most limited application, ACLs should at least be configured to deny access to traffic that never should be allowed on internal enterprise networks. This includes peer-to-peer (P2P) traffic, traffic known to be associated with common worms, NetBIOS and CIFS traffic if it not required for Windows browsing traffic, and other types of traffic that are specific for your particular networking and application requirements. VACLs (VLAN ACLs) if available, should also be used for these purposes.

Encryption

The suite of H.323-related security standards is known as the H.235 hierarchy and is discussed in more detail in Chapter 5. With regards to SIP, Transport Layer Security (TLS) Secure/Multipurpose Internet Mail Extensions (S/MIME), and Secure Real-Time Transfer Protocol (SRTP) are candidates for securing SIP services. SIP architects, sticking with the framework approach, added these security layers below the existing VoIP protocols rather than create new unproven protocols.

Encrypting the entire SIP message end to end is not a workable solution because network intermediaries (like proxy servers) need to view certain header fields (To, From, CSeq, Call-ID, Max-Forwards, and Via) to route messages correctly. The deployment issues for SIP are the same as those for H.323; that is, if you encrypt signaling, firewalls, and other intermediaries that do not know the key, they will not be able to correctly rewrite key signaling information, and SIP messages will fail.

Because RFC 3261 does not define methods for media encryption, supplementary protocols must be added if additional security features are required. Security for the VoIP media layer involves individual media streams, each with its own key generation and exchange mechanism, and its own authentication and encryption methods. IPSec was implemented early on to address these requirements, but performance continues to be a problem. In the future, many VoIP applications will likely use Secure Real-Time Protocol (SRTP) for encryption and SDP (Session Description Protocol) for the key exchange.

Interoperability has been part of VoIP's promise from the start, but in practice secure deployments are rarely interoperable, and interoperable deployments are rarely secure. Even the authors of SIP admit that it "is not an easy protocol to secure," according to RFC 3261.

TLS, on the other hand, has proven to be an efficient, adaptable VoIP security protocol—reducing the computational and consequent processing burden that other protocols generate and providing extensible security between unrelated applications. Use it when you can.

The 802.11i standard describes a more robust security system for WLANs than does 802.1x. Like 802.1x, it makes use of WPA2. It supports both AES and TLS.

Several vendors now include both media encryption and signaling encryption natively with their IP phones and gateway products. Use these tools to encrypt whenever and wherever you can.

Regulations

The past decade has seen an explosion of government regulation that will directly or indirectly affect VoIP implementation security. Although some of these regulations can be addressed by selecting and implementing compliant equipment, the vast majority of these are *operational* in nature, meaning that to ensure compliance you'll need to pay more attention to (1) how your IP communications systems are designed and (2) how your organization's business and IT operations groups are using the equipment once it's live.

We recommend that you ask yourself, your colleagues, and your audit and legal personnel the following questions:

- Does this regulation apply to me and my organization (or client's organization)?

- Who in my organization has responsibility for overall compliance with this regulation? In some cases, the answer may be *you_*if there isn't already someone designated, but for many of these regulations your organization is likely to have a person or group specifically designated as the lead for addressing compliance, particularly with regulations for which security is only an ancillary component of the overall regulation.

- Is it likely that my systems and/or operations are not compliant with this regulation today? If you suspect that remediation is necessary, it's important to raise the concern to the appropriate level of management in a way that allows the issue to be corrected and reduce the risk of fines, negative publicity, or worse.

Summary

There is no out-of-the-box solution for securing VoIP or any other kind of data network. Professional information security in the enterprise is hard. Make no mistake about it; this is not a field for newbies or naive network administrators. Professional, secure VoIP networks are managed, secured, and operated by experienced professionals. Although there is no single key point to accomplish and maintain a secure state, intelligent distribution and operation of your limited resources will allow you and your organization to emulate the level of service and the security levels currently enjoyed by PSTN network users.

Of Layers, Compartments, and Bulkheads

Defense in Depth is based on the concept of layers or *compartments*. You can think of compartments as boxes, and the layers define the edges of the boxes. On a submarine, the greatest threat is that the hull will be breached and that water will flood in and sink the boat. In this analogy, the submarines are your internal network or networks, the hull is the firewall perimeter infrastructure, and the flood of water symbolizes the flood of worm viruses or hacker attacks that can sink the network.

Submarines incorporate bulkheads or compartments that minimize and localize damage when it does occur. Similarly, in VoIP/data networks compartmentalization serves the same function—to limit damage when an attack occurs. Layers or security controls define the boundaries of these compartments.

Each layer or compartment placed between an attacker and his or her goal adds to the time and effort that an attacker must accept if they are to continue. Each layer adds to the *risk* that he or she will be caught. In most cases, our goal is simple: Make the infrastructure environment so unpleasant for an attacker that he or she gives up and goes away, or in some cases, is caught and prosecuted.

Specific Recommendations

We conclude this chapter with the following list of recommendations for securing your VoIP network:

1. Require strong passwords everywhere. Enforce this rule.
2. Then reinforce the password rule again.
3. Update existing security policies, practices, and procedures to reflect the new requirements of converged networks.
4. Distribute, communicate, and enforce these policies.

5. Ensure that users sign a document that states that they understand their responsibilities when using these systems.

6. Train operators and administrators in the latest most relevant tools and techniques.

7. Develop and test secure off-site backup plans.

8. Develop and test disaster recovery plans.

9. Ensure that all networked systems are periodically patched and hardened.

10. Harden server-based IP PBXs.

11. Ensure that antivirus scanners are up-to-date.

12. Employ different subnets with separate RFC 1918 address blocks for voice and data traffic.

13. Segment voice and data traffic by appropriate use of VLANs, firewalls, ALGs and access control lists.

14. Filter private network traffic internally and at the network periphery.

15. Install and monitor tools that protect against ARP spoofing attacks.

16. Install and monitor intrusion detection systems—both host-based and network-based.

17. Exercise diligence in analyzing logs from intrusion detection systems, firewalls, routers, servers and other networked devices.

18. All PC-based phones should be placed behind a firewall or ACL to mediate VOIP traffic.

19. Employ VoIP-aware firewalls, application layer gateways, or session border controllers at the perimeter of the network to process incoming and outgoing voice data.

20. Properly configure these firewalls.

21. Combine your network management tools and integrate their results with data from other monitoring systems. And use these tools daily.

22. Use VoIP-dedicated support servers—TFTP, DHCP, HTTP, SNMP, etc.

23. Turn off SNMP if you can. If not, ensure that community strings are complex.

24. Use IPSec or Secure Shell (SSH) for all remote management and auditing access.

25. Forge strong relationships with your ISPs to defend against external DoS attacks.

26. VoIP components should reside on a separate voice VLAN.

27. VoIP VLAN ports that are not in use should be disabled.

28. If VoIP phones contain a built-in data network port, disable the port when not in use, and if it is use, the port must be configured on the appropriate data VLAN.

29. Approval prior to the use of any IP softphone agent software must be authorized.

30. Personal installation and use of private softphones are prohibited.

31. All softphones must utilize a separate dedicated NIC for VoIP VLAN access.

32. Ensure that all IP phones and softphones are both: VLAN aware and reside in the voice VLAN.

33. All VoIP security perimeter firewalls should be dedicated to VoIP traffic to reduce transmission latency caused by processing latency.

34. The network time protocol (NTP port 123) should be blocked at the security perimeter. Local NTP clients should receive clock information from a local Stratum 2, 3, or 4 clock source.

35. All HTTP connections to VoIP security perimeter firewalls for administrative/management purposes must be tunneled through a VPN or use secure HTTPS.

36. Critical VoIP servers must be secured in compliance with applicable guidelines.

37. All remote administrative connections to critical VoIP servers must be encrypted.

38. All VoIP traffic that is sent over a public IP network (i.e., Internet,) is encrypted.

39. Ensure that the server hosting the voice-mail service is properly hardened and secured.

40. If wireless VoIP (VoWLAN) is used, all of the aforementioned requirements apply.

41. No VoIP systems IP phones, softphones, VoIP-related server hardware and software, or networks will be put into operation without certification that they have complied in every manner with the aforementioned recommendations.

Solutions Fast Track

Reuse Existing Security Infrastructure Wisely

☑ A security policy provides the framework, justification, and metrics for all other security-related development.

☑ A policy that is not consistently enforced is worse than having no policy at all.

☑ The most important step in security policy practices is communicating the policy contents to everyday users—these "human firewalls" are the best security investment an organization can make.

☑ Upgrading a data network to a data and VoIP network is an ideal time to reexamine and revamp the security state of your support infrastructure.

☑ Require more than one type of authentication for access into critical areas.

☑ Remember to lock doors and windows.

☑ Turn off all unnecessary services and listening daemons.

☑ The risk of implementing the service pack or security patch should ALWAYS be LESS than the risk of not implementing it.

☑ If you make the effort to generate log files, then review them regularly. Logged data are a great resource for understanding the day-to-day operation of your infrastructure.

☑ If possible, dedicate your support infrastructure components to either data or VoIP networks, but not both.

☑ Ensure that multiple DHCP servers do not coexist in the same broadcast domain.

☑ Ensure that SNMP community strings are not set to default values.

☑ Replace telnet with SSH at every opportunity.

☑ Delay, jitter, and packet loss are the major network variables that impact VoIP quality.

☑ Always segregate management traffic on a dedicated, secure management network.

Confirm User Identity

☑ Authentication is made up of three factors: "something you have" (a key or certificate), "something you know" (a password or secret handshake), and/or "something you are" (a fingerprint or iris pattern). Authentication mechanisms validate users by one or a combination of these.

☑ The 802.1x protocol defines port-based network access control that is used to provide authenticated network access.

☑ EAP (Extensible Authentication Protocol) is a general authentication protocol that provides a framework for multiple authentication methods.

☑ Most of the more recent EAP types are made up of two components: an outer and an inner authentication type.

☑ The three components of an 802.1x infrastructure are the supplicant (client), the authenticator (NAS), and the authentication server (normally a RADIUS server).

☑ 802.11i is also known as WPA2.

☑ Within the PKI framework, who you are is defined by the private keys you possess.

☑ The fact that the same key is used for both encryption and decryption determines a symmetric exchange.

☑ PKI relies on a public/private key combination.

☑ Public and private keys are mathematical entities that are related. One key is used to encrypt information, and only the related key can decrypt that same information; however, if you know one of the keys, it is computationally unfeasible to calculate the other.

☑ The private key is also used to digitally sign the sent message so that the sender's identity is guaranteed.

☑ Information security is often defined as a number of layers. The basis for this is the idea that every time and place a logical or physical impediment can be created that might reasonably stop an attacker (without hindering normal users' access to network resources) it should be done.

☑ A basic security rule is that endpoints cannot be trusted until the identity of the endpoint is confirmed or authenticated.

☑ In the case of VoIP, a method for authentication of IP phones is the hardware or MAC address.

Active Security Monitoring

☑ A network intrusion detection system (NIDS) is designed to alert administrators when malicious or illegitimate traffic is detected.

☑ A networkk-based IDSs can monitor an entire large network with only a few well-situated nodes or devices and impose little overhead on a network.

☑ NIDSs are normally classified according to the methods they use for attack detection; either as signature-based, or anomaly detection.

☑ NIDS should be located where they can most effectively monitor critical traffic.

☑ Communication between the IDS components (sensors and management console) should be encrypted using strong authentication.

☑ A host-based IDS (HIDS) consists of applications that operate on information collected from individual computer systems.

☑ Tripwire is the reference model for many of the follow-on HIDS.

☑ Most HIDS software establishes a "digital inventory" of files and their attributes in a known state and use that inventory as a baseline for monitoring any system changes.

☑ The key to successful log analysis is to adopt the proper tools for your environment to automatically parse, visualize, and report summarized log data.

☑ Syslog messages use UDP/514 for transport.

☑ The syslog protocol provides a transport to allow a machine to send event notification messages across IP networks to event message collectors, also known as syslog servers.

☑ Syslog messages (ASCII-based) may be sent to local logs, a local console, a remote syslog server, or a remote syslog relay.

☑ The Simple Network Management Protocol (SNMP) is an application layer protocol that facilitates the exchange of management information between network devices.

☑ An SNMP network normally consists of three key components: managed devices, agents, and network-management systems.

☑ If you must use SNMP, immediately change the values of the default read/write community strings.

☑ Penetration/vulnerability tests are useful tools for determining the current security posture of an organization.

☑ Penetration tests (pen-tests) usually refer to tests against perimeter defenses, whereas vulnerability testing refers to tests against specific systems (host, applications, or networks).

☑ The results of a penetration/vulnerability test reflect the security status only during the testing period. Even minor administrative and architectural changes to the environment performed only moments after a penetration test can alter the system's security profile.

Logically Segregate VoIP from Data Traffic

☑ Separate voice and data traffic via VLANs.

☑ VLANs provide security and make smaller broadcast domains by creating logically separated subnets.

☑ Disable unused ports and put them in a unique unused VLAN. This is a simple but effective means to prevent unauthorized access.

☑ For a good discussion of L2 access controls see:
www.cisco.com/en/US/products/hw/switches/ps708/products_white_pap
er09186a008013159f.shtml.

☑ QoS and traffic shaping VoIP have strict performance requirements.

☑ VoIP quality is negatively affected by increased latency, jitter, and packet
loss.

☑ QoS can provide some security against DoS attacks.

☑ Network address translation (NAT) is a method for rewriting the source
and/or destination addresses of IP packet.

☑ NAT also rewrites TCP and UDP checksums based on a pseudo-header

☑ Hosts behind a NAT device do not have true end-to-end Internet
connectivity and cannot directly participate in Internet protocols that
require initiation of TCP connections from outside the NAT device, or
protocols that split signaling and media into separate channels.

☑ The key to the incompatibility of NAT and the IPsec AH mode is the
presence of the Integrity Check Value (ICV).

☑ NAT provides a security function by segregating private hosts from the
publicly routed Internet.

☑ Firewall mechanisms include packet filtering, stateful inspection,
application-layer gateways, and deep packet inspection.

☑ Packet-filtering firewalls inspect only a few header fields in order to make
processing decisions.

☑ Application-layer gateways provide intermediary services for hosts that
reside on different networks, while maintaining complete details of the
TCP connection state and sequencing.

☑ Deep packet inspection analyzes the entire packet, and may buffer,
assemble, and inspect several related packets as part of a session.

☑ H.323 calls are difficult to firewall because IP addresses and ports are embedded in each previous packet stream, because packets are ASN.1 PER encoded, and because media and signaling take place on different channels—some of which are dynamically created.

☑ When used as a VoIP application, SIP is difficult to firewall because NAT often hides the "real" IP address of endpoints, and because, media and signaling take place on different channels—some of which are dynamically created.

☑ Access control lists (ACLs) are tablelike data structures.

☑ A general rule-of-thumb is that outbound ACLs are more efficient than inbound ACLs.

☑ ACLs provide extremely granular control of traffic streams if configured correctly.

Frequently Asked Questions

The following Frequently Asked Questions, answered by the authors of this book, are designed to both measure your understanding of the concepts presented in this chapter and to assist you with real-life implementation of these concepts. To have your questions about this chapter answered by the author, browse to **www.syngress.com/solutions** and click on the **"Ask the Author"** form.

Q: What's the difference between a network intrusion detection system (NIDS) and a host-based intrusion detection system (HIDS)?

A: A NIDS inspects all inbound and outbound network activity and identifies patterns of packet data that may indicate a network or system attack. A HIDS, on the other hand, normally resides as an application on the server that it monitors.

Q: What is the Windows equivalent of syslog?

A: Windows doesn't really have a native equivalent. The eventlog service enables event log messages issued by Windows-based programs and components to be viewed in Event Viewer.

Q: I've setup *<myfile>* to log to syslog, but it's not working. What should I do?

A: Make sure you have an entry in your syslog.conf file to save the apropriate messages. Don't forget to send a SIGHUP to your syslogd so that it re-reads its conf file. Also, remember that syslogd does not create log files. You need to create the file before syslogd will log to it (i.e.: touch /var/log/myfile).

Q: If you have multiple security devices reporting to a remote syslog server, what is the best way to parse or separate the logs?

A: Log parsing is difficult to do in an efficient, scalable manner. A number of commercial products claim to parse various formats and store the information in a backend database. There are numerous open source log parsing projects at Freshmeat or SourceForge. Also simple shell, awk, or perl scripts can be used.

Q: Should my company be running its own honeypot or honeynet?

A: Probably not. Most organizations still have problems completing and maintaining basic security controls. Honeypots and honeynets are primarily learning tools. Most honeynets are run in academia, the military, and government.

Q: I'm looking for a utility that enables me to change community names on multiple devices from a single management console. Where can I find one?

A: Because the methodology for setting community strings is not standardized, every type of device/agent version may have a different mechanism for handling this chore. Therefore, there are no "single console" products for setting community strings. For this to be feasible, you would have to be able to differentiate every agent type, and know how that particular vendor/system/agent handles it.

Q: What is RMON?

A: The Remote Network Monitoring MIB is a SNMP MIB for remote management of networks. Although other MIBs usually are created to support a network device whose primary function is other than management, RMON was created to provide management of a network. RMON is one of the many SNMP based MIBs that are on the IETF Standards track.

Q: What are red-teams or blue-teams?

A: In penetration testing, a red-team approach means that the testers adopt a stealthy posture—that is, they take on the role of untrusted attacker attempting to sneak into the network. Blue-team signifies an approach where the tester is an insider, and test tool collateral "noise" is not an issue.

Index

Syngress: *The Definition of a Serious Security Library*

Syn·gress (sin–gres): *noun, sing.* Freedom from risk or danger; safety. See *security.*